Jews and Gender in Liberation France

This book takes a new look at occupied and liberated France through the dual prism of race, specifically Jewishness, and gender – core components of Vichy ideology.

Imagining liberation, and the potential post-Vichy state, lay at the heart of resistance strategy. The development of these ideas, and their transformation into policy at liberation, form the basis of an enquiry that reveals a society which, while split deeply at the political level, found considerable agreement over questions of race, the family and gender. This is explained through a new analysis of republican assimilation which insists that gender was as important a factor as nationality or ethnicity. A new concept of the 'long liberation' provides a framework for understanding the continuing influence of the liberation in post-war France, where scientific planning came to the fore, but whose exponents were profoundly imbued with reductive beliefs about Jews and women that were familiar during Vichy.

K. H. ADLER is Research Fellow, Department of History, University of Nottingham.

Studies in the Social and Cultural History of Modern Warfare

General Editor
Jay Winter   *Yale University*

Advisory Editors
Paul Kennedy   *Yale University*
Antoine Prost   *Université de Paris-Sorbonne*
Emmanuel Sivan   *The Hebrew University of Jerusalem*

In recent years the field of modern history has been enriched by the exploration of two parallel histories. These are the social and cultural history of armed conflict, and the impact of military events on social and cultural history.

Studies in the Social and Cultural History of Modern Warfare presents the fruits of this growing area of research, reflecting both the colonization of military history by cultural historians and the reciprocal interest of military historians in social and cultural history, to the benefit of both. The series offers the latest scholarship in European and non-European events from the 1850s to the present day.

For a list of titles in the series, please see end of book.

Jews and Gender
in Liberation France

K. H. ADLER

University of Nottingham

CAMBRIDGE
UNIVERSITY PRESS

PUBLISHED BY THE PRESS SYNDICATE OF THE UNIVERSITY OF CAMBRIDGE
The Pitt Building, Trumpington Street, Cambridge CB2 1RP, United Kingdom

CAMBRIDGE UNIVERSITY PRESS
The Edinburgh Building, Cambridge, CB2 2RU, UK
40 West 20th Street, New York, NY 10011–4211, USA
477 Williamstown Road, Port Melbourne, VIC 3207, Australia
Ruiz de Alarcón 13, 28014 Madrid, Spain
Dock House, The Waterfront, Cape Town 8001, South Africa

http://www.cambridge.org

First published 2003

Printed in the United Kingdom at the University Press, Cambridge

Typefaces Palatino 10/12 pt. and Frutiger.   *System* LaTeX 2ε   [TB]

A catalogue record for this book is available from the British Library

ISBN 0 521 79048 4 hardback

For Elli and Henry, and to the memory of
Mimi Goldschmied

Contents

Illustrations

Maps and diagrams

Tables

Abbreviations

AFDAI   Association Française pour la Défense et l'Assimilation des Immigrés
AI   Author's interview
AIU   Alliance Israélite Universelle
AJ   Armée Juive
AN   Archives Nationales
ANCD   Alliance Nationale contre la Dépopulation
BDIC   Bibliothèque de Documentation Internationale Contemporaine
BN   Bibliothèque Nationale de France
CAC   Centre des Archives Contemporaines
CADI   Centre d'Action et de Défense des Immigrés
CCE   Commission Centrale de l'Enfance
CDJC   Centre de Documentation Juive Contemporaine
CFTC   Confédération Française des Travailleurs Chrétiens
CGQJ   Commissariat Général aux Questions Juives
CGT   Confédération Générale du Travail
CNR   Conseil National de la Résistance
CPL   Comité Parisien de la Libération
DP   Displaced Person
FDIF   Fédération Démocratique Internationale des Femmes
FFEPH   Fondation Française pour l'Etude des Problèmes Humains
FLN   Femmes de la Libération Nationale
FNSP   Fondation Nationale des Sciences Politiques
FO   Force Ouvrière
FSJF   Fédération des Sociétés Juives de France
FTP   Francs-Tireurs et Partisans
HCP   Haut Comité de la Population (1939)
HCCPF   Haut Comité Consultatif de la Population et de la Famille (1945–1970)
IEQJ   Institut d'Etudes des Questions Juives (et Ethno-Raciales [from 1942])
IFOP   Institut Français de l'Opinion Publique
INED   Institut National d'Etudes Démographiques

JDC   American Jewish Joint Distribution Committee
JO   Journal Officiel
JOC   Jeunesse Ouvrière Chrétienne
JSS   Jewish Social Studies
LICA   Ligue Internationale contre l'Antisémitisme
LPGF   La Plus Grande Famille
MLN   Mouvement de la Libération Nationale
MOI   Main-d'Œuvre Immigrée
MP   Mauco Papers, Archives Nationales
MPF   Mouvement Populaire des Familles
MRAP   Mouvement contre le Racisme et pour l'Amitié entre les
        Peuples
MRP   Mouvement Républicain Populaire
MUR   Mouvements Unis de la Résistance
OCM   Organisation Civile et Militaire
ORT   Obschestvo Rapotraninia Trouda / Organisation – Reconstruction
        – Travail
OSE   Œuvre de Secours aux Enfants
PCF   Parti Communiste Français
PPF   Parti Populaire Français
SCDI   Service Central des Déportés Israélites
SPP   Société Psychanalytique de Paris
SSAE   Service Social d'Aide aux Emigrants
SSMOE   Service Social de la Main-d'Œuvre Etrangère
STO   Service du Travail Obligatoire
UFF   Union des Femmes Françaises
UFJ   Union des Femmes Juives
UIESP   Union Internationale pour l'Etude Scientifique de la Population
UJRE   Union des Juifs pour la Résistance et l'Entr'aide
UNAF   Union Nationale des Associations Familiales
UNCAF   Union Nationale des Caisses d'Allocations Familiales
UNRRA   United Nations Relief and Rehabilitation Administration

Acknowledgements

Many people have enabled this book to reach publication, perhaps without even realizing it. I am grateful to each of them.

I greatly appreciate the generosity of the British Academy and Cardiff University who provided financial assistance to allow research time in France; a research fellowship from the University of Nottingham gave me time to complete the book. Portions of chapter one were first published in *Jewish Culture and History*, copyright Frank Cass Publishers, 2002.

I am indebted to many archivists and librarians for guidance to their collections. At the Archives Nationales, I thank Chantal de Tourtier-Bonazzi, Paule René-Bazin and Yvonne Poule. Librarians at the Bibliothèque Nationale de France were consistently helpful over many years. I also thank staff at the American Jewish Joint Distribution Committee archives, the Bibliothèque de Documentation Internationale Contemporaine, the Wiener Library, Yad Vashem, Staatsarchiv Detmold, the United States Holocaust Memorial Museum, Karen Taïeb at the Centre de Documentation Juive Contemporaine archives, the Alliance Israélite Universelle, the Bibliothèque Marxiste, the Fondation Nationale des Sciences Politiques, the Bibliothèque Medem, and the Bibliothèque Marguerite Durand. For creating such a convivial research environment, my warmest appreciation goes to Sarah Halperyn and Marcel Meslati at the CDJC library.

The women who so kindly consented to being interviewed provided not just answers in their insights and recollections, but many new questions that provoked my further research. I am grateful to them all. In common with recent archival sources which often prohibit the identification of individuals, their full names are not revealed. Emmanuelle Unal and Stéphane Camus transcribed the interviews with great competence.

I have chewed over aspects of this book with dozens of individuals, and all these conversations – and the meals that almost invariably accompanied them – helped the writing process immeasurably. Some people have been extremely generous. Jackie Clarke and Kevin

Passmore not only read and provided invaluable comments on the entire draft manuscript but were prepared to engage in extensive discussions that were, for me, always productive. Julian Jackson and Nancy Wood's suggestions were tremendously useful. The process of writing would have been far more protracted and difficult without Sylvain Cypel, Hanna Diamond, Peter Gordon, Penelope Hamm, Pat Hudson, Simon Kitson, Reina Lewis, Gail Pheterson, Miranda Pollard, Judith Surkis, Adam Sutcliffe, Garthine Walker and Philippe Zarka. They helped in myriad ways and their support and friendship are inestimable.

I am deeply fortunate to have had the opportunity to work with Rod Kedward. To have benefited from his uncommon combination of scholarship, humour, generosity, democratic openness to new ideas, scepticism and unfailing encouragement has been as much a pleasure as a privilege. Like so many other historians, I will remain forever in his debt.

Always acute, Franziska Meyer read and reread drafts, gave constant encouragement, and much, much more. I dedicate this book to my parents – who connect me to the period and ideas that I discuss – and to the memory of my grandmother. It was she who first awakened my fascination with history, and her unacknowledged resistance in wartime Vienna gave me early insight into many of the themes I explore here.

Chapter 1
Introduction: the long liberation

I remember the day I saw the first Germans... there was a rumour, we went
down to the street and I saw the motorized troops arrive. It was a sort of grey-
green block. It was sparkling, it was backfiring, it was bellowing. They turned
the corner of the road... and in my mind... it was death which advanced.[1]

To begin with, was the invasion. Six weeks later came the defeat, followed by four years of occupation. Riven into pieces (map 2), France
was at war with the occupiers and with itself. The government, demo-
cratically elected in 1936, 'committed suicide' when those parliamentarians still left in the chamber of deputies – the communists had already
been banned and other opponents to the occupation had fled – voted full
powers to the veteran First World War marshal, Philippe Pétain.[2] He and
his collaborationist government would rule with a brand of Catholic,
racist, technocratic and anti-feminist authoritarianism framed by what
was posited as a return to authentic French values, in order to wrest the
nation from the grip of decadence to which it had succumbed. For the
first two years, a large proportion of the population supported Pétain
and his National Revolution. Indeed, many people – and not only those
on the right – had been disturbed for some time about France's weakness
that Pétain seemed set to restore, believing the country to be debil-
itated by, among other elements, degenerate foreigners and a feeble
birth-rate so that it could no longer hold its own on the international
stage.
     To begin with, then, were the fantasmatic ponderings of writers like
Louis-Ferdinand Céline, Pierre Drieu la Rochelle, even Jean Giraudoux.[3]
They found France enfeebled after the First World War and the loss of
more than a million young men which the leaders of the Third Republic –
whom they regarded as decrepit – did little to assuage. Instead of con-
fronting the crisis of the early 1930s with firm controls, the government
permitted the admission of ever greater numbers of foreigners, especially Jews, whose arrival did nothing to aid restabilization. Amid
mounting political polarization and growing membership lists of
communist and far right parties, the installation of the Popular Front

Map 1: French *départements* in 1944 (courtesy Oxford University Press)

government in 1936 was, for those on the right, a final betrayal of their nationalist values. For the ordinary, working immigrants who were increasingly the target of the right's venom, it was a different story.

To begin with, then, was a France embattled against the fascism of its neighbours but whose own 150-year-old values maintained it as a nation of individual freedom and asylum. France welcomed more new-comers than any other country apart from the USA, and in the inter-war years they came from all over southern and eastern Europe, France's colonies and, after 1933, from central Europe too. Those who wanted to be politically active, and they were numerous, could enrol in the Main-d'Œuvre Immigrée (MOI) – communist party sections that operated in their own language – or join native French activists in trade unions, or

A Unoccupied Zone
B Occupied Zone
C Zone attached to German command in Brussels
D 'Reserved' or 'Forbidden' Zone
E Annexed Zone
F Coastal Zone (from Oct. 1941)
G Italian Zone from June 1940–Nov. 1942
H Italian Zone after Nov. 1942
✷ German stronghold until April–May 1945

Map 2: France divided 1940–44 (courtesy Oxford University Press)

subscribe to one of the dozens of social and cultural associations that immigrants themselves established. These organizations offered exciting opportunities. Imagine the significance to poor, working women, for example, who, at a time of strong social divisions when women were still denied contraception and abortion – and providing even information on them was illegal – were given the chance to meet a doctor not only addressed by her first name, but who explained contraceptive methods in detail.[4] To counter their financial hardships, employees benefited for the first time from paid holidays and more limited working hours (though these were inapplicable to that large proportion of Jewish immigrants who bore the insecure conditions in the garment trades). If the mid-1930s offered hope to these individuals, the increasing severity of

3

German Nazism, and the installation of Edouard Daladier's more authoritarian regime in France, followed soon after by war and invasion, were traumatic.

But the majority of the population was neither immigrant nor politically active. After the initial shock of the invasion, and in particular the *exode*, which affected even more than the 8 – perhaps 10 – million individuals trekking across France ahead of the invading armies, most people settled into getting on with their lives as best they could. To begin with, then, was a complex and subtle web of compromise, accommodation, making do and getting by . . .[5]

If there is no single beginning to the story of the German occupation of France, there is even less a single end. In one sense, the Liberation of France was both beginning and end, being the start of a new political and historical era, and the end of the occupation. But only in one sense. It is to challenge the comfortingly neat periodization of 1940–44, and thereby to suggest new interpretations of the history of France at this time, that this book has been written. Even at its most basic level – the liberation of territory in 1944 – the liberation did not start and end with the Normandy landings in June, or the Provence landings in August, or the liberation of Paris the same month, or any other of the multiple events that encompassed the military liberation. It did not even end in 1944. Only in 1945 would the German coastal strongholds and the bases in eastern France annexed to the Reich come once more under French control. Only in 1945 would the approximately 1.5 million people taken from France to Germany as prisoners of war, forced labourers and resisters start to return home.[6] And the settling of scores took many more years yet.

The liberation of French territory was prolonged and violent. More people lost their lives and more property was destroyed during the liberation than at any time since the war began. Two million people became homeless, many as a result of Allied bombing.[7] Communications were chaotic and supplies unreliable, especially to the cities. In the unusually harsh winter of 1944–45, urban inhabitants really started to starve. That winter was particularly arduous in the annexed zone as, in addition to all the terrors of Nazi rule and the knowledge that most of France was now free of it, to say nothing of the dreadful cold, Allied aircraft returning from raids on Germany routinely discharged their unused bombs over the area.[8] Nazi reprisals were devastating, as they had been during the occupation.[9] So the significance of despatching the Nazis from France must not be minimized. But the liberation involved more than ejecting two sets of rulers (Vichy and Nazi) and installing a viable third. Just what kind of rule and, moreover, what kind of France it would govern was the burning question at liberation, and had been constantly discussed during the occupation years.

Liberation started the day the armistice was signed. While many people initially believed in Pétain's promise to protect 'the French' and help them survive the occupation as best they could, his growing number of opponents were anticipating and working to achieve liberation. What would become the highest honour for those who fought to free France, the Compagnon de la Libération, was instituted by General de Gaulle and his supporters as early as November 1940. Throughout the occupation, ideas for a liberated France were defined and refined in a process of 'aspirational liberation'. Plans for the post-occupation future were debated in the resister clandestine press, among the Free French in London and Algiers, and certainly by ordinary people. This protracted process of imagining, hoping for and planning liberation, merged and intersected with discourses emanating from Vichy, and it continued until well after the installation in Paris of the provisional government in August 1944. We could point to a variety of cut-off dates for this liberationism: the inauguration of the Fourth Republic in 1947; the end of the war in Indochina and the start of the one in Algeria in 1954; or the end of the Algerian war in 1962; or possibly the events of May 1968; or even 1995 when, for the first time, a French head of state admitted French responsibility for the deportation of the Jews.[10] My discussion of source material ends in the early 1950s, not with a major historical event, but with commentators' own historicization of the Vichy past. For all its curtailment from the potential longer views that may be explored in the future, though, this book is about the 'long liberation'.

The long liberation and the issues it raises are viewed here through the prism of Jewishness and gender – concerns at the heart of Vichy's idealized France. While Vichy excluded all sorts of groups from its France – freemasons, Roma and communists, for example – its own anti-semitism combined with that of the Nazi occupiers led to a catastrophic policy of deportation and murder. For the racists and xenophobes whose moment seemed to have arrived under Vichy, moreover, Jews had come to represent the very worst dangers that immigration and infiltration by outsiders were supposed to portend. With respect to gender, ever-stricter differentiation between men and women, and their public and private roles, formed one of the most significant foundations on which Vichy's National Revolution was based.[11] These two aspects were adopted and manipulated by resisters too. But studying them reveals more than the sum of their parts: taken together, the combination opens a door to the very conceptualization of the world that resisters wanted to make against that conceived by Vichy. Resisters – whether small groups of communist women producing clandestine newspapers, members of the Free French provisional government in Algiers, or high-status men who worked with Vichy and its agencies but who claimed resister status afterwards – were the people who formed or influenced policy and ideas at the end of the occupation, though they did not do so with equal authority or power. It is their transformations of these notions of race, gender and exclusion within liberationist imaginings that concern us here. Before shifting to an examination of how liberationism cohered with the belief in technocratic planning that became such a force in post-war French politics, this study explores aspirational liberationism as it was expressed in the clandestine press. Subsequently, it investigates the effects and interpretations of these discussions on some of the people most implicated in Vichy's exclusionary policies. To begin with, though, we focus on that classic moment of liberation – Paris in August 1944.

Chapter 2
Narrating liberation

Cramped on tiny wooden school-room chairs in one of the two re-maining rooms belonging to the Union des Juifs pour la Résistance et l'Entr'aide (UJRE), we came, in the summer of 1996, to honour the memory of a former resister. In its post-war heyday, the clinic, news-paper printing and distribution, meeting rooms and orphans' adminis-tration centre took over the entirety of what, fifty years later, had become a crumbling three-storey building not far from the Gare de l'Est in Paris. Early in 1943, this communist affiliated, Jewish resistance organization based in Paris, brought together a number of Jewish clandestine group-ings under a single umbrella, the better to draw all Jews, immigrant and French-born, into the resistance, and to represent Jews in France once the occupation was over.[1] After liberation, its Commission Centrale de l'Enfance, like the Œuvre de Secours aux Enfants, ran a number of orphanages for some of the thousands of children its members, largely women, had helped to hide during the occupation and whose parents had been deported.[2] It continued to publish *Droit et liberté*, the clandestine newspaper that had appeared during the occupation, as well as *La Presse nouvelle* and its Yiddish version, *Di Naïe Presse*, and provide medical assistance. Former resisters still found a home there, and a hundred or so gathered to pay their last respects to the Polish-born resister and lifelong activist Perela Traler. Stories, poems, songs and jokes were succeeded by orations on her resistance character and polit-ical adroitness informed, we were told, by an innate maternalism. They were delivered in a mixture of Yiddish and French, a division apparently dependent on the age of the speaker. Finally, the Kaddish, the Jewish prayer of mourning, signalled the sad ending of the gathering and its palpable sense of losing a generation as well as a comrade. But what to do? Everyone present, it might be assumed, was Jewish, nearly all over the age of sixty-five. But these were also communists or ex-communists who had consciously rescinded any pre-existent Judaic piety in favour of a politicized antipathy to rabbinical doctrine. A few people's sense of propriety forced them to rise, a move most others in the room gradually followed. Led by those at the front, chairs and walking sticks scraped the stained wooden floor as the congregation shuffled to its feet, in noisy competition with the elderly singer's faltering tones. At the same time, he was waving his hands in a furious gesture telling us to sit down, and so, once again from the front of the room to the back, everyone retook their seat. The entire Kaddish, a call for peace within and beyond the unity of the Jewish people, had been disrupted by this creaky indecision. In its small, tragi-comic way, the spectacle symbolized the ambiguities at the heart of this group – an expression, perhaps, of its uncertain relations to religion, to the political party, to the republic. It is these uncertain relations, and their reformulation within the changing nationalized and gendered contexts of occupation and liberation, that will be explored in this book.

Liberation was the moment that France emerged from the politics of exclusion that characterized Vichy and the Nazi occupation of France.[3] The Vichy regime sought to control not only what the inhabitants of France did, in the manner of all legislatures, but to mould the population according to ideals that befitted its National Revolution, embodied in the redrafted state slogan, *Travail, famille, patrie*. It rapidly enacted exclusionist policies. Exactly one month after the armistice of 22 June 1940, Vichy legislation stripped French nationality from those individuals who had been naturalized after 1927. This act was applied rather unevenly, directly affecting some 15,000 of the potential 900,000, and particularly targeted Jews.[4] Within a few months, the regime had barred foreigners (including these newly foreign) and married women (11 October) from public office and the liberal professions, repealed the law against antisemitic publications (27 August), and reduced Jews to inferior civil status, excluding them from many areas of public life and influence (3 October), before diminishing their rights still further the following year and stealing their property under the policy of what it called 'Aryanization'.[5] All Jews, including those born in France, effectively became foreigners in the early stages of the regime, which aided their later transformation into the special threat that would be 'solved' by deportation.[6] Jewish and non-Jewish refugees were forced into internment camps. About 3,000 Roma and Sinti were also rounded up into camps, where they remained until 1946, two years after liberation, and seventy were deported as forced labour to Germany.[7] All sorts of groups were regarded as not appropriately French, including freemasons, Protestants and resisters, 30,000 of whom were executed in France. Approximately 60,000 individuals identified as non-Jewish political resisters were taken to concentration camps in Germany. More than 75,000 Jews, two-thirds of them never having held French nationality, were transported first to transit camps in France and thence to the killing centres in Poland; all but about 5,000 ended their days in Auschwitz-Birkenau. In common with other parts of occupied Europe, more than half the Jewish deportees from France were taken in 1942, and more than a third of the total in just two months, July and August, of that year. They were rounded up across the occupied and non-occupied zones. Less than 3 per cent of the Jewish deportees, and about 60 per cent of the politicals would return.[8]

The politics of exclusion embodied in the National Revolution was not confined to those subject to deportation and internment, and cut still deeper into the social fabric. Vichy's insistence on the priority of the heterosexual Catholic family, which was seen most powerfully in its apparent elevation of motherhood which confined women to the home via its *femme au foyer* policy, the woman at home;[9] its reformulations of gender via youth programmes and labour constraints;[10] its veneration of the figure of Pétain, insisted on in the multifarious uniformed leagues that adults and young people were constrained to join; its introduction of specific legislation against male homosexuality – all these fed a radical new vision for a population deemed appropriate for France. For all its devastating impact on some elements of the population, many people managed to adapt without much difficulty. The regime was inconsistent, and regional differences in people's responses to it were stark. It is important nonetheless to remember the subtle depths at which Vichy ideology acted, as well as to seek the extent to which its legislative efforts achieved their stated ends, which had four years to take effect.

Vichy had new ideals to fulfil and was a radically different regime from its republican predecessors; it was also indebted to them.[11] The authoritarian republican government of Edouard Daladier installed in 1938, signed the Munich Agreement in September that year, and established some of the anti-immigrationist legislative framework and internment camps which were to prosper under Vichy and facilitate its projects. After a new wave of anti-communism had been unleashed by the Red Army's entry into Poland in September 1939, Daladier's government banned the French Communist Party (PCF). Even before the invasion in May 1940, Daladier was interning 'political undesirables'. Populationist concerns too had beset Third Republic governments and commentators since the First World War. Troubled by what they perceived as a falling birth-rate, particularly in comparison with its erstwhile enemy, Germany, pro-natalists had seen their support augment.[12] This was given state support in various ways, not least laws in 1920 and 1923 against abortion and contraception, and legislation that was supposed to support large families. In July 1939 when another war was all but certain, new measures designed to bolster the family and to repress abortion and contraception still further were enacted in the Code de la Famille.

Immigration from the colonies and Europe also increased during the inter-war years. Most of those arriving filled jobs in the industrial and agricultural sectors, whose needs were not met by labour available in France, though some came in search of educational opportunities denied them at home. In a European context of heightened political tension during the 1930s, and in which greater reliance was being placed on biological notions of race, the influx of these immigrants was in many quarters interpreted in terms of the threat and damage they might cause the republic. The arrival of thousands of refugees from the growing German Reich and Spain only exacerbated older tensions, so that by the time war was declared, many commentators and those in government were willing to accept that the non-French really did pose significant threats to national well-being.[13]

The concept that came to define and confine these disparate elements of the population was assimilationism. This was the mechanism whereby people learnt to become French. From its earliest days, the republic demanded that individuals regarded as welcome would need to conform to certain requirements in order to fulfil their duty to the republic and to benefit from the rights it conferred upon them. In defining itself as singular and indivisible, the Jacobin republic also instituted a set of exclusionary principles to identify those individuals permitted citizenship or the potential to become citizens. This dynamic contractual arrangement between the republic and its citizens, as well as those regarded as not, or not yet, appropriate for citizenship, is called here the assimilatory project. Its capacity at once to contain notions of assimilation that inevitably dilute difference, and notions of individualism in which difference resists redefinition, made the assimilatory project open to continual refinement. At the top, the state demanded conformity and excluded those it deemed nonconformist and maverick; at the bottom, the individual internalized assimilationism so as to make it their own. The project's dynamism privileged the individual's feeling that they had fashioned themselves within the universal, itself an inherent part of the project, and fashioned the universal within themselves.

Difference was inherent to assimilationism, not in opposition to it, and it always contained a 'double bind' whereby the community which the outsider was required to join could always reject it on grounds of difference.[14] In a work that provides a very clear analysis of assimilationism in France, Max Silverman argued that the national community was to supersede all other forms of identification in the modern nation-state that the republic inaugurated.[15] This was certainly true for men, who were the only people offered the possibility of citizenship. Women, though, had other primary allegiances. The modern French nation, while excluding women from access to public power and also from the democratic process of choosing which men should have access to it, was scarcely going to proceed entirely without women. But it demanded no single primary allegiance of them. Instead, they were split between identifying with the nation and the home. Women were as implicated in the assimilatory project as much as men, but the processes by which they were enjoined to participate in it were differentiated by gender; for women, nationality was but a part. Even when the Third Republic endeavoured the fullest realization of assimilationism that had been accomplished so far, by ensuring that everybody received an education in the French language that taught them to believe in the republic rather than the church, gender differences remained.[16] And those differences were as inherent to the assimilatory project as were differences based on national origin, which itself was sometimes equated with that other biological attribute, race.[17]

It is this dual interplay of race and gender within assimilationist discourses and the ways that they would help to define a new, liberated, republic after the occupation that will be scrutinized in this book. Quite apart from its denial of citizenship for women until 1944, the republic increasingly constrained women to define themselves in terms of their familial ties. The continuing effects of this would be seen during the Vichy period, as both Vichy and its opponents went to some lengths to represent women as the embodiment of these relations. In the social, political and economic conditions of inter-war France, Jacobin notions of necessary unity and universality were adapted, providing new sets of associations between the individual and the state. Laws on immigration, nationality and the family were all revised. Even if these were on occasion liberalizations of previous legislation, such as the 1927 law on nationality, they served to reconfirm and reconfigure the necessity of assimilationism.

The deep roots of assimilationism explain some of the continuities between Vichy ideology and republicanism. As has been implied, the cleavage between the two was never as clear cut as many republican commentators at liberation hoped. Certainly, republicanism was profoundly anti-clerical, while Catholicism was to triumph under Vichy. Equally, Vichy was deeply anti-republican and went so far as to put the Third Republic on trial. Yet the confluences between the two are manifold, in the systematic categorization and surveillance of non-French nationals, in the rapprochement between church and state, in anti-communism, and in the increasing acceptability of antisemitism.[18] As far as gender roles are concerned, despite profound differences between republicans and Catholics on the issue of motherhood, similarities between Vichy and its predecessors are also traceable. Historically, republicans, although the family was a core part of their world view, assigned to the mother a much less significant role in shaping the child than did Catholics. They expected that the mother would be the guide in the first stages of life, when the child needed a sort of repetitive education based on symbols that appealed on a non-rational level. Thereafter, the male child required an education based on reason and independence. Republicans therefore emphasized state schools, and sometimes even said that the child belonged to the state (since mothers were supposed to be too Catholic and too irrational, attributes that also justified denying women the vote).[19] For sixty years before Vichy, Catholics campaigned fruitlessly for recognition of the rights of the family in the sphere of education. Republican ideas on these issues are closely related to those concerning the assimilation of immigrant children, wherein the excesses of the mother were held to be more pronounced than ever, and the assimilation of girls who were to be trained to grow into mothers. Despite these divergent approaches to motherhood, the family remained a key part of republican thinking. The family's paradoxical rechristianization at liberation, as the secular republic was reinstated against Catholic Vichy, and the war-torn family emerged into a liberated future, will be explored in the next chapter. During the occupation, both the Vichy National Revolution and its dissidents went to some lengths to represent women as the embodiment of familialism. Other points of crossover are indicated by the presence in resister literature of antisemitism and anti-foreigner expression.[20] The extent to which resisters shared populationist ideas with Vichy is confirmed by Gaullist and communist expression. Framed especially, but not solely, by Gaullists, a revived post-war Jacobinism stimulated a public redefinition of uniformity and the assimilatory demands of the state, as our analysis of the state's focus on populationism will show. So, while the resistance protested against the radical *effects* of exclusionism, the categorical *basis* for that exclusionism was, in many ways, taken at face value.

The assimilationist framework sketched above forms the context in which a more detailed examination of aspects of Jewish life in Paris during and after the occupation will proceed. Its sister concept, assimilation, has been a major theme in the historiography of European Jewry. Since the destruction of a third of the Jewish population of Europe and same Jews in North Africa during the war, the assimilation of Jews has sometimes been seen as a negation of Jewish specificity, that reflected Jews' alleged voluntaristic but myopic assumption of the dangerous qualities of an inherently antisemitic society.[21] In conforming to state demands, it has been held, Jews who desired full integration in their societies divested themselves of outward signs of their Jewishness, without ever being able to leave behind the essential qualities that would permit their enemies to identify them as Jews when the time came, as it inevitably would. This move was further complicated by the fact that these Jews are also believed to have rescinded the qualities that formed their internal communities, and so became unrecognizable as Jews, except to those antisemites intent on distinguishing them under whatever guise. While this sort of analysis has pertained in particular to excursions into the reasons behind the rise of murderous antisemitism in Germany, the concern that Jews would stop being Jewish predate the Holocaust by at least a century. In France, as early as 1840, doubts were expressed whether succeeding generations would find anything on which to base their Jewishness:

The grandfather believes, the father doubts and the son denies. Grandfather prays in Hebrew, father reads the prayer in French and the son doesn't pray at all. Grandfather observes all the festivals, father only observes Yom Kippur, and the son observes none whatsoever. Grandfather has remained *Juif*, father has become Israelite, the son simply believes in God – as long as he isn't an atheist...[22]

As this quotation suggests, in France, the dichotomy between *Israélite* and *Juif* has in some senses occupied similar historiographic ground to the worries about assimilation. Under Napoleon, Jews – or at least Jewish men – were emancipated and became citizens of France of Jewish, or Mosaic, faith. Part of the contract with the state entailed the establishment of new administrative structures, the consistories, so that the state played a role in what might be regarded as the private affairs of the community. Around the same time, Jews of France came to be called *Israélites*. No longer did Jewishness form their entire identity, as members of that international and amorphous 'Jewish nation', and Judaism came to be regarded solely as a private religion, rather than in any way being able to determine Jews' public existence, such as which school they could attend or which profession they might carry out. For reasons more to do with what happened in the 1940s than the 1790s, the wholesale adoption of this name has been interpreted as a voluntaristic rejection of Jewishness, with the consequent implication that a secular *Israélite*, in rejecting Judaism as a faith, was in effect no longer Jewish. In this vein, Simon Sibelman noted that 'it is indeed astounding how rapidly and easily an entire community abdicated without regret its traditional Jewishness in favour of the more "universally acceptable" vision of the israélite'.[23] Then again, 'traditional Jewishness' and its exclusionary implications might have seemed a fair exchange for entry to citizenship in the early nineteenth century, when equality with other nationals was systematically denied Jews across Europe. Support for Sibelman's argument centres on public and largely urban pronouncements. It also implies that Jewish self-consciousness was somewhat flimsy in the face of changing state control. Given the noteworthy endurance of recognizable Jewish communities and expression in western Europe during the past millennium, such presumed insubstantiality seems implausible. It should be questioned why the term 'Israélite' implies so strongly for some a *lack* of

Jewishness, when the biblical allusion to the 'the people of Israel' is so plain. Even if 'Israélite' did decouple the sense of peoplehood from the religiosity of 'Juif', it seems doubtful that those drafting the Napoleonic Code had cleverly contrived a neologism and then unproblematically mapped it on to the population concerned.[24]

Prior to later Enlightenment rejection of biblical formulations of history, the terms 'Hebrew', 'Israelite' and 'Jew' (and their appropriate linguistic variants) had been deployed across Europe with a certain degree of accuracy in both Jewish and non-Jewish texts.[25] Thus, 'Hebrews' were positioned in the wilderness, the 'Israelites' were those who had settled the promised land, while 'Jews' were seen as members of the dominant remaining tribe of Judah and ancestors of contemporary Jewry. During the eighteenth century, 'Israelite' drew increasingly derogatory associations with the barbaric primitivism attributed to the age of King David, in distinction to a more respectful appellation, 'Hebrews', as original recipients of the word of God. With the rise of national consciousness and history's newly secular turn, 'Israelite' became a preferred term to impute a settled sense of nationhood, in contrast to the rootless 'Jew'. During the nineteenth century, the term 'Israelite' acquired the respectability attributed to it today, a meaning that was by no means limited to France. Nor was it contrasted in France with 'Juif' to the latter's detriment until the 1890s, which saw changes in antisemitic discourses in general, and the dramas of the Dreyfus Affair in particular, earlier debates over the two terms notwithstanding.[26] By the 1930s, *Israélite* had become associated with Jews whose families had been in France for many generations, and *Juif* with immigrants. The Jewishness of these immigrant, largely Polish, Jews tended to be more distinctive than that of non-immigrants: unlike Jews from France and other western European countries who spoke the local languages, Polish Jews habitually spoke Yiddish, and also wrote in Yiddish, on their shop fronts and in their newspapers. Like other immigrants, they lived and worked in close proximity to each other, establishing the sorts of links that make up a community – shops and businesses, leisure, religious and political, especially left-wing, organizations. They also lived in a society with the antisemitic propensities to notice them.

The view of western European Jewish communities as in flight from their cultural and religious specificities into the welcoming but still suspect arms of the state does not fully explain the complex developments that European Jewry underwent during the nineteenth and the first half of the twentieth centuries. In France, there was, and still is, little coherence between these communities in terms of depth of religious adherence, urban or rural location, manner of their arrival and reception in France, and gender.[27] While public statements from senior male members of some communities might flatter the authorities and bring these two parties into closer harmony, in the home, women were often expected to provide a traditional Jewish upbringing for their children. Where Jews in large cities might find numerous milieux in which to work and socialize, separations based on earlier ideas persisted in smaller towns. Allegiances could be multiple, and the sort of exclusive arrangements anticipated both by those who were suspicious of the entry of Jews into full civil rights, and some historians, do not bear close scrutiny.

Implicit within the condemnation of Jewish assimilation is a rigidity that counterpoises an assumed Jewish self-perception as the 'chosen people' against an exclusionary Catholicism unable to brook internal difference. Is it not the over-determination of hindsight that leads to the assumption that Jews who adopted majority culture automatically internalized the antisemitism that is supposed to have accompanied it, for does this interpretation not depend on the belief that the Holocaust should have loomed large long before it ever occurred? This perception also owes much to a vision of the European diaspora as one, for reasons of centuries of ineluctable antisemitism, essentially unsuitable for Jews. Yet the nature of antisemitism, and the reasons provided for its justification, far from continuous and unchanging, have shifted within varying historical and geographical contexts. For example, in the late nineteenth century, many migrant Jews saw Germany as a safer option than France, while in the 1930s, the situation was reversed.[28] Arguments about whether Europe was appropriate for Jews are indebted to Zionist historiographic inflections that suggest not one, but two places as suitable permanent homes for Jews: the promised land of Israel, and the *goldene medina* of the United States. Not only has the United States the largest Jewish population in the world, but its Jewish communities are by and large self-conscious of their Jewishness. The greatest proportion of the culturally significant Jewish population of the US has its roots in the eastern European communities that the Nazis later destroyed. These communities consisted of the *shtetls*, small towns, and of great centres of Yiddish learning and culture such as Vilna, known before 1939 as the 'Jerusalem of the East'. Since the Second World War, parts of the United States to some extent assumed this central role, but with the critical difference that in a sort of proto-Zionist move, the US itself has come to be seen as an authentic Jewish home. The Jewishness that existed in pre-Holocaust eastern Europe was characterized by economic independence, numerous urban centres with a high density of Jewish population, and particularism expressed through language, education and religion. From the romanticizing viewpoint of bourgeois Jewry, particularly in the United States, these characteristics are represented as immutable, as though they too would not have modernized given the chance. Instead, they have been critically compared to the acculturation and accommodation that Jews made in western Europe, where religious practice was reformed, languages unique to Jews declined in favour of national languages, and Jews, while tending to settle in urban over rural locations, were nowhere so numerous as they had been further east. Eastern European Ashkenazim have come to contain an authenticity denied and, apparently, betrayed by Jews of Germany and France, prior to the destruction of Jewish communities of the east, and their resurrection in Israel and, more particularly, the United States after 1945.

Judaism is a religion practised largely in the home. The examination of lives beyond and behind established, urban and generally male expression, reveal a more nuanced and complicated position *vis-à-vis* Jewish tradition than was suggested by the public utterances about *Israélites* noted above. What might abdication of 'traditional Jewishness' mean in the context of the household of that exemplar of assimilation, Captain Alfred Dreyfus, where an elaborately embroidered cloth depicting important Jewish holidays was displayed?[29] Jewish women in nineteenth-century western Europe were charged with responsibility for the acculturation of their children into the wider, Christian and national community, and yet blamed for their over-rapid assimilation when this came to be seen as problematic. They were also supposed to oversee their offspring's Jewish education. Their control over the domestic was vitiated through the inevitably imperfect fulfilment of these contradictory requirements. The home was a contested site, and the domestic was an affair at once public and private. The Jewish home, and a mother criticized as too Jewish or not Jewish enough – dependent to an extent on her children's relations to the outside world – allows us better to view the home less as a place of private refuge than as a corridor.

To such complex arrangements need to be added the abrupt changes of status that immigration brought about in the period before the Second World War, when people accustomed to life in small towns found themselves in a large city, when those who had kept relatively strict religious rules in Poland submitted to the need to work on Saturdays, when intellectuals became workers in the garment trades, when those who had felt oppressed by religion and small communities discovered the freedom of independent political activity in a vibrant city, or when married women whose lives had been eased by domestic servants found themselves burdened by low wages and full responsibility for running a home, to say nothing of the need rapidly to learn a new language and the rules of French culture.[30] If mothers themselves were anxious about all these changes, nationalist commentators were still more so. Doubts about the home and the mother's role in it in occupied and post-war France will come under further examination in chapters three and five, via discussion of the relationship between mother and child, and the non-French mother's responsibility for assimilation.

French Jewry's self-consciousness was changing after the Second World War. After the deportation of a quarter of the pre-war Jewish population, the meanings attached to '*Juif*' and '*Israélite*' had radically changed. It is not the case, though, that 'those who survived the War sought', through intermarriage, 'to escape their Jewishness in total assimilation'.[31] If that were the case, we would expect minimal particularist expression. Some merging of the particular into the general did occur, as when the Union de la Jeunesse Juive (Union of Jewish Youth) became the Union de la Jeunesse Républicaine de la France (Union of Republican Youth of France).[32] But in the late 1940s and early 1950s, Jewish journals proliferated, covering the full spectrum of political, religious and intellectual interest. They appeared in French, Yiddish and Hebrew, and were published in Paris, Marseilles, Strasbourg, Lyons, Algiers, Toulouse, Grenoble and elsewhere; the interest groups they sought included left- and right-wing Zionist youth, former resisters, the religious from orthodox to reformist, philosophers, anti-racists, students, Sephardim, and medical practitioners, among others.[33] By 1948 there were two Jewish primary schools and five *lycées*, an increase on the pre-war situation.[34] Jewish youth groups began to flourish,[35] and there were a number of children's homes. Oral sources suggest that people consciously sought a new Jewish milieu after the war that would contrast with the Jewishness that Vichy and Nazism had imposed during the occupation.[36] The symptomatic dichotomous approach of some historians, and the choice it enforces on its subjects to question whether they were French or Jewish limits our comprehension and relies for its truth on depicting a sole and unitary Jewish community, as well as a singular version of France. It is further hidebound by the view that individuals who chose a non-Jewish partner would find that person's religion to be inevitably dominant, a natural victor over a frail Jewishness alluded to above.

This picture can be drawn in greater detail via the examination of Jewish women's changing lives and expression during the occupation and will be approached here through the writings of a Jewish woman activist whose war-time diaries and journalism were published in the 1950s. Jacqueline Mesnil-Amar was born into a family of bankers and lived in the sixteenth *arrondissement* of Paris until the invasion. Hers was a classic life of the 'assimilated Jew', growing up with Jewish and non-Jewish friends and rarely, if ever, according to her diaries, questioning her place as a Jewish woman in pre-war France. The occupation changed all that, and the liberation had an even greater impact on her assessment of Jewishness. During the occupation, Mesnil-Amar became involved with the Armée Juive (AJ), the independent Jewish resistance organization founded in Toulouse in 1942. The AJ held dear the desire for a Jewish state, alongside the equally strong commitment to full Jewish rights in the diaspora. It later united other Jewish resistance groupings into the Organisation Juive de Combat. Mesnil-Amar's husband, André Amar, was one of its leaders. Along with thirteen others, he was arrested in July 1944 and imprisoned in Fresnes. When this group was deported in August from Drancy, most of the fourteen managed to escape from the train in northern France and he returned to Paris.[37] Jacqueline Mesnil-Amar provided funding for the AJ and was one of its liaison agents. In 1944 she became one of a group of women (who included Juliette Stern, Nine Jefroykin, Mme Lion, Gisèle Gonse and Tony Lublin) to establish the tracing and information service, the Service Central des Déportés Israélites (SCDI).[38] Between late 1944 and mid-1947, she wrote a column in their fortnightly journal, the *Bulletin du Service Central des Déportés Israélites*. In 1957, Les Editions de Minuit, the celebrated resistance publishing house established in 1942, brought out as one volume a collection of these articles preceded by selections from her war-time diary.[39]

The first entry reads: '18 July 1944. Rue de Seine, 11 p.m. A. hasn't come home tonight,' which immediately marks her as a waiting wife.[40] In occupied France, tens of thousands of women were waiting wives. Wives of prisoners of war had the most public and, for Vichy, respectable, face, but wives of maquis fighters also figured as resistance emblems of feminine virtue (before some of them were punished for their independence).[41] Immigrant Jewish women were denied the possibility of waiting: the threat of deportation made waiting a luxury, and affected many of the gender assumptions that might be made about women, the abnormal conditions of war and occupation notwithstanding. Those immigrant Jews who were apparently doing very little – and a degree of resentment sometimes adhered to people who seemed to spend their time sitting in the sun in southern French villages – were actively hiding, and the constant risks of betrayal deferred 'waiting' for less hazardous times.[42] Jacqueline Mesnil-Amar's ability to speak native French, her wealth, the social connections that arose as a consequence of these factors and her intimate knowledge of France in general endorsed her gendered self-characterization that severed her from immigrant women. Historically, as an active resister, Mesnil-Amar was far more than a waiting wife. That she should write herself as waiting, and thereby create her own discursive disconnection from immigrant Jews, should alert us to the subtle mechanisms of identity that emerge more powerfully elsewhere in the diary.

The text seems to offer a ready-made contrast between the native-born *Israélite* and the incoming *Juif*. Attachment to France is present, but it is the city of Paris that emerges as formative of notions of national belonging. Mesnil-Amar's ruminations on what never quite achieves the stature of alienation expose the limitations of assimilationism that the rest of this work will explore. Mesnil-Amar reflected constantly on whether or not she was foreign, as Vichy had decreed, and whether the city of her birth was indeed hers. On 23 August 1944, in the middle of the week from 19 to 25 August, when Paris was retrieved from the Nazis, she joined a non-Jewish resister whom she admired, Suzanne S. 'Yes,' the author reflects, watching Suzanne as, with the aid of her Black Martinican servant, she selected some special clothes suitable for building barricades, 'Suzanne will rediscover Paris and the Parisians. And I? I find myself between two worlds, between two destinies, subject to a series of hazards; which Paris will be mine?'[43] Meditations on the author's city, and on her position under threat, clarify the extent to which her prior claims on the city have been left intact by the invasion. This only serves to throw into sharper relief the immigrant's absence of security. What she saw, but suspected to be only temporarily unified, was a Paris of class and sexual unity, as diverse individuals emerged into the August sunshine to support the liberation. Hiding had provided her with opportunities to observe the local characters. Now she saw them joined in building barricades, but this did not diminish her disdain, however tender, for the prostitutes, homosexuals and working-class people who had become more visible to her while she attempted to maintain the fiction of her own invisibility:

At our barricade on the rue de Clichy, everyone's working together: the elderly, women, kids, the corner florist arranging her dusty pinks and faded roses, even the local prostitutes, the most painted and the most pale, abandoning their crocodile skin bags, tripping on their platform shoes – everyone is forming a chain for the cobble stones that the patriots are digging up, looking for iron bars, chairs to build crenelated defences, sandbags. The Parisians' uprising is bursting forth from the depths! All the classes are dragged into this frenzied whirlwind! . . . the strait-laced bourgeois, for they've finally ended up joining in, the shopkeepers, the black-market butter dealers, the antique shop owners, even the most 'refined' interior decorators of the Boulevard Saint-Germain have thrown themselves with virility into the chain ('Oh, but I simply must join the freedom fighters!' the blondest of them repeats, with a gentle flick of his wrist), finally the chic people (not too many), the concierges, students, and most definitely the sons of collaborators.

Despite this wonderful zeal [to build barricades everywhere] I do wonder what it's all really for. No matter! It's fantastic![44]

That week, hundreds of barriers built of paving stones, sandbags and old furniture blocked roads across the city to impede German escape and control. It is this image above all that has come to symbolize the popular Paris uprising that preceded liberation. As Mesnil-Amar suspected, the barricade was occasionally a more symbolic than practical measure. Instead of blocking the path of the German forces, they hindered the advance of the US army, and were sometimes taken down as fast as they were built.[45] Equally suspect here is whether the barricade, and its long history in popular Paris protest, really sufficed to erase the underlying differences among Parisians. Yet however conscious Mesnil-Amar was of these distinctions – and Vichy's separation of people from each other is a core theme throughout the diary – they are framed within terms that derive from exclusionism as well as against it.

In the diary, the increasing erasure of the author's sure sense of self reveals how these divergences operate in practice. The greatest impact, apart from the war, comes from the presence of outsiders in the shape of German occupiers and Jewish immigrants. At the book's opening, Mesnil-Amar's occupation-time residences had included Marseilles, Bordeaux and nine Paris addresses. Much of her time was spent seeking safe housing for herself, her parents and her daughter, all lodged separately. This unremarked 'women's work' of resistance as survival was fraught with danger, as it entailed trust and an ever-increasing number of people to be drawn into the secrecy of hiding.[46] The curfew imposed on Jews and their constant danger of arrest, closed down Paris for them as city of the polyglot and international human exchange. Re-establishing the city's former roles along these lines is part of the discursive work that Mesnil-Amar's diary performs towards closure.

The feeling of belonging, she asserted, was indispensable. Imagining that her husband would be deported – and return safely – she reflected on what a homecoming to France should entail. The deportee needed once again to feel at home, with his own armchair, lamp and room, and his own street and city to build on a sense of shared past. She further reflected:

The only decor, the only landscape that he seeks is that which cannot be reconstituted artificially – street life, the monument in the square, the broad accents of bus passengers, a schoolchild reciting the same irregular verbs and the same French history textbook that his father had learnt before him, a brother-in-law who announces a distant cousin's marriage to a former army comrade's nephew. The expatriate will only be cured within the arms of his country.[47]

Like the pious grandfather and his family cited above, the imagined returning deportee and those he has missed are male. Moreover, the implicit distance between the French and the non-French deportee, or the French and the non-French Jew, seems in this account to be permanent. The necessity that home be based on the deep familiarity of language, schooling and a shared historical past is denied immigrants. Their 'broad accents' are not what the deportee yearns to hear. If republican assimilationism was practised via schooling and military service, the significance of learning irregular verbs extends beyond a shared linguistic base, into the very mapping of the meaning of home.

Mesnil-Amar's potential fate as a Jew emerges through her increasing sense of ephemerality. Former certainties that she could gaze at others and see her own undistorted image reflected back have vanished. A telling passage during the evolution of this shift concerns her distant and yet shared subjectivity with a friend referred to as Madame L., who is unaware that the author is Jewish. Early in August 1944, the two friends sit in the Tuileries gardens, awaiting their husbands' return – Mme L.'s from a prisoner of war camp, Mesnil-Amar's from Gestapo detention. The two women watch children at play. Mesnil-Amar's vision of Paris and France is rooted in the solidity and apparent timelessness of the city itself:

my city Paris, such a subtle and secret vision of France. Surely in the thick shadow of your prison, dearest 'absent', wherever you are, wherever beats your heart, surely certain faces of your Paris return to haunt and reassure you. This tapestry of stones and foliage that is France, under the trees' long tresses, the prayers in its cathedrals, the land charged with faith and scepticism, defeats and victories, blood and freedom, crossroads of so many ideas, battles, and with these houses, these roads, these woods, which ever deepen down the centuries...[48]

This is a France that accommodates difference. Mesnil-Amar's identification with resister discourses can be interpreted in part via her adoption of the umbrella term 'the absent', then in widespread use, which referred to the prisoners of war, political deportees and forced labourers (almost all male) that the war had taken from their families, who together numbered more than 1.5 million. Commemoration of 'the absent' having been disallowed by Vichy, the new provisional government sponsored a 'week of the absent' in the period of acute nostalgia between Christmas and new year in 1944.[49] By this time, the end of the war was anticipated, and the government encouraged the belief that these men's successful rehabilitation would depend not merely on the re-establishment of their professional and local lives. The temporary ministry for prisoners of war, deportees and refugees, headed by Henri Frenay, was enjoined to facilitate the large-scale transfer of people from Germany in both practical and ideological terms. Those few surviving individuals who were not in Germany but had been taken 'to the east towards an unknown destination', as deportation to the killing centres in Poland was termed, did not benefit from any of these plans and had to make their own way back, journeys that took many months and, in some cases, years, following spells in displaced persons' camps. Republican reassertion of state assimilationism instrumentalized the notion of the 'absent'. Its unificatory aspects, which refrained from mentioning Jewish deportees, and women, included hefty doses of familialism that would reposition French women back into the republican – as opposed to the

Vichy – home, and restore the heterosexual family with the father at its head.[50] If the returning patriot needed an armchair, then women were to provide the cushions. In Mesnil-Amar's instance in August 1944, some ten months before the repatriation of the 'absent' was to start, her sense of Jewishness and commonality with other women that earlier she had regarded as mutual, had begun to be displaced as a result of her experiences as a Jew in occupied Paris:

> I look at this woman sitting next to me, foreign and similar to me, bound to this earth by so many roots from the past and the future, and at her side, I feel mobile and transitory, coming from far away through the centuries with this other secret face which is also me and which comes to me from 'elsewhere', I don't know where, from nowhere, and despite myself I am also the sister of all these children of Israel whom I don't know, the foreigners, the unknown, the tracked, the lost, my companions in misery, like me hunted and beaten by our Fate, our misunderstood God . . .
>
> And yet, in this torment that grips Europe, in this corner of Paris, in this garden, this evening like so many other evenings, like thousands of other wives without news, Mme L. and I, we wait, we wait . . .[51]

It was noted above that the diary character's resistance activism and Jewishness rendered her more than a waiting wife. Her comparison to the non-Jewish Madame L. clarifies the transience and mysteriousness of her Jewishness, formulated in terms largely adopted from outside. During the second half of the occupation, immigrant Jewish resisters battled against the reluctance prevalent among French-born Jews to form strong Jewish alliances. While it is known that some Armée Juive activists were immigrant, the deeper political ramifications of these alliances seem to have left Mesnil-Amar relatively untouched. Only 'despite herself' does she admit to connections with the 'foreign' and the 'lost'. It should not be forgotten that the author embraced Jewish particularism. Membership of the Armée Juive entailed swearing a secret oath in Hebrew beneath a Star of David flag. There were plenty of Jewish resisters who fought the occupation in organizations that were wholly dedicated to the restoration of the French republic and which paid little attention to the deportation of Jews or to Vichy antisemitism. The sensation of allegiance to the foreign 'despite herself' is therefore not the result of a refusal to recognize herself as Jewish. Such is the power of the combination of a class-infected republican assimilationism with Vichyist exclusionism that Mesnil-Amar cannot discuss her separateness except via discourses that exclude her at the very moment that those discourses become untenable. During the 1920s, the republic had not made Jewishness an issue: never had there been census questions about religion, for example. Now, in occupied France, Jewishness has become primordial, but Mesnil-Amar has no language to hand that allows her to locate herself. Only the materiality of Paris retains its reality in contrast to the ethereal semi-presence of other Jews, identifiable via the tracks and traces they inadvertently leave their hunters.

By the end of the week of the liberation of Paris, when crowds gathered at the Hôtel de Ville and there was dancing in the streets, the two worlds of Jew and non-Jew had seemingly been remade as one:

> That day, for the first time in four years, we were finally like other people; we could wave our false papers under the noses of police officers, burn our stars or pack them away in a drawer, we could shout our names, say who we were on the telephone, in restaurants; we were no longer these 'foreigners', these tourists, secret pedestrians in the city of our birth, or these prison fugitives, tracked from lodge to lodge, from attic to attic. We were returned to our deepest identity, to society, to France – to the war . . . Everything was easy as it had been before, exhilarating with ease, with dangers overcome, and of a common destiny. We were diving into a deep and divine similitude. We were *reconciled*.[52]

The extent to which Mesnil-Amar's occupation-time identity was a temporary one emerges here with force. Inasmuch as Vichy had fatally marked all Jews, it was indeed joyful to relinquish this identity at the end of the occupation. For *what* remains unclear: Madame L. and Suzanne S. both had roots in the future; Mesnil-Amar did not. Her future was defined by her past, and the certainties of that had just been dismantled, if not destroyed. But 'we were reconciled'? Scarcely.

The most striking aspect of her writing in the bulletin of the Service Central des Déportés Israélites, in comparison to the diary, is its profound *lack* of reconciliation. A deep sense of betrayal by her adored France replaces the diary's yearning and loss, with its hymns to Paris and high French culture. This dislocation has several roots: first, there is a difference in genre, as the author switched from writing a secret diary to journalism with a public addressee. Second, the imagined audience was broadened, since a diary's might be conceived as far from that for campaigning articles. The third divergence between the two forms of Mesnil-Amar's writing lay in knowledge of the Holocaust, which surfaced a few months after the newsletter's launch. But perhaps the most crucial distinction was in Mesnil-Amar's discursive transformation from transient onlooker to public political engagement. The diary voice adopted the character of a tourist, a mobile, unrooted passer-by of no fixed abode, whose only consistency was a desire for an unchanging Paris. In the journalism, this diary character gives way to an activist, which further masks the militant resister that the diary author in fact was. Only euphemistic expressions such as 'tourism' reveal clandestine hiding to have been undertaken with autonomy and an anticipated return home. This vision is in contrast to the one she provides of immigrant Jews, where a residual superiority tempers both her sympathy for their fate and her admiration for the combatants who made up the majority of resister Jews fighting against antisemitism:

These people still more alone than we, and poorer too! Sometimes very easy victims, innocent and pathetic prey, offered up to the perpetrators, sometimes combative in the extreme like these young OJC Jewish comrades. Young heroes...whom no one has helped apart from chance neighbours or the concierge who knew no parliamentarians, no ministers, no deputy mayors, not one single person in the world! And, quite frankly, hardly any French Jews either! Sometimes they have remained bitter towards the France that they loved, where they came with their parents, and which abandoned them. I like them however they are, even the badly brought-up, quibbling, difficult, quickly aggressive and fanciful, but often they're full of feeling, generosity, intelligence, and they threw themselves madly into the clandestine war...with their dark eyes, their feverish complexion, their foreign accents, their imprudent words, their over-French 'noms de guerre' and their vengeance. Their sublime vengeance, sacred as God.[53]

Representing immigrant Jews via their aggression and physical appearance suggests that Mesnil-Amar, while regretting the paucity of their contacts with French-born Jews, herself knew them little or at least relied on pre-war public perceptions that the occupation had done little to alter. Her alliance with them – based in part on an imposed love of France – is conditional on immigrant Jewish participation in the resistance. With regard to their false names, it was suggested (by one of Mesnil-Amar's resister comrades) that it was Jews of French origin who took the most French-sounding false names during the clandestine period.[54] Communist immigrant Jewish resisters protested with vehemence these fractures between resister Jews.[55] And yet, despite Mesnil-Amar's self-conscious amalgamation of Jewish and resister values, national, class and cultural divisions among activists seem more marked for her than any cohesiveness that ethnicity, politics or, indeed, persecution might confer. Mesnil-Amar's protest against Jewish divisions is formulated as a complex extension of exclusion.

How far these divisions extended into understandings of suffering tells us a great deal about their nature at liberation. Non-French Jews had been subject to the earliest deportation orders and made up the majority of Jews deported from France. The biggest round-up of the occupation, the Vél d'Hiv *rafle* in Paris on the 16–17 July 1942, for example, targeted only Jews who had never held French nationality including, for the first time, women and children. As women with children were initially taken to the Vélodrome d'Hiver sports stadium in western Paris, the round-up quickly became known as 'Vél d'Hiv'. In liberated Paris, discourses of Christian suffering were widespread in visual and written texts and were not, as one historian suggests, later additions to a historicist canon of suffering.[56] A major meeting of former deportees and prisoners of war in support of world peace, for example, was advertised with a variety of posters that dwelt on this theme. One depicted a deportee in concentration camp stripes, arms spread as though crucified, while another showed a number of saints and more recent martyrs encircling the important Paris churches, to produce an image of Paris as the global representation of suffering in a Catholic frame. Other public images of this time include Raymond Gid's red, white and blue poster to welcome the return of the absent which shows a skeletal man, reminiscent of the concentration camp inmate, with a red sacred heart, and Georges Rouault's sombre anti-war series, the Miserere, which, although it had been planned in the 1920s, was only revealed to the public in 1948.[57] Texts by Jewish immigrants, which might be expected to demonstrate greater claims to notions of suffering (albeit devoid of Catholic references), tended to relinquish this stance in favour of images of strength and renewal. In March 1945, *Droit et liberté*, the UJRE weekly, suggested:

The Jewish community of France has escaped the major Nazi massacres relatively well in comparison with eastern and central European countries. In consequence, it will be called on to play an important role in the renaissance of Jewish life in Europe. Certainly, we have suffered cruelly with our 120,000 deportees. But, thanks to the active solidarity of the French people, we have had the luck to save a great number of our children who were destined for destruction.[58]

Here, it is not prior suffering, but successful resistance – that is, survival – that endows immigrant Jews with value. Implicitly gendered – the article was written by an activist in the Union des Femmes Juives – immigrant Jewish worth is achieved through children, approximately 60,000 of whom were not deported. The author combines here claims for France, since the French helped to save the Jewish people, and for internationalism that made it vital to consider Jews beyond French national boundaries. Her suggestions merge post-Holocaust demands for Jewish reproduction with republican assimilationist pro-natalism that was already underway. Nonetheless, she writes in favour not simply of a French renaissance – a favourite PCF desire at this time – but for an identifiably Jewish future too. Across the political spectrum, commentators reiterated a relatively self-enclosed nationalism after the occupation. In defiance, the internationalism present here invokes a Jewishness which demands recognition while serving to bestow greater merit on the republic.

At liberation, former Jewish resisters emphasized Jewish agency again and again. The photograph captioned 'Freedom rediscovered: liberated Jewish women from the Kaunitz camp show their tattooed arms' (illustration 1) that *Droit et liberté* reproduced in April 1945 is a case in point.[59] Here, women wearing the headscarves of slave labourers

Illustration 1: Liberated Jewish women (YIVO Institute, courtesy of USHMM Photo Archives)

are shown laughing and showing off the tattoos on their forearms. It is difficult to read the photograph unless it is against images of the camp survivor that have become familiar to us. Even in April 1945, stories were appearing daily of the horrors being revealed from concentration camps in Germany, and the gaunt face of the concentration camp survivor was becoming a recurrent figure in the press at this time.[60] Images of men returning from Buchenwald, staring blankly from the windows of trains or leaning on walking sticks as they entered centres set up for their immediate care, formed the majority of those published. The arrival in Paris of the first female political resisters freed from the women's concentration camp, Ravensbrück, was also covered in April 1945 before the news was eclipsed by President Roosevelt's death the following day. Women were described as having aged beyond measure; it was said that people who seemed to be grandmothers turned out to be youngsters. In contrast, the women in the Kaunitz photograph are not skeletal, nor are they shaven. Smiling, they point to the tattooed numbers on their arms as to a prize. Indeed, in the version published in *Droit et liberté*, the tattoos were touched up to increase their prominence and to forge an indisputable link between the tattoo and the smile. The tattoo, while a mark of persecution, was also a sign of survival, as only those not selected for immediate death would receive a number. In accentuating the tattoo, the photograph underlines what might be read as the eroticism of the women's bare arms, which goes some way to sexualizing the tattoo itself, that permanent distinction between Jews transported to die and the rest of the European population. *Droit et liberté*'s publication of the photograph refused the more usual portrayals of moribund concentration camp survivors seen elsewhere. It asserted a Jewish femininity that refused to die, and that moreover declared itself sexual, independent and unbroken. The photograph is also part of a new repertoire that initiated the process whereby Auschwitz, the only camp in which inmates were tattooed, became synonymous with the Holocaust.[61]

The texts in *Droit et liberté* and that of Mesnil-Amar shared a disdain for the dominance of suffering and redemption that pervaded republican discourse at the end of the war. De Gaulle's victory speech on 8 May 1945 is a prime example: 'Not a single effort by [France's] soldiers, her sailors or her aviators, not a single act of courage or of self-effacement by her sons and daughters, no suffering of her prisoners of war and their wives, no mourning, no sacrifice, not a tear will have been lost!'[62] Here, he stressed the worthwhile sacrifice for national good and eternal memory that the French people as a whole had made. Jacqueline Mesnil-Amar reacted in anger, repeating, if misquoting, again and again de Gaulle's phrase, 'no mourning, not a tear in vain,' as a dissident response to his victorious litany. Where the Jewish communist text quoted above applauded the survival of Jewish children, Mesnil-Amar confronted the public instead with children's destruction and irredeemable loss. For her, no national glory was permissible when so many Jews, especially children, were killed. In her reply to the speech, a new connection to non-French-born Jews accompanies her former emphatic and emotive bond with a France that she continues to see as unquestionably her own:

Must I spell out that we, the Jews of France, march on this marvellous night in the joy of France with even more ghosts at our side than everyone else... [ghosts] who arrived [at] Auschwitz where the SS, assisted by their doctors, yelled the call to death so methodically... *All the children*... so many children, massacred because they couldn't work, thrown in the ovens with their mothers because they didn't want to leave them?... All this wasn't in vain? There is some sense in such suffering? And am I to understand this evening, General de Gaulle, that France claims for *itself* not only the misfortune of these French Jews that it can't deny because they belong to it, these French Jews bursting with love for their only country, of whom we know exactly which hymn they were singing as they departed, with which cry they died. But what of the misfortunes of the *others*, those who weren't French? These people to whom France gave asylum, who were taken to its land, who were rounded up by 'summons', or passport checks and held for months in Vichy camps, then handed to the Germans... these foreigners of whom many had lost their sons for France, and these poor French army prisoners who are now returning to find no one, neither wife nor children, taken, alas, by our French police?... Do I take it that none of this

27

suffering will be disowned, even that of the most off-putting, the most distant, the most foreign, and should I think that your 'Vive la France' includes all these dead?

France, my country where I was born, you have rewarded me this evening for my sorrows; I would like to kiss the cobbles on your streets, the walls of your houses, Paris, oh my city, and sleep tonight on your earth which is my land, where I hope one day to sleep forever. And my ghosts and my absent ones and my dead who walk beside me, you have recovered them as well, they have found you again.

But the 'others', distant brothers of the transports and the camps, those who were not born here and who were prey to all kinds of suffering, towards whom will their dead turn?[63]

These are hardly the words of reconciliation. Nine months after liberation, Paris remains the revered and sacred city it was in the diary; Mesnil-Amar's entitlement to the land of her birth and her imagined interment in its earth have not been revoked. Indeed, these prior claims, compared with those who had none and who are presented as lacking any connection to the city, are exposed even more starkly. De Gaulle's insistence on sacrificial unity and his consequent erasure of the death of non-French Jews, now become ghosts, has jarred Mesnil-Amar's conviction of her own place in France, even while she continues to distinguish between the relative certainty of 'home' felt by the French-born and non-French-born Jew. But her new-found necessity to act on behalf of the 'others' serves to underscore again the differentiation between French and non-French Jew within the diary. Her angry mobilization of these unacknowledged dead, figuratively waving them under de Gaulle's nose as she had proposed doing with the false papers of the living, repositions their memory back into an imagined land from which they will physically be forever gone.

And yet . . . France, for Mesnil-Amar as for de Gaulle, has become a holy territory of the dead and she narrates the disarticulation of her rightful place in words that underwrite Gaullist unity even while they deride it. Redemption through war is possible, she suggests, and the problem lies in de Gaulle's exclusion of the foreign dead from the community of the blessed, rather than the fact that they died at all. Mesnil-Amar's dead are glorified through their recovery, they walk side by side with her on Paris streets as ghosts, an image that cannot fail to conjure up that of de Gaulle's triumphal march through the masses along the Champs Elysées on 26 August 1944. Mesnil-Amar's demands that immigrant Jews be included in the war dead nationalizes the immigrants, integrating them into a discourse which never permitted them space when they were alive.

And yet again . . . Mesnil-Amar undeniably celebrates republican assimilationism, and the physical and moral landscape in which it occurs.

She does not, however, unthinkingly embrace assimilationist uniformity or refuse Jewish particularism. She may speak in terms familiar from the language of assimilationism, but she suggests something more complex. We know much about the bilateral versions of national unity that were declared at liberation – on the one hand, de Gaulle's fantasy of a singular France that had liberated itself in unison with him, on the other hand, a vast resistance fused with the clandestine communist party. In her insistence on a place for the immigrant Jewish dead, on recognition of the utter pointlessness of their mass murder, and on France's responsibility for these crimes, Mesnil-Amar departs from these stories of national unity at the very moment of their narration.

Narrating liberation for Mesnil-Amar was in the process of evolution and change even as the liberation progressed. The issues her texts raise map out many of the areas of enquiry that will be deepened in the pages that follow. These refer to Paris as formative of a certain French identity, and of the separation between Jews born in France and those migrating from elsewhere, especially Yiddish-speaking eastern Europeans. The diary drew out some of the meanings of the life of a clandestine, and one under double threat, being targeted as both a resister and a Jew – though those Jewish resisters deported as resisters rather than as Jews had a greater chance of survival in the concentration camps in Germany than in the killing centres in Poland. The absence of much narrative of what Mesnil-Amar the resister did owes something to the diary's necessary secrecy, but also to her gender, and thus the text opens questions associated with women resisters, typically identified as joined familially to men, as well as aspects of the female response to liberation. The disappointments of liberation that many women expressed are evident in Mesnil-Amar's response to de Gaulle's victory speech, and her linkage of that with the Jewish tragedy of the war years lends the glories of liberation a special piquancy. Reading this text of liberation allows the reader to recall how central the question of the Holocaust was for some at the time. This is in sharp contrast to subsequent historical accounts which have started to regard the emphasis on the Holocaust as overdone and anachronistic since, it is said, they come more than fifty years after the events, contradict discourses of the time and are expressed by and large by individuals who were not there.[64] Motherhood also plays its part here, and the maternalism of Mesnil-Amar, Perela Traler and other women resisters is something we will explore further. Ways of narrating the liberation have been in constant shift in the years since the war. Anticipating liberation, however, started as soon as the German authorities had established their rule. How liberation was imagined, and what sort of social divisions would emerge within a France liberated from its Vichy and Nazi rulers, is our next point of departure.

Chapter 3
Anticipating liberation: the gendered nation in print

Late in 1943, when the all-male Fédération Nationale de la Presse Clandestine was founded within the resistance Mouvement de Libération Nationale (MLN), there was plain agreement on what the resistance press was, and that indeed a coherent genre of clandestine journalism existed.[1] When people found the first home-made leaflets protesting against the occupation in their letterboxes, it is doubtful that any such grandiose or collective notions were at play that would permit either actors or recipients to conceive of their work as unified. Nor is it likely in 1940 that many regarded the roughly copied single sheets as journalism inasmuch as they were neither for sale nor did they much resemble newspapers. But in an environment of censorship and the suppression of communications between the different zones, information became as scarce as other goods. People read the clandestine press as much for news that was otherwise impossible to obtain as for the fulfilment of their desire for comment coloured by a politics they shared.[2] The latter is a standard attribute of the press, whether published under conditions of relative freedom or not. The clandestine press also performed a third, but equally important function: it helped to instrumentalize and confirm readers' opposition to the occupation.

Aspirational liberationism – what France would look like after the occupation – was repeatedly exposed in clandestine literature. Alongside aversion to the current regime it discussed a liberated political and social future at a time when this could only be fantasy. This examination of clandestine literature concentrates on the women's press – that 8 per cent of the total number of titles which was aimed at women. In some ways it was no exception to the general trends just outlined, although it had its own interests, styles and concerns. How did it construct an idea of femininity appropriate to France in the context of state racism that was supported by authors and journalists?[3] How far did it oppose Vichy's views of France and femininity, and what were the ramifications for the post-liberation period? What role did constructions of sexuality play in the press's definition of women as French? Finally, what happened at liberation, when the clandestine

Table 1 *Annual clandestine press production in France*

Year	Number of copies
1941	100,000
1942	250,000
1943	1,000,000
1944	2,000,000

Source: André Bendjebbar, *Libérations rêvées, Libérations vécues 1940–1945* (Hachette, 1994), 79.

press metamorphosed from oppositional secrecy into a new hegemonic order after the war?

One of the German authorities' early acts in occupied France was to inaugurate press censorship and control of other publishing through the Propaganda Abteilung (18 July 1940). A month later, Vichy repealed the Marchandeau law that had banned racist publications. Antisemitic weeklies such as *Au pilori* and *Je suis partout* and, later, monthlies like *Le Cahier jaune* and *L'Ethnie française* could be openly distributed.[4] Despite the Propaganda Abteilung's lists of approved and banned publications, contained in the Service W and Liste Otto respectively, its success with books was limited.[5] Other media were subject to stricter and, from the occupier's point of view, more effective surveillance, and newspapers were heavily censored.[6] Much of the earliest resistance, therefore, was dedicated to the publication and dissemination of views oppositional to Vichy, collaboration or occupation. These activities endured throughout the four years of occupation and by 1944, small format publications up to sixteen pages long, such as *Les Lettres françaises* or *Franc-tireur* had grown into recognisable newspapers that appeared with relative regularity. Some – for example, *Défense de la France*, *Combat* or *Libération* – continued after the war. These papers were the exception.[7] Most resistance press remained spasmodic and small-scale; readers shared the rare, poorly printed copies until they were scarcely legible. The authorities' control, and the relatively large number of people involved in finance, journalism, production and distribution, meant that producing this press involved considerable risk and many titles have been lost. Nevertheless, well over a thousand are listed in the largest catalogue of these journals.[8] As the war progressed, annual production increased exponentially; between January and August 1944, it is estimated that about 2 million copies of papers appeared (Table 1), though even these figures may be conservative given that one paper, *Défense de la France*, alone produced 450,000 copies.[9] Certain cases have become celebrated. Growth of the clandestine press was in inverse proportion to that of the official press, whose production figures – at least in Paris – fell from a high in 1940 to a steady low in 1942 and 1943.[10] But there was no correlation between print-run figures and readership, for while the authorities impounded many papers, countless individuals read the surviving copies. As far as the women's press is concerned, print-runs are impossible to ascertain. All that can be stated for certain is that where region of production is known, the proportion of papers produced in the Zone nord was about twice that of those from the Zone sud.

For all their numerical abundance, publishing a clandestine newspaper required some effort. With paper and ink supplies under strict control, finding, acquiring and hiding the necessary materials was only the first step. Type had to be set (or stencils typed for small offset production for the press examined here) at night, printing machines found or stolen, and skilled printers entrusted with the larger papers.[11] Distribution and bill-posting, often undertaken by women, were perhaps even more fraught, as discovery in possession of these forbidden materials could lead to arrest and deportation or execution.[12] 'Chucking a bundle of tracts from the top of a railway bridge was just as perilous as throwing a grenade into a garage,' commented one former resister, confirming figures that show that most women arrested in the Paris region were held on charges relating to tracts or journals.[13] This neatly counteracts the view that armed resistance, largely carried out by men, involved greater bravado than women's, though such an idea has been repeatedly asserted since liberation. It was not unusual for women to cycle hundreds of kilometres, or dart in and out of buildings under the nose of police officers, or develop more creative distribution methods, such as showering cinema-goers with tracts from a balcony at the moment the word 'fin' appeared on screen.[14] While certain writers and politicians made or enhanced their reputation (though hardly their 'name') as anonymous or pseudonymous resistance authors, for the more marginal resistance press, immediacy, small resources and fear of discovery meant that papers were hand-made in small quantities.

All these factors applied to the women's press. Some studies of the clandestine press have emphasized its producers' professional pride in quality, the fact that named individuals were involved with different titles and that the means of production were technically quite advanced.[15] This did not apply to the women's press. Rarely typeset, it consisted of single-sheet, two- or four-page bulletins produced in haste and under penurious conditions. Many had hand-lettered mastheads; every inch of the paper was covered with cramped, typewritten articles and occasional drawings. As the resister Esther Frydman explained, in the summer of 1942, 'our Solidarité committee was made up of women in the twentieth *arrondissement* of Paris. They had decided to publish an appeal to the Jewish population of the *arrondissement*. We got ourselves a primitive "printer" – in fact it was a children's toy – and Sunday afternoons we got down to work at our "new job".'[16] Production conditions may have been makeshift, but that did not undermine the significance of the papers. That they survive at all is a mark of the combined assiduity of the censors on one side and the producers and recipients on the other. Where the regional spread of the 'professional' clandestine press centred on anything between a city and a zone, the smaller publications for women sought a neighbourhood readership. Their typical means of distribution was to be handed out quickly to women waiting in food queues. In the politics of exclusion operating in occupied France, this haphazard and dangerous diffusion method meant that Jewish women were even less likely than others to receive a copy as their shopping was restricted to the last hour of trading each day. It would be a mistake to view the women's press as journals at an earlier stage of evolution, or aspiring to imitate the larger press. Their home-made quality expressed women's own participatory capacities in a way a 'professional' newspaper could not.[17] In consequence, the women's press could capitalize on the relative ease with which readers might perform resistance tasks within or not far from their domestic environment.

Esther Frydman may imply that the decision to publish a paper was independent. In fact, the clandestine communist party or its various fronts, in the form of women's committees that started to meet from 1940, initiated much of the women's press. In 1944 these committees collectively became the Union des Femmes Françaises (Union of French Women, UFF).[18] Towards the end of the occupation, their papers often attributed production to 'the Union of women for the defence of the family and for the liberation of France' – though the journals spoke somewhat more in favour of the former, while enjoining the reader to demonstrate their commitment to the latter. Some papers for women were produced directly by the clandestine communist party. Groups of *marraines* (godmothers) who supported individual Francs-Tireurs et Partisans (FTP) fighting groups also produced papers towards the end of the occupation. Aside from these, two papers had Jewish interests, one came from the Mouvements Unis de la Résistance (MUR), one was trade union and four were for prisoner of war wives.[19] It should not be inferred that non-communist resistance organisms were uninterested in female militants. Instead, they used other recruitment and communications methods, had different objectives and were less interested than communists in building a mass resistance movement.[20] The communist party had long advocated local activism and had developed effective organizational hierarchies. Anticipating illegality arguably formed part of its foundational structure. This helped in its bid to become one of the major organizers of resistance, despite its confusion after the Nazi–Soviet pact, which has in any case been subject to some misrepresentation. More than other groupings, it regarded women as a significant potential resister constituency worthy of being addressed in literature designed for them alone. Nor were women the only group singled out in this way. Resistance papers from various political camps addressed a huge variety of sectors – peasants, cinematographers, teachers, anti-racists, immigrants of diverse origin and in a variety of languages, musicians, Jews, medical personnel and inhabitants of individual districts, towns or regions, to name only a few. Reading the women's press therefore cannot encompass all resistance views.

The pre-war forerunners to this press might help to explain its profusion during the occupation. The PCF, having been banned in September 1939, was already publishing clandestine journals before the occupation, and other political groups were accustomed to publishing bulletins. Immigrant communities had formed networks with journals at their heart.[21] In the 1930s, the PCF's Main-d'Œuvre Immigrée (Immigrant Work-Force, MOI) sections based on language provided a further boost. Between 1936 and 1939, women could read the pro-natalist – and flirtatious – *Jeunes Filles de France* published by the PCF's young women's organization, the Union des Jeunes Filles de France, and edited by the future resistance heroine Danielle Casanova.[22]

During the occupation, the women's press covered issues regarded as resting within women's sphere, and archivists have curated these journals in collections of resistance press. But the question of how far the women's press was *journalism* remains far from simple to determine. In idealistic and contestatory mode shortly after liberation, Albert Camus, then editor of *Combat*, understood a free press in the following terms:

> The press is not an instrument of commercial profit; it is an instrument of culture. Its purpose is to give accurate information, to defend ideas, to serve the cause of human progress ... The press is free when it does not depend on either the power of government or the power of money, but only upon the conscience of its journalists and readers.[23]

Camus was defending the post-clandestine press against government control after the liberation. The provisional government decided on 22 June 1944 that all pre-occupation journals that had continued to appear after June 1940 were by definition collaborationist and at liberation would be forced to cease trading; the same conditions applied to those journals that had begun publishing after the armistice was signed.[24] The sole daily newspaper to be permitted after liberation was *Le Monde*, but it was not only the collaborationist press that was singled out for closure. In the weeks that followed liberation, kiosks displayed a wealth of former clandestine newspapers but many papers could not afford to continue, and others were hampered by new rules governing content.

The resistance tool of which Camus had been an important part thus found itself both celebrated and discouraged and, one by one, papers disappeared. But Camus's idealism did not tell the entire story about the clandestine press. In terms of conscience, it would seem clear from his definition that the women's press did indeed form part of a free press. In terms of accuracy and information provision, however, the women's press did not reach Camus's standard, even if we accept the unconvincing premise that its readership only sought the information actually contained therein. This becomes clearer if, in contrast to Camus's approach as an editor, we investigate the act of reading.

Resisters' reading

It was said at the time, and subsequently, that one of the resistance's primary aims in publishing newspapers was to recruit readers.[25] This suggests that the clandestine press could be transformative of readers' opinions, and that editors were sufficiently knowledgeable of potential resister motivation as to be capable of manufacturing a publication that could aid in a one-way process that led from print via reading to participation. Readers' relationships to the press were rather more nuanced.[26] A journal could help to channel pre-existent desires into action, and provide a set of contacts – to 'feed their courage', as one former resister remarked.[27] Madame Hanna, for instance, attributed her active involvement in the FTP–MOI to the catalyst of a resistance tract. Not long after the Vél d'Hiv round-up, she found a clandestine flyer. By this time she had taken refuge just outside Paris, and her landlord's fear of being discovered with this document on his premises combined with her existing political stance to impel her to leave the relative safety of her housing, find a resistance network and eventually go underground until liberation.[28] It seems to have been as much the landlord's rejection of clandestine literature as that literature's appeal to the nascent resister that provoked Madame Hanna's political conscience. Yet the debate over whether reading constituted an act of resistance in itself was not one that emerged only after the fact. *Mères de France* ironized this self-reflexivity; under a hammer and sickle masthead it shouted, 'A communist journal! The "hammer and sickle"! No! Not that! I don't read that kind of thing! Brrr!!!' before reassuring readers that the party was the sole organization to protect 'the happiness of your maternity'.[29] Madeleine Baudoin, leader of an armed unit in Marseilles, was scathing of those 'resisters' who found reading an adequate form of protest:

You either did something or you were one of the mass who wouldn't do anything. Everyone found ways of getting bread, more vegetables, more food. But they didn't resist the Germans. There were a few individuals in Marseilles before 1942: a few small groups of resisters... but it was mostly a question of discussion and writing tracts. Very few of those who wrote or read tracts went into active, armed resistance after 1942.[30]

Baudoin's isolation in armed resistance notwithstanding, the rigid separation between active resisters and those who 'merely' read and wrote tracts is questionable. Producers of the press, often involved in resistance that went beyond tracts, needed to disseminate their opposition to the occupation, and reader-resisters needed to know that they shared their hatred of the occupation with others; both could encourage each other. Reading could palpably aid resistance: while we do not know figures, many of the 12,000 Jews who escaped the Vél d'Hiv round-up (which had planned for 25,000 but in the event captured slightly under 13,000) hid because they had read about it beforehand in leaflets delivered to the door in defiance of normal resister practice.[31] Moreover, the process of engagement did not necessarily start with words and end in action, but could work in opposite or two-way directions. And yet people who did not read the clandestine press also counted themselves as non-resisters. In response to questions as to whether she had read this press, for example, Madame Denise replied that she played no part in the resistance at all, suggesting that the link between reading and resistance was manifest.[32]

The women's press contained limited and few representational models of femininity. It is therefore easy to comprehend the impatience and disappointment that are evident in one early study of it.[33] Reading it in the hushed and reverent environment of the Bibliothèque Nationale's rare books department reinforces only one aspect of continuity between its original conditions of production and the present day: its scarcity value. Otherwise, the constant demands for greater milk and bread rations and for readers to demonstrate outside this or that town hall seem rather repetitive to the modern reader, and perhaps to former readers too.[34] The restrictive view of women as motherly carers is equally hard to avoid. Yet we should recall the thrill consequent upon reading one of these documents in a bread queue or in the 'privacy' of a woman's home (where it could always be discovered during a raid). Only now do we have the luxury of reading these journals *en bloc*, obscuring the extent to which their clandestine nature augmented their worth and significance.

The women's press shared with the clandestine press in general this excited reading engendered by rarity. Its content was markedly different. The largest proportion of articles in the women's press consisted of calls for campaigns to improve rations and to prevent food and fuel being exported to Germany. The suggested means of protest to achieve these ends were demonstrations and delegations to the town hall and, more rarely, strikes. After 1943, there were protests against the transportation

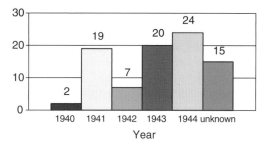

Figure 1: Women's clandestine press: first publication date by year

of STO workers and, occasionally, resisters, and readers were enjoined to demonstrate at embarkation points. It is probably the start of the STO that explains the increase in production, just as it motivated thousands of other resisters (Figure 1). There were also calls to help wives of prisoners of war, complaints about the black market and hoarding, and news of successful actions carried out elsewhere in France. The press called special demonstrations to mark French victory over Germany, such as 11 November or Valmy (whose 150th anniversary fell on 20 September 1942)[35] and attacked Vichy for causing undue suffering to children and the elderly. Finally, it appealed for readers to raise funds. International news was a rarity.[36] In 1944, we find increased encouragement for women to collect medical supplies, clothes and money for resisters and occasionally to join armed units. The lack of political news beyond the domestic interests assigned to readers and the absence of any extended commentary are the initial significant differences between this and the general clandestine press. A few exceptions aside, the female reader's interest was framed in local and domestic terms – similar, in fact, to images evident elsewhere.[37]

One of the strengths of the clandestine press was its instrumentalization of the local and temporal context. In a France hewn into pieces, the acquisition of information in one zone about events in another was vital. The women's press deliberately invoked the familiar in a way that non-resisters could understand: for example, after Allied bombs targeted at industrial areas had devastated the local population, the press called on bombed-out mothers not to let their children be sent away to Vichy camps.[38] Likewise, it confronted Vichy familialism, but here, against the pressure of Vichy policy and its contradictory practice, it could only ironize and invert. Early disgust at the expulsion of women from the labour force and back into the home[39] soon gave way to a recasting of Vichy rhetoric. So, papers demanded a 'real' home, not the removal of women from the confines of the domestic sphere. Young women's 'dearest desire', *Jeunes Filles de France* asserted, was ' "to create a home" where they will no longer be servants, but French women, workers, peasants, intellectuals'.[40] Vichy did not imagine French women as workers, and still less as intellectuals. Like Vichy, though, the clandestine press went some way towards identifying the French nation with the domestic.[41] Far from the Pétainist lie that Vichy protected the family, the birth-rate and the mother and child, papers suggested, Vichy tore families asunder, removed men and so prevented the birth-rate from rising, and provided insufficient means for women and children to maintain their health. For many papers, protection of women and children was in itself an act of opposition, particularly in respect of the STO.[42] These compromised critiques of Pétainism signalled the way for the protectionist pro-natalist policies of the liberation that will be discussed in the next chapter. Exposés of Vichy maternalism were resister inversions of a hated regime; but, as in any inversion, the original was almost as necessary to the clandestine women's press as to Vichy.

The women's press sought not so much the introduction of a new form of democracy in which women might play a fuller part as the restoration of democracy defined in conventionally gendered terms familiar from the 1930s. Marie-France Brive noted the unanimous esteem in this press for women's traditional nurturing roles. She suggested that women adopted positions at odds with each other, reading them as active agents in the construction of this 'unanimity'. While they might have refused the totalizing confines of the home by becoming reader–resisters and as a consequence recognized their anti-Nazi or anti-Pétainist position, they also endorsed the limited range of self-images which Brive argued they had been offered.[43] To be sure, there is little evidence that resistance inevitably implied a commitment to anti-Pétainism, and it should not be assumed that readers of the clandestine press would have necessarily departed from Pétainist domesticizing ideology.[44] Nor should the simultaneity of resistance via reading, and acceptance of limited, and possibly Pétainist, versions of femininity be regarded as contradictory. Anti-Pétainism – or pro-Pétainism, for that matter – were not absolutes, and while the gender perspective of these journals may have followed Pétainist ideology, their demand for better housing in which maternity might flourish contained explicit critique from a social perspective.

Closer investigation of readers' reception of this press provides a further departure from the apparent conundrum of simultaneous pro- and anti-Pétainism. For the recipient, the sparse content of the press might attest to the fact that reading it was not its primary aim. Journals were a kind of symbolic glue that connected opponents of the occupation to each other, and performed a functional syllogism whereby the very act of producing a journal proved an organism's resistance credentials – it was resister *because* it produced a journal. Brive's examination of the women's press analysed the initial interpellation of a reader via the journal's title. Newspapers called 'The housewife' or 'Mothers of

France' were supposed to appeal to individuals so described. But unlike a press not subject to censorship, these journals announced themselves to readers not so much through their titles as via their very clandestinity; production and distribution methods spoke more loudly than any signal a title could make. These were not conditions in which numerous papers were displayed on a newsstand, each clamouring for the reader's attention and choice; acquiring one involved the decision to be receptive, but also the accident of being in the vicinity of a distributor, and it might be months before another could be found. In any case, countless readers shared their copies, so receptivity was confirmed via comradeship and friendship, rather than the more distant relation readers have to newspapers in ordinary conditions.

Acquisition methods aside, the extent to which the authorities tried to suppress this press is testimony to its propagandistic efficacy. It has been argued that women readers' response to literature in general has been conditioned by their historical social exclusion from power.[45] Studies of women's readings of genres such as romance found in the writing an ability to express women's aspirations while simultaneously containing and neutralizing them.[46] Readers were not necessarily duped by what they read, but were in some way conscious of using, within limits, their reading towards a specific end, such as pleasure or, here, resistance. Female readers' capacity for scepticism towards Vichy propaganda and press was not simply abandoned when they read the resistance press, even if the appeal of the latter was made largely in terms of the maternal.[47] The reader might have responded to the resistance text indirectly and creatively; the pleasure of holding a clandestine document directed to them may have been combined with a critical distance from the limited representations it contained. Nor should the limitations be exaggerated. Was it mothers or resisters that one paper called on when it implored, '*MUMS*, our children's lives are in our hands; we won't let them be torn from us. Let's make a rampart of our bodies for our children. Everywhere our cries will resonate: "Our children will not go to Boche-land to die for Hitler"'?[48] Read against other resistance literature, the prosaic content of the women's press, its domesticization of the political, stands out. But read against an existing genre of feminine journalism, the politicization of the domestic becomes more plain.

In the end, at the level of the politics of family and gender, the communist resistance failed to reconcile its conservatism with its expressed desire for women to be politically active. Building on the experience of the non-party political women's committees, it encouraged women into positions of power after liberation.[49] More women would be elected to local and national political seats at this period than at any other time until the 1990s.[50] But submission to familialism militated against women's activism.[51] Women were to be both separate from the greater life of France and essential to its well-being. Their literary aspirations as represented in these texts were not expressed in the poetry published elsewhere in the clandestine press, but limited to slogans, pared down to the essentials of daily life. While women's role in this literature was shot through with the ambiguities of dual ideological allegiances to Vichyist and resister gender politics, the texts themselves showed women's lives to be uncomplicated by the discrepancies of contemporary politics.

Being French: the nationalization of sexuality

Addressed primarily as 'maman', 'ménagère' and 'Française' (mum, housewife, Frenchwoman), women were to be both domestic and patriotic. How did the women's press codify 'French' and 'foreign' femininity in the muddled context wherein both the resistance and Vichy identified the objects of their hatred as foreign – the occupiers for the resistance, and non-French nationals (especially Jews) for Vichy? Claudine Michaut, president of the UFF, suggested at the end of the war that during the occupation, women had learnt 'not to separate the security of the home from the country; the joys of free life and the freedom of the nation'.[52] The women's press regarded Vichy's moves to shift women into the home as a foreign import, inimical to French values.[53] But when Jews were coded as 'foreign', the construction of two competing notions of Frenchness – Vichy and resister – and the equation of 'foreign' with 'undesirable', was highly problematic. Resistance desire to restore a non-fascist, French government in some ways mirrored Vichy's own exclusionism. It removed the focus from the need to protect the victims of Vichy exclusionism, and in part reinforced the very qualities of Frenchness that Vichy promoted. These problems are especially noticeable in the clandestine press with regard to issues of sexuality, which constructed two versions of femininity – an asexual resister, and a sexualized collaborator.

Even towards the end of the war, when papers more frequently asked women to support armed resistance (by nursing wounded men, for instance), women were supposed to be the moral bedrock on which the home rested. 'Despite the exigencies of modern life,' observed *Femmes françaises* in January 1944,

the woman has the advantage of maintaining a more liberated conscience, more vigorous reactions than the man. Thus, the important role of animator falls to her. Our homes must not be centres of defeatism. Every one of you must use your ingenuity to create an atmosphere of courage and confidence. Your fathers, your husbands, your brothers must always be sure of finding there a faithful collaborator, a woman who knows their needs and doesn't distance herself from them.[54]

Femmes françaises insisted that the woman work alone to maintain morale for her company of men. In the clandestine press, the home remains the locus of feminine solitude, without other adult women, despite all the changes that the war and occupation had brought to transform women's lives, and that the press itself frequently recognized (what it calls here 'the exigencies of modern life'). The clandestine press reinforced the values of motherhood and familial instinct by its repeated addresses to women in these terms, while simultaneously protesting against Vichy's negative transformation of them. It regarded 'the anti-France of Vichy'[55] as attached to foreign, German, values, having 'import[ed] from abroad' its *femme au foyer* policy and celebrating Mothers' Day 'in the German manner'. The press's self-avowal as champion of the French family overlapped with the sort of nationalism embedded in Vichy family policy (and centre-right republicanism of the 1930s) and which the new government would reassert without much change after liberation.[56]

The resistance press virtually always positioned the righteous French woman in relation to motherhood – as a young woman looking forward to her mature days as a parent, the legion *ménagères* and *mamans* who were to solicit extra rations for their family, or the *marraines* who were to mother their fighting units, providing food, shelter, comfort and laundry services. In contrast, the public nature of prostitution rendered it open to scrutiny; it was associated on a recurrent and profound level with danger and betrayal. Those represented as bringing this threat into being found that their relation to France itself was seen as transitional and suspect. Prostitution became a metaphor for the uncertain status of national identity, and doubts were raised concerning the right for such individuals to claim to belong to the nation.[57]

Sex work was widespread in France despite various proposals for its control. Many of the regulatory attempts around the time of the First World War were connected to an exaggerated view of syphilis as the root of all moral and physical degeneracy. Before the occupation, the number of brothels in Paris was diminishing; from 1940, as an environment in which disease control could be carried out in regulated conditions, they revived. The German authorities made considerable use of brothels, setting up an elaborate surveillance system that was intended to exclude all but registered, non-Jewish sex workers with a clean bill of health, and designating separate brothels for use by officers and other ranks.[58] In practice, increasing numbers of unregistered, clandestine sex workers were active. The demographics of sex work also evolved as more single mothers and married women took it up, a situation that one commentator at liberation attributed to Vichy's legislative exclusion of married women from the workplace.[59] Shortly before its return to France, the provisional government in Algiers accused the Nazis of a deliberate policy to promote prostitution in pursuit of a Europe-wide attempt to weaken the 'race'. Liberation, it argued, would be a dangerous time of transition, and Allied troops would need to be prevented from using the newly liberated France as a sexual playground. To counter this, the new government of 'pure' resisters should see prostitution as inimical to resistance values. Banning prostitution was thus presented as a form of moral progress bound up in the fight against the occupier and all that was ideologically foreign to the resistance itself.[60]

Sex work in practice differed from the representation of 'prostitution'. In the clandestine press, prostitution was more than a matter of solicited and paid-for sexual services, but encompassed any suspected sexual relationship between a French woman and a German man. Women who anticipated a glimpse of German officers in Lyons, for example, seem to have inspired Yves Farge's very urge to resist:

The trolley-bus from Tassin stopped to let a German motorized column pass, and some type on the bus dared to say in a loud voice, 'The French are at last going to learn what order really is'. I nearly hit him. Then in front of the Grand Hotel there were women waiting to see the German officers emerge. To one of them I said 'Too old for prostitution'. It all began in ways like that.[61]

Farge's easy sexualization of his antipathy to women he interprets as pro-German – 'too old for prostitution' – instantiates feminine fascination with the invading army as though masculine fascination never existed, and proves the banality of the women's gaze. 'Too old for prostitution,' implies that women were motivated by sexuality combined with the desire for material gain. The fantasy of women's urge for financial reward also aided the preservation of French male potency, since women were assumed otherwise to prefer French men. Farge was not alone in his view of women as materialist sexual beings, and the woman-as-prostitute was the immoral inverse of the woman-as-mother seen elsewhere. But prostitution in the clandestine press assumed more serious connotations than either sexuality or greed. To be identified as a prostitute during the occupation was to be marked as having relinquished the right to be French.

The clandestine press presented prostitution as a foreign, not French, affair: prostitutes were malignant Gestapo agents, out to seduce resistance secrets from the male resister at the moment of his greatest vulnerability. Only once in the press sampled here, in a Trotskyist paper, was sex work presented as the ultimate economic recourse for women unable to find other sources of income.[62] More frequently, the mention of prostitution sowed nationalized moral doubt on its practitioners so that not only were prostitutes presented as working for the enemy, but their very national identity became subject to misgiving. French men who paid for sex were portrayed as merely weak. This further reinforced the idea that in order to be upstanding, men required the moral example of the honourable and motherly women around them. 'Prostitution' thus functioned to bolster resister morality, and underscored the importance of patriotic gender roles. Women guilty of sexual intimacy with German men learnt from this press that they could expect a gendered retribution by other women. Both the judged and the judges were addressed apostrophically, the former identified as those who 'have no right to the name of Frenchwoman' and the latter as the French element who 'should punish'.[63] 'Women of Lyons, your patriotism turns to disgust when you see women whom one cannot qualify as Frenchwomen displaying themselves with German troops', wrote *Femmes patriotes* in an unusually bitter piece, giving the name and address of a woman it accused of so acting.[64]

As female sexuality became inscribed as servicing betrayal, it fed the view that it was the responsibility of the stout, righteous woman ('French mothers') to restrain the energetic male libido. Young collaborationist women who acted as German spies ('execrable Gestapo bitches'), bore no comparison with young resister women, who simply had no sexuality as far as this press was concerned. One of the few times vindictiveness emerged in the women's press was on this 'delicate chapter' when men had to be instructed to 'do the necessary': 'pretend to accept their propositions, set them a trap, correct them severely, shave their hair and, finally, take their identity cards. The photo will serve to identify and punish them when the time comes.'[65] The expectation that liberation would provide the opportunity for women to punish was equally explicit, as in the centre right resistance paper, *L'Aurore*, which outlined a 'special measure' that would befall such women, whose foreheads would be marked with swastikas in imitation of the actions of a German who had reportedly carved one on his French lover's abdomen.[66] *Femmes françaises* was clear that women were to be the authorities to whom men would turn for guidance on which treacherous women to punish at liberation and how to go about it. In the event, women did not exert such authority,[67] though the attribution of the punitive function to them increased the chasm between the desexualized French woman and those others. The separation between collaborators and resisters is drawn in the harshest possible terms because of the use in the women's press of a gendered view of collaboration as resting within the female body.

Authentic French women could only be slurred by the attribution of prostitution to them. On the impossible alliance of true French femininity with a marketable sexuality, the Mouvement National contre le Racisme announced under the heading 'outrage to French women' that the Académie de Médecine had 'unanimously protested against the introduction of a gynaecological examination to which women required for work in Germany would have to submit. This examination, which gives no guarantee from a scientific point of view, can only be considered an insult to French women, given that only prostitutes are obliged to undergo such treatment.'[68] In distinguishing between French women and prostitutes, this protest against inhumane treatment legitimized the examination of prostitutes as it demurred from those on the others. We see here a tripartite distinction between images of women – as the prostitute collaborator, the asexual active resister and the good, maternal, French woman. Far from being set in stone, national identity became subject to momentary transformation, its conferment an honour under constant threat of withdrawal. Collaboration, it was suggested, led to the loss of French identity. In the associations of Frenchness and honour, and the subsequent enfranchisement of women in terms of patriotic valour, it is therefore of little surprise that there were calls for female collaborators to forfeit the right to vote, though these were rarely put into practice.[69] As prostitution had become metonymic with the very idea of unease and shifting identity, the exclusion from Frenchness that it enforced further underlined the sexualization of femininity, and dismissed women as real or potential active citizens.

The clandestine women's press rarely concerned itself with people beyond the national family, either women in other occupied countries or those deemed beyond the national interest within France. Not one protested when Jews over the age of six in the occupied zone had to wear the yellow star after May 1942 (paying for them with clothing ration coupons) though at least one did note the Vél d'Hiv *rafle* a couple of months later.[70] How the clandestine press dealt with the starkest assertion of racialization in occupied France, then, may provide clues to the resister imaginary nation, and how far it was able to resist Vichy and Nazi racial discourses. According to one tract addressed to 'Frenchmen, Women and French mothers', it was the duty of those French 'worthy of this name' to protest against the *rafle*.[71] The tract separated readers into three groups, two defined by gender and national identity (Frenchmen and French mothers), and one by gender alone (women), though French mothers were further defined by their gender function. To be scandalized by round-ups, this tract suggests, combines gender and nationality in ways that are inclusive with respect to women, and exclusive when motherhood and masculinity are concerned. *La Franc-Comtoise* also put a feminine gloss on the *rafle*. It marked the round-up as an affront to the nation, since 'Jewish or non-Jewish' women should all feel threatened by its attack on some Jewish women. Protection of all women, it is suggested, was essential for national pride; it was mothers in France, rather than French mothers, who in this instance were in need of security.[72] Here is a France responsible for all its inhabitants, not merely for those who earned the honorific 'French' via displays of national devotion. In underlining the insufficiency of defending solely French motherhood, *La Franc-Comtoise* implicitly contested the conditional conception of Frenchness present in most of the clandestine women's press. When the women's edition of *Humanité* instructed 'French women' to teach their children 'to hate Hitler and to love the little Israelites, innocent victims of fascism', they hint at the contrary inference of guilt – of the government, the arresting police or other, less innocent and more adult *Israélites*.[73] The response to the *rafle* as an opportunity to shore up women's – albeit politicized – maternalism diminishes the round-up's significance, and again confines women's activism to the home. Use of the term 'Israélite' might also indicate *Humanité*'s refusal to employ Vichyist differentiation between French and non-French Jews, and to promote the non-French Jews, threatened by deportation, to the term generally reserved for Jews native to France. Conversely, an established term which avoided immigrant Jews' usual self-nomination as *Juifs* may have assisted the reader to distance herself from the events and individuals of the Vél d'Hiv *rafle*. Neither of these interpretations excludes the other. On this occasion, the internationalist communists protested against antisemitism and also referred to 'Juifs', although the latter were countenanced as part of the Vichy imaginary, since they were enclosed, like 'foreigners' and 'Jewish capitalism', in inverted commas.[74] Only one other paper aimed at women, *La Voix des Dauphinoises*, found the Jewish deportations bruising to the national ego. Here, interpretation expanded beyond the local to the national level under a heading 'what the women of France think'. Quoting a recent sermon, they wrote,

For the women of France, 'Jews are human beings', and they have a right to help and protection. In attacking, deporting, killing the Israelites, Hitler wants not only to annihilate a minority which is odious to him, he wants to humiliate the whole of France in forcing it to renounce the principles on which it has based itself for 150 years and which have given it glory.[75]

This article appears to have been written as a late reaction to the *Affiche rouge*, the notorious German poster produced after the mass arrest, torture and execution of dozens of MOI resisters in late 1943. Twenty-three of these formed part of the network centred around the Armenian poet, Missak Manouchian, and many of their tortured faces were featured on the poster that was plastered across Paris after their execution at the Mont Valérian prison. Olga Bancic, the only woman in the network, was not pictured; she was taken to Germany and decapitated in May 1944. Like the occasion in the Nord–Pas-de-Calais, when only the Ménagère network of housewives remained after the arrest of all known male resisters, Bancic's omission from the poster attests to the authorities' refusal to countenance women as political actors.[76] The poster's accusations that these resisters were foreign terrorists found little public support, and it was often torn down or covered in graffiti. *La Voix des Dauphinoises* had an alternative response: using the feminine language of the family to express attachment to republican principles, it elevated all those foreigners noble enough to join the *maquis* into honorary French and, in the name of universal humanism rather than hatred of antisemitism, found the deportation of Jews humiliating for France.

La Voix de la femme juive, which published its sole issue in August 1943, reflected some of the familialist and nationalist tendencies outlined above but displayed subtle and significant differences.[77] Its title alludes to a reader and producer's dual identificatory potential. It regarded the Jewish woman not as innocent victim, nor as though her entire militant character were encompassed in the access to national identification that resistance patriotism would confer. Published shortly after the Gestapo executed the resistance leader Mendel Langer, the paper expressed outrage at his execution. Langer, leader of the 35th FTP-MOI brigade and described as a 'tender husband' and 'affectionate father' as well as a hero, was to be avenged by Jewish women. The paper's inscription of Langer as a son of 'our people' iterates an ambiguity in which the 'people' is at once French and Jewish. Nor was this imagined reader's political insight limited as it was elsewhere in the women's press. *La Voix de la femme juive* represented women as active agents in their own deliverance, and it recognized their individual, communal and national concerns by discussing international issues, like the liberation of Sicily, alongside those germane to a woman running a household and connected to the French Jewish communities. Encouraging news of allied victories across Europe, with ironic commentary from the Nazi *Völkische Beobachter*, marks it out as unique in this literature. Its presentation of Nazi politics makes it one of only four papers which assumed that women knew anything of Nazism outside France.[78] Unusually, the paper implied no contradiction between the appeal to be French and that to be Jewish. A reader was to gain as much encouragement from the example of heroic Jewish women in the Warsaw ghetto, as from the strikes held the previous year in Lyons to commemorate Vél d'Hiv. Dual ties to Jewishness and Frenchness would pervade the Jewish women's resistance press even after liberation.

In contrast, *Notre voix*, a Jewish paper with no gendered appeal, seemed unable to balance gender and patriotism, differentiating between men and women in its calls for unity. In March 1943 it marked International Women's Day with an article entitled 'Women! Let's take our place in the struggle that will liberate France', quoting extensively from the manifesto of the Anti-Fascist Soviet Women's Committee for 8 March. Here it noted that Soviet women were given equal rights on 8 March 1918, which not only opened occupations hitherto reserved for men, but gave them the chance finally to create happy homes – a gloss with greater Vichyist than Bolshevik overtones, at least for the period immediately after 1917. *Notre voix* was silent on the fact that women had not simply waited to be given equal rights, but that their demands had initiated the October Revolution, as well as that International Women's Day had not started in the Soviet Union. Nonetheless, it was to defend these rights that Soviet women had thrown themselves heroically into the anti-fascist struggle against the German invasion, said the paper. Fascism, it continued, was women's worst enemy since it wanted to reduce women to slavery, transforming them into producers of cannon fodder. 'Jewish women suffer cruelly,' it noted. 'Their husbands, sons, parents and sisters are deported to the East where the Nazis assassinate them at the same time as the unfortunate Jews of Poland, by thousands.' In order to protest against this, Jewish women were instructed to demand at the town hall that more bread and milk be given to their children rather than it being sent to the 'Boches'.[79] Similar calls were standard fare in the press aimed at non-Jewish women, for whom the danger associated with town hall protest was of a different order from the round-ups that threatened Jews. *Notre voix* ignored the far greater retribution that would befall Jews who protested in public, and did not see that the question of rations was but one of the problems that beset them – as the paper itself had noted in its previous issue which proclaimed that 'deportation is certain death, terrible death'.[80] Where readers of *La Voix de la femme juive* were to identify with Jews in France and elsewhere, as well as with other women, the female readers of *Notre voix* were regarded first and foremost as women whose political and racialized position differed little from that of other women in France.

There is one area in the women's press in which women's agency and international regard as well as drive for action was deployed. An element of daring to step beyond the predestined boundaries of gender role is present in the many references to Soviet women. These seem to act as a vehicle for the transference of desire on the part of women in France and indicate how difficult it was for them to speak directly for themselves. The press positioned Soviet women's feats as desirable but as yet unattainable.[81] The textual effects of these projected hopes appear to translate the wishes of the French female resister for a recognized place in the active struggle. Unable to express these yearnings overtly, the papers underlined Soviet women's strength and equality with men, and this provides a clue to the fantasies that French women might themselves hope to realize. Communist literature was full of esteem for the Soviet Union as exemplar of hope for the future, and references to 'Stalin's fantastic politics' abound from the confused period of the Nazi–Soviet pact on.[82] But beyond the rhetoric of glory, and of reverence for Stalin's army, can be glimpsed a more expansive vision of women's capacities. Early during the occupation, *Jeunes Filles de France* alluded to the disruption of feminine roles: 'More than 40,000 [Soviet] girls have completed their training as tractor drivers. Disdain for women and the lack of confidence in their strength that were formerly so characteristic of village life have for a long time been relegated to the past.'[83] Alongside oblique critique of the role assigned to women in the Pétainist *retour à la terre* was recognition that belief in women's physical weakness and the necessity that they undertake different tasks from men was ideologically produced. Even in resistance literature, it was not, or not yet, possible to make the same demands for French women. The paper argued that while young French women wanted work which would guarantee them independence, their real dream of the future was represented by a happy home, a dream turned nightmare by Vichy. Fifteen months later, in January 1942, the paper noted that not only had Soviet women replaced men in heavy industry and agriculture, but some had entered armed combat where, 'knowing neither weakness nor fatigue and moved by sublime courage, they remain proud'.[84] The superhuman quality attributed to these fighters notwithstanding, here is more than a hint that women's capabilities lay far beyond their usual domain in France, represented by the call that they participate in the liberationist movement by claiming bigger milk rations.[85]

The reasons for the disjunction between the idealized Soviet woman and the reality of 'modern life' in France are explained in the discourses of sexual politics discussed above, as well as by the primacy of class struggle. These major divergences between left-wing resisters and Vichy ideology notwithstanding, commonalities among the two sides were not unknown. Vichy had provided a central place to its own version of the pro-natalist dream. This rhetoric, we have argued, crossed political boundaries so that resisters and Vichyists assumed that national strength was founded partly on the productive family. Only very few feminists dared to confront this approach with an alternative ideology that foresaw for women a permanent place beyond the family. After liberation, even some of those who claimed feminism as their own would suggest that these politics flee from the 'ridiculous image' of pre-war suffragism in order to maintain a feminism attractive to men.[86] It was not just that the clandestine women's press refrained from taking seriously or giving much credence to feminist concerns, such as the vote or equal rights at work, but that its representation of women persisted in nationalizing what it regarded as women's innate maternalism and familialism. This was presented as being part of an essential French femininity trying to maintain itself against the distortion of gender roles imposed from outside by imported German values. The problem with such representation lay as much with the limitations on women's lives in and beyond the resistance, as with the continuation of troublesome discourses which pitched 'French' and 'foreign' as eternal opposites, to the detriment of the non-French already under attack in occupied France. Only rarely, such as in the marginal voices of Jewish women or Trotskyists, did these apparent dichotomies between French and foreign cease to be quite so stark. Just how far this adoption of Vichyist familialism would extend after liberation can be seen in the recuperation of the celebration of French motherhood that was the Fête des Mères.

Mothers' Day: the festival of the 'Renaissance of our nation'

Vichy's Journée des Mères represented the apotheosis of its national-ization of motherhood. The Plus Grande Famille, an organization de-voted to the interests of the large family as well as to families of senior rank, originated the Fête des Mères during the First World War.[87] The government supported the fête for the first time in 1920 when, in the post-war upsurge of pro-natalist enthusiasm, it also introduced legisla-tion to limit access to contraception and provide financial benefits for large families. Despite this official respect for pro-natalism, though, the fête attracted little popular attention for two decades.[88] It took Vichy to elevate it, as the Journée des Mères, to pride of place in its famil-ialist calendar, and it is perhaps for this reason that a number of sub-sequent commentators attributed its invention to Vichy, so associated had the two become.[89] Under Vichy, this Sunday in late spring was to be both a national and a local celebration, and it was publicly pro-claimed at all levels of the state, via Pétain's personal radio addresses to French mothers, the conferment of medals on mothers of more than five children, teas held in town halls, and church services to honour French motherhood.[90] Schoolchildren were constrained to prepare spe-cial gifts and girls were taught the tasks of motherhood – though such education was a year-round activity not limited to the weeks preceding the Journée. Whereas nationalist florists had originated Mothers' Day in Weimar Germany, the Vichy Journée des Mères elevated maternal duty and sacrifice to a status beyond that of a 'consumerist holiday'.[91]

As Vichy implanted its Journée des Mères in a timeless French na-tional culture of its own invention, the celebration's cruel ironies became immediate targets for the clandestine women's press. Vichy's separa-tion of parents from their children through war, imprisonment and de-portation and the deprivation engendered by inadequate rations were attacked as a wicked betrayal of the family. Papers took the regime to task for organizing a 'festival' when mothers were mourning their dead children, a 'celebration' for mothers when there was insufficient food for their charges and a 'holiday solely in name' for mothers it had betrayed.[92] In a conscious transformation of Vichy's ideals of mother-hood, the women's press also saw the day as occasion for mothers to protest against these new conditions. Instead of 'German-style' celebrations with a couple of cinema screenings and dreary speeches about the family, it said, 'French mothers' should demand a daily ration of 500 grams of bread, improved clothing allowances and bread for their prisoner of war sons.[93] The clandestine press did not, however, suggest that mothers needed no festival at all.

In the patriotic and pro-natalist mood of the immediate post-liberation period, the Fête des Mères was immediately reinscribed as a celebration worthy of resistance commemoration. The first came just three weeks after VE Day, on 3 June 1945. It was marked by awards of certificates and medals little different from Vichy's.[94] Across France, luminaries presented the 'French family gold medal' to mothers of ten or more children.[95] In Paris, a gendarme's wife and mother of eleven was among twenty-five women to receive theirs from the communist minister for public health and population, François Billoux, at the Hôtel de Ville.[96] In Lyons, representatives of the entire republican elite gathered to confer three gold medals, eleven silver and a number of diplomas: in the chair, Edouard Herriot, former president of the Chamber of Deputies and anti-Pétainist, symbolically reinstated republican continuity. He was joined by the prefect of the Rhône, the archbishop of Lyons, Cardinal Gerlier, the city's military governor and the family delegate to the regional assembly.[97] In an era of medal ceremonies the award of medals to mothers might be read as compensation for women's exclusion from the highest resistance honour, the Compagnon de la Libération, the 1,038 recipients of which, bar six, were all men.[98] Otherwise, the Fête des Mères gifts of medals – which numbered nearly 5,000 in 1946 – and household goods offered to those mothers of large families who, according to the prefect of the Seine, were 'at the top level of the artisans of Victory', could be seen as small crumbs indeed.[99] Mothers were also supposed to be content with being glorified for a single day. 'For French mothers, today is a wonderful day three times over,' crowed the *Parisien libéré*, though it seems to have been difficult for them to find much to applaud, beyond it being 'a Sunday, better still their Sunday and, better again, their first "day" of peace'.[100]

Commentary on the fête was far from unified. The Catholic *La Croix*, with barely disguised Vichyism, proclaimed war a lesser evil than the murder of the soul and the death of the nation engendered by the modern selfish refusal to sacrifice oneself to the duty of bearing children.[101] At the other end of the spectrum, *Front national* complained that women's issues were reduced to platitudes pronounced on a single day of the year.[102] Attention here will focus mainly on those responses that emerged from the former resistance, to explore the legacy of resister discourses on women which have been outlined above, and how the ubiquity of maternalism and the sacrifice it contained allowed the

Fête des Mères to have projected on to it hopes for the reconstitution and unity of the familial nation.

A new natalist magazine, *Maman*, was born on the day of the first postwar fête. Its editor, Robert Wolf-Wolney, had formerly been associated with two clandestine journals, *La Gazette du temps* and *Le Lot résistant*. Although neither reveals evidence of his later natalist concerns, the first issue of *Maman* declared that the magazine had been' conceived in clandestinity' and called on 'all the French to fight for a new and beautiful France by increasing the strength, size and moral influence of the French Family'.[103] According to *Maman*, protecting the French family involved not only social, medical and cultural questions, but the regulation of immigration and the spread of foreigners on French territory, just as de Gaulle had announced and which will be explored in more detail in the next chapter. The article 'Mothers' Day' in issue one, recognized that Vichy had given 'the greatest possible acclaim' to the day, only serving to underline how far its slogan 'Labour, Family, Fatherland' ought to have been '*forced* labour, *far* from the family and *against* the Fatherland'.[104] Somehow, though, the day could be unproblematically reinstated as 'the return of Liberty and Democracy gives Mothers' Day its full, moving, meaning.' Now, the 'millions' of French women who had been 'deliberately rejected from the national community' as mothers of STO workers, political deportees, *réfractaires* or *maquisards* (though not of Jews) were to be welcomed back, to fulfil their motherly duties.[105] Like much of the clandestine women's press, *Maman* believed in a 'real' family, conceived as one in which the son had been an active resister. Not content merely to celebrate the joyous bounty of motherhood, at the heart of *Maman*'s new France was a pro-natalism at once resister and Christian. In common with the first Christian mother, motherhood was a matter of suffering the loss of her son, a theme that recurred in much liberation literature. *Maman* reminded its version of the Marian mother that 'The mothers that we must celebrate today are first and foremost all the "sorrowful mothers" [mères douloureuses] who have suffered the greatest sacrifice of all.'[106] *Maman* was self-conscious that its mother should be symbolic of a new France. The infantile woman of yesteryear contrasted with the new mother who had proved her sense of responsibility, maturity and experience, to lead the new French family. Just as women's resistance activity was immediately mythologized as the reason for the introduction of universal suffrage, so the fact that women had given up their sons 'for France' became inscribed as allowing them entry to a newly familialist nation which, in its devotion to reproduction and control of outsiders, shared much with Vichy's own vision of the 'real' French family.

The presence of the 'real' French family was confirmed in the most widely distributed daily, the PCF's *Humanité*. It was moved to call

Mothers' Day 'the celebration *par excellence* of the Renaissance of our nation'.[107] The link between national rebirth and reproduction could not be clearer. Its commentary, again with Christian echoes, sustained the sacrificial value which had been so distinctive a part of the pre-liberation clandestine press, itself imitative of Vichy's own rendition of the sacrificial mother. The nationalization of motherhood under Vichy had involved the sacrifice of women's individuality for the benefit of the nation which had demanded that she surrender her children to work in the German Reich. In post-liberation France, mothers were called on to assume the burden of the nation's grief. Mourning became established as a national motherly duty. 'The heroic mothers, the sorrowful mums of those who died for France have not been forgotten,' it intoned. 'They have received as homage the admiration and respectful sympathy to which they have the right by reason of their most burdensome sacrifice.'[108] It has been argued that the mater dolorosa acted as a 'symbol for maternal peacekeeping [who]... provides a great deterrent to the politics of war.'[109] The symbolic value attached to maternity at the end of the occupation, however, elevated and separated mothers from the rest of society at the very moment that women were supposed to cede employment and positions of responsibility to men returning from Germany. Consequently, the weeping woman encumbered by national grief was part of the division of sexual labour that accompanied men's re-entry into French society and reconfirmed the duty of war. The simultaneous nationalization and feminization of grief that Catholic *and* communist discourses promoted, underscored not only the necessity to mother. For the symbol suggests that motherhood was the essential accompaniment to mourning and that men were excluded from grief.[110]

The variations on this figure of maternal suffering suggest that she was not entirely satisfactory. The communist women's journal, *Femmes françaises*, recast the Fête des Mères as Family Day (Fête de la Famille), though the change of name had little impact on the view of the mother as repository of all things familial. *Femmes françaises*' 1945 Mothers' Day issue was illustrated with a picture of two typhus-ridden children in a displaced persons camp. 'But where is their mum, and will they rediscover the tenderness of the lost home?' it captioned. Here, it counterpoised mothers' 'immense joy' at rediscovering family life with their experience of Vichy which had, 'with ghastly cynicism dared to glorify its "Fête des Mères"' after deporting mothers whose children had been snatched from their arms. *Femmes françaises* was not in the least cynical about motherhood and the family, but it was reluctant to allow women to exercise functions other than the maternal (though not necessarily within the confines of traditional marriage, as Catholic respectability was less important than the care and reproduction of children).[111]

With men returning to France, the state emphasized their war-time sacrifice, and suggested that resolution of the anticipated marital difficulties should start with the wife's recognition of all that her husband had renounced during these years. Now that the war was over, the tables should be turned so that women might relinquish their desires for the good of the home, and of the nation – as though there had been no difficulties comparable to those endured by men in German prisoner of war camps or factories for women who had remained in France.[112] The clandestine women's press had by no means shared the view that women in France had not suffered during the occupation. Out of clandestinity, though, the familialism that this press had brokered conformed with that propagated by a government eager to see the heterosexual family restored to its imagined erstwhile place at the centre of French life.

Not everyone spoke of mothers as sacrificial vessels into which were poured the nation's miseries. Some continued to prioritize resistance humanism above unity-at-any-price, distancing themselves from the suffocating visions of national redemption via the Fête des Mères. Militants in the Union des Femmes Juives (UFJ) used the Fête to relaunch and revive their children's welfare campaign. At a public meeting with the Minister for Population and the Union des Femmes Françaises, the UFJ stated that 'it was natural that Jewish Women were at the head of the movement to save children'.[113] Childcare was urgent after the deportation of so many parents, and was one of the few ways open to women who wanted to continue as activists. Yet describing this action as natural, obscured the fact that even more non-Jews might have helped to hide Jewish children (not to mention adults) and that children were not necessarily the sole responsibility of women, let alone women of the children's own ethnic group. In the event, the UFJ commemorations that day made a point of marking Jewish women's international armed resistance.[114] While women's sacrifice was not absent from the commentary, the celebrations encompassed greater resistance continuity than in the natalist and nationalistic blandishments found elsewhere.

The Christian resistance paper *Témoignage chrétien* explicitly saw motherhood as 'the future of France', yet it too suggested that its readers continue the militancy for which they had become renowned and, instead of passive spectatorship at medal ceremonies, asked them to help refugee and impoverished mothers. Far from underlining the indissoluble relationship between the nation and the heterosexual family, *Témoignage chrétien* made a rare appeal to counter the widespread vilification of volunteer female workers returning from Germany. These women had joined the German work force without being drafted by the STO. As female traitors, the hatred with which collaborators were regarded in general was coloured by the gender contempt that flourished at liberation. *Témoignage chrétien* insisted on the context of the volunteer women's departure. 'Are they all guilty?' it demanded, differentiating between women returning to France who may have been non-French nationals, deportees, adolescent at the time of their 'voluntary' departure, pregnant, or forced to 'choose' between imprisonment in France and labour in Germany after being arrested as resisters. Even those who had left willingly had paid a heavy price for their eagerness and, before being judged, should be fed and clothed rather than threatened with violence, the paper said.[115] The delineation between women's circumstances offered by *Témoignage chrétien* confronted the ways that other former resistance papers continued to view the nation as divided between the 'true' and the excluded, which countered Vichyism only by turning it on its head. Less concerned with the imaginary nation as a whole, *Témoignage chrétien*'s careful regard for all inhabitants highlighted the judgemental tone of unity and mass that was pronounced elsewhere.

The new liberation Fête des Mères was the logical outcome of resister national familialism. Understanding the liberationist underscoring of the family as part of a necessary populationist framework for a reborn France allows us to see why contemporary analyses that departed from this view were so marginal. Suzanne Normand's scathing account of Mothers' Day was one of these rare instances. 'It reminds me a bit of the defunct "Week of Bounty": be good for eight days on the trot, all the while giving free rein to indifference, egoism and harshness for the other fifty-one weeks.' Thus, one had endured radio speeches 'of sickening sentimentality and poems whose quality, alas, does not really accord with their good intentions'.[116] What was really necessary was an end to the rudeness and insolence that faced women – 'and above all, we mean women' – Normand wrote, questioning discourses that set women apart as inferior.[117] Although limited and contained, Normand's feminism found little public reflection, and remained isolated, as can be seen from the case of the post-clandestine feminist press.

A word in edgeways? The post-clandestine women's press

At liberation, most of the small clandestine periodicals folded while the larger, better-funded journals transformed themselves into legal papers. Initially, the spirit of the press's primary resisting role during the occupation as an assertion of independence from the authorities became transferred to the legal press. Quickly, though, this press came to be controlled by a government that elements of the resistance press had itself fought to install. Editors berated those in power for the paper shortages that led to decrees restricting the size of their papers, and complained against control of content. For several months, no authorized newspaper apart from the new *Le Monde* was permitted to publish more than a small single sheet (reduced still further in 1945), which led some to compare conditions to those that had prevailed during the occupation.[118] Several papers were censored: all Forces Françaises de l'Intérieur (FFI) journals were suppressed from mid-January 1945, and Spanish-language journals (of which there were many in the south), from the following month.[119] The Syndicat de la Presse Hebdomadaire Parisienne protested that while the former clandestine press was being closed down, other journals with no 'patriotic' (i.e., resister) background were allowed to launch.[120] It almost goes without saying that scarcely any of the tiny, hand-made women's press survived beyond August 1944. Yet other journals started in their wake and it is to some of these that we now turn in order to explore the continuities and ruptures of liberation as presented in the press born directly out of their clandestine forebears.

La Femme and *Privilèges des femmes* were edited by Lyons-based Libération-sud resister, Lucie Aubrac. Both were short-lived women's magazines which started publication in 1945; *La Femme* was the mouthpiece of the MLN women's section, Femmes de la Libération Nationale (FLN), and its first issue appeared in March, while the independent *Privilèges*, which resembles *La Femme* in all respects, came out from October. Lucie Aubrac was one of those few unmartyred, named women whose resistance was recognized at the time. Her story as an evasion specialist is now well known through her autobiography and a feature film based on it.[121] Even at liberation, Aubrac had ensured that women's resistance was not hidden from view, and made the now-familiar universalist demand that their war-time participation should permit them entry into full citizenship. They had learnt, she said, 'how to stay charming and feminine, but they have acquired qualities of initiative, endurance and seriousness that they did not have before the war.'[122] At a London press conference she noted that, 'there is a higher number of women than men in the resistance'.[123] This quantitative assertion depended on a view of resistance as an endeavour that encompassed more than the armed struggle, and her two magazines were edited in favour of women's political, civil and social advancement.[124]

Privilèges spoke to readers as though they had concerns beyond the domestic. Features on education, politics and women's place in the complexities of national reconstruction reflected many of Aubrac's own interests as a teacher, resister and delegate to the Provisional Consultative Assembly. They joined opinion, fashion, fiction and reportage – such as Gertrude Stein's feature on a tour of Germany with the US army (issue one). The journal also provided information – such as on how to register a birth, or vaccinations for babies – at a time when change was happening at a pace difficult for the public to follow. The magazine was abundantly illustrated, and included that form popular among female readers, the photo-story. (Issue two, for example, contained the story

'So take a taxi if you're not in a hurry!' This ridiculed the restrictions, petty corruption and convoluted bureaucracy that faced a pregnant woman, legally entitled to a taxi, trying to cross Paris at a time of severe petrol shortages.) Fashion was treated to comparatively lavish coverage in each issue, while other material was more didactic. Taking an anti-Eurocentric, non-exoticized view that was rare at the time, an article on beauty, for example, compared cultural variations and constructions of femininity in less developed countries. The magazine also escaped from the confines of the maternal, and refrained from the widely expressed derision of the 'masculinization' of female sexuality. The return of men, and the concern to cede them positions of relative power (such as heads of household or farm) that women had held during the occupation, put feminists in an awkward position. They were faced with what they represented as a problem of trying to maintain the political activism of the occupation years, while remaining available for appropriate men and establishing their respectability. This meant that resister sexual codes applicable to the occupation needed to be redrafted. As we have seen, in the clandestine women's press, active sexuality and desire became associated with treachery, as the available objects of desire were German occupiers or collaborators whose status put them out of bounds. Nor, according to this press, was there much time for sexual activity in the resistance, and narratives of resister romance were not reflected in the clandestine women's press.[125] Now, with men back in circulation, heterosexual desire once again became sanctioned to the extent that even prostitution could be regarded as patriotic, as long as it occurred between French women and French men.[126] Feminists faced with the 'triple bind' tried not to antagonize their readers – but it was not a very solid starting point. Some sneered at their pre-war counterparts' adoption of 'masculine' clothes and attitudes instead of instrumentalizing the power that flirtatiousness and housewifery could afford women. Others viewed women serving in the French armed forces in occupied Germany as either swaggering and smoking 'garçons manqués', or silly coquettes, 'grinning like cats on heat' and wearing skirts of indecent length.[127] It was virtually impossible for women in this situation to succeed, since they were assessed via their gender rather than professional role. *Privilèges* was one of the rare instances whose content envisaged a world in which women could be successful on their own terms. Instead of the appeasement and implicit anti-lesbianism found in other sections of the press, the magazine's first editorial approved the 'feminization' of the contemporary world, which it regarded as women's increased access to public areas from which they had hitherto been barred. Its mature sense of self-irony and multiple registers allowed it to publish reviews of works such as Jean-Paul Sartre's *Les Chemins de la liberté*, and to ridicule abstract concerns in cartoons (two women queuing outside the dairy: 'with butter at 500 francs a kilo and you're telling me that existentialism is becoming a problem!')[128] Likewise, though they did not ignore motherhood, Aubrac's journals extended their presentation of women in modes other than the maternal by daring to condemn pro-natalism.[129]

A striking feature that sets *La Femme* and *Privilèges* apart from other women's political publications is the fashion pages. The new glossy, *Elle*, which introduced colour photography to French women's journals, was about to provide an original vision for and of a French woman. Other political journals for women, such as *Femmes françaises*, attempted to combine nationalist communist politics with a nod towards what they assumed to be their readers' desire for adornment. It is hard to tell whether readers were convinced that in crocheting the lacy '[national] renaissance collar' to enhance a drab old dress ('of such rich ornamen-tation...all you need is a bit of pearlized cotton...and above all a great deal of patience and care') they would be supporting the patriotic effort for a reborn nation.[130] Readers accustomed to features of the 'turn an old handkerchief into a cheeky summer skirt!' genre that proliferated after liberation may have been surprised to find haute couture in *Privilèges* and *La Femme*. Schiaparelli hats and Worth suits were commonplace on the full-colour double-page spread devoted to fashion in each issue. Further, at a time when images of concentration camp survivors showed their gaunt subjects bravely facing up to the still uncertain renewal of life, *Privilèges* pictured one former deportee to Ravensbrück in a com-fortable salon modelling a new woollen dress donated by the haute couturier, Lucien Lelong.[131] This designer (and haggard concentration camp survivors) appeared in *Femmes françaises*, too. Saint Catherine's day was traditionally observed by Paris models holding a millinery contest. Some fanciful hand-drawn 'Lelong' hats adorned the heads of various models, and the paper declared, 'Catherinette 45 we wish you a husband – because France needs cradles'.[132] Aubrac editorialized in the first issue of *Privilèges* on the recent gains to feminine 'privilege' – that to vote, study or fight for one's country was no longer a male pre-serve. These privileges also included an assertion of agency, as the teach-ing, medical and legal professions were being feminized.[133] Aubrac had performed her own femininity to devastating effect when, disguised as a well-dressed, aristocratic wife, she gained an audience with Gestapo officers and so acquired the information necessary to lead the escape unit that would rescue a number of condemned men. Simone de Beau-voir may have turned the turban – that necessity for the shaven or hairdresser-less post-liberation woman – into a fashion statement, but Lucie Aubrac took another path.[134] There is nothing down at heel about the look of *la renaissance française* in these two journals. If read as particu-larist feminine fantasy, rather than as advertising for goods unavailable to all but wealthy readers – that is, as an extension of the political and sartorial acuity Aubrac performed during the occupation – then the fashion pages underline a move into a confident, public place for women.

During its first few months, *La Femme* contained a similar mix in the same quarto format as *Privilèges*. Its first issue in March 1945 opened with Emmanuel Mounier anticipating the journal's efforts to 'raise women from their ghetto'. Its internationalism and broad political spectrum disappeared along with Lucie Aubrac's editorship after a few months. In interview, she avoided discussing the decline of her involvement with these journals, beyond noting that sales of the self-financed *Privilèges* were too small. In Aubrac's view, a clue was in the subtitle, 'for evolved women', and perhaps then as now, she suggested, most women were insufficiently evolved to appreciate its content.[135] But the magazine, and Aubrac herself, also suffered from political hostility elsewhere on the left. 'It was exactly the same as conformity under Hitler, as conformity under Mussolini, as conformity under Pétain,' complained others on the independent left:

We struggled for four years in the clandestine press to abolish it. Are we seriously to believe that today we will tolerate its revival? Is it credible that we will once again suffer a regime at the heart of which the government, at the behest of its friends, gags its enemies, a regime which would grant the minister of information the right to sack newspaper editors just as he appoints and sacks civil service chiefs?[136]

Lucie Aubrac's departure from *La Femme* was interpreted as the failure of the resistance to defend its former ideals – and reminds us that her encounter with those eager to query her resistance politics in the 1990s was not her first brush with hostility from 'her own side'.[137] In *La Femme*, internationalism and controversial opinion gave way to domestic trivia so that by its demise in December 1946 after sixty-six issues, it was as full of knitting patterns and handy recipe tips ('steak without meat') as any other women's magazine, and even lacked the intriguing gossip and gloss with which the new magazines were starting to allure their readers. Symbolic of the changes to women's political economy as a whole, the watered-down *La Femme* was neither dedicated political commentary nor glamorous fashion temptation, and it failed on both counts.

Aubrac's autobiographical account of her daring resistance and escape has been read as 'feminine humanism' which, it is suggested, is 'a merging of humanitarian concerns and women's issues.'[138] This may offer a useful insight into later conceptualizations of the period, but does not encompass all the efforts that were made at the time. While the phrase 'feminine humanism' has been attributed to the communist resister Edith Thomas, other readings regard it as a Vichyist Catholic interpretation of ' "true" feminine qualities' that would do nothing to counter normative rules about relations between men and women.[139] The feminism of *Privilèges* and *La Femme* under Aubrac's editorship was more radical than the term 'feminine humanism' implies. Both magazines mapped new terrain in post-liberation France that would permit women to depart from traditional values, without denying feminine particularity. Anti-essentialist, feminist and internationalist, these views lost out to those which insisted on 'true' feminine qualities, as they had done during the occupation, and which paid only lip service to advancing women's position. For some, it was a depressing culmination to resistance. Adrienne Weill, for example, was a doctor involved with a London-based United Nations international working party organizing the return of women deportees from Nazi-occupied Europe.[140] On her return to Paris, she attempted to track down former feminist comrades and organizations. In the freezing winter of 1944–45, she found politics in a dismal state:

Don't be surprised at the hardships I encounter. France is a country which sets itself back to work in an atmosphere of suffering and difficulty which we can scarcely suspect at first glance, and which becomes increasingly accentuated the more one deepens one's questions. Yes, the façade remains, but all those active people you knew before who had their fingers on the pulse, completely lost contact with each other during the years of isolation, relying on themselves, to say nothing of the constant threat of arrest and deportation. We're paying for that now. All the papers burnt, either carefully by the resistance or by the Germans when they left, and the lack of communications with the provinces – this is sufficient to paralyse quite a lot. Add to that the victims of the cold (we have no heating at work or at home) so don't ask too much of us at the moment unless it's a question of immediate life or death. Right now, that's where we are.[141]

The failure of the sort of feminism expressed in Aubrac's two magazines or by Adrienne Weill was not inevitable. But the commitment to nationalized familialism and all it implied for women permitted even political adversaries to find accord. The views expressed by 'the anti-feminist' in 'Allow me a word in edgeways', *La Femme*'s regular satirical column during Aubrac's editorship, prevailed.

Motherhood and assimilationism

If maternalist assimilationism prevented the feminist press from succeeding after liberation, how were similar issues portrayed in the Jewish clandestine and post-clandestine press? Here, the notion of Jewish agency was an insistent counterpoint to the persecution of Jews under Vichy. At liberation, discourses of the active Jew, provoked by assimilationism as well as by the recognition of the importance of survival, represented a means to reintegrate these marginalized inhabitants into the French polity. At the same time, though, they helped to obscure the extent of antisemitism during the war, and of French responsibility for it. Those who insisted on assimilationism believed that the acknowledgement of difference would bring it into being and thereby threaten the unity of the republic and, to a lesser extent, those marked as different. The strength of republican assimilationism explains in part why the issue of French participation in the Holocaust was neglected for so long after the war. As far as women were concerned, assimilationism contended that their interests were largely consumed by family and maternity. We cannot view the question of children at liberation simply as a matter of discourse, however, and Jewish resisters in particular paid special attention to those orphaned by deportation.

It was noted in the last chapter that ideas of suffering were adopted in the general post-clandestine press, and rejected in favour of notions of agency in the Jewish press. This differentiation is borne out in considerations of the hidden child, a topic frequently discussed on *Droit et liberté*'s women's page. The issue of the orphan was also studied in detail by Alexis Danan in his unusually long series 'The war against children', published daily in *Libération* from 18 December 1944 to 3 January 1945. That first liberation Christmas and New Year – called the 'week of the absent' – was used to honour and prepare for the return of prisoners of war and political deportees, and an extensive programme of fundraising and commemorative events took place. Danan had campaigned during the 1930s to improve conditions for underprivileged children in concert with Suzanne Lacore, under-secretary of state for children and one of three women members of the Popular Front government.[142] His moving series is coloured by the enduring expectation that, even in the face of overwhelming and unpredictable state power, the mother would keep continual and all-knowing watch over her home and children. He represented these mothers as passive rather than resister, watching in agony as their children were torn from them, or were sought out by caring doctors, social workers or teachers willing to hide them. Danan did not mention mothers who actively sought safe places for their own children. The children's helplessness and ignorance evoke the reader's sympathy in equal measure:

He was five when a Protestant organization collected him. Impossible, you understand, to know anything from he himself. He was even ignorant of the fact that he had so many brothers and sisters. As for his surname, he had only the vaguest idea once they sent him to school. In any case, this surname made everyone laugh because of its barbarous inflections. He thought it was a trick. 'I'm called Raymond,' he told his classmates, 'and only Raymond.'[143]

Droit et liberté's treatment of the same subject showed a hidden child, Micou, in an active rather than passive mode. Not only had her mother deliberately sought refuge, but the toddler even understood what resistance meant:

she still knew her real name. Because Micou is her *nom de combat*. Yes, Micou is a *réfractaire*. She didn't want to let herself be taken by the Boches. Micou defended herself, she changed her name and went to find shelter at Auntie Julie's, who welcomed her with open arms. And once when her mother mistakenly called her by her real name, Micou, a fat little finger on her lips, said with a mysterious air and wide open eyes, 'Don't say that any more, maman. I'm called Micou.' Yes, at the age of two-and-a-half, Micou knew conspiracy, applied the rules of vigilance and taught her own mother.[144]

The two narratives are presented here not to argue for greater authenticity of one over the other, but to contrast constructions of the Jewish child. Where *Droit et liberté* underlined consciousness, individual resister agency and the chosen separation of mother and child, Danan applauded an organized resistance that had to compete not only against a ferocious government, but against maternal ignorance and obstinacy to prevent their children's departure, often to disastrous results.

Danan's commentary on the future of hidden children provoked outrage. Jewish resistance organizations had succeeded in rescuing about 10,000 children, placing them in rural Christian institutions and private homes in France or over the Swiss border. With many parents deported, the large number of orphans, many of whom had undergone a change in identity, posed real problems. First, they had to be found; just as in other areas of resistance, hiding a child successfully meant keeping the network of those involved as small as possible, and retaining few written records. Lists of children, their original names and addresses, and where they had been taken, had themselves been hidden or destroyed, and the restitution of these registers was one of the first tasks to be completed, before establishing what had become of their parents. The major resister organizations to have undertaken mass rescue of children in France, the UJRE's Commission Centrale de l'Enfance, and the Œuvre de Secours aux Enfants, succeeded in finding thousands of the children it had helped to hide, and both established children's homes where many lived to adulthood.[145] Some children hidden with families came up for adoption, and Lucie Aubrac, as a delegate to the Provisional Consultative Assembly, proposed a law to ease the process. For the first time, this would grant passed rights to single people, widows and divorcees of either sex as well as to non-French individuals and couples over the age of thirty. The law was adopted for a limited period without further discussion in the chamber.[146] Aubrac regarded the adoption of children into families already having children as ideal, a state of affairs until then forbidden by law. Noting that the vast majority of Spanish republican refugee and Jewish children who had been hidden in France went to such families, now was their chance to become entirely assimilated into existing French families, with the same rights and civic status as the biological children. But the conferment of these rights meant the abrogation of the child's original civic status.[147] It was this matter of civic status (état civil) and its embedded cultural assumptions that were to be so problematic.

The government began to discuss the question even before the return of the deportees, and before news of the Holocaust broke. In light of concerns about the assimilation of foreigners, it seemed to wish to take advantage of the fact that the children of non-French deportees who had been living with French families had become, in its terminology, 'semi-assimilated'. While their 'full assimilation' might be costly and demanding in terms of education, some suggested, their potential to the nation could be worthwhile. But the commission set up to discuss this matter took seriously an alternative proposal that such children should be sent abroad, even before the possible return of their parents.[148] The view of the non-French parent–child relationship suggested by this discussion is concomitant, first, with the importance attached to increasing the young population of France and, second, with the perceived necessity to render all elements within the nation as French as possible. We will explore more fully how these debates operated in later chapters. Let us recall here that the deportation of Jews from France, most of whom held non-French nationality or no nationality at all, had been assisted by Vichy's law that withdrew French nationality from those citizens naturalized after 1927. Having rescinded its commitment to its own population, the administrations of both Vichy and now the incoming republic pushed still further its rejection of the deportees by severing the normally inviolable relationship between biological parent and child – a position that Jacqueline Mesnil-Amar implicitly criticized in her response to de Gaulle's Victory Day speech in May 1945 discussed in the previous chapter.[149] This it did by instrumentalizing to national needs the child born to non-French parents. Danan's approach to this was apparently based on sentiment, but was just as instrumental. Of a four-year-old child who was the sole known survivor of a family of ten, he wrote:

If his mother returned one day from among the dead, what will she be to him? And what will he be to her? They believe they can recall that he was handed over to some benevolent country priest . . . Should his parents ever return, who would like to say that, according to a set of completely theoretical rights based on blood and civic status, this child belongs more to these survivors than to the farmers who, for nearly four years, have nourished him with their bread and tenderness, as and with their own? . . . We must say something cruel . . . They will not find each other unchanged . . . the certain truth . . . is that these children, should they still dream of a mother whom they idealize ... in reality don't really wish to find her again and, on the contrary, at the bottom of their hearts, the most lucid clearly never want to find her again. The new milieu has absorbed them without return.[150]

In being deported, Danan suggests, parents had rescinded their right to overall care of their children, placing responsibility on the deported parent rather than on the state then in the process of deciding what to do with such children. The question of Danan's irony is moot; his apostrophic address to deported Jews is so preposterous – 'We can count on your wisdom. You will never come back ... If you are not dead, your children are dead to you. Everything has been consumed' – that it is difficult to read other than as hyperbolic incitement to readers' outrage. But the irony was lost in certain quarters, and angry ripostes appeared in sections of the Jewish press. In an open letter published three days before the death marches were to start from Auschwitz, and less than a fortnight before the camp's liberation, the *Bulletin du Service Central des Déportés Israélites* condemned Danan's call that the hidden children of deported parents remain with their protectors even in the event of their parents' return.[151] They complained that severing the links between children and their deported parents had 'scandalized and disgusted' them and 'seemed completely unnatural'. The left Zionist paper *La Terre retrouvée* gave him the benefit of the doubt, fearing that 'his words had betrayed his thoughts'. However, to his suggestion that Jewish children would not wish to see their parents in such a distressed condition, 'ugly, shadowy, dramatically foreign to the world of the living', it asked whether children of Christian resister deportees would 'prefer' eternal separation from their parents, or whether poor working-class parents would be willing to relinquish their children even if other carers could offer greater financial security.[152] Beneath the complaints, though, lies a sense that Danan had betrayed Jewish hopes for the deportees' return – a hope that by this time was becoming increasingly slim. Danan's brutal honesty disturbed the impossible fantasy of an eventual restoration of pre-war life; but it was further coloured by his differentiation in the value placed on the French non-Jew and the Jew in France. In the context of familialism coupled with an assimilatory drive, discussions such as these once again placed deported Jews outside the national frame, discursively denying them the familial approbation that French families could expect. Motherhood itself, the condition that all agreed was the most important role for adult women, became dependent on a prior relationship to the nation.

Immigrant organizations responded to this gendered differentiation of the assimilatory project by conforming to its gender and ethnic requirements while attempting to contest the republic on its own terms. The Centre d'Action et de Défense des Immigrés (CADI), a federation dedicated to the defence of immigrants' rights and status, highlighted immigrant participation in the resistance and war.[153] Immigrants were important to France, they stressed, providing examples and statistics to prove the utility of immigrant labour and creativity in the effort to renew the economy and birth-rate. The CADI weekly *Unir* (later *Unis*) provided little opposition to conservative discourses, unlike more critical voices in *Droit et liberté*. 'Today [the immigrants] put their intelligence to service for France in war and France under reconstruction. Tomorrow, via the progressive assimilation of youth, they will work in ever greater numbers for France's reputation and development.'[154] While *Unis* instructed its female readers to use the holidays as a chance to brighten up an old tablecloth with embroidery,[155] *Droit et liberté* instituted from its first non-clandestine issue a women's page devoted to political and social issues. Its initial statement, from the UFJ, interpreted the public and private face of engaged Jewish womanhood as though she were committed to areas beyond, though including, the familial.[156] CADI's efforts to propel its readers towards a model Frenchness explain their more conformist view of femininity. *Unis* joined the general tendency to collapse France into the resistance, and offered women the least radical version of how they might be French. *Droit et liberté*, whose early women's page masthead shows women engaged in five different activities (working a factory machine; a nurse holding a baby; with a child; reading a book by a bookshelf; and in military uniform, describing an educated, socially and politically involved working woman), demonstrates confidence with respect to its connections to France. CADI's subscription to a behaviourist school of assimilation allowed it to project an unjeopardized image of its reader as just like the French (she owns an embroidered tablecloth), always undermined by adjacent articles demanding legal status for immigrants.[157] Less perturbed by issues of national status, *Droit et liberté*'s political stance allowed it to recognize a more equal access to work and public life for both genders. In contrast to other immigrant and Jewish organizations that wanted women to work in domestic and low-grade support roles, they demanded training in radio manufacture, metal work and electrics for women who had become independent heads of household.[158] The constant dangers of exclusion and the shifting fault line of assimilation which the immigrant bestrode lay at the heart of whether a woman was expected to be an active thinker or an active embroiderer.

No knitting

The clandestine and post-clandestine press was one agent in the construction of femininity in France that defined how women could belong to or be excluded from the nation. It circumscribed the family in national and gendered terms, and those few voices raised against the main trend were rapidly isolated and marginalized. Women were held responsible not only for bringing more babies into the world, but for the well-being of the nation – an extension of their role during the occupation. Vichy and resister France had described exclusion from the community of the tolerated in terms of the national, determined as much by clear gender lines as by the differentiation between nationalities.

In the years immediately after the war, the space for women's activism declined. Such was the identification between the interests of mothers and children that by 1950 the UFF had founded a new international 'week of the child'.[159] It had gone so far along the pro-natalist road that the date chosen for this annual memorialization of care and protective instinct was 8 March. This date had once been proudly commemorated in the clandestine press as International Women's Day, when courageous women would take inspiration from Clara Zetkin or the indefatigable boldness of Soviet women. The 'village values' that the clandestine press had so derided as restraining the woman under Tsarist rule and, by extension, her daughter under Vichy, seemed, in this respect at least, to have been restored.[160] Not everybody greeted the downturn in women's political militancy with equanimity, and many expressed disappointment that after years of clandestine resistance, the opportunities for long-term political activity seemed to have faded. Yet the germs for this exclusion were present in the very way that the clandestine women's press defined and represented its readership. Vichy discourses on women, though powerful and given material support, were contradictory, assigning women to a domestic sphere while requiring many to work outside the home. Wartime conditions accentuated these embedded ambiguities still further. As material circumstances changed after the war, the familialist values shared by the collaborationist state and many of its opponents alike could make an impact on a longer-term basis than that accomplished by Vichy. 'Let's be absolutely frank,' despaired Corinne, general secretary of Femmes de la Libération Nationale, early in 1947. 'These two years that have just rolled by since the liberation have been dreadfully disappointing.'[161] Women who saw themselves as once united in resistance had become split, subject more to party rather than to grass-roots politics.[162] But in setting its own agenda with respect to women, the resistance had not encouraged them to strive beyond a form of patriotic domesticity. Paradoxically, because some Jewish women's resistance had been precisely in the area of childcare, a continued resister identity was available in ways that were closed to non-Jewish women.

The next chapter will examine the natalist–Gaullist Haut Comité Consultatif de la Population et de la Famille, which was to codify pro-natalist policy for legislative purposes. At the outset, this committee, dominated by the right, had two female members; by 1947 it was seeking a third, specifically to represent family organizations. Rather than turn to the major organism in this area, the Union Nationale des Associations Familiales, or the smaller, workerist Mouvement Populaire des Familles, the committee appointed Eugénie Cotton, president of the UFF. So acceptable to the natalist establishment had the UFF become just two years after the war that her appointment seems to have inspired no opposition.[163] Unlike Corinne of the FLN, the UFF's retrospective gaze on the two years since the war found its organization and journal to be in a better condition than in the immediate liberation period: 'How did [*Femmes françaises*] appear in those days? Text, a lot of text, very long articles in small type, covering whole pages without a single illustration. Practically no fashion. Minuscule drawings, and no knitting. Nothing on interior decoration, cooking, children. Too much political news removing the feminine character from our journal.' Gradually, it said, the journal became easier to read, introduced serials, practical fashion tips, and a mother and baby page. By 1947, the editorial committee claimed that the weekly's print run had risen from 80,000 in July 1945 to 170,000 eighteen months later, while the illustrated supplement attained a figure of 120,000 copies before being reduced because of paper shortages.[164] Contrary to these statements, the post-war publication was in fact illustrated. The UFF also claimed a million members.[165] By 1949, it was sure of its status as a family organization. 'Childhood,' announced its cover headline, 'our reason for living. Defence of the family and childhood, that's the UFF *raison d'être*.'[166] Despite the alleged popularity of its pro-natalism, income from sales of *Femmes françaises* is unlikely to have supported its impressive print run. Reading was related to economics, however much Camus may have abhorred such an equation. *Privilèges des femmes* had no party or charitable funding on which it could call, and was unable to compete financially, but it was not solely economics that forced its closure.[167] In the anti-feminist atmosphere of post-war France, the propagandistic familialism of *Femmes françaises* helped the UFF to establish itself at government level, while *Privilèges* – politically and financially independent – foundered.

The secrecy necessary for the clandestine press to survive during the occupation may have played a part in women's return to obscurity after the war. Not only were women involved in the production and distribution of this press forced, like all resisters, to hide as best they could from the authorities, but their instrumentalization of femininity that had led many of them to be successful as resisters worked against their peace-time public participation. This also operated at the level of production: the 'make do and mend' tendency of the liberation period was equally present in the clandestine press mode of production. The success of the women's press had relied partly on the fact that any woman could produce a journal in her own kitchen; now, after liberation, the kitchen remained to all intents and purposes her place, and it would be another twenty-five years before it once again became a site of resistance. The anonymity of women's press authors, the perceived lack of necessity to assume even a pseudonym during the war, may also have contributed to women's rapid disappearance from public view. Perhaps female readers' expectations had been so conditioned by the paucity of 'high' politics in the clandestine press that even when it did appear, as in *Privilèges des femmes*, they did not appreciate it.

One of the few public areas available to women was social work, that ambiguous, semi-public, semi-private feminine maternal profession. UFF journals, among others, were used to recruit social workers and nurses for work in reception centres for returning deportees or to care for hidden children and other deserving families. As Madame Jeanne claimed, there was nothing to be done after the occupation except care for children. Here, though, was labour imbued with a strict sense of gendered morality.[168] It was also work which, when carried out with immigrants, provided the field for the foreigner's first assimilatory encounter. But in establishing a link between social service, maternity and appropriate femininity, French women themselves, as much as the non-French, were assigned strict roles of how they might fit in to the newly reconstructing nation after liberation.

Chapter 4
Limiting liberation: 'the French for France'

'France for the French', Charles Maurras and his followers in the extreme right Action Française insisted and, between 1940 and 1944, exclusion of all that was deemed foreign in terms of gender role, ethnicity and nationality had been Vichy's driving force. In 1946, Robert Debré, a respected paediatrician, and Alfred Sauvy, the demographer and econometrist, both advisers to Charles de Gaulle, published a book in which they outlined their populationist vision for the post-war development of France. Here, they inverted the Maurrassian slogan, demanding not France for the French, but French people for France, 'des Français pour la France'. Neither Debré nor Sauvy had much time for Maurras (Debré had been a clandestine resister, and Sauvy claimed to have been).[1] But of what did these 'French' consist whom the authors suggested should repopulate the diminished nation and restore its former greatness?

The provisional government based in Algiers issued the clarion call for population policies to take centre stage after the war. 'In post-war politics, there can be no doubt that the first concern, the only consideration to which all others must be subordinated, must be the reconstitution of the population in France', wrote one of its members who had designs on a ministerial post.[2] Liberation was the demographers' moment. Amid all the conflict and discord already present in the resistance, despite its unity of opposition to the occupation, there persisted one field of stark agreement: France was underpopulated. On this, socialists, communists, Gaullists and Christian republicans all concurred with the now-disgraced collaborationist right.[3] Only a few politically marginal and now scarce feminists, remnants of pre-war movements, remained sceptical, as we have seen. Population was hardly a new concern, especially for the militants who had been trying for several decades to bring France to its natalist senses and revitalize the country through a rise in the birth-rate that would at once increase the population, and redress what they regarded as the unhealthy balance between too many elderly and too few young.[4] But why was it after the Second World War that populationist campaigners' wishes cohered so closely with those of a post-resister government set on restoring the republic? What do the terms of discussion for the repopulation of France reveal? And how did the government and its allies seek to embed populationist policy and thought among its inhabitants?

Populationism was not a static set of discourses. At liberation, it consisted of a dual vision for national revival: an increase in the birth-rate, and an increase in immigration. Together, these would provide the framework on which the new republic could be built. It was perceived that, for the birth-rate to rise, conditions for mothers needed to be improved, and to this end a range of new family benefits was planned to encourage women to devote their time to reproducing and raising children. New adult residents were to be sought and rigorously selected to be of maximum benefit to the nation. Limited in terms of ethnicity and gender, post-liberation pro-natalism was in continual flux, redefining itself and those it categorized. The racialization that these limitations produced affected those already defined as French as much as new-comers, or those whose origins lay beyond French borders. The assimilatory project itself, therefore, far from being open to all as its ideal might suggest, was restricted to those deemed suitable candidates. The project to 'make people French' was deemed applicable only to those already perceived as sufficiently similar to 'the French' for its actions to take effect.

From the late nineteenth century, France was second only to the United States as a nation of mass immigration. Between the two world wars, there persisted a utilitarian approach to immigration. The government sought migrants in times of economic need, and despatched or restricted them during recessions – although those who favoured new restrictive legislation after liberation insisted that immigration had never before been controlled.[5] Legislation after the Second World War was enacted on the widespread understanding that progressive measures were being pursued, and that in order to protect the nation, the population had to come under far more vigorous control than had been the case hitherto. A brief account of immigrant expulsions from the end of the First World War should show how contrary to reality this pervasive notion was. In 1919, non-European workers among the 400,000 introduced during the First World War were repatriated, and immigration from the colonies was restricted. During the 1921 and 1927 recessions, immigration was once again limited, and work permits introduced which sent labour to unpopular jobs. By the early 1930s, repatriations were so frequent that, even with the rise in other forms of immigration, foreign population figures fell. Labour quotas were introduced in 1932 while, two years later, legislation was enacted to expel undesirables. The first four months of 1935 saw more than 3,000 expulsions, and the economic crisis led to discriminatory sackings. Between 1921 and 1940, over 1 million workers left France either through expulsion or 'voluntarily'.[6] Despite their constant departure, though, fears of immigrants already detectable after the First World War were only exacerbated during the 1930s 'refugee crisis'.[7] By any measure it is evident that the influx of labour had come under both scrutiny and control in the years before the Second World War. Myths about refugees coloured ideas of the dangers of immigrant population and its control after Vichy. But after the war the fate during the occupation of those whom Vichy defined as foreign came in for very little overt comment at all.

Fears attached to immigration were coupled with those concerning the birth-rate. Falling reproduction rates were perceived as both symbol and cause of national decline. Pro-natalists, increasingly strident after the First World War, believed that France suffered from both a catastrophically low birth-rate and a burdensome proportion of elderly population.[8] They constantly cited figures from Germany, and later Japan and Italy as these became enemies, in harsh comparison with both the perceived reproductive lack at home, and with a fecund past. As fascist Italy and the Third Reich put their faith in youth during the 1930s, pro-natalists began to see the preponderance of elderly people in France in even more catastrophic terms, that the loss and disablement of young men during the First World War had only accelerated. Terrible projections were made of the death of France itself, based on the middle years of the 1930s when deaths did outnumber births. Despite the rise in the birth-rate during the occupation, a fact which took many demographers by surprise, after liberation they continued to suggest that the birth-rate was falling. Predictions that by 1985, the population of France would be 29 million were quite standard, though subsequent analysis has shown that even during the 1930s, trends were upwards.[9] Demographers' view of history was imbued with nostalgia for a distant and lost past, and yet when it came to their assessment of current conditions, they took little notice of the long view, and preferred instead to regard the disequilibrium between births and deaths in the mid-1930s as clear support for their pessimism. In fact, there were numerous ways of calculating the birth-rate, all of them more or less approximate and none taking into account all the variables.[10] The horrifying data that seemed to demonstrate beyond doubt that Frenchwomen were lax in fulfilling their childbearing duties sustained the beliefs of those ideologically committed to the need for women to have more children, and to imagine France as a nation that had lost its greatness.

Reconstructing the population

The post-liberation government set out to tackle head-on what it insisted was the demographic 'problem', and Charles de Gaulle announced the framework of reconstruction during the spring of 1945.[11] In a long 'state of the nation' speech he spelt out the often quoted national need for 'twelve million bonny babies' to be produced within ten years. The lack of population was, he said, 'the profound cause of our misfortune' and 'the principle obstacle against our recovery ... so that France can be no more than a bright light going out'. New legislation, however, would come into play, 'at the moment, for which we have waited so long, that our mobilized men, prisoners and deportees return, and when a large number of French households are founded or reborn'.[12] The return of prisoners of war, political deportees and forced labourers from Germany was a sensitive issue, and many objected to the proposal to hold elections – the first in which women would be able to vote – before all the men had been repatriated. Shortly after the end of the European war, de Gaulle outlined in greater depth three major areas of reform – modernization of the *fonction publique*, the nationalization programme and the introduction of family and immigration policies. 'Finally,' he concluded, 'measures are required concerning the peopling of France as much by financial guarantees to families as by rational rules concerning immigration'.[13] The 'intimate connection' that de Gaulle sketched between immigration and the French family was repeatedly expressed during the liberation years.[14] But 'rationalization' of immigration and family policy was not, as many claimed, the institution of some sensible rules in a muddled area in which none had previously existed.[15] Instead, it would be the implementation of a set of ideas in which the development of the French populace could, it was hoped, be as scientifically planned as its future economic progress.[16] It was against the perceived chaos of immigration during the 1920s and 1930s that such rationalization, or regulation based on 'natural' and scientifically identifiable laws, was to take place.

Pro-natalism was far from new to post-war France, but it would be a mistake to view its transformation from propaganda to legislation as simply incremental. Inter-war campaigners were certainly adept, and the organization that became the Alliance Nationale contre la Dépopulation was prolific and successful in making its mark – sometimes quite literally, as when their demands appeared on a themed postage stamp in 1939. Pro-natalism made an impact immediately after the First World War as contraception and abortion were suppressed and benefits introduced for *familles nombreuses*. It was not until 1939 that various elements of pro-natalism were assembled into the package called the Code de la Famille. The promulgation of the Code scarcely more than a month before the invasion of Poland is significant here for two reasons. First, it was formulated at a time of heightened fear – of war, and of immigration. Second, post-war interpretation of the Code emphasized its original date. Pro-natalists welcomed Vichy familialism, but afterwards maintained the conceit that the Code's republican origins less than a year before the armistice qualified its work as unfinished. The return of the republic permitted the Code's ambitions to be fully realized, therefore, without explicit reference to Vichy.[17] These political aspects lead me to problematize the term 'pro-natalism' itself. For pro-natalism was never solely about reproduction: the question of *which* babies, and what sort of population was desirable for the nation, always lay at its heart. As de Gaulle made explicit, the politics of demography concerned nation, race, ethnicity and gender, and demographers undertook the project to form a population appropriate for France. For these reasons I prefer the term populationism.

The wave of demographic enthusiasm in 1945 saw the creation of numerous new official bodies. In place of the former Ministry of Health, the government established a new Ministry of Population and Public Health, in a bid to end the pre-war atomization of the various government departments that dealt with family and population issues. The new ministry had executive powers in all the key areas of population – naturalization, the family, preventive health and social security – a situation even the first minister of population deplored.[18] Action did not stop there, and before the war was over, a further interconnected set of populationist agencies was set up to protect what the first and second ministers of population, the communist François Billoux and the centrist Robert Prigent (MRP), both referred to as 'human capital'.[19] The one which endures to this day is the Institut National d'Etudes Démographiques (INED), born less from the ashes than from the still-burning flames of the Vichy research institute, the Fondation Française pour l'Etude des Problèmes Humains (FFEPH) that had been founded in 1941 under the 'regency' of Nobel prize-winner, Alexis Carrel.[20] As François Billoux announced, 'just like the National Institute of Hygiene, we must have a National Institute of Demographic Studies which, every morning, will remind all the French that we need other French for France to continue, which will practise a reasoned policy of immigration or at least the progressive assimilation of immigrant elements'.[21] The Institut National d'Etudes Démographiques became the key instrument of populationist research and policy, and a few months after its foundation in April 1945, its links to the ministry and influence over policy were tightened still further, as it at once came under ministry supervision, and was officially required to provide training for ministry staff.[22]

Within the ministry itself, three new organisms were to administer and formulate population policy. The Secrétariat Général à la Famille et à la Population was headed by Alfred Sauvy, who was also the director of INED; he was charged with coordinating the activities and decisions of the various ministries still concerned with questions of population. The Comité Interministériel de la Population et de la Famille was to bring together representatives of all these ministries. Finally, the Haut Comité Consultatif de la Population et de la Famille (HCCPF) was formed under de Gaulle's personal chairmanship.[23] According to the decree that established the HCCPF, whose members were chosen by the president himself, it was to be 'consulted by the government on all measures concerning the protection of the family, the development of natality, rural population, urban deconcentration, the establishment of foreigners on French soil and their integration into the French population'.[24] It met frequently in 1945 – more than once a week in June – and its deliberations lay behind much of the slew of populationist legislation that was passed in the first two years after the war.

Commentators at liberation insisted that these structural moves in favour of the family and population control were new. In some significant respects they were, such as the elevation of scientists and scientific planning to the centre of government thinking. They also owed much to the recent past. INED had its Vichy predecessor, the FFEPH.[25] Likewise, the first Haut Comité de la Population had formulated the Code de la Famille in 1939. At the time, Edouard Daladier envisaged this extension of 1920 and 1923 anti-abortion and anti-contraception legislation in favour of the *famille nombreuse* as an opportunity to shore up the nation against its perceived numerical weakness. 'A deserted country cannot be a free country,' he famously said. 'It is a route open to all invasions, willing prey for the greedy.' The new policy would 'permit France to remain that which it was in the last century'.[26] Daladier's glorification of the nineteenth century was unusual, as most demographers believed that France's golden past lay further back in the eighteenth century. In this vein, Jacques Doublet, secretary to the 1939 Haut Comité, commented that it was to redress the over-emphasis since 1789 on the individual in favour of the collectivity, and particularly the family, that the Code de la Famille proceeded.[27] Indeed, in a move away from individualism that had been criticized as having fostered an anti-communitarian spirit, the new constitution after liberation specified that both the individual and the family were to be assured the necessary conditions for their development.[28] So much for shifts from the past. Robert Prigent, resister and member of the provisional government in Algiers, later clarified just how far familialist militants were prepared to compromise with Vichy. Vichy's Gounot Law had established a representative body of familialist organizations, so that familialism was brought into the direct sphere of the state. Prigent, active in Christian, working-class familialism, and founder of the Mouvement Populaire des Familles, saw the chance in Vichy for the concerns of his organizations to remain central to government populationism after liberation.[29] Nor was Vichy's

Table 2 *Links between populationist organizations*

HCCPF	INED	FFEPH	SSAE	Other
Maxime Blocq-Mascart				CNR
Fernand Boverat		*		ANCD
Simone Collet				UNAF
Robert Debré	*			PGF
Jeanne Delabit				CGT-FO
Jacques Doublet	*	*		
Adolphe Landry	*	*	*	UIESP
				ANCD
Georges Mauco			*	UIESP
Maurice Monsaingeon		*		UNAF
Alfred Sauvy	*	*		LPGF

Commission Générale à la Famille so distant from the new Secrétariat Général à la Famille et à la Population. It might even be said that Vichy initiatives were strengthened after liberation. While the Vichy Commission Générale à la Famille had little legislative power, its inheritor at liberation did not suffer from such handicaps.

Beyond the strict remit of the state, other organisms were charged with putting into practice many of the ideas regarding immigrants and their 'progressive assimilation' into France. The Service Social d'Aide aux Emigrants was one of these. It operated on a relatively small scale, and indeed complained to the ministry that its lack of funds prevented the satisfactory fulfilment of its tasks.[30] Yet it was a significant organization whose examination will help us to understand the ways that familialism, assimilation and immigration became enmeshed. The crossover between these agencies and committees was significant, and Table 2 shows just how few individuals were able to have an impact across the field. Each of these bodies understood population in the dual terms of the family and reproduction on one side, and immigration on the other. They framed the very process of immigration in terms of the family, so that through successful assimilation, immigrants would be able to found families and have children, becoming worthy bearers of the title 'French'. The terms in which demographers discussed the family concerned not only the bringing together of women and men in heterosexual, productive union, but also the nationality of the family. Just as the Union des Femmes Françaises addressed French women as reproducers, so demographers talked of the productive family as French. This did not emerge suddenly at liberation: even during the débâcle in early June 1940 and shortly before the government left Paris, the prime minister Paul Reynaud established a new Ministry of the French Family to replace that of Public Health whose minister, Marcel Héraud, had just resigned.

Nobody, wrote Jean-François Gravier in 1947, could any longer ignore the problem of population given the fine contributions from Adolphe Landry, Alfred Sauvy, Robert Debré, Georges Mauco and Fernand Boverat.[31] Gravier's influential work, *Paris et le désert français*, asserted that French centralization encouraged rural depopulation and turned Paris into a vast parasite that fed off the rest of an inevitably depleted France. As a former Vichy senior civil servant reintegrated into the administration after liberation, he was perhaps partisan.[32] Each of the individuals he mentioned, plus a number of other notable commentators on population, were members of the HCCPF. All were prolific authors who, in common with the other Committee members bar one, had remained in metropolitan France during the occupation. Each had published work on populationism during or immediately after the occupation. Who were they, and what credentials did they hold that encouraged de Gaulle to seek their authority on matters of population?

A new member of the HCCPF in 1945, Maxime Blocq-Mascart was a right-wing, corporatist critic of the Third Republic.[33] A former First World War pilot, Blocq-Mascart studied economics and later formed the Service Social des Travailleurs Intellectuels, assuming its vice-presidency after the Second World War. He was an early member of the centrist resistance group Organisation Civile et Militaire (OCM), and much criticized for his detailed fifty-page discussion of the 'problem of minorities' in their 1942 clandestine publication, the OCM *Cahiers*.[34] Although these proposals for exclusion went some way beyond Vichy's, he became the OCM representative on the Conseil National de la Résistance (CNR) and vice-president of that body.[35] The 'problem of minorities' was explicitly one of Jews. In a tone that at times seemed to justify antisemitism, and was certainly sympathetic to the reasons for its preponderance, Blocq-Mascart traced its historical roots and formulations in pre-war France. He criticized Léon Blum in terms more normally expected from Blum's Vichyist opponents who had sent him – and in effect the Third Republic – to trial at Riom. Writing just after measures had been promulgated to force all Jews in the Northern Zone to wear the yellow star, Blocq-Mascart remained silent on the matter of Vichy or Nazi antisemitic legislation. Those members of national and non-Christian minorities who could not prove four generations of Christian ascendancy, or three generations of birth on French soil, he concluded, should be excluded from various occupations and be deprived of the choice of where to settle.[36] While these were not necessarily common sentiments in the resistance overall, we will see that elements would be taken up at liberation. After liberation, Blocq-Mascart became a delegate to the Provisional Consultative Assembly and founded the centrist newspaper, *Parisien libéré*. He was president of Entr'aide Française (the republican version of Vichy's social work organization, Secours National) and after 1951, became a Conseiller d'Etat, representing French interests in its African colonies as they moved to independence. He was instrumental in de Gaulle's return in 1958, though later distanced himself from the president over Algeria.

An obsessive populationist, Fernand Boverat began his publishing career in 1913 with *Patriotisme et paternité*, a call to arms in the war against depopulation. He held senior positions from 1912 until after the Second World War in the organization that became the Alliance Nationale contre la Dépopulation (ANCD) and described himself as an expert demographer, though his only qualification was a diploma from a business school. The son of a well-established stockbroker, it might be speculated that Boverat's febrile insistence that others have children be attributed to his own childlessness.[37] His attraction to extreme populationism was pronounced during the 1920s and especially the 1930s, as fascist Italy and then Nazi Germany engaged in what he regarded as active population development, and as refugees began to arrive in France.[38] In 1939 he was invited to join the Haut Comité de la Population that formulated the Code de la Famille. During the occupation, Boverat continued to write for the ANCD – now with bases in the occupied and non-occupied zones – and joined the FFEPH in 1943 as chair of its new Natality team.[39] The ANCD publications of this period were aimed particularly at young readers in Vichy's youth organizations, the Chantiers de la Jeunesse and the Eclaireurs de France.[40] After the war, some accused Boverat of collaboration; in his defence, he claimed instead to have attempted to join de Gaulle in London, only to receive the humiliating news that his presence was superfluous, at which point he returned to France.[41] There he found that Vichy's familialism coincided with his own, and the ANCD responded to Vichy's call for a unified family movement by joining with similar organizations, including the Fédération des Associations des Familles Nombreuses and La Plus Grande Famille, to become Vichy's official representative of the family movement in July 1941.[42] After the war, Boverat became one of the HCCPF's most vociferous members, a prolixity matched only by his monomaniacal publication record.[43]

Robert Debré was professor of paediatrics at the Paris Faculty of Medicine, and fathered a dynasty of prominent Gaullists.[44] He too had been involved with the 1939 Haut Comité, and became a key member of its 1945 incarnation. His family were pious Alsatian Jews, and he grew up in Paris, where his father taught at the yeshiva of which his grandfather was director.[45] Debré later abandoned Judaism, which he associated with Zionist excess and small-minded particularism, a point of view that led him to regret the influence that Jewish organizations would have on child concentration camp survivors who had come to France in 1945.[46] After the invasion, Debré remained in Paris and was one of the handful of Jews in medicine, education, law or public service permitted by Article 8 of the Statut des Juifs to remain in work after the same legislation had excluded the rest from these areas. Like other Jewish medical professionals, though, he was forbidden to treat non-Jewish patients and worked at the Rothschild Hospital, now limited to Jews alone. Even after the hospital came under constant police surveillance and was surrounded by barbed wire, some staff delayed the deportation of patients by faking illnesses and helping them escape. Despite these efforts, there were frequent round-ups at the hospital between November 1942 and April 1944.[47] Debré used his laboratory to produce false papers; he also helped to establish a network of medical personnel to assist refugees and resisters, and two medical resistance groups. These – the Comité Médical de la Résistance, affiliated to the OCM, and the Front National des Médecins, allied to the Front National – aimed to bring together politically divergent wings of the resistance. The Rothschild Hospital was thus the site of round-ups and arrests, as well as of succour and resistance. In September 1943, Debré went underground, and later assisted Gaullists to plan the Paris uprising.[48] His research focused on infectious diseases among children, interests that keyed with his populationist preoccupations. These received full expression in his 1946 publication, *Des Français pour la France*, co-authored with Alfred Sauvy, whose appointment as director of INED he was instrumental in procuring and whom he joined as chair of INED's first technical committee.[49]

Simone Collet, née Brunet (known on the Committee under her husband's name as Mme Olry Collet) was president of La Plus Grande Famille. This organization for parents of more than five children used the same address as many other populationist groups, an impressive building in central Paris that Philippe Renaudin, Vichy's general commissioner for the family, inaugurated as the Maison de la Famille in 1942. La Plus Grande Famille was created during the First World War in a consciously élitist move, its name reflecting concerns not just for the biggest families, but those deemed socially most worthy, who would show the way to those less fortunate.[50] Funding came from industrialists to help other family organizations to orientate themselves 'from an intellectual and moral point of view'. During the occupation, Simone Collet headed their welfare committee, helping middle-class mothers in Paris through the crisis, for which she was awarded the Chevalier de la Légion d'Honneur in 1946, gaining Officier status in 1966.[51] La Plus Grande Famille published the populationist journal *Pour la vie*, which began its new series in 1945 and was intended to span all family movements.[52]

The Committee records present her concerns to be the family as the primary unit of social organization, and hostility to immigration of anything other than families.[53] Collet seems not to have been considered an important member: when the British Royal Commission on Population invited the Committee to send a delegation, she was excluded at the last minute, despite her protestations and appearance on the original list.[54]

Jeanne Marcelle Delabit, née Hartmann, was the only left-wing member of the Committee, although as a founding member of the Confédération Générale du Travail–Force-Ouvrière (CGT–FO) trade union bloc, her sympathies were anti-communist. Born in 1892 in eastern Paris, where she remained all her life, she began work as a cigarette maker, becoming a factory welfare supervisor (*surintendante d'usine*) during the First World War shortly after such responsibilities for women were introduced. She was first elected to trade union office in 1922 and held senior posts in the tobacco workers' union, the Fédération Nationale CGT des Ouvriers et Ouvrières des Manufactures de Tabacs, as under-secretary, secretary-general and editor of the monthly newspaper. As an anti-communist on the left, she might well have clashed with her only potential political ally on the Committee, François Billoux. At the same time, her politics isolated her from all the other members. As a trade union organizer of many years' standing, though, she was familiar with being in a minority position: until 1945, only two unions, the tobacco workers and the clothing workers, had any women among their leadership.[55] In 1932, she spoke on behalf of the women's section at the CGT congress organized by the Comité d'Action pour la Paix, and as secretary of her union's welfare section, she ensured that the interests of women workers as well as men were defended. She was a member of the Fédération Démocratique Internationale des Femmes (FDIF), the communist-organized international women's peace organization initiated at the end of the Second World War by the Union des Femmes Françaises.[56] In 1945, she was elected to the CGT administrative commission and to the Force-Ouvrière executive commission at its first conference in April 1948, where she remained for thirteen years.[57] This brief biography implies considerable oratorical and organizational prowess; the HCCPF archives silence her almost completely, though Delabit was occasionally noted as voicing opposition to measures such as the family vote, opinions on which the right-wing majority generally overruled her and Blocq-Mascart. Nonetheless, the presence of two women on the HCCPF did represent a change from its Vichy forebears; while women had been a major focus for familialism, they played less part in the formulation of policy.[58] Here, though, it is difficult for the historian to reach far beyond Collet's and Delabit's femininity as it all but excised them from the written record.

The *fonctionnaire* Jacques Doublet had been secretary to the 1939 Haut Comité before becoming a fully fledged member in 1945. He first entered the Ministry of the Interior (foreigners' section) in 1930 before moving to the Conseil d'Etat in 1932. During the 1930s he prepared a doctorate in law on the Nazi Arbeitsfront.[59] 'Relieved of his functions' to organize peasants at the Ministry of Agriculture at the end of 1942, he was hardly in disgrace with Vichy since he immediately joined the Rural Economy research team at the FFEPH.[60] His claim to have remained in clandestine contact throughout the occupation with other HCP members Alfred Sauvy, Fernand Boverat and Adolphe Landry, as well as undertaking unspecified resistance work with Jean Lefebvre and Pasteur Vallery-Radot (with whom Robert Debré was also connected) would seem to be stretching a point since only the latter were underground, and the former were all working with the FFEPH.[61] At liberation, he was briefly involved with the short-lived Ministry of Prisoners, Deportees and Refugees.[62] After the war, Doublet published a number of commentaries on welfare benefits whose chief interest here is their hesitation vis-à-vis the easy transferability of legislative desires to social change assumed elsewhere.

Populationists generally credit Adolphe Landry as father of the 1939 Code de la Famille. As deputy for Corsica, government minister and, briefly, senator, he began to introduce populationist measures such as reduced rail fares for large families shortly after the First World War. Landry was president of the Union Internationale pour l'Etude Scientifique de la Population in the 1930s, was a senior member of the ANCD, and published numerous works on demography before, during and after the occupation, most notably, *La Démographie française* and *Traité de démographie*.[63] His contributions to the HCCPF were especially concerned with the details of family welfare benefits, and he succeeded in his determination that child benefit should apply to all and not just the first child, but be disallowed for the first child if it were born more than two years after marriage or if the mother were over twenty-five years old.[64] His party loyalties remained in the republican–radical ambit, and he was appointed to the Ministries of Marine (January 1920–January 1921, as a deputy for Action Républicaine et Sociale, a group interested in linking technocracy with natalism) and Instruction Publique, Beaux-Arts and Enseignement Technique (but for only twenty-four hours in June 1924 before the cabinet fell); finally, in Pierre Laval's government he was at Travail et Prévoyance Sociale (as a Gauche Radicale between January 1931 and February 1932). After 1933, Landry took a principled stand and joined what became the Comité National Français de Secours aux Réfugiés Allemands, Victimes de l'Antisémitisme, and in 1940, he abstained in the vote to grant Pétain full powers.[65] Landry joined Robert Debré on the first technical committee that helped to formulate the direction that INED would pursue.[66]

If Landry was the father of populationist legislation, the paternity of demographics could be attributed to Alfred Sauvy. His professional career in this field spanned more than five decades, and his output was prolific and influential in the construction not only of a fundamental belief in the workability of a planned econometric demographic policy, but of a scientistic, historicist view of France, past, present and future. A graduate of the Ecole Polytechnique, Sauvy worked in Paris for the Statistique Générale de la France from 1922, where, apart from a brief period of mobilization at the outbreak of war, he was director of the Institut de Conjoncture throughout the occupation. It was in this capacity that he joined Vichy's Conseil Supérieur de la Famille. Among other duties, the Statistique Générale helped to compile the census of Jews during the occupation.[67] During the occupation Sauvy published a major work on demography, *Richesse et population*.[68] Having been a member of the 1939 Haut Comité, he claimed to have remained in clandestine contact with others to plan post-war policy, particularly with regard to abortion, family and housing benefits and retirement pensions, a process greatly eased given his appointment as technical advisor to the FFEPH Bio-sociology department.[69] In 1945, he became head of INED and remained editor of their journal, *Population*, until 1976.[70] The transformation of the Fondation Française pour l'Etude des Problèmes Humains established by Vichy in 1941 to INED was almost seamless. The same legislation dissolved the first and created the second, paving the way for the FFEPH to persist in a new republican incarnation.[71] INED researchers wrote up the results of FFEPH enquiries,[72] and continuity was evident in objectives, personnel and methods.[73] Of twenty-five researchers at INED, more than half had been employed at the FFEPH, and a number of projects that the first initiated were completed by the second. The first issue of *Population* from mid-1946 contained a variety of articles by former FFEPH employees. Implicit in the FFEPH's conversion to INED was the disappearance of the occupation from the demographer's mind. In his introduction to the first issue of *Population*, Sauvy noted two dates – the promulgation of the Code de la Famille in July 1939, and the creation of the Secrétariat Général à la Famille et à la Population in April 1945 – as the only ones worthy of recollection, despite the fact that this Secrétariat owed a great deal to Vichy's organization of family at government level.[74]

Maurice Monsaingeon was a medical practitioner and Catholic familialist whose official Committee role was to represent the new Union Nationale des Associations Familiales (UNAF). Another former member of the FFEPH (he sat on its executive committee), Monsaingeon was also vice-president of La Plus Grande Famille and almost as prolific a correspondent as Boverat.[75] Like his son André, he was an outspoken opponent of abortion. Monsaingeon expressed pious arguments in favour of the Catholic family, which he regarded as 'the providential institution animated by spirituality, intelligence and love which together make the familial trinity of man, woman and child'.[76] As a Catholic, his populationism differed constitutively from Boverat's, whose primary concern was increased national reproductivity, though this too was to be achieved within a family setting.[77] Shortly before liberation, Monsaingeon published a Vichyist defence of the family as sole bedrock of a healthy society which should be constituted to form 'la Patrie, Famille de familles', a position he probably defended as member of the permanent section of Vichy's Conseil Supérieur de la Famille and president of its Centre National de Coordination des Activités Familiales.[78] Hostile to immigration, which he compared to invasion, he subscribed to a biologistic view of population movement as 'a veritable human transplant or blood transfusion', a view that echoed the extreme racism of René Martial, whom we shall meet again in the next chapter.[79]

Robert Prigent was also a Christian familialist whose religious convictions, while profound, were coupled with a working-class sensibility and were more generous than those of Monsaingeon. Born in 1910 in the Nord, Prigent was a Christian trade unionist from an early age, and co-founded the Ligue Ouvrière Chrétienne in 1936. In 1941, he founded the Mouvement Populaire des Familles, representing both these organizations on Vichy's various family coordination committees. He left France in 1942, and by 1943 had been elected to the Consultative Provisional Assembly in Algiers for the OCM. At liberation, as well as working with Lucie Aubrac on *Privilèges des femmes* (he had supported universal suffrage during the vote in Algiers), he remained a parliamentarian, and was deputy for the Nord until 1951. For two years from autumn 1945 he was minister for population. After leaving parliament, he remained active until the 1980s in a variety of social welfare, Catholic and familialist organizations. Prigent had for many years campaigned for the rights of working-class families, and the family in general, which he suggested was, 'isolated, underrated and mocked, and moreover bears the weight of a terrible inferiority complex which makes it seek only timid remedies for its suffering'.[80] While he wished to raise the status of the family, his democratic inclinations opposed the family vote in whose favour right-wing familialists routinely campaigned. The family vote would give parents a vote on behalf of each child; its supporters variously suggested that mothers should vote on behalf of their daughters, or for their children under the age of ten, and fathers for sons or older children. At liberation, proponents tried to insist that the family vote would introduce truly universal suffrage, imagining that families would vote only in their familial, rather than class, regional or other interests.[81] Against this trend, which had received state support from Vichy in theory (though in practice it abandoned voting rights for all), Prigent regarded as imperative the need for familialist organizations to have a recognized advisory council at state level, as the economy had done.[82]

The last person on the Committee was Georges Mauco. As its secretary, he is important for the historian inasmuch as he was in charge of its papers. His work on immigration and assimilationism forms the basis of the next chapter. Here, it is important to consider his place on the Committee. At its first meeting on 30 April 1945, members were asked to consider immigration. As an expert on this matter since the early 1930s when he published *Les Etrangers en France*, a book that rapidly achieved pre-eminence in the field, Mauco's hand in the formulation of the Committee's published proposals is evident.[83] In common with many specialists, Mauco was convinced that some categories of foreigner would adapt to France better than others. It was necessary, therefore, to adopt a policy whereby the proportion of desirables would be maintained. The minutes of that first meeting record that,

The Secretary [Georges Mauco] presented the project devoted to the initial organization of immigration. He first proposed discussion of the principle of ethnic selection: Nordics, Mediterraneans, Slavs. This choice rests on experience and on studies carried out in the last two decades. It further rests on selection carried out in the United States.

The President [Charles de Gaulle] confirmed the necessity for such a choice.[84]

It was universally accepted that, even without immigrants, France was an ethnically mixed nation, and from this, even the intellectual acrobatics of the ardent biological racists could not depart. Before turning our attention to the reasons 'Nordics' held such appeal at liberation, let us examine the ideas behind the new structural arrangements on population a little more closely.

French people for France

The establishment of the Ministry of Population, and its constituent committee and secretariat, owed much to a visionary plan that Robert Debré devised.[85] 'Inspired by a new spirit', he aimed to put populationism at the forefront of public consciousness. More far-reaching than a similar plan by his Algiers-based colleague, Bernard Mélamède,[86] Debré's departed from prior administrative arrangements to propose a new ministry whose independent budget and cabinet membership would lend it the strategic status equivalent to that of a ministry of economy. The ministry would be dedicated to supporting populationism across the entire range of government functions. The new body should prioritize rebirth, natality and immigration, and sweep away old ideas of a ministry of health that Debré suggested took an unproductive interest in death via its curative, rather than preventive, attitude to medicine. In addition to a coordinated effort among legislators, educators and social workers to ensure that France was repopulated with healthy families and diligent immigrants, a policy of population distribution to key areas should be undertaken. The ministry would be organized into three divisions – health, social welfare, and population. This last would be subdivided into two sections – first, family, and second, population, immigration and population distribution (*peuplement*). Mindful of his 'new spirit', Debré insisted that the family section be 'haunted by the concern to restore the French birth-rate' via an increase in the number of families with more than three children – a departure from Daladier's promotion of *very* large families. Immigrants in the Debré plan were to be 'fixed by a system of appropriate proportions according to the categories of foreigners'. Assimilation would be achieved step by step, and immigrants would be granted new status in three stages: first, their initial admission, then the 'wanderer' (*pérégrin*) status which would award them economic but not political benefits, and finally naturalization, which could be granted, or refused, only after this apprenticeship.[87] Debré's plan depended on a nationalized approach to the question of population, that would involve educators and the armed forces as well as the administration. To this end, he proposed the introduction of national service for women whereby young women would be obliged to act as medical social workers, nursing assistants or mothers' helps, thereby taking populationism right to the cradle.

With significant modifications proposed by the HCCPF, many aspects of the Debré plan were realized, both in the establishment of the new ministry and in the quantity and content of legislation on nationality and the family passed between 1945 and 1947. The main legislation consisted of revisions to the Code de la Famille in 1945 and 1946, and the Code de la Nationalité of 19 October 1945.[88] There were also dozens of other laws on housing, demography, welfare benefits and the problems known as 'social scourges' – chiefly tuberculosis, alcoholism and prostitution. These extensive pieces of legislation introduced and amended a whole raft of measures. As far as the family was concerned, the HCCPF voted for changes in benefits to the family such as payments made to expectant and neo-natal mothers, and measures to counter infant mortality and abortion (which it called 'protection of the family'). It was also concerned to 'protect the race' by stamping out alcoholism and the sale of hard spirits, and by outlawing 'moral outrage' (homosexuality and prostitution) and illegal drugs. Many of the committee's deliberations were adopted in law. Their wishes to educate the children of foreigners in 'intellectual and spiritual' issues, though, and their suggestion that parents of three or more living and legitimate children brought up 'with dignity' be honoured with a special title and a distinctive badge to be worn at all times, did not reach the statute books.[89] Among other laws that were passed at this time was one that brought private establishments that trained housewives under state control, for instance, and there were new measures for ante- and neo-natal care.[90] Women who disobeyed measures designed to encourage childbirth and who failed to attend medical examinations during and after their pregnancy, would lose their maternity allowances. In any case, these benefits were far from universal. In a bid to rejuvenate the country, allowances would only be paid to parents if the mother were under twenty-five years old, or if the child were born within the first two years of marriage, followed by the subsequent children within three years of the last.[91]

In the realm of nationality, the new Code de la Nationalité specified precisely how French nationality was to be acquired, on whom it could be conferred, and how it could be lost. Naturalization was at once encouraged, and yet subject to new measures whereby the degree of an applicant's assimilation was taken into account for the first time. New residents were forbidden to change their profession from that written on their identity card for ten years, a situation that some found to be 'in flagrant contradiction' with the government's professed hopes for speedy assimilation.[92] These hopes were encompassed in legislation to encourage the Gallicization of surnames, until then permitted only under special parliamentary order on a case-by-case basis, so that individuals might lose their 'foreign sound or look'.[93] As far as professionals were concerned, the non-French were excluded from architecture, law, accountancy and pharmacy, and could not run travel agencies or direct plays. The medical establishment had for many years been hostile to the admission of immigrants to their ranks, and ministerial permission was required before any non-French national could practise medicine, or its branches such as dentistry, optometry, veterinary science or massage.[94] The importance of the HCCPF in respect of this legislation should not be underestimated, given that the Code de la Nationalité and the new Code de la Famille, plus many other laws, were *ordonnances*, a type of legislation not subject to parliamentary debate.[95] The significance of the HCCPF deliberations was further compounded by the friction between the various ministries with which they consulted – labour, finance, justice and interior – which meant that the inter-ministerial council met only rarely.[96]

Debré's plan was not the only document available for the Committee's consultation. Between them, the members had published dozens of works and each was considered an expert. If there were any senior members of the Committee, though, these were Georges Mauco, whose propositions for immigration legislation formed the basis of the law that would eventually be passed (and that is discussed in the next chapter), Robert Debré and Alfred Sauvy. It is worth examining more closely the collaborative explorations of the last two in *Des Français pour la France*, published in 1946.

Debré's and Sauvy's claims to authority stemmed initially from their scientific backgrounds. *Des Français pour la France* argued for social planning on every level, and stemmed from their belief in the legislated management of progress. Population, for them, was a physical, unified mass, and the low birth-rate was tantamount to an earthquake that caused 'cracks, subsidence and cavings in [to be] produced in the social body'.[97] Society as an earthy crust presented the French social fabric not only as brittle but geo-physical, intrinsically attached to its land. The view of the French populace as bound to and created by their land had long formed part of nationalist discourse of which Vichy's *retour à la terre* could be interpreted as but one version. People, such as immigrants and city-dwellers, who were held to be remote from the land were seen as problematic, a theme to be developed in the next chapter. As far as immigration was concerned, *Des Français pour la France* is suffused with a profound ambivalence. The authors rejected biological racism and asserted that 'the idea of a "pure race", of the "protection of racial purity", is merely political polemic with neither foundation nor value'.[98] Antisemitism was a 'false problem' instrumentalized in the service of pan-German propaganda.[99] At the same time, the authors believed in definite cultural differences between immigrant groups and that immigrants thus varied in value. The temporary migration of colonial subjects notwithstanding, Debré and Sauvy asserted that pre-war immigration proportions were changing from a domination of Belgians, Italians and Spanish (i.e., 'Nordics' and 'Mediterraneans') to Slavs, North Africans and Asians. 'One could say,' they remarked, 'that foreign immigration comprises a greater number of "exotic" elements than previously.'[100] It has been suggested that Debré and Sauvy anticipated mass immigration open to all. The scholar and former immigration service civil servant Patrick Weil compared Sauvy with Georges Mauco, the Conseiller d'Etat, Pierre Tissier, and minister for labour Alexandre Parodi. He wrote, 'And if they considered in respect of the assimilation of foreigners that a hierarchy exists in the capacity of assimilation according to nationality or origin, they nonetheless think that "in the case of assimilation and Gallicization the individual element must prevail over all others. The character of each immigrant must be examined".'[101] Debré and Sauvy did reject biological notions of race. But Weil's quotation was selective, and over-emphasized the role of the individual in relation to the mass. In the passage in *Des Français pour la France* which preceded Weil's citation, the authors worried about the sort of foreigner whose assimilation was considered more problematic than that of the Scandinavian or the Belgian:

There remain the Orientals, Levantines, Balkanics, etc. Their influx is far from being as desirable as that of the Belgians and Dutch, or even the Italians and Spanish. Here again, one must not raise racial objections but, on the contrary, realize that these subjects are too far from our civilization and that its level risks modification after contact with them. The situation in a city like Marseilles, largely open to these immigrants, authorizes certain fears. Severe selection must preside over their admission.[102]

Immigrants, in other words, had to be selected as individuals, but individuals from some categories were less likely to pass muster than others. The examination of the 'character of each immigrant' was far from benign. This 'character' would have to be scrutinized *in addition* to that conferred by membership of a particular ethnic or national grouping, making entry conditions for members of 'undesirable' categories even harder. Debré and Sauvy considered Germans, though, to be capable of making an important contribution to France. While certain precautions needed to be taken to ensure their re-education and prevent clustering ('nothing is more annoying' than colonies of immigrants, they said, underlining again the assimilation of individuals),[103] 'a contribution of German blood in reasonable quantity could be particularly precious since undeniable Germanic qualities could certainly contribute to the moderation of certain imbalances and compensate for too great an influx of Latins or Slavs'.[104] Many populationists shared the belief that these 'undeniable qualities' included industry, creative and rational farming methods, reliability, order – and reproductivity.[105]

When the HCCPF came to discuss the proportions of the new immigrant influx, they decided to return to nineteenth-century immigration scales. At that point, it was claimed, 'Nordics' had made up 65 per cent, 'Mediterraneans' 32 per cent and 'Slavs' a mere 3 per cent of the immigrant population to France.[106] After the First World War, these trends had been inverted, but it was now becoming clear to the Committee that the order of preference had to return to the former hierarchy. Planning was to be total, to the extent that the HCCPF wished to fix an annual figure to the number of foreigners permitted to reside in each *département*.[107] This would be facilitated with the establishment of a register of all foreigners working in France. Immigrants should not 'risk changing the physical, spiritual and moral values which we hold dear ... for this reason these foreigners could not be any foreigners regardless'.[108] Georges Mauco's proposals to the Committee vis-à-vis immigration drew particular attention to the possibilities that new German immigration could hold in helping the French economy and weakening the German nation: 'The interest should be pointed out of tapping the German population... the only demographic source from which we could hope for a numerically significant Nordic contribution, potentially counterbalancing the surplus of Mediterraneans in France. This complement could furnish the work force immediately necessary for French reconstruction, and at the same time weaken Germany demographically.'[109] It is difficult to see a clear-cut division between what are normally analysed as 'biological' or 'cultural' aspects of a population, so intertwined have they become. When Debré and Sauvy talk about German 'blood' they slip into the language of biology, showing how unclear is the demarcation between biological and cultural ideas of race. Even if it is still possible to distinguish between them, the aversion to difference within cultural racism is no less harsh than that which pertains in its biological version. The German nation was considered dangerous, but whether the value of Germans stemmed from their presumed biological or cultural qualities is less apparent. Similar overlaps are visible in *Des Français pour la France*. Being 'too far from our civilization' is construed in cultural terms, but the strength of a foreign culture, and the weakness of French culture in the encounter between the two, are presented as though something permanent – and biological – is at work.[110] Opposition to these selection criteria was sparse. In response to an article in *Le Monde* by Jacques Fauvet, *Action* provided one of the rare counters to the idea that France was in need of 'Nordics' to maintain a balance so as not to 'risk aggravating a rupture that is already marked in the country's human structure':[111] 'One could appeal to... the least contested findings of contemporary science and respond... that [Fauvet's] peculiar anthropology harks back to the steam age. One could reply to him that the conception of Mediterranean–Nordic balance means absolutely nothing, and that nothing would permit one to confirm whether France today is a "Latin country" or a Nordic country.'[112] According to *Action*, the logical conclusion of recourse to these 'Nordics' was 'the good and brave population disciplined by Hitler'. Their irony was unwittingly close to the truth.

The German question

Enthusiasm for an increased birth-rate, *de rigueur* among demographers, was not a new phenomenon to France in 1945. Pétain famously pinned the defeat of 1940 on 'too few children, too few arms, too few allies'.[113] Earlier populationists had blamed national weakness during war on the low birth-rate, and their credo gained significant boosts in popularity after 1870 and especially after the 1914–18 war. Until the Cold War and the transformation of the Soviet Union into a new political threat, for populationists, France's main competitor by virtue of its high birth-rate was Germany. Populationist interpretation of Germany's consequent numerical advantage – witnessed in France via successive invasions of French territory – insisted on the greater quality of German offspring in comparison to the French.

Populationist fear of Germany as a bellicose neighbour, then, was tempered by admiration for its all too obvious efforts to regenerate its numbers. During the 1930s, many demographers in France took seriously Nazi presumptions about youth, and were much impressed by German rejuvenation. As France emerged from one war that had opened with its rapid defeat in 1940, only to embark on a further eighteen years of colonial war, many found attractive the potential to retrieve warrior success through the creation of a strong and virile population.[114] Before the Second World War, many French populationists aimed to emulate the Nazi programme. Republican populationism's creed of state intervention with support from Catholic doctrine that criticized the selfish egoism behind the French refusal to have babies nourished an admiration for the Nazi state which was seen to be tackling these questions head-on. This was particularly clear after the *Anschluss*, the Nazi takeover of Austria, in March 1938.

As Europe hurtled towards war, French populationists turned their admiring gaze on Nazi efforts to increase German natality. Fernand Boverat was not alone in the belief that abortion was the major reason for the low French birth-rate, and that principles of social engineering could be directly applied to minimize the deleterious effects of individual choice. He had subscribed to this view since before the First World War, and became increasingly vociferous in its defence during the 1930s.[115] Boverat was encouraged by the apparently miraculous alterations to Austrian reproduction rates since the *Anschluss*, and applauded the 'immense' results since 1933 which had been obtained in Germany from sending abortionists to concentration camps. He suggested that in Austria, a 20 per cent increase in the birth-rate a few months after March 1938 was due entirely to the suppression of abortion, rather than to other 'encouragements towards marriage and natality [which] have not yet had time to produce their effect'.[116] Lessons to be learnt in France from such efforts included identifying the unscrupulous foreign doctors behind profit-making French abortion clinics.[117] These individuals, he argued, along with 'repugnant' midwives, should face the firing squad.

Lest it be imagined that only the more extreme populationists maintained positions such as these, it should be noted that Alfred Sauvy veered towards a similarly radical stance. He too found the Austrian example compelling as it supported his conviction that improvements to the population could be scientifically planned. In late 1938, he argued that this type of planning was clear, cheap and 'certainly efficacious'. As proof, he advised sceptics to examine demographic statistics from

Germany 'since the demographic problem has been taken in hand by the authorities'. With regard to the birth-rate, he applauded the benefit that would accrue to the nation if the state applied its will, instead of leaving decisions to the vagaries of individual conscience as liberal populationists were prone to advise. As evidence, he cited 'astonishing results from Austria where, since the *Anschluss*, the number of marriages has quadrupled over the previous year. The problem of natality is merely a question of will and forward thinking.'[118] Admiration for Hitler's transformation of German social mores was not confined to the quantitative increase in the birth-rate that populationists alleged he alone produced. In contrast to complaints about the Third Republic's ageing leadership and consequently faltering abilities, commentators in France took to heart Nazi visions that German vitality and strength stemmed from the young.[119] The fact that statisticians routinely calculated annual national death rates without taking military losses into account may go some, but not all, the way to explaining their enduring captivation by Nazi youth.

Praise for the remarkable upturn in the Austrian birth-rate continued during the occupation. In late 1941, shortly before Vichy made abortion a capital offence, Adolphe Landry argued for more repressive measures. Personal antagonism to the occupation and the Vichy government did not dent his admiration for the rapid rise in the Austrian birth-rate. Anti-abortion legislation had achieved this, he explained, since too little time had passed for other populationist measures to have taken effect.[120] In similar vein, Sauvy also drew support from Germany and Austria during the occupation to suggest that repression of abortion was one of the main ways that the birth-rate could be made to rise in a short space of time. So convinced was he that improvements to population quality would result from an increase in its quantity, that he wished to take advantage not only of Vichy and Nazi attitudes to abortion and familialism but of their very form of authoritarian government that made it 'possible to plan a population policy'.[121] Sauvy hedged his bets regarding Vichy in *Richesse et population*, published in 1943. As a state functionary, he did not oppose its existence in print, but neither did he rule out a change of political scene, which allowed him to imagine that democratic elections would once again be held – at which point children as well as men should vote, in order to rejuvenate the nation's politics. While critical of the fact that what was known in France as universal suffrage only enfranchised about a third of the population, he was silent on the question of whether women should vote alongside children, and also refrained from imagining precisely how minors would exercise these new 'democratic' rights.[122]

After liberation, these commentators – all of whom held key posts within or allied to the post-war governments – maintained their approval for Nazi reproduction policies, which they sought to distinguish from the Nazi regime in general, if only by ignoring it. Eight years after the first edition of Boverat's grotesque anti-abortion pamphlet, *Le Massacre des innocents*,[123] the newly formed Union Nationale des Associations Familiales published its own arguments against abortion. This 1947 work made considerable use not only of Boverat, but of J. E. Roy's work on abortion, published in two editions during the occupation (which Simone de Beauvoir described as 'masculine sadism') as well as reiterating approbation for Nazi measures against abortionists.[124] It did so, despite the fact that the meaning of incarceration in a concentration camp was of a somewhat different order in 1947 than it had been even in 1939: 'We see how by introducing severe penalties (concentration camps, forced labour and even the death penalty) and developing controls (a 1939 law required all property-owners to denounce any abortion carried out on their premises within three days), Hitler's regime obtained an extraordinary diminution in the number of abortions.'[125] A year earlier, similar arguments had been advanced in *Population*, INED's scholarly review: 'Hitler's invasion of Austria and Czechoslovakia was translated into a considerable rise in the number of births,' it argued, as a result, predictably, of the Nazi suppression of abortion – a view shared by Landry.[126] According to Sauvy, this was the least painful method. In *Richesse et population* he insisted, 'while it cannot be employed alone, repression of abortion is, according to German and Austrian experience, the most efficient and least onerous procedure to act on the birth-rate'.[127] Immediately after liberation, he reiterated this conviction that the Third Reich had proved that repression of abortion was the least burdensome of populationist measures.[128]

One reason for Sauvy's view that repression of abortion was benign might be the fact that in France, the 1942 legislation that made abortion an offence of treason was applied anything but universally. As Miranda Pollard has argued, in the main it targeted women who had transgressed Vichyist social mores in addition to having carried out abortions.[129] Further, if we examine the Austrian birth-rate more closely, we might find reasons for its increase other than those that the populationists proposed. It is true that from 1925, the Austrian birth-rate had fallen from its peak after the First World War. This trend was reversed in 1938, and there was a considerable upturn in 1939 (before reverting to its pre-war rate immediately after the war).[130] However, the overall population fell between 1938 and 1939, and it was probably medical advances that contributed to a 33 per cent drop in infant mortality between 1925 and 1938, and over 8 per cent in the year 1938 to 1939. If some of these earlier deaths were neo-natal, it would account for a great deal of the rise in the birth-rate.[131] This longer-term view of demographic change suggests that trends were already in place before the Nazis imposed their stringent laws. In any case, while reasons for the rise are not understood, my interest is in the ways that French demographers and populationists interpreted them.

Not all French demographers were as convinced about the effects of the *Anschluss*, beneficial or otherwise. In 1939, Jacques Doublet had commented on abortion in relation to the recently formulated Code de la Famille that 'the future will teach us whether the law is sufficient guard against moral deregulation; the example of Austria is nonetheless intriguing: less than nine months after the incorporation of the Danubian State into the Third Reich, the number of births has risen by 20 per cent'.[132] After the war, he was more guarded in attributing the rising birth-rate solely to Nazi legislation and claimed that it was in the first six months after the *Anschluss* that the birth-rate began to rise in Austria. This should, he suggested, be attributed to home-grown anti-abortion legislation that the 'Austrian Republic' passed in January 1938, three months before the Nazis officially arrived.[133] Doublet regretted that, because of its association with Nazism, the continuation of such legislation was posing major problems vis-à-vis its acceptability in France:

Austria... shows how politics can penetrate all domains; it also shows how politics can, at any given moment, prevent demographically useful measures; it teaches that steps taken to help the family by one regime are easily discredited by the next, even if their utility seemed to be independent of all partisan conceptualization. Current conditions in Austria make the institution not of National Socialist ideas, but simply the protection of the family, extremely delicate. All directive measures risk reminding people, at least in part, of National Socialist ideas.[134]

There were parallels to be drawn between one discredited regime and another, but Doublet was wrong to imply that Vichy's familialist measures were so frowned upon by post-liberation governments as to ensure that all their efforts would be abandoned. The way he historicized his own interpretation is as significant as his deployment of the terms 'family' and 'republic'. Whatever its political provenance, Doublet supported the potential social benefits of populationist legislation because the family was beyond the realm of politics, being 'independent of all partisan conceptualization'. The family and familialism, though, were anything but independent of political manoeuvring, as their interest to the Vichy and post-war governments proves. Doublet's explanation rested on an invocation of the Austrian 'Republic' that ignored constitutional changes that had taken place in Austria before 1938. As such, it echoed the introduction of similar legislation in the new French republic of 1945 wishing to forget its own recent anti-republican manifestations under Vichy.[135] For it was in 1934, with the new right-wing state, and not in January 1938, that populationist legislation had been introduced in Austria. Having closed down counselling centres for pre-marital couples when it came to power, for example, these were reopened in June 1935 under new auspices.[136] In an entirely populationist move, these centres tried to 'preserve' pregnancy, paving the way for the passage of Nazi-style legislation three years later, before the *Anschluss*. In France, both the populationist right in the form of Boverat, and more liberal republicans, such as Doublet, laid claim to Austria as a potent example of the positive benefits of populationist legislation. They did so by taking a view of history that accorded with their own inclinations for either the powerful authoritarian state or the powerful republic. We will return below to this flexible view of history.

At liberation, anti-abortion legislation and practice benefited from the approval that similar measures had received before and during the occupation. While Vichy's most severe, capital, penalties for abortion were repealed, active antagonism to it did not diminish. In line with the resurgence of populationist thinking and legislation described here, prosecutions for abortion rose to such an extent that, compared to the late 1930s, gross numbers of prosecuted individuals increased ten-fold between 1937 and 1946. The great majority received custodial sentences, although it lay within judges' power to fine offenders. Not only did the figures themselves increase, but in 1946, a higher proportion of defendants was imprisoned than had been the case ten years previously, and the percentage of acquittals fell from its pre-war rate of 16 per cent to between 8 and 9 per cent in the late 1940s.[137] Those critical demographers who have argued that pro-natalism was an empty discourse not reflected in shifts to the birth-rate have failed to take into account its workings on all those involved in abortion.[138] Whatever the effect these measures may have had on the birth-rate, they had a negative effect on women.

These statistics and the ideological support given in post-war France to Nazi Austria's radical 'population management' demonstrate one aspect of the dynamic relationship between wider discourses and government measures. As populationism took the centre stage after the war, so other factors associated with a populationist regime receded into unimportance. In their post-war evaluation of Nazi populationism, 'The Biological War', for example, Alfred Sauvy and his co-author, Sully Ledermann, regarded Nazi measures as 'successful', going so far as to suggest that, considered on its own terms, Hitler's realization of his wish to rid Europe of Jews ought to be seen as 'entirely successful'. After the war, as before, Sauvy judged that Hitler's programme had made a positive impact on the birth-rate, and admired the regime for its foresight in engineering a demographic shift that would result in a higher proportion of young and fewer elderly people in Germany from the mid-1950s.[139]

Despite the title of this 1946 article, the authors made no reference to the biological racism that underlay Nazi population policy. This is hardly because the language to analyse racism in these terms did not exist. As noted above, Sauvy himself, in *Des Français pour la France*, made explicit the contention that to speak of 'pure races' was meaningless.[140] Such reticence stemmed from elsewhere. Sauvy and Ledermann omitted to mention that racial qualities were fundamental to Nazi populationism. Moreover, their citation of Friedrich Burgdörfer, a Nazi race theorist, seems to have been made within a spirit of scientistic equivalence.[141] Just as the Third Reich had demanded of scientists that they legitimate the regime, so Sauvy was keen that the new French republic provide him and other scientists with similar accreditation. Sauvy and Ledermann failed to point out that Nazi Germany achieved its ends by first, the suppression of any science that departed from the regime's principles; second, the exclusion of Jewish and dissident scientists; and third, the practice of torture under the guise of science. Throughout Sauvy's work, quantity was accorded greater significance than any other factor in the improvement of a population. It was not that quality was immaterial, but that quantity would produce quality – the greater the number of individuals, the more likely it was that geniuses would materialize across the social spectrum. As a consequence, Sauvy and Ledermann addressed only the quantifiable changes to birth- and death-rates under – and as a result of – Nazism, and ignored the quality of life, and death, that the regime produced. Sauvy, for all his econometric training, seems never to have posed the question 'at what cost?'

Although the threat from Germany was still explicit as a result of the 'benefit' it would gain from the 'Hitlerite births' from 1954 onwards,[142] Sauvy reached these conclusions less as a result of his vision of Germany as a permanent enemy[143] than from demographers' evacuation of recent history from their purview. As we noted above, when he launched the INED journal *Population* in 1946, only two dates were significant for him – July 1939, when the Code de la Famille was promulgated, and April 1945, when the Secrétariat Général à la Famille et à la Population (which he headed) was created.[144] It has been proposed that French demographers found Nazi populationism persuasive only between the Munich crisis and the start of the war, having 'inherited' the attitude that Germany was populous and reproductive from successive generations of populationists.[145] Not only were they by and large responsible for this attitude, but the 'German question' remained both pertinent and a focus for their admiration during and after the occupation, even when the full savagery of the Nazi biological war had been revealed. As Sauvy had said in 1938, for the state to take in hand and transform the 'problem' of population was only a matter of 'will'.[146] Telling only half the story about Nazi Germany and the supposed qualities inherent to the Germanic population served distinct purposes for post-war French demographers: it proved a demonstrable relationship between cause and effect (in this case, policy and social change), and it accorded the technocratic advisor an indispensable position in the state. For those advisors, the Nazi state showed that the potential to improve a population could indeed lie at the behest of politically motivated scientists who, blessed with foresight and a clear view of the desired outcome, could act on legislators and see their visions blossom. But there were other demographic concerns for population improvement planned for post-liberation and Cold-War France, whose interpretation also owed much to demographers' view of history, and it is to one of these that we now turn.

Historicizing eugenics

The challenge for legislators at liberation was the procreation of numerous, healthy children. They combined coercion with encouragement – the bans on abortion and contraception were upheld, while families were to receive a variety of financial benefits when women bore children. In contrast to Sauvy's chronology, the new 1945 law to protect mother and child was founded explicitly on both the pre-war Code de la Famille and Vichy's 1942 family legislation.[147] Among other protective measures, marriage could not proceed without a pre-marital certificate, the *certificat prénuptial*, a eugenic measure still in force today. Intending partners would receive a certificate if, in medical opinion, they were fit to marry. The law of December 1942, introduced after an inter-war campaign,[148] somewhat vaguely declared that marriage could not proceed unless each partner had been issued with a certificate to prove that they had been medically examined 'with a view to marriage'. Post-war legislators favoured more explicit instructions. Just as they spelt out which chemical and surgical abortifacients were to be banned from sale or advertising,[149] so the 1945 marriage legislation required the doctor's examination to focus especially on 'contagious or chronic afflictions, likely to have dangerous consequences for the spouse or offspring'.[150] The stipulation that the spouse be protected from infection owed its origins to moves against sexually transmitted disease that can be traced throughout the twentieth century.[151] Vichy's more radical stance on the family innovated the *certificat prénuptial*, a shift that was consolidated at liberation. There was much discussion of whether the certificate should protect partners from infection, or go still further to encourage productive unions between 'the best stock'.[152]

Supporters of eugenics argued that its adoption after the Second World War was founded on its inter-disciplinary mix[153] – positions similar to those held in favour of demographic science as a whole. Whereas neither biology nor sociology alone could provide satisfactory answers to the problem of raising the birth-rate, they suggested, enthusiasts regarded eugenics, as a discipline founded on the social as much as the physiological, as the science of the future.[154] By the late 1940s, eugenics might just as easily have been regarded as a science of the past. Yet some saw moral value in the pre-marital certificate. Unlike Alfred Sauvy, for whom quantity was all, Maxime Blocq-Mascart adduced that the poor quality of marriage was to blame for the low birth-rate. In his opinion, a simple certificate was insufficient. Instead, couples should receive training prior to marriage, and the population in general be taught its gravity, rapidly becoming lost in the assembly line processing of town hall weddings.[155] There seemed to be no satisfying populationists. As heterosexual couples rushed to marry at the end of the war, apparently in line with demographers' wishes, so such weddings gave rise to complaints that marriage was taken too lightly. Blocq-Mascart also suggested that the certificate be more prognostic than diagnostic, and stipulate the examiner's opinion on whether a union should proceed; if not, the intending couple should be forced to undertake 'additional research'.[156] It was less a concern for the individual that informed this sort of eugenic marriage in which undesirables would be isolated according to medical opinion, than the enforcement of the state's ability to control its population towards national improvement.

One of the problems with this sort of thinking was that even the experts had little idea of its outcome – as can be seen from the extended commentary by Jean Sutter, a major exponent of eugenics. From 1942, he was head of the FFEPH team for research into nutrition and made the transition to INED. He believed that France should be grateful to Vichy for translating a century-long national aspiration for the certificate into legislated reality. In his long defence of eugenics that INED published in 1950,[157] he underlined the universal approval with which he said the certificate was blessed, despite a distinct lack of clarity as to its usefulness: 'the services provided by the certificate are certainly extremely important', he noted, 'even though it is very difficult to evaluate them with any precision'.[158] Obvious though the limits may have been, they in no way deflected from their purpose those demographers who anticipated a planned future. Against all evidence, they found the scientific basis of eugenic predictions convincing – in other words, that it was possible to know which couplings would produce healthy and nationally desirable offspring. The sociological perception that 'the most talented groups' unfortunately had the smallest families only served to enhance eugenics' perceived powers of augury. Sutter considered that an interventionist government should offer material encouragement so that the 'best' types of family would bear the most children.[159] When Francis Galton had devised eugenics some eighty years earlier, he considered social class to be more or less immutable, and disregarded other factors that put the 'talented groups' into that bracket. Despite radical developments in the social sciences since then – not least, the contribution of French sociology – post-war French demographers averred that simply adding to the number of the 'talented' via reproduction would automatically improve the quality of the population. Instead of better education or reductions in poverty, for example, they contended that increasing the quantity of individuals in a nation would inevitably allow inherited talent to emerge.[160]

Demographers admitted that eugenics was not universally admired. Despite its decline into disfavour, it would, said Sauvy, 'undoubtedly give us the most vital and profound debates for tomorrow's society,' though perhaps under 'other forms' or 'other names'.[161] Renaming eugenics in pursuit of acceptability echoed Sauvy's intention to Gallicize non-French surnames to aid immigrant assimilation.[162] Under whichever name, the *certificat prénuptial* combined a modern, demographic economy with more sinister forebears. Only slightly critical of the eugenic 'excesses' practised in Nazi Germany, Sutter remained convinced that the scientific objectivity of a properly mediated eugenics would inspire politicians to act in the best interests of the population. As other commentators saw family improvement measures as beyond politics or ideology, so Sauvy and Sutter discerned similar common sense values in eugenics.[163] By the same token, their claims that the wish for eugenic legislation had historical precedence of at least a century situated such measures as native to France and disguised any explicit link to Vichy.[164]

After liberation, populationists often invoked the glories of pre- or non-republican periods. For them, the caesura of 1789 heralded the quickening of French decline. According to their account, the Revolution generated the twin factors of French demographic deterioration – a falling birth-rate and a rise in immigration. In his introduction to a 700-page critical bibliography of French works on population published prior to 1800, Sauvy applauded the abundance of literature on the subject published before the Revolution and regretted its sudden decline afterwards.[165] The Revolution, it would seem, far from ushering in reforms that transformed France into the civilized republic that remained recognizable into the twentieth century and whose values liberation restored, had inaugurated an excessive individualism that led women to choose themselves over the nation, and childlessness over childbearing. The bibliography was only one work among a number that recalled a more fecund pre-revolutionary era on which INED focused in its first decade.[166] These elaborated the *philosophes*' derision of celibacy and encouragement of prolific union – as long as free benefits to poor people were avoided. The Revolution, INED commented, abandoned these precepts when it rejected traditional *ancien régime* power bases. Instead of making children, the Revolution's advocates preferred to make money.[167] These arguments relied on a perception of the eighteenth century as a period fertile for population *and* populationist ideas, whose ideological base was entirely commensurate with that of twentieth-century demographers. The decline was perceived less as attributable to changes during the period in general than as a direct result of the Revolution. Without a republic to disrupt the belief in fertility, the nation was at liberty to pursue what demographers presented as its natural pro-natalist inclinations. Sutter's location of the earliest demands for the *certificat prénuptial* during the reign of Louis Philippe underscored once again the disregard for population improvement that the republic itself was said to foster.[168]

It was at the moment of the republic's restoration after the violence and authoritarianism of Vichy that demographers turned their gaze to the pre-republican era. That they, among others, were keen to erase the memory of the Vichy years is not in doubt; that they did so by sweeping away the republic as a whole, while participating in and profiting from its very centre, was one of the more subtle mechanisms by which their scientistic historicism might distance the nation from its recent past. It has been suggested that Catholic protection of the sanctity of life underlay a lack of interest in eugenics in France.[169] Not only were aspects of eugenics adopted, but populationists applauded some of Nazi Germany's eugenic instruments, including its concentration camps.[170] After liberation, the body remained the battleground it had become under Vichy.[171] In comparison to the 1930s, prosecutions for abortion increased sharply, and the acquittal rate halved. Against the idea that all Vichy legislation was repealed, its homophobic legislation and the *certificat prénuptial* were not only retained, but were adjusted to greater precision. Only after the occupation did the physical and mental health of an applicant for naturalization become so explicit a concern that it was codified into legislation.[172] New republican structures also benefited from the success of Vichy's familialist discourses. Central as populationism was to Vichy, state apparatuses for its development were less coherent. Now, with a new Ministry of Population, a Secrétariat Général à la Famille et à la Population, and a national institute dedicated to demographic research whose members were enjoined to train ministry *fonctionnaires*, populationism could enter the state at levels that pre-war populationists could only have dreamt.

Becoming French

When immigration resumed after the Second World War, Germans were not numerous amongst them, nor were certain efforts to integrate 'Nordics' charmed with success.[173] The new 1945 Code de la Nationalité was introduced to regulate immigration and, while it moderated some of the HCCPF proposals, it did not, contrary to Patrick Weil's assertions, reject assimilation.[174] The Code introduced various categories of foreigner – temporary, ordinary, or privileged residents, though Debré's 'wanderer' was not confirmed in law. Temporary residents were forbidden to marry in France without authorization from the ministries of Justice and the Interior. Ordinary residents' stay was limited to three years, although their papers could be renewed, while those who had entered France under the age of thirty-five could obtain privileged status after three years. For parents whose children lived in France, each child added five years to the age at which they could acquire privileged status. Women would still lose their French nationality on marriage to a non-French man, though they could retrieve it on application.[175]

The lack of specific reference to assimilation did not mean its absence. Although never defined, the Code entailed a relinquishment of particularism overall. Before permitting naturalization, authorities would note that the applicant spoke French, had received some French education, had French friends and undertook French activities, rather than being exclusively involved with immigrant-run sports or social clubs, trades unions or religious organizations – an area of particular suspicion.[176] Their children should receive French education and immigrants should have been 'emancipated' from their original national milieu. The feelings they exhibited about France, particularly during the occupation, were also taken into account.[177] Those unable to be successfully assimilated and who would be denied naturalization as a matter of course included anyone who had suffered from mental illness.[178]

By the early 1950s, at the depth of the Cold War, conditions for immigrants had deteriorated. Raymond Sarraute, who campaigned for the restoration of property and accommodation to Jews after liberation, wrote in despair of the conditions facing immigrants and against 'the cycle of persecution against immigrants which has developed in France over the last five years and which constitutes, with our colonial policies, one of the saddest aspects of post-war French politics'.[179] Despite their patriotic resistance during the occupation, Sarraute argued that these individuals' civil rights were being suppressed – 'democratic' immigrant journals and organizations were banned, while monarchist or nationalist groups, especially those expressing antipathy to the Soviet Union, were allowed to flourish.[180] Political activists were being deported, as was the case of interviewee Madame Paulette, whose husband was arrested while bill-posting communist material in Paris.[181] Refugees were being sent back to the border and surrendered to their former persecutors. 'No French government until now, even Pétain's government, has dared to violate this moral rule,' Sarraute maintained with some exaggeration.[182] After the 'period of euphoria' which for Sarraute characterized the immediate post-war period, life for immigrants had become intolerable, he said, with a particular cause for concern contained in the Code de la Nationalité itself. Article 96 stipulated that, 'the French person who behaves in fact like the national of a foreign country can, if he has the nationality of that country, be declared by decree to have lost French nationality...measures taken with regard to him can be extended to his wife and children if they themselves have foreign nationality.'[183] The code thus initiated particularism and decried its existence; it legislated to retain difference among those it insisted should assimilate. So committed to the integrity of the family was the government that female immigrants were allowed no independence of thought and could be routinely despatched with the men. 'Frenchness' had assumed such definite attributes – though they were not spelt out in legislation – that civil servants were empowered to classify individuals on the basis of generalized behaviour, rather than specific actions, behaviour that was deeply gendered. Under-attachment to France could, and did, lead to expulsion.

Any doubts that assimilation was not a gendered process can be dismissed when it becomes clear that INED's major study of assimilation among immigrants was carried out in their homes.[184] Although only heads of household were interviewed, so that of thousands of reports, the number of female respondents stayed in single figures, INED concluded that assimilation was most clearly visible in the home environment. While women were rarely questioned in person, they were addressed by the report's methodology and conclusions. The assessment of the relative Frenchness of a family was based on indicators such as what they ate, what sort of education the children received, what language was spoken at home, and how the family socialized. Given that men were often absent from home – at work during the day and frequently in male social groups in the evening – all these aspects were largely or wholly the responsibility of the mother.

Maternal responsibility for delinquency – or its apparent opposite, Frenchness – was confirmed in an important study of immigrant crime carried out by the FFEPH during the war and written up by INED in 1947. In line with the FFEPH's biological orientation, the report confined its interest to those regarded as foreign in their enduring 'biological' rather than temporary juridical sense whereby a naturalized immigrant would disappear from the category 'foreigner'.[185] That is to say, a foreigner remained categorically foreign regardless of the passport they might carry. The study focused on Russians and Armenians and was undertaken by Madeleine Doré, secretary to the FFEPH commission on immigration from 1943.[186] It corroborated the centrality of the mother for assimilation. The ability to speak French was not a good indicator of assimilation, Doré noted, since this was the ruling-class language in Tsarist Russia. More important was 'the orientation imprinted by the mother', for 'when the mother is French, the children are French, not only juridically but in their own thoughts'.[187] Doré was scrupulous in her analysis of foreigners' participation in crime. According to the police, foreigners, largely Jews, were responsible for customs fraud and currency smuggling. Her examination of serious cases, however, pointed to equal French involvement. This capacity for precision was based less on an analysis of bias that from the perspective of 1947 might have been suspected of the police in 1943, than a belief in the truth of figures. In the case of foreign involvement in collaboration during the occupation, Doré found that the non-French accounted for only 2.8 per cent of arrests for collaboration, yet they made up nearly 8 per cent of those held in prison. For her, this was proof not of any tendency among the courts to imprison the non-French, but of their guilt. Crime, formerly associated solely with foreigners, was thought to have increased among the French because the occupation had 'put the population in conditions of insecurity until now reserved for immigrants, and this provoked a collapse of morality in all sections of society'.[188] Much literature at this time echoed the inversion whereby the French were repositioned in a situation that the immigrant normally inhabited. Arguments such as these did nothing to remove the notion of a criminal tendency residing within the foreign. Instead, the suggestion that during the occupation, the French had been made to feel foreign within their own borders emphasized still further the necessary re-Gallicization of those already defined as French at liberation, while simultaneously insisting on the necessity for those yet to be thus defined to assimilate to French principles as quickly as possible, and that those incapable of so doing be barred from remaining.

The French family

The intermediary intended to supervise the correct behaviour of immigrant mothers in respect of their children was the social worker. Their activities demonstrate how the re-establishment of the French family involved the assimilation of immigrants into gender as well as national roles. As Vichy had envisaged France as a family, and a nation based on the unit of the family, so the post-war government and its demographers found in the family the root for Frenchness. Motherhood was the dual key to assimilation and to reproduction, and the role of 'the family in the nation' was felt to be an area worthy of special study.[189] For their part, Debré and Sauvy insisted that 'the child, eternally forgotten, must become public friend No. 1'.[190] Parents should receive compensation for bringing babies into the world, and all 'material and moral assistance' be provided for pregnant women and mothers at birth.[191] By the same token, Debré and Sauvy submitted that the childless or insufficiently fecund be more heavily taxed than those with children.[192] Similarities here with Italian fascist policy are noteworthy, with which the authors were familiar, the 1939 Haut Comité de la Population having sought advice from the Italian government on its populationist plans.[193] Debré and Sauvy insisted that this measure was conceived not as a penalty but as compensation for those who brought up the subsequent generation who in turn would support the childless in their old age.

The World Congress on the Family and the Population was held in Paris in June 1947 and marked the international centring of family demographics in France.[194] The HCCPF itself as well as individual members were key organizers, particularly Maurice Monsaingeon as head of the Union Nationale des Associations Familiales, which was officially represented in decision-making forums on welfare benefits. Delegates came from twenty-six countries in addition to France, including Latin America, Eastern Europe and the Soviet Union, China, North America and Europe. Scientific advances were cited in support of conservative arguments in favour of women's return to the home and it was believed that 'only the rural family continues to remain a really normal family unit' as emblem and instrument of conservatism.[195] The HCCPF motion in favour of the family vote for all elected assemblies reflected this commitment to the family.[196]

The family became a crucial organism both for France's domestic politics and as part of its international self-representation. It was also seen as the best place for immigrant stability. Research suggested that 'the family, limited to the couple and their children, offers . . . the immigrant the best external structure whose form is needed for him to reinforce his life and forge a future . . . [The family] constitutes a protected island where situations of conflict between himself and his entourage can cease'.[197] In contrast to the barracks-like *foyers* where single male immigrants were often housed, a family home was probably a great deal more comfortable, but assimilationism did not prioritize the individual immigrant's comfort, nor was it free from ideological constraints. As assimilation became a national undertaking, it was logical that organizations with direct personal contact to the immigrant should see assimilation as part of their task. It fell to the Service Social d'Aide aux Emigrants (SSAE), founded in 1924 as the French branch of the Social Service International, to perform this mission.[198]

During the occupation, many social workers drew a logical link between their pre-war profession and the need to resist the occupation, and the resister Berthy Albrecht is but the most celebrated example of the many social workers who were active in resistance. Likewise, many women who undertook resistance tasks found themselves working in areas that could broadly be encompassed under a social work brief.[199]

This does not indicate that social workers' political commitment leant automatically towards the left, and women members of extreme right organizations also forged a place for themselves in welfare work, where they were expressly forbidden to have immigrant clients.[200] The political inclinations of social workers themselves are of less interest therefore than the structures that they regarded as fundamental and which they sought to defend.

At all levels, women undertook the organization and day to day labour involved in social service, and often complained about lack of funds.[201] Organizationally, the SSAE had familial links with the HCCPF, as their vice-president, Dr Lucie Thuillier Landry, was married to Adolphe Landry, while Georges Mauco sat on their board.[202] Lucie Chevalley, president of the SSAE and of the Section des Migrations at the Conseil National des Femmes Françaises, was clear how far the remit of the dedicated social worker should extend.[203] Her private correspondence notes that social workers could not act bilaterally, both protective of their clients, and informing against them. Chevalley spelt out the duties of, and problems facing, social workers in a specialized team working for the Ministry of Justice that would carry out enquiries into families that had requested naturalization:

Neither workers responsible for a district, nor social workers in the foreign labour sector can carry out these enquiries, because these social workers have slowly gained the family's confidence and cannot then provide potentially harmful information on it. However, specialized social workers under the Ministry of Justice could, in response to a request for naturalization, find themselves in a completely different situation with respect to the family. In this case, she could fulfil her role both as investigator and, with the agreement of the Foreign Labour Social Services and the district workers, an educational role, pointing out to the family the necessary improvements to be made in order to obtain a favourable response to their request for naturalization.[204]

As a senior professional social worker, Chevalley's resolute commitment in public to the national good was unassailable. No one, she claimed, contested the essential role of social workers in modern life. Family women themselves, social workers 'understand the needs of families, help them at difficult times, are familiar with the services that one might expect from the administration and other bodies, know how to accomplish the necessary formalities, etc'.[205] For the SSAE, working within strict egalitarian principles meant aiding the assimilatory process: 'the fundamental principle for social work with foreigners is to treat foreign families exactly like French families in order to obtain integration into the French population and progressive assimilation as quickly as possible'.[206] But an underlying contradiction arose in that immigrants were *unlike* other families, because they were 'all more or less disconcerted by their deracination, their ignorance of our language, laws and institutions'. A view of the immigrant as dependent and infantile was commensurate with the unequal status assumed between social worker and client in general. Where it departed from this rule, however, was in the policing of difference. While this was expressed in terms of helping integration and not abandoning immigrants to themselves 'like a separate class', it necessitated a concomitant elevation in status for the social worker:

Social workers must be made aware of the problems of immigration in general, and given specialized sessions on foreign families, so that they can understand whether these families are really assimilable or whether it would be better to make them return to their original country or to remigrate to another country. Under normal circumstances, ordinary social services would be the best agent of assimilation.[207]

Helping people to return or re-emigrate would have economic benefits, too: compared to the cost of keeping 'inadaptable foreigners' in 'our hospitals, our prisons, or our centres', the cost of running a repatriation service would be negligible.[208] The reiterated ownership of these centres – *'our* hospitals' – reconfirms the inappropriateness of the unwelcome immigrant. The conscientious social worker was intended to comprehend her work within a national perspective, assessment of the immigrant family's appropriateness to France coming to override the more traditional social work brief that took account of the client's individual difficulties: 'Before examining any social problems, one must first know whether a foreign family is worthy of the welcome they received from us, whether it is worthwhile and useful that they settle down here even more and, after progressive assimilation that has been carefully supervised, become a new element in the French collectivity'.[209] Nor was this simply a question of proper training, either on the part of the social worker or the immigrant. 'It is absolutely useless,' intoned Mme Chevalley, 'to try and stabilize and assimilate a family in France which is inadaptable or unassimilable; this would be time lost and a waste of resources'. Just like the new Code de la Nationalité, assimilability, or its opposite, were conceived as absolutes that nothing could alter. As a consequence – and here the social worker's training did assume importance – it was vital for her to know 'in which collectivity' – i.e. country – 'this family would have some chance one day to become useful and happy'.[210] As an international organization, the SSAE itself could be the conduit by which such an unfortunate family might find happiness and utility.

The feminine connections between the social worker and the client family – the unit which formed the majority of the SSAE case load – underpinned the familial role that was necessary for immigrants to be considered 'worthy' or 'useful'.[211] In interview, Madame Rivka complained of the suspicion with which her social worker regarded her household management skills during her repeated, and repeatedly denied, attempts in the 1950s to obtain subsidized housing.[212] Although the authors of the report on assimilation of Poles and Italians referred to above realized after research had been completed that little information had been obtained on women as a result of questions having been confined to men, it is clear from the type of question posed that women were expected to play a central role in family assimilation.[213] Responses to rigorous enquiries as to the family's preferred domestic celebrations or food that was eaten on Sundays were taken as real indicators of 'emancipation' from their original national environment, and one might suppose that had the interviewees answered other than the standard *pot au feu* (stew) which seems universally to have been consumed, the interviewer's commentaries may have regarded the family's attempts to assimilate with still more suspicion. Reinstated in the family themselves after the occupation, social workers (especially those with a resistance background) remained in a split feminine world of half-public, half-private operation.

The oscillating referent of *la famille française* – at once the nuclear family in France and French society overall – clarifies the extent to which immigration became gendered at this time. This 'French family' was the organism into which the migrant – and her social worker – were supposed to fit. In creating the conditions whereby the normative heterosexual imperative became nationalized, populationist organisms within and beyond the government widened the scope of assimilationism to encompass gender roles as well as nationality and ethnicity. Already suspected as deracinated, immigrants who refused to be absorbed into a familial milieu became tarnished as free-floating and unrooted, qualities which were held to militate against their successful assimilation in France. Single men were damned either way – too young and they were thought flighty and unstable, too old and suspicions could be raised against the fact that they had not yet managed to marry.[214] Nor was a couple without children considered a family, but derided as a 'celibate pair'.[215] Because of the pro-natalist leanings of demographers, population increase via immigration was always seen through the prism of familialism. The corollary of this was that the family itself was regarded not simply as the ideal milieu for absorption into France, but as a unit in which special 'French' qualities were to be developed. These ideal qualities had deep roots in the French past, and the historicization of France at liberation that excised Vichy and the occupation from demographic consciousness assisted in the recuperation of those aspects of Vichy – and Nazi – populationism that demographers had found attractive.

The historian of immigration Gérard Noiriel offered a new view of immigration in *Le Creuset français*, deepened in *Les Origines républicaines de Vichy*.[216] The approach of the earlier work privileged the idea as well as the 'fact' of the immigrant, but was ultimately confined by its own definition of the linguistic problem of 'the immigrant' which, expressed in classic economistic terms, not only failed to take gender into account, but buried it. Quoting the theorist of immigration, Abdelmalik Sayad, Noiriel remarked that, 'in industrial societies, "labour gives 'birth' to the immigrant, gives him being; it is this too, when it ends, which 'kills' the immigrant, articulates his negation or his return to non-existence" '.[217] Economic need undoubtedly governed part of the desire for increased immigration after the war. But the immigrant 'subject', the produced idea of what an immigrant was, is not coterminous with the worker 'subject' – however much the Ministry of Labour may have wished that to be the case during negotiations on the Code de la Nationalité.[218] Populationist desires for a larger population rated immigration as less desirable than reproduction among the native French. Moreover, given immigrant mothers' responsibility for the successful acquisition of Frenchness in her children, the immigrant was always viewed through a familialist lens. However, since Frenchness was at base considered an absolute and, to a very large extent, a permanent quality, the mother–child endeavour would inevitably be an uphill struggle. The distinction between cultural and biological racism that is believed to distinguish French racism from other European versions starts to blur if one explores more carefully the sorts of roles accorded to women in the family (in effect, their only legitimated social role), and the expectation that a particular family could be recognized as assimilable or unassimilable. The insistence on assimilation as a familial process, and the allocation of strict roles to women, made assimilation a requirement to acquire 'Frenchness' at once an ethnic–cultural attribute, and a gendered one.

Chapter 5
Controlling liberation: Georges Mauco and a population fit for France

For Georges Mauco, a renaissance man during the *renaissance française*, the liberation appears at first glance to have been transformative. Until recently, Mauco was claimed as the major expert on immigration in the 1930s.[1] He combined this expertise with interests in population, education and psychoanalysis. All were situated within a belief in the necessary defence of France – as place, as civilization and as idea. We have already explored the populationist principles that informed the scientific and political terrain on which the reconstruction of France was to take place after liberation. We concluded that the formation of, and conformity to, a set of ethnicized and gendered relationships to the nation were prerequisite for an individual to be considered properly French. Here, the construction of these relationships is explored in greater depth through the institutions with which Mauco was associated, and his published and unpublished texts. Beyond his work on immigration, *Les Etrangers en France*, published in 1932, little attention was paid to Mauco before the 1990s.[2] Towards the end of the twentieth century, his expertise and role in the administration started to come under greater scrutiny.[3] These discussions reflected increased recognition of Mauco's importance as an individual, as well as of changing conceptualizations of political history that was now more inclined to address the inner structures and discourses of government and policy than was formerly the case. The years 1940 to 1944 were absent from Mauco's official curriculum vitae.[4] In re-establishing those years, the paradigmatic themes of his life and work will be reconceptualized as a wider shift to centrist political thought between the mid-1930s and the late 1940s. As a whole, these themes connect a set of powerful ideas and organisms whose interest extends beyond that of the individual to the political structure of post-war France itself.

Mauco's view of population development was informed by three fears: of the mass arrival of immigrants; of depopulation; and that the social misfit would fail in their obligatory adaptation to norms. His assimilationist model relied on a view of France as a glorified civilization into which it was only natural that outsiders, of various types, would desire to flow. To counter these desires, the assimilationist nation would be required to remould the outsiders in accordance with national needs. Mauco's concern with Jews, or more specifically, 'the Jew' – less the collectivity of diverse individuals than their imagined spectral threat – lay at the core. In Mauco's work, and in liberation France more generally, 'the Jew' was represented at once as 'French' and 'foreign', assimilated and unassimilable. Moreover, the 'immigrant' was frequently coded as Jewish. At the historical juncture of the liberation, framed by the Holocaust, the investigation of these codes will serve our understanding of the full implications of assimilationism. In so doing, we will reconstruct, and subsequently deconstruct, the gendering of immigration and assimilationist discourse which, because it is already and essentially othered, is frequently understood as ungendered.[5] This will lead me to argue that Mauco's attention to France was as much about defending a certain form of gender relations as it was about ethnicity.

Mauco was as old as the century, of the generation that came of age after the First World War. Born into a modest family in 1899, he traced his native Frenchness – and courtly status – back to the fourteenth century via a singer at the court of Louis XV. Towards the end of the nineteenth century, both sides of his family lost their wealth and he was brought up in relative poverty in central Paris on his father's income as a café waiter. Since Mauco became a psychoanalyst, he might have compared his own early twentieth-century genealogy to Sigmund Freud's discussions of the 'family romance'. Freud observed that in order to correct 'actual life', the child freed itself from 'the parents of whom he now has a low opinion and [replaces] them by others, who, as a rule, are of higher social standing' – not unlike claiming a lineage that substituted royal servants for those who served cups of coffee to harried urban workers.[6] By the time Mauco was ten, and just as Freud was publishing these remarks, Mauco's family had acquired their own café, and they moved just beyond the city's western limits. During the lean years, as was customary at the time, he and two siblings were sent to lodge in spartan conditions with a family of agricultural labourers. The First World War broke out before Mauco could complete his education and, after a brief stint as a junior clerk at the Ministry of Finance, he was called up in 1918. He left the army in 1922, after a posting to Constantinople and further studies. He then entered teaching and spent about ten years at the Ecole Normale d'Instituteurs de la Seine, a men's teaching college. In an unimaginative atmosphere that separated 'intelligence from the heart',[7] he was responsible for discipline among the residential trainees and assisted with the civic and moral aspects of teaching.[8] Students themselves subverted the rigorous discipline – actions which, it might be assumed, were to an extent tolerated, since they published accounts of the nocturnal editorial meetings in their own newspapers.[9] By 1928,

Mauco's approach to the punitive environment was influenced by reading Freud and undertaking analysis with René Laforgue, one of the twelve founders of France's first, and only pre-war, psychoanalytic organization, the Société Psychanalytique de Paris (SPP).[10] It was possibly while working at the Ecole Normale that Mauco first encountered the sex educator and racial ideologue René Martial, when he came in 1924 to speak on sexually transmitted disease as part of his mission to 'educate the educators'.[11] After leaving the Ecole Normale in 1933, Mauco taught in the wealthy districts of St-Germain-en-Laye and the sixteenth *arrondissement* of Paris, where he remained until after the war, though much of the time on secondment.

During his period at the Ecole Normale, Mauco gained a history degree before preparing his doctoral thesis on immigration while acting as assistant to the Sorbonne geographer Albert Demangeon.[12] From 1936, he worked at the foreign section at the Ministry of Labour under Alexandre Parodi.[13] The Popular Front fell while Mauco was at the ministry, and in 1938 he helped to draft the Daladier government's new legislation concerning foreigners. These laws introduced strict new rules that forbade immigrants to change their occupation, and included clauses that would enable the government to intern undesirables. At the very least, it seems likely that Mauco influenced references to the need for 'rational discrimination' between immigrants based on their 'degree of assimilation and attachment to our country'.[14] Relationships with populationists developed during the 1930s, and an association with Adolphe Landry led Mauco to become secretary of the short-lived Centre d'Etudes du Problème des Etrangers en France, established in 1935 by the diplomat and former senator Henry de Jouvenal. Here, he was joined by thirty prominent men, and one woman, concerned with demography and immigration. Of eclectic political persuasion, they ranged from the race hygienist René Martial (who chaired the sub-group concerned with ethnic selection and sanitary aspects of immigration) to the future Popular Frontist and former Dreyfusard Paul Grunebaum-Ballin.[15] Two years later, Mauco became secretary of the Union Internationale pour l'Etude Scientifique des Problèmes de la Population, of which Adolphe Landry was president. Mauco retained his position until the 1950s. Apart from a brief period of mobilization at the outbreak of the Second World War, he remained in Paris throughout the occupation. From 1945 to 1970 he was secretary of the Haut Comité Consultatif de la Population et de la Famille (HCCPF), and in 1946, founded the Centre Psycho-Pédagogique, the first psychological retraining centre in France for what at the time were called maladjusted children.[16] He continued to publish on immigration and psychology until his death in 1988, whereafter a number of his books remained in print.

Mauco published more than twenty books with reputable publishers, and dozens of articles in learned and general journals. In his autobiography, *Vécu 1899–1982*, though, we find a questionable historical record. This is only the starkest example of the author's unreliability, the ramifications of which will be taken up below. Many of his publications were essentially reconfigurations of material written earlier.[17] The fact that an audience remained available for work undertaken decades before may provide a clue to the immense durability of Mauco's version of populationism within a variety of French political systems. Sufficiently malleable to survive radicalization by Vichy, populationism remained embedded within, though not unchanged by, republican milieux. The resilience of the field was mirrored in Mauco's work, and this underlay the reasons for his incorporation into the new resister-based government at liberation, just as it had enabled his co-option by its predecessors. Out of the direct gaze of the public eye, his position as an educator, senior member of the administration and prolific author ensured that his voice echoed at numerous levels.

A protectionist perspective informs Mauco's work, protectionism that set the nation at its heart. Trained in the school of geographical studies that developed in France in the early twentieth century, chiefly under the influence of Paul Vidal de la Blache,[18] he shared with other practitioners a humanized view of geography. This geographical school formalized an enduring conception of France as essentially more beautiful than other nations as a result of its human cultivation. It contrasted this to other geographical traditions, as well as to other nations, whose emphasis lay more on the transformation of landscape by nature and time.[19] Yet, milieu was also held to influence national and regional character. In the French school were revealed tensions between what was considered permanent and natural, and the transformative power of human influence. Core aspects of these conceptions persisted for at least the first half of the twentieth century. As trainers of immigrant applicants for naturalization were instructed to teach their candidates in 1946, 'there are many beautiful countries in Europe including those from which the immigrants come. But French soil alone has the charm which results from a varied landscape uniquely combined with its humanity. French nature is, as nowhere else, completely penetrated by history, that is to say, by the labour and genius of man.'[20] French culture's potential mutability at the hands of certain immigrants, too dissimilar to the French to be easily assimilated, however, was at odds with the view of that culture as something lodged within the nation's geographical development. It was the latent *mal*formative power of this human influence that gave rise to the controlling desire at the core of Mauco's project.

The Haut Comité Consultatif de la Population et de la Famille, reconstituted anew in 1945, exemplified this expression of control. As we have seen, Mauco was instrumental in the Committee's adoption of a dual remit at its first meeting: first, to extend the Code de la Famille, restructure family benefits and attack the 'social scourges' of alcoholism, prostitution, tuberculosis and abortion. Second, it would organize immigration on the basis of priority for 'Nordic', then 'Mediterranean' and, lastly, 'Slav' candidates.[21] This selection, proposed by Mauco and agreed by de Gaulle, was to be rigorously imposed by border controls and recruitment agencies posted abroad. We have explored the extent to which belief in the importance of ethnic selection was shared by populationists; let us now trace the conceptualization of ethnic selection itself, which was informed by the notion of fixed ethnic character, or *ethnie*.

Assimilationism and its discontents

The need to assimilate the individual within society remained paramount for Mauco. His work was imbued with a clear sense of normative behaviour, language and character. Frenchness implied unproblematic superiority. All those who spoke a different language, were conditioned by different cultures or exhibited anomalous psychological tendencies were expected, if capable, to conform. The logical conclusion of their failure to do so was exclusion. This was not at odds with a vision of the authoritarian state founded on traditional principles embodied in the Vichyist National Revolution, which Mauco addressed at the beginning of the war.[22] Faced with the inadequacies of capitalist liberal democracy, his article 'Révolution 1940' outlined a four-phase consensual social revolution in economy, politics, morals and demography. The revolution would be led by an educated élite, evolved from the desiccated condition of French intellectualism. The current rulers were criticized for their over-reliance on qualification instead of the creative pursuit of knowledge. The French needed to create a world where 'individualism cedes to collectivism, the rights of the community take precedence over the rights of man', he said. Rejecting the outworn principles of 1789 as over-determined by individualism, and contemporary politics and economics as an anachronistic legacy of the nineteenth century, Mauco argued for a 'thoughtful' fascist revolution. Communism was suffused by Jewish-influenced, semi-Asiatic internationalism, ethnically inappropriate for Europe, and subject to the diminished mentality of Jews who had been persecuted for centuries: 'The Stalinist Soviet Union,' he wrote, 'evokes Jeovah [*sic*], that inhumane God, inaccessible to mercy, who weighs on Jewish mentality, even while Jews believe themselves to be free.' Fascism, in contrast, proffered a 'less brutal' revolution that would leave intact traditional, middle-class values. 'It operates more via enthusiasm than via hatred,' he mused, 'it seeks to construct more than to destroy.' In retaining valuable principles from the past, fascism 'makes for an orderly socialist revolution, while communism makes for destruction and general ruin', in support of which Goethe's maxim 'better injustice than disorder' was invoked.[23]

All this redevelopment depended on the revirilization of society, Mauco continued. Destructive expression – gloomy songs, narcissistic cinema and morbid art – would have to be banned for the public good. In common with the extreme right that had represented the Jewish left – and especially the Popular Front prime minister Léon Blum – as a decrepit and decadent Marianne, Mauco made explicit the degenerate and feminizing role of Jews in prevailing political values.[24] Likewise, the mentally sick and undesirable foreigners sapped the nation's masculinity and would have to be barred, either by eugenic sterilization or 'draconian' exclusions. The bourgeois especially were to be ostracized from a 'humane and virile' society, which would depend on productive labour – quite simply, those who didn't produce wouldn't eat. Nonetheless, only during the period of transition would strict measures be necessary; afterwards, the individual would be freer than under liberal capitalism. Decline was most visible in demographic change, where the 'peaceful invasion' of immigrants had already altered national unity.[25]

These fascist sentiments expressed on the cusp of Vichy echoed themes Mauco elaborated elsewhere. His view of immigration as 'a peaceful invasion' – a metaphor to which we will return – spanned the pre- and post-war periods. His own learning notwithstanding, he held the intellectual, as well as the Jew and the bourgeois, in contempt. More originally, he proposed that it was not biological characteristics that rendered Jews unfit, but what he termed their persecuted psychology. This idea of collective ethnic psychology underlay his vision for immigration and population policy overall. While not confined to Jews, it was that group above all which represented the worst aspects of uncontrolled immigration, and raised the disturbing question of gender confusion. The search for a proper relationship between native and incomer, between masculine and feminine was, to express it another way, the search for the correct balance between authority and subject. It was in the new science of psychoanalysis that some were seeking solutions to these problems.[26]

The comparatively late arrival of psychoanalysis in France in the mid-1920s has been attributed to anti-German sentiment that often masked antisemitism, and suspicion from within a moralistic psychiatric tradition that condemned Freudian 'pansexualism'.[27] That should not be interpreted as a lack of interest in psychology, whose scientific study had long and distinctive roots in France. Freud himself had studied in Paris in the 1880s. Ideas of collective psychology had been popularized from the 1890s onwards, especially by Gustave Le Bon. His notion that institutions had no effect on a people's psychology, or 'soul',[28] ran

counter to republican efforts to improve the French population via institutions such as the school.[29] Such ideas had obvious appeal on the
right, and Maurice Barrès was not alone in finding them attractive,[30]
but there were more subtle overlaps with the geographical understanding of the influence of land on its inhabitants, however much that
was framed within a republican model. Mauco merged many of these
ideas with newer ones from psychoanalysis. He entered analysis with
René Laforgue while writing his doctorate on foreigners in France, and
began to practise shortly after its publication. The tessellation of these
twin interests in psychoanalysis and immigration emerges most clearly
from Mauco's belief in ethnic psychological character: each ethnic
group, known as *ethnie*, could be recognized by its fixed psychological
traits. This idea was in turn indebted to reformulations of Jean-Baptiste
Lamarck's late eighteenth-century theories of the inheritance of acquired
characteristics whereby the environment's actions on an organism
would be both permanent and inherited by future generations. Collective experience among a group of people, it was held, would leave a psychological imprint for generations to come. For example, Jews' perceived
migratory tendencies were not the result of antisemitic exclusion, but
because Jews had inherited the characteristic to migrate from the time
of the exodus. Lamarck's views of evolution also depended on a balance
between active (masculine) and passive (feminine) elements, whether
sperm and ovum, change and tradition, elite and mass. Rejected by many
natural scientists, in particular those outside France after the populariza-
tion of Darwinian evolutionism, Lamarck's beliefs were readopted in the
early twentieth century by some social scientists and psychologists.[31] Indeed, Freud found here a possible solution to the problem of the infant's
rapid acquisition of what he perceived to be cultural phenomena so universal that he termed them 'laws'.[32] Towards the end of his life, in 'Moses
and Monotheism', Freud proposed possible relationships between these
laws and Jewishness.[33] These explorations of the relationship of a people
to the individual unconscious or preconscious state were highly tentative. 'Moses and Monotheism' was published in German and English
only in 1939 (the French translation appeared in 1948). Freud had, however, begun to formulate some of these connections between the environment and collective ethnic psychology earlier. In private correspondence
from 1922, he complained to Sandor Ferenczi about the vicissitudes that
he faced, noting his 'strange secret longings ... perhaps from the heritage of my ancestors from the Orient and the Mediterranean, and for a
life of quite another kind, wishes from late childhood unrealizable and
ill-adapted to reality'.[34] Ten years later he suggested to Arnold Zweig,
recently returned from Palestine, that 'we hail from there ... our ancestors have perhaps lived there through half a millennium, perhaps a
whole one (but even this only perhaps) and it is impossible to say what

we have taken along in blood and nerves (as one incorrectly puts it) as a heritage from life in that country'.[35] It has been argued that these ideas of an inherited Jewish ethno-psychology were Freud's – nothing if not cautious – responses, not to the 'ancient traditions of religious identity, but to the suppressed discourse of anti-Semitism', which, it is said, 'haunted Freud'.[36] Analysis of the effects on Freud of the antisemitic milieu within which he worked lies beyond the scope of this discussion. What is stressed here is that for Freud, the relation between individual psyche and collective memory was founded on and activated by fantasy and remained in considerable tension.

In Mauco's hands, the notion of ethno-psychology cohered with the generative kernel of all his work, the necessity for control. He admitted no inkling of the fantasy that informed Freud's hesitant formulations, translating what we might regard as his, Mauco's, own fantasmatic fears into definite reality. Ethno-psychology informed Mauco's understanding of the collective unconscious, which, like others in the French tradition, he regarded as conditioned by biology, environment and social relations. All were genetically reproduced from social and natural experience. But as an authoritarian, the individual and the small group were of less account for Mauco than the large collectivity, as he made clear in 'Révolution 1940'. This psycho-social thinking is especially evident in frequent references to the anguish and uprootedness of refugees. From his Lamarckian position – and for all Freud's tantalizingly vague appreciation of Lamarck, Mauco's search for a correct balance between authority and subject might be considered a Lamarckianization of Freud – Mauco argued not for refugees to be given special help, but for their exclusion. This was because the shared collective agony rooted in refugees' ethnic character was immutable even to civilizing French forces. Such characteristics were applied more widely to foreigners' capacities – or assimilability – for labour, politics, mental health and adherence to the law, to become grounds for their inclusion or exclusion from the nation.

A fundamental belief in the malevolent anti-assimilatory drive among immigrants informed Mauco's imaginary. In the 1930s, this became elevated to a doctrinaire refusal to allow immigrant communities to retain their own social or religious organizations.[37] These, he held, were repositories of nationalism, language and culture, all of them inherently anti-French. His antipathy rested on a binary opposition between immigrants, who, he said, remained essentially hostile to France (despite departing their original country) and the French, hierarchically placed above them by virtue of their better civilization. He regarded immigrants' wish to keep something of their national, political or cultural past as an anti-modernist clinging to backwardness. Those who had arrived in France because of persecution and might therefore be well disposed towards it, were no better off, since this very fact would form in them a collective memory of either victimization or the latent desire to conquer.[38] The dichotomy between the backward immigrants and a modern France suggests that Mauco held dear a view of France as modernizing and progressive. Yet this was far from the case.

When the League of Nations invited Mauco in 1937 to present his expert views on assimilation, even an appeal to his audience's liberal tendencies could not disguise the exclusionism of his argument.[39] His lengthy presentation contained all his hopes and fears of assimilation that had been in development since the early 1930s, and it provides a useful contrast, from a distance of only three years, to 'Révolution 1940'. Immigration would be desirable only if tightly controlled and formed of groups ethnically appropriate for France. French immigration controls, Mauco insisted, were non-existent – a point of view that would inform the stricter entry and residence requirements imposed after 1945. French civilization was undeniably superior, he argued, and its prestige made it attractive and thus easier for the immigrant to assimilate. But certain ethnic groups, or *ethnies*, were by definition unassimilable. The linguistic difficulties that Slavs, for instance, encountered when faced with the French language underlay their inability to put down roots, unlike Italians or Spaniards whose languages had much in common with local dialects in the borderland French regions that they favoured.[40] Immigrants' isolation could result in mental illness, schizophrenia, paranoia or criminality. But here we meet one of many internal contradictions: steps that immigrants took to avoid isolation, such as by moving to big cities, were feared to such an extent that measures were deemed necessary to prevent them so doing. Foreigners, argued Mauco, had an instinctive resistance to their new country, a sort of 'psychological inertia'. Immigrants could never make good republicans because they were contemptuous of the common good, taking to crime or going mad in a society reliant on individual autonomy.[41]

But it was important, Mauco noted, not to imagine immigrants as a single block, without taking account of ethnic, class and professional differences. These made Asians, Africans and Levantines impossible to assimilate, and morally and physically undesirable. Nonetheless, France itself was scarcely ethnically pure, so there could be no objection to migration on biological grounds and nothing could hurt immigrant workers more than to feel part of an inferior caste.[42] They should therefore be accorded the same housing and social rights as the French. But here he differentiated between productive manual labourers and the unproductive, trafficking immigrant, strongly coded as Jewish. Nevertheless, Jews were not absolutely incapable of productive activity, as their (ancient) history as shepherds proved; they had simply lost the aptitude from centuries of ghettoization.[43]

Mixed marriage was another area of dubiety. As a populationist, Mauco focused more on children than on their parents, and so referred to this as *métissage*, or interbreeding. The ideal means for speedy adaptation, it would result in disaster if differences were too great. 'In general,' Mauco suggested, 'the Frenchwoman has a finesse and consequently, a capacity to suffer, which renders painful these unions in which the foreigner frequently seems brutal. This is above all true when ethnic differences are accentuated.'[44] Almost daily, unfortunate marriages between French women and Arabic or Asian men showed how difficult assimilation could be. Successful marriages were often dependent on the French wife, given 'the great power of the woman to fix and Gallicize'. Assimilation among Europeans (with certain 'Levantine' exceptions) was rather more likely, given the greater ethnic homogeneity of the continent.

By mid-1937, when this paper was presented, the number of refugees in France was growing, though the difficulties they would face in finding a safe haven were to become acute from 1938. Mauco's conclusions implicitly separated refugees from other, more worthy, immigrants. Soft and hard legislative instruments were to be brought into play. Worker immigrants should be protected from the police and given proper legislative status. The rest – the 'degenerate elements' who reinforced criminality, the intellectuals and artisans who flocked to the cities and the ethnically different – should be excluded. While clusters of Jewish refugees should be avoided since they provoked hostility, repatriation should be instituted only as a last resort, a point developed in the 1938 legislation on foreigners that provided for 'places', that is to say camps, in which undesirables might be contained.[45] Adaptation should be aided by preventing the isolation of immigrants, creating institutions to protect them and reducing 'anti-assimilationist' propaganda from churches and political institutions of the countries of origin, which acted as arsenals of conservative nationalism. The formation of immigrant colonies in France should be avoided and original language schools or trades unions diminished. Manual workers were more worthy for naturalization than intellectuals, and other desirable workers should be attracted through loans so that they could establish farms.[46]

Mauco's equivocation here was dependent less on the basic liberalism of his views than on his environmentalism.[47] While the emphasis would change by the time he wrote 'Révolution 1940', all the important elements were present, including the rejection of values espoused on both the right and the left that would make fascism attractive: the belief in the assimilable and unassimilable, the necessity for markers of immigrant difference to be obliterated; and the innateness of psychological characteristics. Difference had to be ironed out, old connections replaced by new ones and an ethnic uniformity established in order to create 'generations of authentic French people'.[48] The possibility that assimilation might operate in two directions, that France and its inhabitants could alter and adapt along with the immigrants, was ever-present, but repressed. In other words, it formed an originating loathing for difference. The most that could be admitted was that foreigners 'assimilate France within themselves'.[49] This is *ethnie*'s central ambivalence: on the one hand, environmental factors were dynamic; on the other hand, ethnic psychology had become somehow fixed. Mauco was happy to explain its roots, but refused to admit the potential for revision. Psychology, the curative science of the mind, was unable to initiate its habitual processes of change when applied to the ethnic collectivity. This ethnic collectivity was thus immune to the very psychological processes that defined and in large measure created it.

Two interconnected concerns asserted themselves here: the perceived inaptitude for manual labour among Jews and refugees and the tendency for immigrants to settle in cities. Both of these beliefs coalesced in a hatred concentrated on the trafficker (more likely in practice to be a shopkeeper than a major entrepreneur): unproductive, parasitic, dependent on an urban economy, and probably Jewish or, more rarely, Armenian. Four times – for his doctoral research in the early 1930s, for a study on agricultural labour at the end of the decade, at the outbreak of war and at liberation – Mauco undertook a series of local studies in areas with high densities of immigrant population. Each time he found the propensities for city settlement and labour inaptitude – but nuanced by the context of the time. In the 1930s, the need for a rural return to the land lay uppermost, and Mauco believed that immigrants should be encouraged to take up farming instead of forming urban clusters.[50] This would provide a practical solution to overcrowding and reduce the threat that groups of immigrants were held to pose. It would further exchange the idea of rootlessness and mobility ascribed to the immigrant for that prime image of fixity and worth, that of the peasant wedded to his land. The desire to repopulate rural areas, and the investment of the countryside with an authentic Frenchness lacking in the city, were sentiments that historians have long associated with, but which were not confined to, Vichy.[51] The various, doomed, schemes to encourage immigrants to the land[52] cannot, therefore, automatically be attributed to Vichyist, or even conservative, trends, given the Popular Front's enthusiasm for rural repopulation and folklore.[53] The opportunity to develop these ideas into concrete proposals came when Mauco worked with undersecretary of state for immigration Philippe Serre in early 1938. Serre and Mauco more or less forced Jewish organizations to accept their plan to resettle thousands of Jewish refugees in agricultural collectives by the threat of expulsion for any refugee who refused. The plan only foundered when the government fell.[54] But resettlement plans were not simply based on practical considerations. More certain is that the concomitant suspicion of the city – with its mass of strange peoples perceived to be speaking incomprehensible languages and unfettered by the need to conform – was associated with anti-modernism and authoritarianism. Here, the correlation that French geography made between the people and the land attained its reactionary apotheosis.

After the war, Mauco was commissioned to investigate levels of patriotism among immigrants. The reports he furnished to the Ministry of Population were informed by a ready typologism that reduced immigrant groups to single motifs.[55] North Africans, for example, he found to be ruled by an excessive libido, and Jews by money, while northern Italians were solid and industrious, and the Flemish excellent farmers. This sort of information led the army, during discussions on the closure of brothels in 1946, to argue not only that brothels remain open in Metropolitan garrison towns, but that, given 'the morals and mentality of the North African population,' sex workers be of the same 'race' as their North African clients.[56] For Mauco, especial unease focused on what he saw as the inherently Jewish characteristics of an incapacity for manual labour, coupled with an innate mercantilism.[57] Jewish refugees were inscribed as traffickers even when they were engineers or doctors, and the fact that of 202 German and Austrian refugees in the Grenoble area, fifty-five – more than a quarter – *were* manual labourers, went unremarked.[58]

The effects of this reductive approach were stark. Called up at the outbreak of war, Mauco successfully argued for his transfer to a unit that would investigate whether foreigners could be useful for national defence.[59] At this point, about 8,000 foreigners (5,000 of them Jewish refugees) were interned in camps in southern France as a threat to national security. Many of the non-Jews were Spanish republicans. By the end of 1940, with the camps under Vichy control, the figure had risen to 40,000 (28,000 Jewish refugees), while two months later, in February 1941, there were 47,000 foreigners, 40,000 of whom were Jewish.[60] The period between the outbreak of war and the invasion was one of confusion and arbitrary decision. A ministerial circular of 21 December 1939 outlined conditions under which men over the age of forty could be released if they were, for instance, ex-legionnaires, married to French women, or in the process of naturalization. These potential liberties were undermined by the fact that those regarded as communists or black marketeers were declared dangers to national defence, while pimps and vagrants were seen to threaten public safety. Refugees were by definition without a home, and often short of money and contacts. To define, and then incarcerate, them on the basis of 'vagrancy' was one of the more cynical self-fulfilling categories applied to them. Even those who might have been released were subject to the lethargy of the committees established to decide their cases.[61] The type of evidence with which the committees were provided was hardly encouraging. According to the lists he compiled, Mauco's interest in the internees' occupations was confined to the far from numerous agricultural workers, miners, butchers and bakers, and ignored the carpenters, industrial workers, shoemakers, metalworkers, engineers and financial and business workers.[62] His efforts were not the only ones being carried out in the camps. David Vogel, of Russian origin, who was interned in three camps, released, rearrested and deported, never to return, described in a manuscript found buried after the war,

Lists of Austrians, of other foreigners, lists of everybody's profession, lists of ages, of precise former addresses, of spouses of French women or fathers of French children, lists of those who possessed certificates of loyalty and of those who did not, a frenetic monstrosity of lists. What need they had for these lists, what they would do with them, we didn't know. Lists of those who possessed blankets and of those who didn't, then the number of blankets of those who possessed blankets; lists of those who needed clothes, and shoes, and underwear . . . As far as the use they would make of all this information, everybody offered their opinion with as much assurance as if they had been in the captain's confidence himself. The Austrians would definitely be liberated. The other foreigners too. And the husbands of French women. And those who possessed certificates of loyalty (some had about thirty, from their baker, grocer, butcher, concierge). Those who had an income would be liberated and so would those who were needed at work. In short, we didn't stop being liberated. As proof, the lists! If not, what function would they serve? We would receive blankets, clothes, shoes, underwear. As proof, the lists!
No one was liberated. They didn't distribute any blankets.[63]

Retraining refugees for new occupations was not seriously contemplated. In any case, under legislation of December 1938, a foreigner's profession had to be noted on their identity card, and alteration could lead to expulsion.[64] As far as engagement in armed service was concerned, the military considered most non-French people to be unfit, and that Jews were 'temperamentally' unsuited to soldiering.[65] Even legitimate cases of internees who came under the ministerial remit as suitable for release remained hidden in files, and large proportions of Jews in the camps were deported.[66] Mauco seems to have disagreed with the army on immigrants' overall unsuitability for the forces, especially where Italians were concerned.[67] This opposition did not, however, extend to the Jews, who made up the majority of those interned in the camps he visited. Liberal beliefs in the utility of an immigrant work force collided with his own restrictive analysis, and the results for the thousands interned in French camps who were later deported were catastrophic. During the Holocaust, prior skills very occasionally helped some deportees to survive. Primo Levi's training as a chemist, and Anita Lasker-Wallfisch's virtuosity on the cello, for example, coalesced with other factors such as their youth, fitness, the relatively late dates of their deportation, as well as luck, to let them see the arrival of liberation troops at Auschwitz and Bergen-Belsen respectively.[68] It must not be concluded from this that skills necessarily promised survival. On the contrary, and against any expectations of 'economic rationalism', millions of potentially useful labourers perished in the Nazi drive towards the elimination of Jews. In the early months of the occupation, the refusal of the authorities in France to consider the people held in its camps as able workers may well have helped to condemn most of them to death.

The idea of trafficking became a metaphor for Jewishness itself, though it mutated according to the period and context within which Mauco was writing. He ignored the specific historical contexts – not least, the ban on usury among Christians, and the *numerus clausus* that denied Jews education and entry to the professions in many European countries – within which trade was adopted among some parts of some European Jewish communities from the medieval period onwards.[69] Instead, he ascribed to Jews an innate tendency towards trafficking, which came to signify the totality of their economic and social behaviour – and thus the Jewish *ethnie* itself. The year after liberation, he declared that intermediaries were bleeding major cities and rural areas dry, a view shared by Jean-François Gravier, adviser to the new Ministry of Urbanism and Reconstruction, and one that the Ministry of Population used in their decisions to discourage the naturalization of shopkeepers and intermediaries.[70]

In *Les Etrangers en France*, Mauco had noted that:

Along with the mass of immigrants, there is equally the arrival of too great a number of elements unfit for manual work, and who only come to France from their innate disposition for traffic and business. This is the case of Polish, Russian or Romanian Jews, Armenians, Levantines, and in general all the Semites and certain Greeks and Arabs. Now, there are only too many parasitic intermediaries who interpose themselves between the producer and the consumer . . . The too frequently artificial stimulus they can give certain businesses is not that which should be sought in a healthy economy.[71]

A footnote followed this remark: 'These wogs [métèques], often recently naturalized, are frequently found in shady businesses, fraudulent bankruptcies and swindles.' Just in case readers failed to notice the Jewishness of these intermediaries, they were cast in five varieties in a single sentence. Shortly before the outbreak of war, Mauco noted that refugees, 'psychically diminished by anguish', were now compounding the problem of unproductive immigrant labour that increased criminality by a third, demoralized commerce and depressed the 'French collectivity' which had reached 'saturation limits that put at risk the very spirit of the nation'.[72] The very process of becoming a refugee caused such mental affliction as to disable their capacity to become fully formed French inhabitants. Examination of individual cases, it is implied, was unnecessary, since membership of the group took its inevitable toll. Mauco's association of Jewishness with parasitic speculation was constant, yet revealed that the time necessary for ethnic psychology to become permanent was somewhat elastic. Sometimes only a few years appeared necessary, as in the case of refugees, while at other times, centuries of one aspect of life, such as ghettoization, had imprinted stains so indelible that subsequent decades outside the ghetto failed to remove them. Dismissive of biological explanations of race – and often of the concept 'race' itself – recourse to an idea of *ethnie* presupposed not only permanent characteristics but the rapid acquisition of new, generally detrimental ones.

Evaluating nationality

Mauco approved of immigration; he just didn't like immigrants very much. If the disquieting uncertainty that the immigrant held in the conservative French imaginary was to be solved in part by defining their *ethnie*, then it was a short step to imagine that one *ethnie* might be more valuable than the next. As the HCCPF was considering immigration controls in April 1945, ready for presentation to the Provisional Consultative Assembly, Mauco furnished the Committee with data on the value of different nationalities, in the form of an assessment of immigrant labour (Table 3). Research for the table had evidently been carried out before the war. Indeed, Mauco had used it in *Les Etrangers en France* and as supporting evidence to his presentation in 1937 to the League of Nations, and would continue to cite it until the 1950s.[73] Yet the origins of these evaluations lay further back still, and it first appeared in 1926, in a work by André Pairault on immigrant industrial labour.[74] Pairault had begun his investigation of 258 factories in 1924, as a new wave of migrant labour arrived in France, and as US quotas closed the doors on mass migration from Europe. Of particular importance were data collected from eight heads of department on a single day in February 1926 in an anonymous Paris-based motor manufacturer that employed more than 17,000 workers, nearly 30 per cent of whom were not French, though the largest single group came from French colonies in North Africa (the vast majority of whom, being neither French settlers nor Jewish, were never granted citizenship). The heads of department had been asked to judge the quality of their work force. Easily quantifiable data such as output per individual or number of days sick leave taken might have been reliable as long as proper statistics had been kept. More

Table 3 *Value of foreign workers according to nationality*

Nationality in order of value	Number of foreigners	Percentage of work force*	Physical appearance	Regularity at work	Daily production	Piece rate	Mentality/ Discipline	Work force (a)	Language (b)	Total	Overall mark
Belgian/ Luxemburg	297	1.72	10.0	8.1	8.1	10.0	6.8	10.0	10.0	63.0	9.0
Swiss	109	0.63	10.0	7.5	8.1	9.2	8.1	8.5	8.1	59.5	8.5
Italian	427	2.48	7.5	7.5	6.2	7.8	5.3	8.5	8.7	51.5	7.3
Czech/ Yugoslav	162	0.94	8.1	6.2	6.8	7.1	6.2	8.5	4.3	47.2	6.7
Russian	994	5.77	8.7	7.5	4.3	7.8	6.8	8.5	3.1	46.7	6.6
Spanish/ Portuguese	296	1.72	5.1	7.5	4.2	6.6	5.7	9.1	7.1	45.9	6.5
Polish	295	1.71	8.7	6.8	6.2	8.5	6.5	5.0	3.1	44.8	6.4
Armenian	411	2.38	6.2	6.8	2.8	6.5	7.8	8.0	5.6	43.8	6.3
Chinese	212	1.23	4.3	7.1	5.0	8.0	8.0	8.0	2.1	42.5	6.1
Greek	141	0.82	5.6	5.0	3.7	5.8	6.4	5.7	4.3	36.5	5.2
Arab	1,730	10.04	1.2	4.4	1.2	3.2	2.8	4.2	3.7	20.7	2.9
Total	5,074	29.44									

*column added to original: percentage of total work force of 17,229.
(a) Is one satisfied with this work force?
(b) How well do they speak French?
Source: CAC: 860269 1.

subjective categories, such as the workers' appearance or their aptitude for the French language, were presented with equal numerical certainty, though they were largely reliant on late-nineteenth-century notions of visible deviance.

No nationality scored higher than the imaginary French worker whose worth was fixed at a notional ten points, and who formed the basis for comparison. In the 'test', Belgians scored highest and 'Arabs' lowest, by a large margin. Neither in the commentary on, nor in the use of the table, was the contradiction noted between the apparent undesirability of 'Arab' workers, and the fact that numerically they represented almost as much of the work force as all the other non-French nationalities combined. In any case, only the Russians and the Arabs constituted any statistical relevance, as can be seen from the italicized column added to the table to show how small was the proportion of the work force filled by other nationalities.[75] It has been suggested that French statistical methodology, in taking account only of nationality rather than ethnicity, has created great difficulties for the accurate charting of ethnic demography.[76] That does not mean that ethnic tropes were non-existent. In the case of North Africans, the inaccurate designation 'Arab' came to signify many of the reservations about the mutability of France, against the need that it remain unaltered. The table presents stark evidence of the racialized conditions that they faced in the 1920s.

Pairault regarded the results of his research as of sufficient significance to apply across the industry. Under Mauco's pen, their applicability stretched not just beyond motor manufacture, but across time. In 1937, he pronounced, 'naturally, we cite these appreciations because they conform for the most part to those recorded in numerous other establishments, in all regions and in all professions'.[77] More than a decade later, he contended that 'experience proves that uprooting and insufficient professional preparation makes the foreign worker inferior to the French worker, with resultant consequences for discipline, stability and productivity'.[78] Judgements formed in the social, economic and technological context of the aftermath of the First World War remained consistent for Mauco twenty years on, despite radical change in all these areas. In addition to the dislocations of the occupation, the proportion of non-French inhabitants of the Paris region dropped by 50 per cent between 1926 and 1946, and the gross numbers of non-French and naturalized fell by a quarter.[79] Change was just as significant in the industry on which the statistics had been based. Whereas the period after the First World War had inaugurated its most rapid period of growth, many workers had been sacked during the economic crisis of the early 1930s, and it was the non-French who were the hardest hit.[80] Labour and production conditions after the Second World War were incomparable to those after the First, when mass production was in its infancy, trade union membership more rare, and staff–management relations still based on deference. By the 1950s, moreover, external signs of deviance were in general no longer so readily appropriated to indicate a morally suspect character.

The implications of Mauco's plagiarism and constant use of the table were significant. Its echoes are embedded in the very substance of the 1945 Code de la Nationalité since his presentations to the Haut Comité formed the basis of that legislation. In 1950, twenty-five years after the original study, Mauco cited a slightly revised version of the table.[81] Belgians remained at the top and 'Arabs' at the bottom. Indeed, the table remained almost indistinguishable from its 1926 original. In a bid to increase its appearance of scientific enquiry, the column on whether a particular nationality was judged satisfactory was dropped and the 'physical aspect' was now determined by a doctor, though it is a matter of conjecture whether medical practitioners would have examined nearly 5,000 individuals. Mauco proposed that 'the personal attitudes of the foremen influence the marks...but even these attitudes are a factor to be borne in mind for assimilation because they contribute to the climate in which the immigrant must work.'[82] Similarly, he attributed Jewish 'faults' ('contempt, underhandedness, being too skilful [*trop grande habileté*]') to the 'inevitable consequences to which oppression automatically leads'.[83] Even prejudice could be instrumentalized, and recognizing 'oppression' was in no way connected to countering it. The assimilationist circle was complete. From a definite and calculable value of a foreigner's *ethnie*, assimilation now seemed dependent on the imaginary place that the foreigner inhabited in the eyes of the French. Mauco now admitted what had remained hidden until then: the assessment of assimilability rested on the prejudice or toleration of the beholder, and not on the innate characteristics of the incomer. For the immigrant, it would amount to the same thing. The native needed protection and it was the native's rejection or acceptance of the foreigner that determined their assimilability and, ultimately, admission to the nation.

L'Ethnie française

Admission to and exclusion from the nation became vital issues during the occupation, and the determination of *ethnie* a matter of life and death. Notorious as a scientific authority underpinning the Holocaust in France, George Montandon and other right-wing racial ideologues were far more influential on Mauco than he ever gave credit.[84] One of the chief architects of ethnic anthropology in France, by the 1930s Montandon was retreating from his earlier study of Siberia, Japan and Ethiopia in favour of areas closer to home. His book, *L'Ethnie française* (1935), attempted to pin down and categorically define the French, not in terms of biological race, but via a dynamic relationship between biology, language, place and psychology. Along the way he rejected the idea of a Jewish race, insisting instead on a Jewish 'racial type' that was descended from two races.[85] Already attracted to German nomenclature and racial explanation, *L'Ethnie française* differentiated between the 'political' idea of the nation and the 'natural' one of nationality. Linguistically, Montandon explained, the challenge to grasp these concepts was troubling for the Francophone, who could distinguish little between the sound of the words *nation* and *nationalité*, while the German speaker was unlikely to confuse *Nation* with *Volkstum*.[86] Montandon was beguiled by the installation of the Nazi regime in Germany, and was closing down the liberal potentials a more subtle analysis might have offered. For it was against the nationalist aspirations of pan-Germanism that the coherence of the French *ethnie* with the territory of France was contrasted. *Volkstum*, overladen with pan-Germanist and Nazi nuances, was by no means the only available German translation for 'nationality'. Montandon elucidated that French speakers were unaware that elsewhere, the linguistic nation did not necessarily correspond with the main bloc of nationality, as he said was the case in France. With respect to linguistic minorities in France, not only did he distinguish these from French-speakers, but the French themselves were split into seven racial categories.[87] All, however, consolidated into the French *ethnie*. Yet, while Montandon refused the idea of a pure race, he speculated that future studies may have proved the correlation between race and culture.[88] An examination of the development of the term *ethnie* shows how far from liberal its origins, and continuing usage, were.

The term 'ethnie' has its origins in *fin-de-siècle* conservative racial typologism. It seems to have entered the printed language in 1896, when the extreme right-wing Georges Vacher de Lapouge distinguished 'race', an adjunct of zoology, from 'ethnie', a descriptor of human groupings.[89] The linguist Ferdinand de Saussure, rejecting any correlation between language and physical characteristics (consanguinité) later spoke of *ethnisme*, 'a unity resting on multiple relations of religion, civilization, common defence, etc., which can even be established between peoples of different races and in the absence of any political link'.[90] Notwithstanding the attraction of Nazi analyses for many who used the term *ethnie* in the 1930s, the French context forced them to critique the notion of the Aryan super race. In a nation where the assertion of racial unity was absurd even for many of those who found its principles compelling, they had to reach a definition uniquely French. It was to this task that Montandon and René Martial both applied themselves. By the mid-1930s, when Montandon's *L'Ethnie française* joined Martial's *La Race française* (1934), the term was more widely accepted, though its application to the French case was complex and solipsistic:

An *ethnie,* a people, is thus the result of interbreeding [métissages] many races or parts of races, and a simple look at contemporary peoples is sufficient to demonstrate the profound differences which separate the *ethnies* thus formed. These differences express themselves far more by psychology than by anatomy, because in the same populace there may be greatly varied anatomies precisely because they come from the hybridization of races, but there is but one single psychology . . . From the psychological point of view – the most important – race is constituted by the hereditary moral, mental, intellectual, emotional and relational unity of any given people, whatever the amount, nature or quality of interbreeding which has concluded in forming this race, this people, at the moment that one comes to consider it. It is this psychological ensemble which constitutes the 'ethnie' . . . The good hybrid, from the point of view of race, is not so much one of fine physical stature, as he whose individual psychology synchronizes well with national psychology.[91]

Martial's explanation rested not so much on the circular interdependence of national psychology with ethnic psychology, as on a belief in the imperative of national unity. This preconditioned his view of *ethnie* and determined his opposition to admission of the outsider. Mauco's understanding of ethnic psychology integrated Montandon and Martial's explanations with his own reactionary interpretations derived from psychoanalysis. For him, the trauma necessarily undergone by the refugee and, to an even greater extent, the European Jew after generations of anti-semitism, proved so formative as to determine the innate and hereditary psychology of the collectivity.

Though his extreme and active racism only developed during the 1930s, Montandon's fascination with race had developed far earlier. During the First World War he had published an ironic commentary on Arthur Gobineau's treatise and Friedrich Nietzsche's opinions on the subject.[92] Following medical training in Zurich, he emigrated to practise medicine in France. His move into anthropology was rapid, and he carried out field work before the First World War in Ethiopia, continuing afterwards in Siberia, where he worked with the Red Cross. In 1933 he became professor of ethnology at the Paris Ecole d'Anthropologie and published *La Race. Les races.* By the time that *L'Ethnie française* appeared, his growing obsession with Jews was evident. Apart from pinning down their characteristics, his 'solution to the social problem' of Jewish cohesiveness and the residual expression of Jewish biological characteristics in spite of a variance of milieu was 'the creation of a completely independent Palestine which would have its own legations and consulates in other countries. Israelites who opted for Palestine would be furnished with Palestinian passports, and be regarded as foreigners since they would be away from home; the others would have no reason not to assimilate.'[93] Montandon was preoccupied by the maintenance of Jewishness among communities with long experience of mobility: why, when the environment was so formative, were Jews so Jewish? It would appear that Lamarckian environmentalism was not so clear cut. After the German invasion, Montandon's increasingly virulent antisemitism was nourished under the regime installed in Paris, where he became consultant to Louis Darquier de Pellepoix's reinvigorated Institut d'Etude des Questions Juives et Ethno-raciales after the departure of Xavier Vallat. This post he combined with the issue of certificates to prove whether or not the holder was of the 'Jewish race' [Certificat d'appartenance à la race juive] that sent thousands of Jews to the killing centres, and earned Montandon a good income in fees and bribes.[94] His views were exposed in *L'Ethnie française*, a journal established and edited by Gérard Mauger, a former student, which accepted only 'Aryan' advertising and pointedly refused publicity for plays or films starring Jewish actors.[95] Ten issues of this formidable example of Nazi racial science in a French context appeared between March 1941 and April 1944.[96] The print run has been estimated at 10,000.[97] The first issue established its aims for socionational renewal by means of Franco-German collaboration. As far as the editors were concerned, the French were an Aryan ethno-race, and the meaning of Aryanism and 'analogous notions' would be clearly and scientifically explored in the journal, via 'anthropo-somatics ... raciology and ethnology ... heredity and its consequences, eugenics or racial hygiene, natality and its demographic repercussions, the ethnic aspects of comparative religion, ethnography or the study of past and current civilization, sociology in its ethnic aspects and even linguistics'.[98]

As an immigration specialist, it was Mauco's scholarly and civic function to follow current intellectual trends. Despite later disavowals, it is clear from his article 'Géographie et Etnographie' [*sic*] that Montandon informed his thinking.[99] Critical of slapdash school geography manuals which ignored scientific accuracy in respect of race, this article argued that the key factor was the prevalence of a certain type, the 'ethnic germ', dominant in France since prehistoric times.[100] In observing that 'the first distinction to be made is that of race and civilization or *ethnie*', Mauco followed the anthropological theses of the 1930s explored above, and approvingly cited unspecified works by Montandon and the first four issues of *L'Ethnie française*. From this he lifted the division of the peoples of France into racial sub-groups, the Nordics, Alpines and Mediterraneans.[101] In contrast, the *ethnie*, he explained, could include those from different races but whose shared characteristics derived from similar experience. This could even cause physical change, such as that undergone by emigrant Anglo-Saxons who became Yankees under climatic influence. The French seemed to made of stronger stuff: transplanted across the Atlantic to Canada, they remained faithful to their origins even after 250 years, an example Montandon had likewise treated.[102] Mauco illustrated how *ethnie* operated in Europe with a

Figure 2: George Montandon's European *ethnies*
Source: George Montandon, *La Race. Les races.* Payot, 1933, 238

diagram (Figure 2) found on the front cover of Montandon's *La Race. Les races.*[103] He traced the prehistoric racial origins of the French, concluding that the French *ethnie* was the only appropriate term for the national commonality 'which incorporates and moulds together the diversity of the races, without removing from each its own characteristics and qualities'. Montandon had reached similar conclusions in his book *L'Ethnie française.*[104]

Mauco published two articles in issues six and seven of the journal *L'Ethnie française.*[105] These traced the unchecked flood of refugees into France and their essential unassimilability. Armenians, Russians and, notably, Jews were unassimilable because they spoke a different language and exhibited an innate incapacity to a sense of national affiliation. Somewhat paradoxically (a paradox visible in much antisemitic discourse at this time), they also managed to insert themselves almost immediately into senior professional positions to become a major influence on French leadership. Their isolation led to increased criminality and mental problems. Throughout these articles was woven a fear of outsiders who tricked and transformed themselves. Uncontrollable and unstable, Jewish immigration was to be particularly dreaded because of Jews' ability to 'mask' difference 'by completely oriental suppleness'[106] and the fact that French Jews lost their Frenchness on contact with the foreign ones. These eastern tricksters were not what they seemed,

because [the alteration of character] is the product not only of education and the action of the milieu on the individual, but in part from heredity. Modern psychology – and especially psychoanalysis – has shown that these traits, transmitted with the influence of the parents from the infants' very first years, modify the very unconscious of the subject and can only be absorbed after many generations' submission to satisfactory conditions and the complete escape from the influence of the hereditary milieu.[107]

The only hope, therefore, was to make Jews less Jewish, but this action was more or less impossible under normal conditions since it would imply their removal from the parental home and local community. Only more radical measures, it is implied, could achieve the task. Of particular alarm was Jews' 'inversion' of gender roles whereby aggressive Jewish women complemented weak men:

Criminality reveals their quite singular behaviour. Jews commit few brutal crimes against the person. In an inversion frequently noted among them, Jewish women were often more combative than the men. Male Jewish criminality is less than a third of that among the French. It is even inferior to that of non-Jewish women, which reveals a singular repression of aggression and physical combativeness.[108]

Furthermore, Mauco added, Jews occupied the country's 'nervous centres' and thereby 'devirilized' authority.[109] Disruptive Jewish sexuality was a theme that antisemites often projected on to Jewish authors as an obsession of the latter, and was one of the rhetorical devices used to justify the deportation of women, as we shall see below.[110] All 'Jewish' qualities, such as intelligence, assumed the seductive power of masking and fantasy: the brilliance of so-called intellectuals was merely a veneer of abstract theory which had 'departed from reality'.[111] The 'Jewish' professions that Mauco singled out were all connected with over-layering, dressing, decorating and masking – culminating in his deathless example of Jewish trade-union infiltrationism, their take-over among cinema make-up artists.

Mauco later defended the publication of his second *Ethnie française* article on the grounds that it had formerly appeared in the scholarly quarterly, *Annales de géographie*, though this reflects more the coincidence of interests between Montandon and the geographic establishment.[112] Indeed, Mauco owed his introduction to Montandon to Maurice Grandazzi, general secretary of the *Annales*.[113] In *L'Ethnie française*, the article was preceded by a signed note suggesting that the previous article had been overly harsh on Armenians who, as Christians, were more easily assimilable than Jews.[114] While it displayed little of the virulence of the first, its rehearsal of populationist arguments that the low birth- and high mortality rates in France put it at the bottom of European registers, included cause for especial disquiet because of the presence of large numbers of foreigners. The appearance of such classic demographics in *L'Ethnie française* is especially noteworthy in the context of its obsessive antisemitism and ultra-collaboration. Here, Mauco cited only pre-war statistics. In work written later during the occupation, he demonstrated his continued immersion in demographic studies which were based on more up-to-date material.[115] Approving the effects of Vichy pro-family propaganda and anti-divorce legislation, he was pleased that even the reduction in the sense of well-being provoked by the war had produced less egocentrism and a greater likelihood that individuals would reproduce to complete their interior, family, life.

It has been suggested that the basis for the first *Ethnie française* piece was Mauco's submission to the Riom trial.[116] The trial was a mismanaged showcase designed to pin blame for the defeat on military and political leaders of the Third Republic. Mauco's deposition aimed to clarify how the Third Republic government had failed to pay attention to warnings about the decadent effect of inappropriate immigration.[117] Whether the Riom deposition preceded the *Ethnie française* piece is unclear, but the two were almost identical. It is evident that Mauco publicly expressed the same sentiments in two different environments and with ample time to assess Montandon. The Riom text complained of the subversion of French character by uncontrolled immigration:

> A number of problems remained unsolved – ethnic choice, selection, the protection of health, the formation of clusters, assimilation, the alteration of the French spirit by the invasion of the liberal professions and urban activities. Moreover, the political principles of equality and absolute respect for the human person were contrary to measures regarding the quality of immigration. This resulted in allowing, surely but silently, the alteration of the human structure of France in permitting without choice the most diverse foreign elements to penetrate it ... Numerous individuals judged politically undesirable (communists, socialists, royalists, etc) or ethnically undesirable (Armenians, Jews) surged towards France.[118]

Immigrants, the former Popular Front civil servant told the court, carried with them the burden of their sense of failure and feverish desire for revenge, but no capacity for productive labour. Their solidarity enabled them to slide into the most influential positions, while Russians, and above all Jews, never stopped complaining of France's failure to intervene in their original countries. To gain admittance, Jews had also tricked the French authorities with regard to Germany's real power (though it is unclear why French intelligence services had been unable to provide counter-evidence). The weakness of the French in the face of the German invasion was, for Mauco, less an issue of too few tanks and soldiers, or even demography, than the responsibility of Jewish spies and liars, just as the catastrophically low birth-rate was the responsibility of foreign, Jewish abortionists.[119] The weakening of the French spirit, and specifically its demasculinization, was also laid at Jews' door.[120]

The left-wing journal *Action* issued a public complaint against Mauco's associations with *L'Ethnie française* in November 1947, followed by one in *Droit et liberté* the following year.[121] Calling into question Montandon's science, *Droit et liberté* demanded that Mauco's senior at Matignon, Louis Joxe, investigate how one of Montandon's collaborators could have acceded to an elevated government position. Noting that Mauco, as head of the Centre Psycho-Pédagogique, was lecturing on children's sensitivity, the author, a former resister who had helped rescue many Jews in the southern zone, accused him of 'enormous responsibilities' in the deportation of Jewish children and that personal experience should demonstrate how sensitive they could indeed be.

A Ministry of Education purge committee subpoenaed Mauco in June 1947 after Maurice Thorez, leader of the Communist Party and France's vice-president, had brought the *Ethnie française* articles to its attention.[122] Mauco's main defence was total ignorance of Montandon's aims and opinions. He argued that his first *Ethnie française* piece had been 'deformed' from the original, turning it from a balanced scientific study into a nasty antisemitic tract. Although he provided no evidence to this effect, Mauco claimed and the committee accepted that the article had been commissioned to explain the facts regarding the Jewish community in France against Vichy propaganda by none other than 'Israelite personalities (Ancel, Halphen, Milhaud, Seror, de [sic] Laforgue, of the Executive Committee of the Antisemitic League [sic], etc.)'.[123] In any case, Mauco claimed to have submitted the article to the *Annales de géographie* in December 1940. A month earlier, Montandon's handbook *Comment reconnaître et expliquer le Juif* had appeared.[124] Mauco failed to mention, and the committee did not notice, that the same piece had been submitted to Riom.

It is true that a manuscript of the first *Ethnie française* article was edited – 'Israélite' replaced by 'juif', 'Nordic elements' changed to 'racially Nordic elements', and an implication of the 'final solution' introduced into a section demanding help for France from other democratic countries with respect to refugees. Rarely modest, Mauco maintained to the committee that in this case he had opted for anonymity, only to be confounded when Montandon printed the author's name and his position as secretary of the Union Internationale pour l'Etude Scientifique de la Population above the article.[125] According to his presentation to the committee, Mauco's work showed 'constantly how important geographical and psychological factors work against racism' and that he had believed Montandon's review to be '*scientific*' (his emphasis). Mauco remained bitter about the post-war purge, though his acquisition of testimonials for his participation for three days on the barricades during the liberation of Paris suggests that he might have anticipated difficulties. According to *Vécu*, at this time, 'the notion of justice disappeared, dominated by the desire, notably among Jewish jurists, for overtly expressed revenge'.[126] Furthermore, his participation in Montandon's publication had 'brought me death threats from badly informed Jews who, at liberation, had killed Professor Montandon at his home, in front of his wife and children'.[127] Mauco attributed criticisms in the former Jewish and non-Jewish resistance press to the same badly informed Jews who erroneously executed Montandon. He was not the only person to report Montandon's death, and many historians have followed suit. Against these claims, it has been suggested that Montandon and his three children survived the assassination attempt, though his wife did not and, after hospital treatment, all four were evacuated to Germany in August 1944. According to this account, Montandon lived until 1961. However, the Paris court of justice abandoned his case as early as June 1945, after his lawyer provided what was probably a faked death certificate.[128]

Mauco alone appears to have been unaware of Montandon's pre-war antisemitism. On the left, Montandon was vilified, especially for an article in the Italian journal *Difesa della Razza* in 1938.[129] Harsh criticism of Montandon's pseudo-scientific antisemitism appeared in *La Lumière*, *Le Droit de vivre*, *Nouvel âge* and the right-wing anti-fascist journal, *L'Ordre*.[130] With the antisemite's absurd quest for accuracy, Montandon corresponded with the authors of these critical pieces, and succeeded in obtaining a right to reply in *La Lumière*.[131] Mauco might not have been a regular reader of the left and anti-racist press, yet Montandon's reputation was equally widespread on the right.[132] 'Our mutual friend', Céline, had recommended Montandon's services apropos 'the anti-Jewish struggle with which our organism deals' to Henry Robert Petit, director of the antisemitic newspaper *Au pilori*, who requested an article on 'the French race and the demographic principles [which] above all should discuss the Jewish *ethnie*' in September 1938. On this occasion, Montandon regretted his inability to comply with Petit's 'amiable proposition', and recommended that Petit condense another of Montandon's articles on the topic. This, for which Montandon claimed support from Mussolini, concluded with 'concrete propositions . . . to regulate the Jewish problem definitively' in a way far better than others, including Action Française, had so far imagined.[133] Montandon was likewise in regular correspondence with Darquier de Pellepoix and Robert Vallery-Radot over questions of Jewish racial typology and antisemitic action in France before the outbreak of war.[134] The senior Nazi race scientist, Hans Günther, of the Anstalt für Rassenkunde in Berlin, was delighted with Montandon's work, whose proposals for the 'solution to the Jewish question' he found remarkably similar to his own *Rassenkunde des jüdischen Volkes* (though the appreciation was not reciprocated).[135] Montandon's reply to the professor elaborated still further his plans for solving the eternal question. Apart from forcibly transferring all Jews to Palestine, he had read with approval of

branding with red-hot irons . . . and, personally, in certain cases, I would welcome the amputation of the tip of the nose as the appropriate measure for female Jewish persons, since Jewish bitches are no less dangerous than the men; in one such case, in my own practice as a young doctor in Zurich, I discovered the best effects of such an operation to be achieved by biting.[136]

This is presumably his idea of a joke (though some early psychologists had favoured rhinoplasty as a cure for hysteria). Using largely nineteenth-century German sources, Sander Gilman argued that the antisemitic trope of the distorted Jewish nose represented the equally disfigured, because circumcised, penis.[137] Jewish male sexuality was so widely regarded as having been feminized by Jews' economic position and by the perceived mutilation of their sexual organs, that Otto Weininger, in a widely distributed work, imagined a third, uniquely Jewish, sex.[138] While there were manifold representations of overbearing Jewish women, Montandon's fellated circumcision positioned female, Jewish sexuality as qualitatively parallel to, and equally noxious as, the male. Given their outrageous phallic possession, the necessity to reduce Jewish women's potency permanently then becomes obvious.

The occupation was infinitely variable in Mauco's account. As early as 1941, he said, he was distributing tracts for the resistance Les Petites Ailes de France – an unusual activity, given that between 1939 and 1942, he was a member of the fascist Parti Populaire Français.[139] He even met its leader, Jacques Doriot, who had requested an article on population from Mauco.[140] There, he recalled 'a fine and sensitive man, while I expected to find an authoritarian fanatic'.[141] When he was not writing for Montandon or meeting Doriot, his claims to active resistance are generally difficult to substantiate from the available evidence. Mauco did join the barricades for three days during the liberation of Paris, acting on one night as look-out for German positions in the Bois de Boulogne just behind his flat.[142] There is no substantive evidence for his claim to have saved any refugees and no copies of replies to the few pre-war requests for help from refugee organizations. As a civil servant and recognized consultant on immigration, Mauco was better-placed than many to assist refugees, and a number of organizations attempted to persuade him to help. Despite his later boasts, it would appear that he did little even before the outbreak of war. In the absence of evidence, his assertion to the Association Internationale d'Histoire de la Psychanalyse that he had helped the Freuds escape from Vienna[143] rests on the possibility that he could have advised Freud's former analysand and senior member of the SPP, Marie Bonaparte, of official procedures, while she used her high-society international diplomatic contacts to make the journey as safe as possible.[144] Finally, he claimed to have hidden throughout the occupation all the Union Internationale pour l'Etude Scientifique de la Population files that Adolphe Landry entrusted to him. As Landry noted at the first meeting to reconstitute the Union after the war, 'the minutes of that 1937 Assembly are missing. They disappeared, with most of the Union's documents, as a result of the occupation of our central office by the Germans.'[145]

Evidence of what Mauco did achieve during the occupation points in another direction. One of his activities was to prepare a new gloss on the 1939 Code de la Famille. After 1945, the Code was generally presented in terms that suggested its suppression by Vichy and its happy resurrection in times of retrieved liberty at liberation. Under the heading 'Race protection', Mauco explained that the intentions of those who had formulated the Code had been blocked, leaving them with what could be considered, at best, a partial achievement:

Other measures were envisaged concerning housing, protection of the race against the influx of foreign refugees, especially Jews – who, diminished by anguish and illness, infiltrated all the country's nerve centres, the educational role of the press, radio and cinema then in large part in foreign hands, etc.

In sum, for the first time in France an exceptional effort was attempted to fight the country's demographic decline. For the first time, a little justice was imposed on the distribution of family expenditure. Battle lines were drawn up which would submit egoism and excessive individualism, which were mortally bleeding France, to the general interest. An effort was also initiated to extricate the French race from the invasion and delinquent influence of wogs [métèques] which were altering it more and more. But here the deaf resistance of those concerned paralysed the rapid discharge of the necessary measures and the Foreigners' Statute could not appear.[146]

Mauco's contribution to *L'Ethnie française* had been no aberration, but coincided with the development of his thought during – and, crucially, after – the occupation.

Had Mauco's purge committee been a little more tenacious, it might have uncovered the fabrications that made up his defence. The hearing, held six days after he was called to account, was brisk and superficial.[147] The committee chair provided adequate analysis of Mauco's anti-semitism that quite accurately noted the similarity to familiar 1930s arguments against Jews. Yet Mauco's habitual hiding behind others, claiming that responsibility for the *Ethnie française* articles lay with senior Jewish academics, was sufficient to convince them that he had 'commit-ted an error of judgement to believe that it was possible to continue to publish objective articles on such a burning question during the occupa-tion. Yet he cannot be accused of antisemitism.'[148] Mauco was vindicated in February 1948 when he was informed that the committee saw no case to answer.[149]

Mauco's defence rested on science and, in certain ways, the case was represented as a struggle between science and politics. Neither element was neutral in the way that Mauco and the *épuration* committee assumed. No better illustration than Montandon is needed to show the extent to which politics inevitably imbue science. Our earlier discussions of demography in the previous chapter provided no less stark examples. It would have been impossible, asserted Mauco's supporters, to guess that a 'man of science' would so deform his knowledge in the service of racial hatred.[150] But, as far as his own work was concerned, it was not about racism, but innate psychological factors which, as a scientist, he believed himself objectively able to describe. Far from being a matter of Jewish qualities, Mauco further maintained that 'the particularism for which Israelites were reproached was a consequence not of racial factors, but of a psychology common to all refugees, Armenians and White Russians as well as Israelites'.[151] Meanwhile, in the context of the need to ease former Vichyists and their skills in government and management into the liberation administration, the acquittal placed politics above the scientific rigour demanded of a court.

'Five tonnes for the demographic struggle'[152]

Exoneration left Mauco free to pursue his interest in children, the major concern for populationists. In the previous chapter we noted how discourses of immigration and populationism reinforced each other at liberation. In Mauco's case, they joined in the form of populationist education. Pro-natalist propaganda for children, known by its supporters as 'demographic education', was introduced officially in 1939. It was planned and prepared under Vichy, but only realized after liberation.[153] In 1943, the Ministry of Information had asked experts at the Fondation Française pour l'Etude des Problèmes Humains – including the director, Alexis Carrel, Alfred Sauvy, Fernand Boverat, Paul Haury and Adolphe Landry – to take charge of all materials and methods for teaching demography in *lycées*.[154] So convinced was the ANCD that the liberation government would look favourably on Vichy policy in this respect, that it referred to Vichy decisions to strengthen its post-liberation demands, remarking that it was only 'the events of the war of liberation [which] upset and delayed the execution of the programme currently underway'.[155] As early as the end of 1944 when the *épuration* was at its most fierce, it recalled that 'Our relations with the Government itself were facilitated by the fact that the words "Family and Fatherland" figured in its slogan and that on this twin terrain our demands could not but be warmly welcomed'.[156] In the bellicose rhetoric of the new Cold War, the liberation government declared that all students from secondary school to doctoral candidates were to study the 'sanitary armament of France and, in particular, French demography'.[157] Indeed, by 1949, Mauco's lectures to military recruits had acquired official sanction so that the Ministry of Defence stipulated that all recruits were to be taught their 'responsibilities as citizens' to reproduce, especially given that 'the upturn in French natality following the end of the Second World War has been realized to have been frequently overestimated'.[158] Similar material was provided to prisoners of war still in German camps, to novice parents and their children, young professionals and military cadets.[159] At a time of severe paper shortage, Mauco helped furnish five tonnes of paper for the quarter of a million textbooks on populationist history and geography that were distributed to schools from 1946.[160] These included diagrams and explanations culled from Montandon's journal, L'Ethnie française, including the observation that Judaism could explain the 'characteristic traits of the Jewish spirit: instability and the aspiration for unity'.[161]

Mauco's contribution to this literature, La Démographie à l'école, was co-authored with his épuration defence witness and editor of the Annales de géographie, Maurice Grandazzi, and published in 1948. An interdisciplinary teachers' manual, it provided geo-historical background to diminishing population figures. Apart from rehearsing urges to increase the birth-rate, its new historicization of the French past rendered the immigrant an economic necessity, yet a demographic liability. In a period of rising birth-rate, populationists needed to retrieve a new raison d'être, which they found in racism.[162] Immigrant reproductivity, said Grandazzi and Mauco, had 'masked' the 'deficit' in French reproduction.[163] Simply being born in France was insufficient to conceal one's difference from the truly French. Despite its 'strong national unity', and calls for marriage between French and non-French partners to accelerate assimilation, France was revealed as a nation in which generations of residence could not obscure the taint of non-French national origins.[164] The incipient danger of immigration was reflected in figures that declared that as many as one in seven people in France was of 're-cent foreign origin'. 'Recent' here referred not to the refugee influx of the 1930s, nor even to the post-First World War wave of immigration, but dated from 1801. In line with populationism's veneration of the eighteenth century as a golden age, so the dawn of the nineteenth, and the telescopic intimacy with which the Napoleonic era was viewed, heralded the decline and dissolution of Frenchness. And although it was 'almost' impossible to distinguish races in France from one another, the authors reprinted the schematic grid from the front cover of Montandon's La Race. Les races (Figure 2) and explored the character and physical differences between the various types.[165] Once again, arguments that assimilation could overcome racial difference were contradicted by the certainty that even the great grandchild of the foreigner would remain forever foreign. Assimilation could only be an imitative approximation.

Populationist propaganda tended to situate what it called the foreign demographic threat – countries with higher birth-rates than France – as coeval with the military–political one. Before the war, Germany had been represented as the major competitor to France. Now, propaganda attempted to reconcile itself to the new politics of nation and gender of the liberation and Cold-War world. With the Allies victorious and Nazi Germany – in this respect at least – substantially vindicated for what were applauded as its successful pro-natalist and anti-abortion policies, the external threat shifted. In the 1930s, populationist propaganda had generally illustrated international reproduction rates with babies of pro-portionately different sizes, while nostalgia for a fecund past was shown with adults of varied size in appropriate period costume.[166] In Mauco's work, international reproduction rates were shown by differently sized workers. In order of political threat, retranslated into reproduction rates, the newcomer, the USSR, was a huge worker whose naked arms wielded an enormous mallet, Germany a farmer holding a rake, Britain a country gent in plus fours, and Italy a gondolier, while France, ever the exception, was represented by a minuscule Marianne. Germany's benign represen-tation here by a key *retour à la terre* image is significant in the transfer of political hostility to the Soviet Union.[167] Similarly, to illustrate the glo-rious past, *La Démographie à l'école* showed an eighteenth-century man standing beside someone half his height, diminished because his lower half has been severed, while the remnants of his upper body rest in a pool of blood. The modern man's gaze, enhanced by a dotted line, is directed towards eighteenth-century man's loins, these accentuated in their turn by his cane held at a saucy angle. This dramatic castration of the present internally supported the representation of Marianne as a feeble refugee, unable to work and sapped of strength and prowess. The historical revisionism at work here iconographically manifested a continued threat to French masculinity – externally from the excessively virile Russian with his mallet–phallus, and internally from the dismem-bering tendencies of the French female, encouraged by the decadent effects of immigration.

Official congratulations for the book came from the president, Vincent Auriol, the Ministries of Education, Armed Forces and Social Se-curity as well as INED. The HCCPF demanded that it receive the fullest backing.[168] Mauco's expertise was now in some demand, and his talks to naval cadets framed demographic alarmism in geopolitical terms.[169] France, he said, was at the centre of a European zone of falling birth-rate, 'mathematically' on the road to extinction.[170] What he called the 'population centre of gravity' had shifted from its pre-war location in Bavaria to somewhere near the Polish border; it was the responsibility of the French military to wrest it back again. The resolution of the Cold War seemed to lie in the reproductive capacity of French men. Only by fathering large families could international French power be rebuilt. For Mauco, as for other populationists, the parent of one or two children – the majority in France – was an evident egoist, who put their own comfort before national welfare.[171] The outcome of this self-interest was physical weakness and lassitude of the parent and, by extension, the nation. The devirilization of France that Mauco had detected before the war could now be countered by a combination of militarism and reproductivity. Setting out a position from which he never retreated, Mauco asserted that only through parenting could an adult achieve full development and that without children, death was 'more complete'. Even the baby boom was insufficient defence against depopulationist tendencies; other demographic means to improve the quality of the population would have to be sought.

At liberation, Mauco pursued his professional expertise as a psychoanalyst and educator with young people. He claimed that during the occupation he had continued working as a school teacher. But his post-war interest in 'maladjusted children' resulted not solely from his wartime teaching and psychoanalytic connections. In line with his interest in a 'strong and disciplined' France,[172] he had become active in the Association des Centres de Réadaptation Sociale des Jeunes Chômeurs (Association of Centres for Retraining the Young Unemployed). Based in a poor residential district of north-east Paris, this centre was established in 1938 to retrain young unemployed men, and Mauco's failed attempt to be elected vice-president in 1941 testifies to his activity there during the war, in contradiction to his curriculum vitae, which dated his involvement, as vice-president, between 1937 and 1939.[173] In 1941, he was compensated with a post as administrator, and he took his place on the governing body alongside the government's general secretary for youth, the prefect of the Seine, the labour secretariat's director of labour, and the director of youth labour and technical training.[174] Philippe Serre, former undersecretary of state for immigration with whom Mauco had worked on immigration plans and legislation before the war, and member of the 1939 Haut Comité de la Population, was president. Six months later, at the end of July 1942, Mauco gained his coveted vice-presidency.[175] The management committee considered the centre's associations with Vichy with a certain amount of euphemistic regret when, in October 1941, it was explained that some former colleagues, including the director, Guy de Beaumont, were no longer available owing to 'certain incompatibilities'.[176] The compatible residue soldiered on. Alongside learning a new profession, the young trainees followed a course plan imbued with Pétainist principles (the final week examined the life of Pétain himself),[177] though Mauco remained critical of the individual's total submersion into the collectivity.[178] In the centre, the ideas of worthwhile labour, as opposed to unproductive mercantilism, were realized, in a setting that would exclude Jews as a matter of principle. The association with retraining and adaptation to a set of nationally predetermined values would again figure in the Centre Psycho-Pédagogique that Mauco founded immediately after the war.

Within a classic populationist concern to increase the number and quality of the population,[179] the centre placed 'infantile mental hygiene' to the fore.[180] The conservative psychological circles in which Mauco moved after the war were fortified with the inauguration of the Societé Française de Psychanalyse.[181] More nationalist than the SPP, its espousal of Christian values bolstered the Centre Psycho-Pédagogique's conformist retraining programme. The Centre regarded parents as the root of most children's ills and they, alongside teachers, were alleged to be responsible for any failures of treatment.[182] While it was at pains to stress the affective inadequacy of French education, which, it was held, placed too little emphasis on children's emotions, and the need for children to break free of excessive parental control, it aimed less for children's free expression than their integration of traditional norms, such as success at the *baccaleuréat* for a pupil considered slow.[183] At practical and theoretical levels, Mauco's previous experience coalesced with this post-war work to produce a vision of containment and enforced belonging. Using a discourse of liberty, the Centre Psycho-Pédagogique was as informed by populationist preoccupations to increase the quantity and quality of the French populace as were Mauco's views of immigration. Quality would be maintained within a secure notion of the greater collectivity into which the 'maladjusted' child would have to fit.[184]

Populationists were concerned above all with children, and this question governed Mauco's application of psychoanalytic principles. After the First World War, it seemed to some as though traditional locations of authority were being swept away. Conservatives worried that the paternal head of the family no longer wielded as much power over his wife or children as formerly, and that young people and women had become newly arrogant and unconstrained by the pre-existent order. It was in this context that psychologists in France erected the concept of the symbolic father.[185] Here, the newly weakened normal, everyday father was replaced by a new, powerful, symbolic one. For Mauco the psychologist, symbolic paternal authority resided in the familial father; for Mauco the educator, in the teacher; and for Mauco the immigration expert in the state. The immigrant's social past contaminated their present: the more different a migrant was from the French, the less they were worth to the country, in terms of labour and sociability.[186] In an apparent projection of his own disregard for the foreigner, he ascribed them a dislike for the new milieu as a 'variable contempt according to nationality and the degree of misadaptation',[187] a resentment particularly marked among refugees. But for Mauco, the prior, regressive authority of the foreign nation or culture was waiting to be replaced by a new, desired one. His critique of authority thus implied its inherent retention. As the 'dogma of the irreproachable family must be abandoned' and parental love recognized as 'heavy, carnal power which suffocates the infant',[188] so the immigrant should be released from the stifling, pre-modern tendencies of the country of origin. As long as, it would appear, that didn't take place in France.

With respect to the family, Mauco steered a course that veered from that of Catholic populationists. Maurice Monsaingeon, for example, placed the familial trinity above the state, a view only modified when the state itself was seen to embody the family, as during Vichy.[189] In this regard, Mauco touched the core of republican anti-clericalism. His co-operation with a school for parents in 1946 (housed in the Maison de la Famille, the same building as Boverat's Alliance Nationale contre la Dépopulation), could be seen as an expression of this.[190] While the school was a private initiative, institutional intervention into what Catholics regarded as the private realm of the family was within the frame of republican demands that its citizens behave appropriately. But Mauco's psychoanalytic perspectives meant his rhetoric of the family extended beyond republican echoes.

Within the nuclear family, the child could suffer from its father's brutality and the mother's excessive maternalistic smothering of her son's virility.[191] Mauco's 'enormous contempt' for the foreigner has been recognized;[192] his contempt was equal for the woman who broke free of her preordained gendered bounds. Women inhabited a position that was nothing if not ambivalent. Female immigrants were supposedly orderly and exerted a stabilizing influence. They founded families, had babies, weakened men's ambulatory tendencies and represented conservatism. 'The woman,' Mauco wrote, 'assists greatly in stabilization and adaptation, not only because she allows a family to be founded, but also because she needs to root herself, and because life routines are stronger in her than in the man who is more enterprising and tends to flit about'.[193] Yet this had the unfortunate additional effect of preventing the child from forming a proper relationship with the symbolic father, the new nation, via language. The home was reduced to a site of atavism that repressed the child's natural assimilationist tendencies because there reigned, quite literally, the mother-tongue.[194] The remote incomprehension assumed to exist between the autochthon and the immigrant was laid at the door of immigrant women, who were held to prolong the use of non-French languages.

Women who were either not maternal at all, or were overly maternal, were equally dangerous. Like Jacques Lacan (from whose views Mauco otherwise distanced himself), Mauco believed that in conjunction with an authoritarian father, these non- or overly maternal women could produce a homosexual son.[195] This was apparently more the responsibility of the mother, since children would be damaged in general were paternal authority absent.[196] Although it might be postulated that Mauco was himself homosexual, his populationist politics insisted that parenthood was the chief fulfilment for an adult.[197] Those who were obviously homosexual either needed to be cured of their sexuality or Mauco refused to recognize it at all.[198] Nonetheless, it was in a variety of homosocial milieux that Mauco achieved his own fulfilment, and recognized that success could take place. The liberation of Paris was a week of intense celebration of male bonding and heroic discourse when men in shirt-sleeves sweated together behind piles of sandbags and cobblestones, rifles at the ready. The most absent player in this scenario of political and sexual excess was, perhaps, the stifling mother. The citation for Mauco's own three-day participation on the barricades read, 'Georges Mauco (Georges in the underground) was a particularly active element of opposition to the occupier as much by his action on his own pupils (of whom fourteen fought at his side at the liberation) as a teacher at the JB Say College, as by his active participation in the clandestine organization of the resistance' – a moment of vaunted, virile and spectacular fatherhood.[199] Thanks to him, fourteen young men were at his side. But his activity here also confirmed his own youth as the relationship became multiplied as both one of brother to brother, and father to a great many sons.

In her study of the inter-war period, Carolyn Dean described how, after the First World War, a new discourse of deviance emerged regarding the dangerous invisibility of the new criminal, particularly the criminal woman, prostitute or homosexual.[200] Lombrosan typology, whose uptake had been swift in the late nineteenth century, had relied on physical characteristics such as the squint or prominent ears of the criminal to detect alterity.[201] By the end of the First World War, the invert or the prostitute who looked like anybody else had become discursively dominant. The especial insidiousness of this invisible threat lurking within became gendered, Dean argues, not because crime was committed by women, but because of the inherent qualities of crime itself. No longer based on brute force, crime was delinquent, cowardly, cunning and manipulative, 'characterized above all by a rejection of "honest" work and by sloth; they were motivated less by greed or necessity than by pleasure'.[202] Mauco's views of immigration and assimilation dovetailed with and extended this earlier view of the deviant.

Immigrants, Mauco stressed again and again, silently crept up on France. Whether he framed immigration as a 'silent invasion', a 'peaceful invasion' or, still more frequently, that immigrants arrived 'surely but silently', beneath the representation of the immigrant lay fear for a nation under siege.[203] So devilish was the invasion, it is implied, that those invaded were oblivious to its occurrence. Earlier discourses of the deviant criminal woman were mapped on to the foreigner who had assumed her cunning attributes. Slippery, hidden away in workshops, unsupervised and uncontrolled, the supreme exemplar of this independence was the odious intermediary and artisan. Self-determining yet socio-economically connected both upwards and downwards, these intermediaries aroused Mauco's apprehension to such an extent that he even saw them when they were not there – as in the case of the Grenoble refugees cited earlier. By presenting immigrants as essentially uncontrollable, linked to their weakness and innate deviance, those tropes previously inhabited by the female acted to gender immigration itself. But the formation of what he perceived as monoglottal clusters, and the restrictions forced on children by their mother-tongue, prove this 'invasion' to have been anything but silent.

Whether he was writing on immigration, demography or childhood, the same factor remained primordial: France needed protection from 'degenerate elements'. In populationist anthropomorphization of France, portentous discourses of its ageing population were transferred on to the nation itself, in the process of losing its dynamism and adaptability.[204] Within this syndrome lay an implicit gendering of France and, by extension, its constituent populations. It would be simplistic to mark the penetrative ingress of the immigrant as masculine. Rather, the immigration process described here was smothering, atavistic and dissimulating. The way Mauco expressed the feminine, as regressive and seductive, allied forcefully with his view of immigrants. Sometimes this was explicit, as in his call for special institutions that would oversee the protection of all immigrants, 'as has been done for female Polish workers'.[205] He stressed immigrants' resistance to assimilation, their simultaneous visibility and invisibility, pre-linguistic maternal condition, and the endurance of unassimilable *ethnies*. Ultimately, the discursive fear of immigration lay in its vacillatory and feminized threat to gender fixity.

According to Patrick Weil, Mauco 'favoured a selection policy that was not only ethnic, but also professional and sanitary'.[206] To separate profession, health and class from ethnicity is to misconstrue ethnic typologization for sociology. It was the very incorporation of all these classifications under the single umbrella of *ethnie* that refused the immigrant as complex, individual and unbound by the categories into which she or he was placed. The value-laden approach to different categories of immigrant established Jews as a model liable to absorb all others. Though formulated in terms of economic protectionism, this categorization was driven by the pervasive idea of a type whose inescapable tendencies would inevitably materialize like a sort of recessive psycho-bio-cultural gene. France was forced to look beyond its own borders to recruit workers, but Mauco's warnings cohered with the extreme ambivalence regarding modernity that in France lay at the heart of anxieties over depopulation, and that were symbolized in the sacred value placed on the countryside against the dangers of the city. Keen to avoid the introduction of regressive elements that the immigrant allegedly brought, this ambivalence expressed equal fear of change from within. Only the native French, trained to reproduce and conform, would be fully capable and appropriate for this task.

For the historian of psychology Elisabeth Roudinesco Mauco was guilty of racial prejudice, a catch-all that condemns at a stroke many writers and thinkers in twentieth-century France, and whose reductiveness obscures cultural or historical specificity.[207] Seen at its most blatant in the *Ethnie française* articles, the fear of seduction by a masked and disguised figure of indeterminate gender was a core theme throughout Mauco's work. Immigration controls were, he maintained, necessary for economic reasons, and to reinforce the strict gender values that pertained at the end of the Second World War – and which would triumph in the 1950s. Mauco's interest to the historian is not to place him within one extreme camp or another, to prove him either a man driven by extreme antisemitism, or to demonstrate his effort and benevolence towards immigrants.[208] This is the central mistake: he wasn't either. He was both. This was the man excited enough to join the extreme right demonstrations in Paris on 6 February 1934 – but who, by his own account, remained an observer at the corner.[209] The foundation of Mauco's thought was a temporal taxonomy that undercut and formed a versatile but enduring structure for the political imaginary. His challenge to the historian is to escape from an over-rigid classification of individuals as *either* antisemites *or* tireless refugee workers and to resituate a subjectivity capable of incorporating a variety of simultaneous possibilities. This is not to suggest that historiography become as unscrupulous as Mauco, nor to propose a facile relativism. On the contrary, specificity remains vital. It would not be incorrect to suggest that, politically, Mauco was sycophantic, publishing ambivalent prevarications with the League of Nations, National Revolution echoes in 1940, Nazi racism during the occupation, Gaullist Cold War rhetoric in 1946 and *gauchiste*, though deeply misogynist, defences of sex education and liberation after 1968.[210] To do so would not be wrong, but it would miss the point. Liberal institutions of the 1930s, as much as arch-collaborationists and Vichy agencies during the occupation, and government institutions at liberation, all welcomed the idea that France, embattled and attacked by unsuitable outsiders trying to gain admittance, could be controlled. Mauco was accused of collaboration in 1947–48, a charge which, like so many, failed to stick. His detractors were correct, too, but limited: Mauco collaborated with any political current that admitted his perceived necessity for restriction and conformity, and he discovered it within each. Our determining focus should, therefore, be as much on the underlying structures as on traditional overarching political positions, for these remain consistent throughout and, still more, consistently plausible in liberated France.

Chapter 6
Liberation in place: Jewish women in the city

At liberation, the assimilatory project loomed large in resister and demographer discourses. But how was the project received and interpreted by those who had been its targets during the occupation? Some answers to this question will be sought from testimony from interviews with a number of immigrant Jewish women from Paris. There is no sense that the interviews together form a sociologically representative sample, though it is also unclear quite how such a sample might be constituted. Women, immigrants and Jews had faced Vichy exclusionism from a variety of standpoints. I chose to interview a number of individuals on the basis of their femininity, Jewishness and foreignness – essentialized traits, perhaps – rather than on the basis of their actions that might in some small way express their agency, such as joining resistance groups, going into hiding or having babies, for instance. It has been a central contention of this study that gender in general, and references to maternity in particular, framed the assimilatory project. Motherhood provided one of the areas of reflection in interviews, although the people concerned did not necessarily see themselves primarily as mothers. All had undertaken paid work, though many suspected that their femininity and loss of education while in hiding had hindered the type of employment available. A number had been political activists before, during and after the war. All had married and had children, and all were in Paris during the period of liberation. It is instructive, therefore, initially to explore the places of their existence, and the meanings attached to them.

The district of Belleville in north-east Paris lies at the edge of the tourist map. Its place on the city's memory map is more secure. Historically, Belleville's left-wing traditions were regarded from outside with suspicion, and from inside with pride. Today, nostalgia and exoticism percolate popular views of the area, as a result of the twin factors of immigration and post-war urban renewal.[1] Towards the end of the twentieth century, a longing for Belleville's lost urban texture, much of which had been condemned as slum, and for its former inhabitants became combined with a vision of its contemporary local culture as oriental and exotic. Willy Ronis was only the best-known of the photographers who humanized Belleville's poverty and architectural decline after the Second World War.[2] Robert Bober turned absence and loss into poetry in his film, *En remontant la rue Vilin* (the double meaning suggests as much remembering as climbing the rue Vilin).[3] A homage to his novelist friend, the late Georges Perec, the film traces the life of a steep and narrow street that no longer exists except in photographic and personal memory, where Perec and his scarcely remembered mother had lived before she was deported, along with thousands of other Belleville residents.[4]

Formerly a number of villages, the poor, hilly district of Belleville was incorporated into Paris in the 1850s – though it could be argued that it was only connected to the centre after 1935, when a new metro line, planned in 1907, finally opened. Belleville has long been perceived as an area of immigration, an assessment accentuated by the North African origins of many of its current inhabitants.[5] Yet until the end of the Second World War, the proportion of foreign population in Belleville was actually lower than in Paris overall.[6] The image of pre-war Belleville as one of the main sites of Yiddish Paris remains nonetheless intact, for immigrant Jews and their descendents, as much as for onlookers. Attracted by low rents and an anti-clerical, left-wing tradition that pre-dated the Paris Commune (the last barricade of the Commune fell here in 1871), many politically active eastern European Jews settled in Belleville between the wars.[7] It was perhaps their radicalism and their foreignness that made them especially visible in a society of increasing right-wing extremism and xenophobia. So pervasive was the sense of left activism that one interviewee attributes her father's joining the Communist Party to his quest for speedy assimilation.[8] Jewish immigrants joined resident French, Armenians and Greeks, and were followed by refugees from Spain and the Third Reich. A large proportion of the immigrant population worked in clothing and footwear manufacture, and was as a result subject to the annual impoverishment of the slack season. Their politics left them at best suspicious, if not contemptuous, of religious piety.[9] While there was a lone consistorial synagogue, the Jewish population had been sufficiently numerous to account for three branches of the childcare organization, the Œuvre de Secours aux Enfants (OSE) in a single street in the years immediately after the Second World War. Later assurances of Belleville's inter-war devotionalism were no more than vain attempts to inject religiosity where little existed.[10] It was only after the arrival of Jews from North Africa that religious observance increased, though within their Sephardi, rather than the eastern European Ashkenazi, traditions.[11]

Almost half the immigrant Jewish women interviewed had lived or worked in Belleville, and some still did.[12] Of those who had not, some drew attention to the slightly greater wealth, or dedication to religious practice, that left their families disdainful of the Belleville inhabitants.[13] In other words, Belleville figured in the imagination, even when it played little role in daily life. It was echoed by another Parisian district, the Marais, which summons up images of a different Jewishness. Known by its Yiddish-speaking inhabitants as the Pletsl (little square), Jews had inhabited this area of central Paris in the Middle Ages, but there is no reason to believe that it saw continuous Jewish settlement. Eastern European Jews, arriving from the 1880s, found affordable housing in a district that had escaped Haussmann's reconstruction in the mid-nineteenth century, and descendents of the Alsatian Jews who had moved there after the Revolution.[14] The Marais was mainly settled by eastern Europeans, both Jewish and Catholic, though Turkish Sephardim lived in the southern part of the district.

The perception of these distinct neighbourhoods is remarkably similar. Yet even before gentrification, the Marais's villas and proximity to the most ancient part of Paris made visible its antiquity and prior wealth. In contrast, for decades after the Revolution, Belleville remained largely farmland. In the 1960s, the geographer and demographer Louis Chevalier found it almost axiomatic to invoke Belleville when speaking of the Marais, whose loss of authenticity he regretted in comparison to its retention in Belleville (at least until what he termed the 'North African invasion').[15] Today, Parisians and non-Parisians alike flock to the Marais for its mix of airy elegance, chic boutiques, gay village and the falafel-and-Holocaust of the rue des Rosiers. 'For everyone,' states US-born sociologist Jeanne Brody in her essay *Rue des Rosiers: une manière d'être juif* (Rue des Rosiers: a Way of Being Jewish), 'the rue des Rosiers is not simply "a" Jewish quarter, it's "the" Jewish quarter'.[16] It is always awkward to substantiate 'everyone', but the assertion is characteristic of tendencies that need deeper exploration. For the rue des Rosiers plays a more complex role even than the very broad one that Brody attributes it as 'the' Jewish quarter not merely of Paris but, it might be suggested, of France itself.

Brody's ascription relies less on a way of Jews *being* Jewish, perhaps, than on a way of non-Jews *thinking* Jewish in an orientalizing process of imagining.[17] In another oriental context, the British colonial administrator Lord Cromer compared what he regarded as European civilization and rationality to Egyptian deficiencies. His lengthy exegesis opened with the observation that 'the mind of the Oriental . . . like his picturesque streets, is eminently wanting in symmetry. His reasoning is of the most slipshod description'.[18] That the places inhabited by 'Orientals' reflect their difference from westerners is borne out in numerous narratives of their neighbourhoods, even in so deeply 'rational' a city as Paris. In the 1990s, Brody described her discovery of 'another universe' that was the Jewish Marais. Almost invoking a ghetto, she observed that, 'surrounded by large perpendicular roads or avenues, these little hemmed in and tortuous streets haven't been broached'.[19] Twenty years earlier, David Weinberg, in his discussion of Jewish immigration in the 1930s, referred to that 'labyrinth of narrow streets around the Saint-Paul metro station', and proceeded to argue that increasing immigration, low birth-rate among native-born Jews and constant creation of new Jewish organizations meant that the Paris Jewish community (he spoke of a singular entity) was 'one of the most unstable'.[20] For his part, Georges Mauco in the 1940s noted the maze-like squalor of the district when recommending potential photographic sites to illustrate immigration in Paris.[21] The association of this urban maze with its oriental inhabitants has a long precedent. In the seventeenth century, the historian Sauval regarded the streets of the medieval Jewish settlement as 'narrow, tortuous and obscure' at a time when much of the city would have had such an aspect.[22] Nancy Green dehistoricizes Sauval's observations with the implication that the streets were little changed after six centuries.[23] Is the Marais that much more labyrinthine than other parts of pre-Haussmann Paris, such as the area around the Saint Michel metro station? Does the vision of another world made up of tortuous streets not owe more to the alterity of its inhabitants than to its architecture? In her 1962 work *Du ghetto à l'occident* Charlotte Roland echoes these narratives of the Marais when she describes tiny, winding streets teeming with people and noise, which 'make this neighbourhood like a non-stop open-air market'. Here, though, she is writing not of the Marais but of Jewish Belleville. The title of her work, From the Ghetto to the West, implies that progress inevitably accrues to east–west migration, an implication belied in the book's content. That these migrants did not leave ghettos but cities and small towns, albeit many of them with densities of Jewish population unknown in the west, is obscured, at least in the title of this otherwise fascinating work. 'Despite their dilapidation, overcrowding and the narrowness of the streets,' writes Roland,

these centres in which the population under study is concentrated don't seem at all pitiful. Like oriental or southern European cities, they share the liveliness of places where the coexistence of work and everyday life concentrates the crowds in incessant activity, a confused brouhaha that combines noise, smells and the gestures of labour with the general colour of life. Mixed with an architectural ensemble full of surprises and the absence of those large and monotonous modern industrial complexes, the whole seems picturesque in a way that easily hides the painful reality of life for the local inhabitants.[24]

This 'picturesque' Belleville is informed by Roland's enthusiasm. Robert Anchel, in contrast, scorned the Marais and the 'unpleasant habits' of its oriental Jews.[25] But almost regardless of an author's standpoint, Belleville and the Marais have been subject to similar geographic orientalism that signifies an impenetrability of their inhabitants' culture as much as their terrain, with the former encoded before the latter is observed. The equation of place with mentality, by observers often keen to stress their status as outsiders, contains repercussions in contemporary interplays of memory of these two areas.

Thanks to the census of Jews that the German military authorities ordered in September 1940, they and the French police were well informed that Belleville and the Marais housed significant numbers of non-French Jews. They deported thousands from both districts, and concentrated their efforts also on other areas in Paris with high densities of non-French Jewish population. If there was slippage in the commentaries on Belleville and the Marais, and mass round-ups in each, a relative unity of memory might be assumed. That is not the case; notable divergences persist in the experience and memorialization of the occupation. This is chiefly related to pre-war communal politics, and debates about Jewish resistance. Far from the Marais functioning as 'the' Jewish neighbourhood in the memory of occupied Paris, it is Belleville that has become predominant. It commands this position largely from the claim made on its behalf as 'the' site of Jewish resistance.[26] In lists of Jewish communist resisters responsible in 1944 for different parts of Paris, for example, only Belleville and Avron (another part of the twentieth *arrondissement*) are named, all the other areas being denoted by their *arrondissement* number.[27] Resister Marais has been sidelined, represented as concentrating on communal politicking rather than national politics.

Much of the debate turns on the role and definition of Jewish resistance.[28] In simple terms, the debate considers whether Jews in France were to resist the Nazi occupation, and so identify as French, or to resist antisemitism, and so identify as Jews. Being identified as Jews was, particularly for republican non-immigrants, associated with antisemitic persecution. For many communists, it reduced anti-fascism to unwarranted segmentation that sidelined the issue of class. Communists, among others, further emphasized that French people as a whole were subject to exterminatory measures just as much as Jews, and so not only was the distinction unnecessary, but interests other than the common anti-occupation one could not but damage unity.[29] Historiographic endeavours have highlighted Jewish activity in various resistance branches. Some historians have emphasized the vital rescue aspect of resistance whereby thousands of children and adults were hidden in France or helped over the borders to Switzerland or Spain.[30] Rescue, though, sometimes involved treading a fine line between resister instrumentalization of official bodies and a more dubious conformism, even trust in Pétain's government.[31] Others have examined the activity of clandestine Jewish communists. Often in the front line of communist resistance, they were of central importance to the resistance effort overall. On the deportation of Jews, there is little evidence that the communist national leadership paid this much attention at the time.[32] It is clear, though, that immigrant and French-born Jews were among the first resisters (for example, in London with de Gaulle; in the Musée de l'Homme and Solidarité networks; or as part of the Libération-sud and Défense de la France leadership teams), and that their proportions in all branches of resistance far outweighed their numerical representation in the population at large.

The problem with framing 'Jewish resistance' as an alternative between being French or being Jewish is that it allows little space for multiple allegiances of the sort with which Jacqueline Mesnil-Amar grappled and which were discussed in the first chapter. Given the high proportion of Jews among resisters, it is unlikely that either the various factions represented in pre-war Jewish politics, or the individual political tendencies, should suddenly be eclipsed after the invasion. While the politicizing effects on Jews of the rise and arrival of Nazism should not be minimized, the universal identification of a single enemy, or unity regarding means of combat, should no more be anticipated among Jews in France than among any other inhabitants. Points of crossover and convergence of interests abound. While the communist leadership tended to eschew the idea of Jews as a special case, the communist-affiliated Mouvement National contre le Racisme (MNCR) actively focused on the effects of antisemitism.[33] In the case of the interviewees, two pre-war residents of the Marais made vehement claims for it as a site of resistance. One operated, for pragmatic reasons, with a communist resister cell in Belleville (and attended school under her real name, wearing the yellow star, at least until she went underground in 1943), while the other joined Hashomer Hatzair, left-wing Zionists, in the south, assisting children's escape to Switzerland.[34] A parallel contest emerges for ownership of resistance origins, alongside a counter-claim from the Marais and non-communists that Jewish politics and memory be divested of the communist aura they have assumed since the upsurge of interest in Jewish memory of the occupation. Instead of dichotomy, a many-layered, sometimes ambivalent, series of belongings emerges from witness testimony, of a kind far more subtle than any imagined by the demographers whose works were explored in the previous two chapters. Primary belonging, as the demographers well knew, is rarely to a nation, but to one's home. What, then, did home mean to immigrant Jewish women before and after liberation?

Coming home

Women's place was in the home. Vichy insisted on this point and, as we saw in chapter three, so did much of the resistance that addressed women directly. That the economy of occupied France required many women to work outside the home was but one of Vichy's myriad contradictions. The pro-natalist nationalism that flourished at liberation relied on and reinforced the tenet of the woman in the home. During the occupation, though, the home and the neighbourhood became increasingly perilous places for Jews subject to round-up and deportation. From 1941, Jews in Paris were rounded up out of doors, and locations such as metro station exits became notorious. Dozens of stories of lucky escape feature the chance decision to use 'the other' exit. Yet for more than a year, the mass arrest of working-age men provoked little protest beyond the communities affected. This situation changed when Jewish women and children started to be arrested in their homes from the summer of 1942. Home then became the site not of refuge, but of terror. The differences between the first mass round-up in May 1941 and that of July 1942 were stark. In 1941, men were issued with a summons to local meeting points such as schools or garages, and thence transported to purpose-built camps in the Paris region, such as Beaune-la-Rolande. Visitors could not enter the camp, but were permitted to talk with inmates through the barbed wire. Despite the huge risk involved, one group of women even successfully protested for them to be allowed food parcels.[35] Deportations of these men started in March 1942. During the largest single mass arrest of the occupation, in contrast, French police entered the homes of non-French Jews in Paris during the night of 16–17 July 1942 and arrested 12,884 people, of whom a third (4,051) were children.[36] After the inhabitants of a flat had been arrested and the property removed, the doors were sealed and entry forbidden. Women's clandestine literature mocked Vichy's sacramentalization of the home that it was in the process of destroying. This, however, was not because doors were barred against the home's former inhabitants, but because with men sent away, the heterosexual matrix, and the economy it sustained, became unviable. What did an allegedly stable position in the home mean for women whose survival necessitated their forced departure?

Recent studies have argued that women in occupied France enjoyed a relative degree of autonomy, which some translated into feelings of emancipation. Despite shortages, and Vichy's restrictions, the absence of men forced women into positions of responsibility that few had known in peace-time.[37] Resister women often felt equal to men, even though historians have pointed out that their roles often continued to be gendered.[38] Jewish women *did* on occasion more often assume resister roles that were equal to men, such as bomb manufacture.[39] In general, though, they underwent a significant loss of freedom. When Jews as a whole, and non-French Jews in particular, experienced this loss, is there any sense in which gender played a part? Let us explore this through one aspect of resister women's work. Women in hiding, like Jacqueline Mesnil-Amar, took responsibility for their own domestic security, and often that of their families and resister comrades. Mesnil-Amar sought safe housing in the Paris area for four individuals (herself, both parents and her daughter), all lodged separately. By 1944, Mesnil-Amar alone had lived at nine addresses; the danger multiplied with each new lodging in which the family members would be safe, fed and able to trust the landlord and concierge. The working-class immigrant Madame Jeanne had to locate safe housing for the leaders of her resistance network, whose leases she signed under constantly changing false names. The experience is replicated many times over. Exposure could come in a variety of guises. In fear of imminent arrest, Madame Jeanne and her resister partner fled their apartment in April 1942, taking nothing with them. Forced to rely on others, Madame Jeanne, now pregnant, spent the next six months clothed in an unsuitable black satin dress donated by a friend's relative. The tawdriness of her outfit, and her foreign accent, would have raised suspicions against her, and those like her. It was via interviews with former resisters that H. R. Kedward developed the concept of 'the woman at the door'.[40] Forgotten even by local, resister history, this vital figure acted as buffer between hostile visitors such as the police or militia and a male resister. Her dissembling, prevarication or pretend slow-wittedness could provide him with time to escape, or send search parties in the wrong direction. In the case of immigrant Jewish women seeking safe housing, two women were at the door: one, the concierge, was inside while the other, outside, was forced into snap decisions about whether to trust the interlocutor on whom she must depend. Like Kedward's woman at the door, the concierge could activate ruses similar to those that protected resisters. In this case, though, she could denounce a tenant or refuse her entry. This is not to mark concierges as informers, but to note their power as doorkeepers and watchers. Urban resisters came to rely on them, but concierges are also known to have betrayed countless potential deportees. Immigrant women, visibly impoverished and revealed as foreign by their accents, were placed in positions of extreme risk when seeking safe housing.

The gendering of the war and occupation in France has been described as a situation in which men departed (as soldiers, resisters, forced labourers), while women stayed. This may have been the case for non-Jews, but did not apply to immigrant Jews. Not one of the interviewees remained at home during the occupation. The sole individual among the sample who stayed in the same district was forced into hiding, and the fact that this was only about a kilometre from her former home in no way decreased the danger.[41] On the contrary, familiar to locals as pre-war shopkeepers, the family could have been denounced at any moment. Not only did they leave home, but all the other interviewees were separated from those to whom they were closest. Family members who managed to survive were often far from each other (Madame Fanny's father was in the Pyrenees while she remained in Paris, for example, a predicament she greatly resented); others were deported. Memories of the liberation inevitably interweave with those of the discovery of the Holocaust a few months later. Madame Rachel was unique in remaining with her entire immediate family (both parents and a brother) throughout the occupation. Madame Magda, deported from Hungary to Auschwitz in 1944, lost all her family except her sister and a cousin. Four of Madame Jeanne's siblings were killed at Treblinka, 6 kilometres from the home she had left as a young teenager. Her Jewish resister partner was arrested and executed while she was pregnant in 1942. Madame Perla's close relatives had also remained, and perished, in Poland; she was deported with FTP–MOI comrades to Auschwitz in 1943. Madame Sara witnessed the massacre of her whole community by an Einsatzgruppe near Bialystok. Madame Rivka's parents, Polish Jews who arrived in France with the *exode* from Belgium via Berlin, were deported from a southern zone camp and her brother was killed in the resistance. Many of Madame Frida's resistance comrades were arrested and killed. Madame Hanna's father was arrested during a round-up in October 1941. Madame Paulette's parents were both taken during the Vél d'Hiv round-up and her brother was delivered to the Germans as he was crossing the Spanish border to join the Forces Françaises de l'Intérieur (FFI). The Vél d'Hiv *rafle* saw the arrest too of Madame Sarah's mother (her father had died in hospital in 1941), Madame Nechuma's mother and the best friends of Madame Fanny and Madame Hanna. Madame Esther's mother and sister survived Vél d'Hiv, only to be deported later in the year.

After the liberation of territory, young women returned home to face the consequences of this shattering of family and community. Almost all the interviewees were of Polish origin, and the end of the war brought knowledge of the terrible losses in Poland, and that Poland had been the location of all the killing centres. In addition to the direct murder of parents and siblings, many lost those close to them in the years after the war. Their partners' health broken in the camps or by war, Madame Fanny and Madame Magda were forced in the 1950s into early widowhood; Madame Denise was mourning her mother who, already weakened by cancer, succumbed to the strain of going into hiding and crossing the demarcation line on foot. Madame Rachel's father's last moment with his family was her twentieth birthday in July 1947. Madame Esther's father died in July 1945, immediately after his arduous return from Switzerland. Madame Paulette's brother was killed in a cycling accident while she was on honeymoon in 1945. Madame Hanna's mother died in 1948, the same year her fiancé was killed in the Arab–Israeli war. We know of the inmates who survived the camps only to die at liberation, but not of the number of Jewish deaths after May 1945 that could be attributable to the privations inflicted in Nazi-occupied Europe on Jews who were not deported. In the small, unrepresentative sample here, and counting only those individuals whose demise is related to the effects of the war in Europe, 30 per cent lost close family members in the seven years after 1945.

In order to understand the significance of the return home after the violence of the occupation, it will be situated in the context of renewed violence that took place not in the home but on the doorstep. If local violence was overwhelmingly at the behest of Nazi and Vichy authorities during the occupation (outlaw resister violence notwithstanding),[42] at liberation, the local community and resisters often undertook violent revenge on women accused of collaboration. In a retributive humiliation of women and remasculinization of space, about 20,000 women accused of collaboration were publicly shaved and paraded through the streets.[43] The home played a central part in the shavings, as women, whose traditional place was the 'private' home, were violently dragged from it and installed in public. The confusion of public and private that these acts entailed displaces the idea that the home was a private refuge while simultaneously insisting that it was women's rightful place. Afraid and ashamed to be seen in public, they were forced back into seclusion.[44] Numerous interviewees witnessed the shavings in the streets of Paris, and their recollections half a century after the events help us to situate their own reclamation of their city homes. By August 1944, Madame Hanna was a clandestine resister transporting explosives. She encountered the *femmes tondues*, shaven women, in Belleville. Her account of this episode is entwined with her view of liberation as 'a very deep disappointment', a moment when no action was taken against an important bureaucrat working for the Union Générale des Israélites Français (UGIF) whom she had held at gunpoint over two days in a UGIF community clinic. Rifling their files led to her discovery of UGIF's involvement in the deportations. Of the *femmes tondues*, she said:

I found it abominable. I fled. I saw two *femmes tondues* with a swastika on their heads in a street in Belleville ... It wasn't political action. OK, they'd slept with some Germans, that wasn't so bad. In the clinic that we'd occupied, they brought in a couple of concierges who had denounced a Jewish family ... we kept them two or three days until the police station opened. I was in charge of writing the

153

reports . . . there were about half a dozen collaborators and I had to take the files to the police so they could go and find them. I arrived with my files . . . and [the policeman] looked at my reports, 'Oh là là, very well written, well done,' then he noticed those concierges who had denounced the Jews. And he said to me, 'Oh, the Jews, give them an inch and they take a mile.' I didn't know what to say I was so flabbergasted. And . . . the police came to get them and, two or three days later . . . I met the man, the concierge's husband, who recognized me, and he said, 'Watch it, we'll get you.' So, when I saw people who had denounced Jews being liberated, and women who'd slept with Germans being shaved and arrested . . . it was brutal – if they had arrested the Germans and shaved them, that wouldn't have upset me, but the women – no.[45]

Madame Hanna's disapproval of the shaving rests here on a relativistic approach to justice and retribution. It is not any intrinsic unfairness of the women's treatment that provokes her comment, but the refusal of the French authorities to acknowledge their greater crime at the moment of its discovery.

Madame Rachel privileges both Jewishness and gender as factors in her understanding of the shavings, and the liberation more generally. Her account allows us to understand further the relationship of these Jewish women to their liberated environment. Madame Rachel was not a resister, and spent the last eighteen months of the occupation in hiding. Only afterwards did she discover that her father had been active in a resistance cell. Her background was atypical of immigrant Jews, her parents having worked alongside non-Jewish Poles in the coal mines of northern France before moving to Issy-les-Moulineaux, an industrial suburb south-west of Paris.[46] She was alone in offering an account of liberation in Paris which parallels, though departs from, classic, non-Jewish, versions. In recollection, her reactions reflected a mix of fear and thrill that are now set within a frame of femininity.

Her initial response to being asked about the liberation was its 'joy'. Female joy and male heroism were the chief features emphasized in public commemoration of the liberation drama, given vast media coverage during the fiftieth anniversary of liberation two years before the interview took place. The commemorative public image offered scant place to liberation as a moment of discovery of horror, or the start of mourning or, in Madame Rachel's terms, as an explosion of revenge.[47] The testimony demonstrates its development from this public image – adolescent girls flirting with American soldiers – to a story that had been concealed.[48]

Issy-les-Moulineaux was a working-class area of diverse immigrant communities, hard by a major German encampment and home to a number of strategic industries, including Renault. Liberation was preceded by Allied bombing and accompanied by a great deal of violence. With

German gunfire from the Meudon hill a few kilometres south-west, the Americans arrived:

we hugged the Americans, we climbed on their lorries, we tried to talk to them, we were madly happy, and during that time, what was most extraordinary is that . . . we behaved as though there was nothing unusual – it's incredible when I think about it. And not only that, they were shooting mortar bombs, full of shrapnel . . . and there were young people who were wounded and the Red Cross were lifting the wounded onto stretchers and we just carried on singing, being happy, while everything was mixed up – it was amazing – we saw the wounded passing in front of us and we carried on talking to the Americans and the guns went on firing, it was crazy! It was completely mad![49]

Contemporary photographs and footage of the liberation of Paris confirm this mélange.[50] It is almost as if the account needed to launch itself with familiar elements of wild happiness and the simultaneous shooting that both tempers and heightens it. If this image of liberation was itself gender- and age-specific – the image of young women aboard the liberators' vehicles is no less well known than that of crowds sheltering from sniper fire – then what followed in Madame Rachel's account is filtered by the teller through later reflections on her youth and femininity. The occupation had not only produced long-term fear, though of what, precisely, remained unknown, but necessitated protection from adolescent sexual experience that we understand would normally have accrued to a young woman growing up in an urban environment in the 1940s. The account echoes that of another witness, whose 'memory is split between traditional versions of the Holocaust and her own experience', when she spoke for the first time of having been abused by the family of those hiding her as a young adolescent in Poland.[51]

When the Germans came out of the military encampment . . . [and were] handed over to the Americans, they were in rows like soldiers, one behind the other with their hands behind their necks, and I remember that my mother, who already knew that in Poland she had already lost practically everyone in her family, one of her brothers and everyone, and she already knew all that, and she spat in the face of one of the soldiers, so much did she hold against him. She didn't know how to express herself yet at the time, and we didn't know precisely what had happened, we didn't know yet about the dramas of the concentration camps . . . and I remember seeing my mother spitting in a German's face.

A justification for her mother spitting in a German soldier's face here struggles for articulation. It is possible – but only possible – that by August 1944 Madame Rachel's mother did know of the family deaths in Poland. In her daughter's memory, the mother's unrespectable and shocking behaviour can only be tied to a wider German crime and cannot be justified solely on the grounds of her mother's recent personal torments. It is still more shameful that the mother might have mimicked – or even initiated – similar actions among non-Jewish women. The spitting seems to require a larger context than France – in stark contrast to widespread patriotic sentiments of suffering that we explored in chapter two. There is little reason to think that Madame Rachel's mother responded to the German soldier in a particularly Jewish way. As we will see, local loathing was forceful and could easily have accommodated, if not encouraged, this action. The speaker continues:

I was terribly afraid of the Germans, very, very frightened, at that moment I was *very* upset to see the Germans who had made us so frightened. I suddenly realized that my life had been in suspense – I knew at the time that it would have taken so little to have been deported – I still didn't know exactly what that would have meant, but I knew I could have been taken . . . How did I react? I was *very* disturbed because they were really upsetting days. There was the arrival of the Americans, there were the Germans who came out with their hands behind their necks, it was very upsetting to see, as there were several thousand Germans . . . inside [the encampment] with weapons [and] factories inside, it was extremely big. And we lived in the middle of it all!

It was the kind of fear that made you tremble, I remember shaking, with fear, with emotion, shaking about everything that had happened and, just to add to the picture, at the same time as the Germans came out as prisoners, they were shaving the women . . . who had been with them! . . .

It was dreadful, atrocious, and it scared me, disturbed me dreadfully. I was very shocked by it all because they took the women who were still hidden inside. They knew that they would be denounced . . . These men caught them, young girls for the most part. And opposite the military compound, my parents had their shop, right there. There were numerous shops – there was my parents', there was a greengrocer, a fabric shop, a florist and there was a hairdresser. It all happened there, where the shops were. And they took the women out of the military compound to the hairdresser. And we – my mother and me and my brother and my father – were in front of the shop, though it had been closed down and nobody was inside. And we stood there and saw the Germans coming out and the women coming out and they took them right in front of us to the hairdresser and they shaved them. And two days later, maybe three – oh it was horrible, really horrible – the FFI organized a march with all these women, there were a lot of them, they were naked, and they painted swastikas on their heads and their bodies with brushes dipped in tar. And there were the men, and someone was beating a drum. There was a column of FFI on both sides and the women in the middle and they made them march from Issy-les-Moulineaux to Meudon, some kilometres away, all the time with the drum and the escort of people from Issy-les-Moulineaux. It was very disturbing . . . one doesn't know what to think or say. There was such a reaction of hatred, stronger than anything else, stronger than reason, and the people following shouted awful things at the women, it was a sort of revenge.

At the time I thought it was right! Hah! I was against the Germans, therefore I was against these women. What did I know, what did I understand, I think I didn't understand, all I understood was the hatred that we had. I wasn't yet a woman, it was only later that I learnt a form of tolerance, that I asked myself questions, why did those women do that, maybe they really needed to, maybe it was a way for them to survive, but at the time I saw it as revenge. I hadn't had any sexual experience, I hadn't known any boys. Actually I was still a child, even though I was sixteen, I'd had no opportunity to live like a teenager . . .

KHA: Did you participate in the procession?

Mme R: I remember having marched a bit and then . . . we got to where we'd been hidden, about a kilometre, and then they climbed up to Meudon but I didn't go up, I stayed where we'd been living, and didn't go any further. Nor did my mother, nor my brother, nor my father, but there was a huge crowd . . . I remember seeing them coming back again . . . completely naked, with bare feet . . .

We knew what we'd risked, but in fact it wasn't even us who did it, it was the French. It's strange to take the time to recall . . . such very powerful memories. There was such indignation between the Germans, the women who were shaved, the Americans, it was complete turmoil, awful. The guns were still firing, even then, because not all the Germans had given themselves up, so there were Germans still firing at the same time as all that. A whirlwind like that. That was the liberation.[52]

Madame Rachel paints a vivid picture of the liberation of her neighbourhood. The creation of spectacle was a fundamental element in the reiterated ritual that the shaving of women became. As on many other occasions when it occurred, the shaving appears here to have been premeditated. If 'the visible constitutes . . . the contemporary theater of our fundamental options . . . two practices of space clash in the field of visibility, the one ordered by discipline, the other based on astonishment', then nowhere is this more apparent than in the imagined boundary between the shuttered shop and the public space of the women's humiliation.[53] The restitution of the family's space was coincident with the vengeance being enacted at the hairdresser a few doors away. They participate in the parade of women, yet leave it once they reach the safety of their former hiding place, thereby re-enacting the fearful visibility that they themselves had undergone until that moment. At liberation, they become voyeurs, indeed actors, where they had for so long attempted an impossible invisibility as Jews hiding in an urban environment in which they had previously been well-known neighbourhood shopkeepers. Knowledge, as much as spectacle, informs this memory – knowledge as duty, and as justification, a particularist feminine Jewish knowledge that resists culpability and yet is haunted by it. In the original French, this is evidenced in the slippage between the use of an othering 'on' (they), of those French shaving the women, and the first person 'on' (we) of her family, twice enumerated as 'me . . . my mother . . . my brother . . . my father'. Their partial complicity in the procession that they leave early might be read as an assimilatory moment, a reconstitution of this small space as their own among the other inhabitants. The rage against 'the Germans' that they share with other locals is extenuated by the knowledge that their experience of the occupation was wholly dissimilar. The geography present in this account replicates the particularity of Madame Rachel's family's experience of the occupation. In hiding, and yet sometimes at work, they relied on neighbours and colleagues to protect them when round-ups were imminent. As a consequence, the family was within the local community to an exaggerated degree in comparison with more mundane times, and yet excluded from it. Their participation in the communal violence against the women was similarly partial and uncertain. Above all, it was measured by their personal geography. Together the family supported the procession of naked women from their old shop to their hiding place. Neither place was home – the shop no longer belonged to them, and they had no further need of the safe house – but the line between these two locations delimited the space that for the past two years had, in only the most tentative of ways, been theirs. Madame Rachel's testimony cannot be read without understanding the Jewish and feminine costs of this war and this liberation.

Again and again, the interviewees' accounts refer to the streets in which they experienced the liberation. Far from Mesnil-Amar's deep yearning to reclaim tree-lined avenues of whose possession she was once sure, these references to urban geography instantiate a lack of certainty that the street had now become safe. It is difficult to disentangle the Jewish from the feminine aspects of this: women are often made to feel that city streets are unsuitable, or unrespectable, locations for them, and during the occupation Jews were often in danger out of doors. Both aspects should be borne in mind when interpreting the material. Let us recall the few, highly gendered, visual tropes that have come to encompass liberation: the barricade, with men in shirtsleeves and guns; the Allies' armoured vehicles, with smiling young women in summer dresses sitting high up beside the soldiers; the parades, with generals and troops striding down broad avenues; the jubilant crowds. Images of women reclaiming the streets for themselves are rare, and certainly do not form part of the visual cannon, in contrast to images of armed, yet obviously civilian, men. Neither are they present in these tentative accounts. The street remained unsafe for Jewish immigrant women at liberation and Madame Hanna would have received the concierge's husband's threat – 'watch it, we'll get you' – both as a Jew and as a young woman who knows that the danger would not vanish with the liberation of territory. The image of the city as dangerous for women, or a place in which women are invisible, has a long history, most of which has been bad for women.[54] Instrumentalized by pro-natalists, it provided the evidence they needed to dispatch women to the home and to the countryside.[55] It is not the picture that I intend to paint of liberated Paris. It is, however, important to contextualize the story of unmitigated joy that has sidelined the feminine and the Jewish in favour of masculine, non-Jewish versions of events.

A question of authority

If the interviewees explain the *femmes tondues* in relation to their positioning as Jews during the occupation, an exploration of their perspectives on national authority might clarify the picture of their adjustments to view themselves as French. One outcome of these sources was the way that respect for the republic's institutions and the nation, in the guise of the police, emerged. No questions were asked about the police during interviews. It might be expected that these respondents would disparage the behaviour of the Paris police during the occupation, and all did indeed make a point of mentioning their role in the Vél d'Hiv arrests. As agents of the state, and the uniformed face of collaboration, the police were among the first to be accused of responsibility for deportations, crimes that affected many of the respondents. Not one referred to police participation during the Paris uprising from 19 August 1944, an event quickly mythologized that helped for many years to obscure their more nefarious activities during the occupation.[56] For while the police helped to ensure that only about half the planned arrests took place during the Vél d'Hiv *rafle*, they still managed, in a single city, to arrest nearly 13,000 individuals in the space of thirty-seven hours.[57] That the police should emerge as a topic of praise is worthy of some investigation.

We have already seen how the police formed part of Madame Hanna's realization of disappointment, if not betrayal, at the liberation, in her account of their failure to act against some local informers. Elsewhere in her account are ambivalent tales of the police. In 1942, she was living in the Marais. A week before Vél d'Hiv, a non-Jewish school-friend whose father was a policeman was told to inform his Jewish friends to beware. The afternoon before the round-up, he suggested that Madame Hanna should sleep away from home. On this occasion, she tried to persuade some friends to join her at her occasional lodgings in Vincennes, a district east of Paris; two came, but a third was preparing an exam and refused to move. She was arrested and deported.[58] Nine months earlier, Hanna had been walking with her father and his friend when they were stopped by a policeman checking papers. The officer allowed the two men time to escape by insisting he had to verify procedures with his superior. The friend took his chance and ran; Madame Hanna's father, whose papers were always in order, waited patiently to be arrested. He too was deported. 'I hate the police, but I can nonetheless say that it was a policeman who saved us,' she reflects.

Madame Madeleine's communist family, living in the tenth *arrondissement*, had also heard rumours about the July 1942 round-up. They assumed that, like the year before, adult men would be targeted, so her father stayed elsewhere that night. At four in the morning (just as the *rafle* began), a policeman knocked on the door accompanied by the concierge. He announced that her mother should pack for herself and the children, and he would return in half an hour. Snatching a few belongings, the children and the dog, and rushing past the protesting concierge, her mother found refuge at the nearby Italian shoe mender's which had become a communist meeting place. Of the policeman's behaviour, Madame Madeleine says,

For me it was an admirable act of resistance, because there were many French police officers who couldn't tolerate the arrest of women and children. It wasn't easy for them to become perpetrators, even if they'd got used to obeying the occupier. There were many police officers who wanted to arrest wrong-doers, who stayed in the police because it was their profession – I mean, they had to eat . . . but it was unthinkable to take women and children.[59]

Later, in the spring of 1943, the police intervened in ways that reflect the full panoply of their behaviour during the occupation. Madame Madeleine's cousins were active, and later celebrated, resisters, and it was in their mother's flat that Madeleine and her family found occa-sional refuge. During the period of intense activity against the FTP–MOI in 1943, another police officer visited to warn that the flat had been denounced as harbouring resisters. The next few days were spent burning incriminating material but as nothing else untoward occurred, the family gradually came to believe that it had been a false alarm. Madeleine had fallen ill and remembers that one afternoon, her father (a former university lecturer in Warsaw, now a knitter) was in the pro-cess of explaining the meaning of 'utopia' to her. At this point, five police officers arrived and, after handcuffing her father and uncle, proceeded to ransack the flat. The girl's illness meant that instead of returning in the early evening, Madeleine's mother came back during the afternoon. 'Bonsoir, Madame,' she reports the police chief as saying triumphantly, 'just the person we've been waiting for.' On this occasion, her parents, both stateless, were taken, in the daughter's view as trophies to replace the real prey, the resister brothers.[60]

Madame Perla was an active resister in 1942 (though had not yet gone underground) when a friend went to renew his identity card at the local police station, only to be informed that there was little point since all the Jews would be arrested the following day. When the police came knocking, Madame Perla refused to open the door.[61] Madame Rachel attributes her family's survival to 'left-wing French gendarmes', as well as resisters at the nearby Renault factory. The police would alert the family each time the threats became more serious, and they would go to sleep in someone's storeroom or attic.[62] Madame Esther was living in the thirteenth *arrondissement* when, the afternoon before the *rafle*, a policeman fell into step beside her and her sister and, without making eye contact, advised them not to sleep at home that night.[63] The same afternoon, Madame Nechuma reports that she was sitting with some friends on the pavement when a policeman approached them, saying, 'We're going to do a round-up; try not to be here.' Like many others, they had no idea who would be targeted, so that night Madame Nechuma stayed with her best friend, a non-Jewish girl, while her father slept in an attic. Feeling it unlikely that a middle-aged woman would be in any danger, her mother remained at home. At six in the morning, Nechuma remembers her friend's mother waking her. 'She said, "Chuma, they're taking your mother!"' The girls rushed down to the street, where Nechuma's mother refused to look at her daughter but mouthed, 'Gaye veg,' get away, as the friend tore Nechuma's yellow star off her coat.[64] Madame Paulette believes that 'there was probably a resister who was a senior person at the police station'. She attributes this individual with letting her free along with her brother when her parents were arrested; once again, they had heard rumours of a *rafle* and so her father and older brother had avoided staying at home that night. However, the concierge gave the police the addresses of relatives where her father might have hidden, and he was tracked down to his sister-in-law's. After both parents had been arrested, the police returned for the children, who were taken to the town hall of the nineteenth *arrondissement*, where an unknown officer apparently ensured their release.[65]

The grudging gratitude present in these accounts coheres with their tellers' ambivalent reclamation of French identity and its attendant administrative structures as their own. But perhaps the starkest rapprochement with the natural power invested in the state is expressed by Madame Paulette, whose husband was deported to Poland in 1951 for bill-posting PCF material:

There was a law in France which said that a foreigner had no right to get mixed up in politics. Well, he was mixed up in politics, they knew he was a member of the Communist Party and they expelled him. It was within Cold War logic and French law ... we had certain disillusions regarding the Communist Party, and ended up understanding the position of the French government with regard to communist activists.[66]

They stayed in Poland (where she claims they were treated as French rather than as Jews) for nine years. Even though her husband had been a political deportee and could have applied for naturalization, and she was entitled to return, there is apparently no bitterness in Madame Paulette's recollection of this expulsion.[67] This suggests an overriding respect for the French state, an attitude imparted above all via its educational system, and that endures despite its perversion by Vichy and the continuation after liberation of bio-geographical categorizations of the type favoured by Sauvy or Mauco.[68] These accounts together allude to a reconciliation tempered by an ambivalence itself determined by experience. While, as was argued above, Mesnil-Amar's pronouncement of reconciliation at the moment of liberation was premature, a recomposition of memory in relation to the police, adjusted through the prism of assimilation, allows it to emerge as more settled.

These stories of the police as agents of assistance as well as of repression help to draw out gender as a factor of the Holocaust. Even at the limits of its greatest terror and excess, the Holocaust was not experienced equally. Vichy and Nazi discourses of motherhood were each connected to their separate ideologies of race. The Nazis applied to Jewish mothers the reverse of the protective praise showered on Aryans, and indicted Jewish women for their capacity to reproduce what the Nazis feared would be a generation of vengeful Jewish children. This lay behind the reason that a quarter of all Holocaust deaths consisted of Jewish children. In the camps, women experienced sexual violence and were separated from their children. Pregnancy was a terrible liability, and women were subject to experimentation on their reproductive systems. In Paris, real or simulated pregnancy occasionally provided a means of escape, whereby women might be sent to hospital instead of to Drancy.[69] But the figures are stark. Of transports from France to Auschwitz in 1943 and 1944, the number of women selected for work, as opposed to immediate gassing – inmates who might have at least a remote chance of survival – was roughly half that of men (2,707 women against 5,494 men).[70] During the Vél d'Hiv *rafle*, as the German military command noted at the time, many men had already been arrested, and others hid in the belief that women and children were not threatened.[71] Madame Nechuma and Madame Madeleine's parents were far from alone in suspecting that mothers would not be targeted. In the event, adult women outnumbered men by almost two to one (5,802 to 3,031), while women and children together outnumbered men by more than three to one. But we must not forget that the home was supposed to be safe for women. Their internalization of this belief, even in the face of warnings to the contrary, led to tragedy. Discourses of home were not only powerful but, in this case, treacherous.

'I love this country, but...'[72]

Mauco, Sauvy, and their contemporaries refused to countenance the possibility that immigrant Jews could ever sufficiently divest themselves of their particularity to assimilate properly. The overwhelming evidence from the interviewees underlines the poverty of this type of thinking and its reductive categories. The ambivalence that all interviewees expressed about their French status rested on the pragmatic, and more or less accidental fact of their residence. But while such ambivalence may be manifest, the accounts reveal significant debts to French republican discourses of national identity as well as to Jewish and other discourses. In response to questions about her reactions to the atmosphere of resistance patriotism which permeated Paris at liberation, Madame Hanna said,

I was never a patriot... France? Well, when I was in the resistance, there were two Frances – resistance France, and then there was Pétainist France, which was the majority. Of course, I detested that France. And there was no question that I was going to stay in France, I wanted to go to Palestine – I didn't feel French. And today I still don't feel French, I couldn't care less about France, I couldn't care less about any country except Israel. Having said that, it's the country where I live and if France were threatened I would do just as I did during the war... To some extent, my Jewishness connects to the idea of universality which drives Judaism, even if the universal of the Jewish religion is that when the Messiah comes everyone will be Jewish. Hmm. Everyone will become Jewish? Personally I don't believe that. But this universality that I have experienced because being born in Poland, and not having lived in Jewish environments all the time, having lived side by side with good French people, having gone to a school where I had an English teacher who incidentally was Jewish – she was marvellous, that woman... she disappeared after the Pétainist laws... Personally I felt universal, I felt part of everything, of everyone, and I believe that it was my Jewishness which drove that.[73]

It is not the hierarchization whereby Madame Hanna's sense of Jewishness towers over her attachment to France that emerges here, but the infusion of French universalist values by which her Jewishness is interpreted. Madame Hanna does not suggest that she would re-engage in resistance if the *Jews* were threatened again, but if the *nation* were – and moreover, a nation that she admits to disparaging. Madame Hanna is hardly a classic Zionist; while she lived briefly in Israel, returning to France in part because she wanted to divorce her husband (whom she married in order to acquire nationality), she also describes herself as attracted to Trotskyist ideals of permanent international revolution. It was among these groups that she found her political home after the disappointments of liberation.[74] Her uneasy relationship with France in spatial terms (she also lived in Belgium from the late 1950s, working for the Common Market) is less fraught, therefore, in intellectual ones.

We could compare this to Madame Magda's liberalism and sense of being a 'citizen of the world' that could, she suggested, be 'one of the consequences [of] deportation'. When lived in the context of France, with whose image of freedom and asylum she grew up, this antipathy to nationalism assumes a similar tenor as that of Madame Hanna, of French and Jewish universal values.[75] Madame Sara echoed these ideas. For her, France was 'the best country that exists. Germany didn't exist for me, nor Poland, nor the Soviet Union...when we arrived, France was the country of the rights of man...to be able to walk about in the evening without being frightened...was something really special.'[76] These discourses of Frenchness and Jewishness and the impossibility of prioritizing one over another extend beyond the realm of nationality. 'We can't be put in a category, we were beyond categorization,' Madame Fanny stated of herself and her husband, a Jewish resister deported as political to Buchenwald and expelled from the PCF after the war:

We weren't workers, we weren't intellectuals, we weren't bourgeois – certainly not bourgeois – we didn't know what we were...We believed that a category exists but had nonetheless noticed that some people had their own family ethics, ethics for their own milieu. And in comparison to our parents, we jumped numerous generations, but with respect to our friends we were completely downgraded. I mean, how can you explain that today?[77]

The perplexity of explanation is part of what forms this disparate group into a community of sorts. They share a common disregard for the agony that the lack of national belonging was supposed by demographers to impart. All express ambivalence about French non-Jewish culture, though few suggested French non-Jews themselves were indistinguishable from each other. Madame Rivka retained visceral hatred of what she regards as an inherent conservative traditionalism which renders them untrustworthy, while Madame Magda was bored with incessant discourses of war-time suffering. Madame Jeanne disliked their inquisitiveness about national origins (she retorts that she's been French for longer than her interlocutor). Some have similar suspicion of French Jews. Madame Jeanne detected a chasm of misunderstanding that separated immigrant Jews from French Jews who felt 'completely 105 per cent French' and who found eastern European Jews 'annoying' and 'inferior'. France itself is sometimes regarded as cultural home, a place of refuge, and the location of a pleasing language – but never somewhere of total belonging. This is not, however, cause for anxiety, but of taxonomic contingency:

My country isn't Poland, it's not Israel, it's a floating country which is the country of the Jews...Though when I find myself in a Jewish environment, I get profoundly irritated by the constant remarks between Sephardim and Ashkenazim because I was always against 'racism'...It's always like that in a floating country...I was always attached to a country, this country, and I always knew that I wasn't quite French, I hitched myself to France but I knew that I wasn't French. When I was asked to assess what I was, I understood that I was of Polish origin...for a long time I believed that Poland was my country because my entire childhood was cradled in my mother's Polish stories of her life there – it was a miserable life . . . It's a cocktail . . . I'm a French Jewish woman [*Je suis Juive française*].[78]

A number of these interviewees appear to inhabit this imaginary country, managing to live and work successfully in France while remaining unattached to the nation. It could be argued that 'Juive française' is less the emphatic reclamation of a name than an announcement of the inadequacy of the terminology that assimilationist compunction supplies. The past is neither to be wholly rejected nor wholly embraced in romantic nostalgia in the ways that *Des Français pour la France* and Mauco feared. More than a lost Poland, it is the paucity of available language that seems to emerge through Madame Fanny's search. 'Je suis Juive française' sounds an incomplete finale to what has gone before. 'How do you explain that today?' retains its piercing pertinence.

Each of these women encompasses the fractured sense of self that Jacobin universalism would deny but that remains paradoxically widespread within the Republic. To attempt to confine them analytically into this or that category by foregrounding the unique and univocal would be to act in similar fashion.[79] The resistance that they mount against any such imposed unity is borne out most clearly in they ways they speak of their children. Of traditional generational assimilation (which assimilationists hope becomes stronger further down the ancestral line), Madame Paulette says:

My children, for example, are married to non-Jews . . . Assimilation is the fact that children no longer feel Jewish. That is to say, they identify with France for the French, with the dominant religion, etc., and that's what I call assimilation, but I must say that deep down I don't have the impression that that is the case . . . my son and daughter feel completely Jewish. They haven't renounced their Judaism – on the contrary.[80]

Unspecific national and ethnic definitions imparted by these mothers exist as a legacy of the female immigrant generation that survived the Holocaust. The emergence of a community certain of, and even content with, its own mutable Jewishness was provoked by the war and took place within an atmosphere of insistent, and effective, assimilation. Let us recall the picture of the meeting that opened this book: one of indecision, of standing and sitting down again while Kaddish was sung for Perela Traler. We could read that as confusion. In the context of the diverse allegiances of which these women spoke (some of whom were present at the memorial), let us read the occasion instead as one that conceded multiplicity, which only becomes uncertain because it occurs within a French national context that itself is nervous of cultural plurality.[81] That gathering is reminiscent of another that took place nearly fifty years earlier, when a group of Jewish political activists would meet shortly after the war. 'The atmosphere is a rather curious mixture of Yiddish, Russian, Zionist and French traditions,' noted the observer. 'They play the Marseillaise, the March of Stalin and the Hatik-vah in order to reconcile all the political tendencies of the participants, of whom only half stand, while the rest manifests its disapproval or indifference.'[82] What seems important to underline here is less the fac-tionalism than the fact that these oppositional tendencies were meeting together at all. This *was* the community, and any assumption that it be single-minded either in the face of or after the occupation fails to anticipate the potential for proliferating belongings that the immigrant generation produced, and that is retained and developed by its children. Discourses of the universal might be internalized, but resistance to them persists.

It was, in part, through their roles as mothers that these women ful-filled one of the assimilationist prerequisites, while at the same time resisting the assimilationism that the rest of this book has described. The imperative to mother is one of the avenues that we have explored. Widely regarded as a necessity for the French woman in her duty to the nation, and the means by which the immigrant woman would im-plant her husband, children and herself as worthy inhabitants of France, maternalism appealed to Vichyists and to its deepest opponents. The immigrant Jewish women interviewed here did not primarily present themselves as mothers. They portrayed themselves as leather work-ers, garment makers, psychologists, market-stall holders, resisters, sur-vivors and embattled or appreciative political militants. They revealed post-war occupations as workers, students and professionals, often in psychology or social work. The list is not exhaustive. Nevertheless, the power of the notion that the assimilationist project be completed by and within the family is palpable in the ways that so many presented the family as the lens through which they viewed assimilation. All had children, and the only one not to marry had lived with the father of her child. Yet they spoke both within and against dominant notions of assimilation. Some voiced the impulse to marry as emergent from the tragedy of the Holocaust.[83] The oral evidence suggests that the baby boom operated differently among Jewish and non-Jewish women in France. Women whose marriages had ended in divorce claimed that not only had the injunction to marry been powerful, but that the pos-sibility of creating life out of the Holocaust had been stronger than the evidence that the men they were about to marry were unsuitable.[84] The birth-rate among Jews may have been similar to that among non-Jews in France, and is to be distinguished from the birth-rate in the Displaced Persons (DP) camps, which was higher than in any other post-war Jewish community.[85] Like the displaced persons, though, women who were often the sole survivor of their family may have felt a pressing need to form new, if unwise, familial relationships.[86] These they framed as a response to the Holocaust, not to the French national 'need' outlined by populationists, but it seems likely that populationist ideas informed their decisions too.

It was through children that the populationist choice between the maintenance of a clear-cut ethnic identity and the creation of a unitary Frenchness, was refused. Some interviewees were proud that their children had married non-Jewish North Africans, or had become professional Arabists or anti-racist lawyers. The marriage of their children to non-Jews, often feared within the Jewish establishment as an abandonment of Jewish lineage, was regarded by these mothers more as an act of confirmation of their children's Jewishness that expressed the rejection of the unitary, in either its Jewish or French versions. Madame Jeanne articulated this most clearly, and became conscious of a political necessity to cross cultures as early as the 1930s, when she took the unusual step of marrying a non-Jewish man (whom she divorced early during the occupation, losing her non-Jewish surname in the process). Her rejection of Jewish and French exclusivity stemmed from a considered political stance. She grew up in a non-Jewish area of rural north-east Poland and moved to Warsaw to attend high school and escape the stifling domination of her father. In Warsaw, though, she was excluded from non-Jewish organizations and joined the Bund, the Jewish, non-Zionist socialist organization notable for its high proportion of women members.

As a child, as a young woman, I tried to break the barrier... when I came to France I said to myself, 'We must break that barrier, Jews can't be eternally isolated... We live in the same country, we aren't in a ghetto, we aren't surrounded by walls, we surround ourselves by a wall!' Mentally. We don't mix with others. I was always conscious of this, and personally I broke that wall. Between 1930 and 1939... my best friends were not Jewish... the fact that I had close friends who weren't Jewish helped me enormously during the occupation... I could help my family and other people through the fact that I had friends on the left.[87]

It must be admitted that Madame Jeanne's perspective was rare. While a relatively large proportion of Jewish immigrants were communist activists, few were so conscious of political communalism. Madame Sara's experience of a different kind of ghetto raised linked questions from an alternative perspective:

Persecution... wasn't a privilege... It was a secret just for myself. They destroyed us in the flesh, and in the head. I remember in Poland when they arrived in '39, the Germans were blond and tall and handsome... I said, 'So they really are superior to us.' They stripped off to wash, they were great-looking guys, blond and everything. And I thought, 'Maybe it's true what they say.' It was awful. And in the ghetto... they made us feel guilty, they said that the Jews were shit, they smell awful, and so on. It was they who made us smell bad, but we were doubly guilt-ridden ... they *conditioned* us![88]

This is just the sort of conditioning that Mauco would have regarded as sufficient reason to refuse ghetto Jews entry to France.

Interviewees repeatedly contrasted their sense of distance from France with one of being settled and at ease in Paris. The single entity of the nation seemed at once too overwhelming and too restricting for most respondents to feel comfortable with it. Paris, though, answered to their identificatory needs for a particular place. It was not, as Mesnil-Amar romanticized, on account of birth that made one identify with that place, although Madame Jeanne thought it 'inevitable' that one remained attached to the country of one's birth.[89] For most, though, residence in a country was contingent and patriotism remained irrelevant. While some interpreted their residence in France as being in the country of the rights of man, they stayed less from love of the country than a sense of familiarity. Madame Madeleine regards the restoration of the tricolour in what had been 'swastika-infested Paris'[90] as 'a fantastic symbol of rediscovered liberty. Even if one is not a chauvinist, to have seen these swastika flags on public buildings was absolutely unbearable ... It was a dreadful symbol.'[91] The flag of the restored republic became then a counter-symbol that represented the swastika's defeat, rather than an evocation of pride in and for itself. Yet it cannot be disconnected from the context in which the tricolour was raised. If the country was too problematic, the city was an entity to which interviewees were deeply attached and in which they were implicated. With a long history for European Jewry, it provided space to enact the sort of Jewishness claimed by Madame Fanny, who suggested that being Jewish is 'to be not like the others'. Being 'not like the others', then, becomes normative within its radical Jewish context. A legitimation of immigration and resistance, it compels those so defined to remain vigilant about current social norms and to contest them where necessary – an endeavour undertaken with pleasure according to accounts of many of these interviewees, whose children refuse traditional versions of assimilation, and continue to battle with received ideas of race.

The reflections that have been analysed above were articulated at the end of the twentieth century. They were formed with the benefit of hindsight, and certain factors – such as the memorialization of the Holocaust, the dismantling of state socialism in eastern Europe and the rise of the French far right, to name only a few – undoubtedly played a part in their composition. What interested me was less the search for new facts than the ways that the interviewees understood the sorts of ideas that have been explored in the rest of this book. To end with, let us consider the status of the interview. Oral sources have come under close and critical scrutiny since the 1970s, when historians, eager to break from the elitism of positivism, began to question people who had witnessed particular movements, events or aspects of history, especially those that had been marginalized.[92] Critics sometimes suggest that questions go only one way, from the historian to the respondent. Like any other source though, issues that arose from interviewee testimony informed the progress of research elsewhere. That this needs elucidation is one of the peculiarities of oral history's position in the broader historical discipline.

Oral accounts are necessarily mediated by the context in which they arise. Responses, and indeed questions, are determined by contemporary discourses, as is their interpretation by the historian. In a recent work on testimony, Annette Wieviorka, who has undertaken hundreds of interviews with survivors, regards this as so problematic as to dismiss the witness from History (her capitalization).[93] While it might add colour, she says, witness testimony is too embedded in its moment of articulation, too washed by emotion, to be instrumentalized as a document could be. It is generally assumed that, since most witnesses to the Holocaust were murdered and, even before their death, had little access to the requisite tools to document their plight, written sources from the victims' point of view are rare. To counter this notion, Wieviorka describes some extensive archives prepared by the inhabitants of the Lodz and Warsaw ghettos. These collections were started in October 1938 when the German government deposited 12,000 formerly Polish and now stateless Jews over the border into Poland, where they lived in penurious conditions. The archives eventually consisted of daily chronicles, even monographs, of ghetto life, diaries, theatre posters, ration cards, clandestine newspapers, Nazi decrees, and other memorabilia. Buried in milk churns shortly before the destruction of the Warsaw ghetto in April 1943, some of these documents were found after the war and are now stored at the Institute for Jewish History in Warsaw. Wieviorka cites the existence of this extraordinary archive to invalidate the need to record the, necessarily unreliable, living witness. For this witness is bound to contemporary cultural politics and ideology in ways that to Wieviorka are restrictive and inauthentic. Today, she insists, '*not one* witness any longer recalls, as he did before, how he kissed French soil on his return or cried with emotion on hearing the Marseillaise. The witness *always* fixes his tale with a finality that transcends it.'[94] Are witness accounts really that unreliable, or uniform? Is their only use to add colour to the past, and not allow us new ways to interpret the relationship between the present and the past?[95] And are witnesses not permitted to temper memories of their joy of return to France with subsequent encounters that they interpreted as rejection?

The witness testimony presented here does not much resemble Wieviorka's experience of finality. Certainly, the interviewees' accounts are imbued with myth and received ideas, that we have analysed as forming part of their contested notions of national belonging. The accounts also reveal plenty of differentiation. Some former members of the PCF (the most Stalinist of post-war western European communist parties) allude to the party in ways that invoke the details that emerged after 1989. Others remained proud members, or had fond memories, while a further set explored their expulsion from the party in terms that connected gender and Jewishness. The differences between the accounts, and their composition that incorporates elements from 'outside', do not invalidate the accounts, but allow the historian to read them through other reflections on the time, just as a historian would take the context of a written document into account. The very discrepancy of the accounts throws light on the myth-making and historical construction that for Wieviorka is irrelevant in our analysis of the past.

Her example of the milk churns is instructive, but their contents remain unusual. Most historians who privilege the written above the oral account find their sources in archives, and these often belong to the state or its local derivatives. Most of the documents emanate from official sources. Entry to archives and the time necessary to read them are largely restricted to professional historians. The claim against the oral account not only discards the witness, but requires 'History' to be confined to an elite whose scientific credentials are founded on criteria that are themselves ideologically constructed.[96] Nor are other contemporary written accounts necessarily the transparent truth. Bias of some sort is likely in official documents, especially those prepared for an authoritarian regime during a war. Victim accounts, such as a Jewish resister diary written at the time (one of this book's sources), could scarcely be claimed as a free or true mode of expression. Fear of its discovery by the police meant that much was left unwritten. Indeed, as an account of resister activity, Jacqueline Mesnil-Amar's diary is disappointing since it excludes almost all her clandestine operations. As an insight into a world of the female Jewish resister, though, it is inspiring, passionate and suggestive.

As far as allegations of uniformity are concerned, this is also disproved in the accounts collected here. One interviewee found her husband uncomprehending of her own search for Jewishness. Having lived in a non-Jewish environment, and despite her family's continued attendance of a synagogue during the occupation, her only sense of Jewishness at that time was that imposed by persecution. Others were fully confident of their Jewishness, that they expressed in secular and religious ways. Some were ardent anti-communists, while others remained members of the party. Stories of divorce, of political disagreements, of factionalism were all present. None of it adds up to uniformity. While the accounts are necessarily produced within and from available discourses, they are not obliged to run along parallel tracks.

Wieviorka draws a false dichotomy between the emotionality of the living witness and the utilitarian dryness of the written account.[97] I cannot be the only reader who, immersed day after day in memoranda, newspaper accounts, published diaries, inter-ministerial correspondence and other types of written document, each of which was in some way concerned with death on a mass scale, found the emotional onslaught sometimes hard to bear. The interviewees, in contrast, rarely cried; on the few occasions that they did, it was generally when recounting the death of a parent, or even a pet, before the start of the war. Not a tear was shed when these women spoke of the deportation of their parents or siblings.

Listening to individuals allows us to hear about personal experience, which in turn provokes the analysis of factors that are difficult to grasp from written accounts. There is no denying that individual agency is affected by external factors – indeed, the interplay between the two has been one of this book's overriding concerns. Above all, thinking about the ways that the interviewees told their stories led me to try to understand how contemporary discourses and practices about the home and the neighbourhood interwove with the way that Vichy antisemitism proceeded in occupied Paris. Without these oral accounts, it is unlikely that we would have been able to reach these conclusions, because written records would not have provoked their analysis. If the street and the kitchen are gendered and racialized sites, then we need to hear how they were inhabited in order to enlarge our understanding that would otherwise be at best generalized or at worst ignored. Police and court records do contain information about the street, if rather less about the kitchen, but only once tensions have reached a certain, dangerous point. It was precisely because of prior relations with the police that Madame Hanna's encounters on the street with antisemites and crowds attacking women led to no court records at all. Hearing about them later permits us to enrich our conceptualization of the streets of liberated Paris beyond the image of the vast open-air dance hall that it became on the 25 August 1944. Unpoliced crowds became menacing in new ways at liberation for young Jewish women, who only a few days before would have found the presence of police even more alarming.

The fact that the accounts come years after the event may not make the historian's task any easier, but does lend them more than the richness of reflection. Elements may be missing that would have been underlined at the time, but that is the case for historiography too. Inscribed in current concerns, writing and talking more than fifty years after the events allows us to bring to the forefront the theoretical issues of today in order to achieve ever greater understanding of the past. Madame Rachel's story of the *femmes tondues*, for example, had, she said, been concealed until the interview. Only once the language of women's history had became more widespread could she articulate this episode. In many ways her entire story is one *of* concealment – of herself during the occupation, and of her memories until public discourses gave them permission for expression. Far from damaging the oral account, public discourses allow witnesses to tell things that they may not otherwise have dared.

Finally, let us examine more closely the question of accuracy, whose absence Wieviorka so deplores in witness testimony. Madame Magda relates that she, and her entire extended family, were deported in 1944 to Auschwitz-Birkenau from a small Transylvanian town then under Hungarian rule. She, her sister and a cousin were selected for labour; the rest of her family was murdered on arrival at Birkenau, at the start of the frenetic period when 400,000 Hungarian Jews were deported during the second half of 1944. In December that year, Madame Magda and her sister were moved to the Gross Rosen concentration camp, where she worked as a slave labourer and, as Soviet troops came westwards, to two other camps in Germany. In April 1945, US troops liberated her. Against all injunctions, the two sisters befriended some French prisoners of war in a camp near by, and it was on their lorry that they arrived in France. A felicitous encounter with a Jewish colonel at the border ensured that their passage was relatively speedy and untroubled.

In late May 1945, Madame Magda says she arrived at the Hôtel Lutétia in Paris. For deportees, the Lutétia was the first stop on the path towards reintegration in French society or, in the case of Madame Magda, her first French resting place. The hotel represented the epitome of comfort for what she recalls as the three days of her stay. Her impressions of it are filtered through the eyes of someone who had spent a year in conditions of terror and privation:

It was a marvel, I tell you, because when you leave a camp, even after the liberation – the Americans had put us in a barracks and we were better housed but even so it was a military barracks and therefore incomparable with the Hôtel Lutétia.
  KHA: Were there a lot of people at the Hôtel Lutétia at that point?
  Mme M: I believe we were the only ones.[98]

Madame Magda's impressions would have surprised managers of the Lutétia, for whom conditions were far from desirable. Intended as a calm, restful environment reserved for high-status political deportees, it quickly became overcrowded.[99] On 2 June 1945, a few days after

Madame Magda's arrival, the Ministry of Prisoners, Deportees and Refugees received complaints of chaos and disorder that threatened to overwhelm staff. The ministry was further informed that the welfare and the medical sections seemed ignorant of each other's work, that residents lacked basic care in their rooms and that medical attention was negligible.[100] Madame Magda, though, found in the Lutétia an oasis of welcoming ease. Are we to dismiss her narrative on grounds of factual error? Not at all. It points instead to the profound contrast between the conditions she had endured in concentration camps and the ones she met on arrival in France. Moreover, her first impression of France was supported by ideas from her childhood, where she had learnt that 'France is the country – how do they put it? – a very welcoming country, where they welcome refugees.' We hear also the former deportee who admits to a willing suppression of the more unpleasant aspects of her past. Does this invalidate her testimony, or make it too emotional? Does it confirm the failure of all deportees to recall their joy at arriving in France?

Implicit among critics of oral history is the suggestion that the interviewee be innocent and pure. When they prove to be imbued with contemporary cultural politics, their contributions are to be rejected. But rarely were these respondents unreflective. Formal education may have been denied many, and their backgrounds may have been modest, but they were often conscious of the problems of transmission. Madame Sara realized that neither keeping silent, nor informing her children of the suffering associated with the Holocaust, could be satisfactory: 'If one said nothing after the war, one was at fault,' she said, 'and if one spoke, I know people who say, "My mother has poisoned me with everything about the Shoah."'[101] Madame Madeleine remembers her first view of the occupying troops: 'There was a rumour, we went down to the street and I saw the motorized troops arrive. It was a sort of grey-green block. It was sparkling, it was backfiring, it was bellowing. They turned the corner of the road...and in my mind – I must have seen some horror films – it was death which advanced.'[102] It is improbable that a young girl in pre-war France had seen many horror films. The attribution to cinema of her childhood reactions indicates Madame Madeleine's own consciousness of the 'impurity' of memory and its composure from various public and private sources.[103] Oral accounts of the Holocaust are often read through a filter of either heroism and sorrow.[104] I gained little impression from the interviewees that they regarded themselves as either heroines or transmitters of sorrow, and I have aimed to acknowledge their position within local and national contexts that have undergone enormous change. Growing old in a France of whose mounting racial tensions most were keenly aware, as they were of the increasingly reductive terms via which those tensions were understood, they could not but connect the moment at which they spoke to the period under discussion. Above all, they remind us of the complexities of national belonging by referring us back to a time when the state was dedicated to reducing and instrumentalizing national allegiances at their simplest, and most devastating, level.

Chapter 7
Conclusion

Sixty years after the events described in this book and as it was going to press, France was undergoing what might be read as a crisis of assimilationism. Some people of immigrant origin born in the country were believed to feel a lesser sense of belonging than they should, and the same went for immigrants who had lived in France for many years. In any case, the two categories were often confused. Whether the 'crisis' was crystallized by Muslim girls who sought to identify their religion in that bulwark of state secularism, the school; or the largely male football fans who booed the national anthem at matches between teams whose Frenchness – being Corsican or Algerian – was highly contested; or the increasing respectability of the extreme right, especially among male voters, problems of assimilation were coming into ever-sharper focus at the turn of the twenty-first century. As each of these examples suggests, the crisis was one in which questions of race and racialization were deeply entwined with and affected by gender.

This book has traced some of the historical foundations of another crisis of assimilationism and national identity. In its incarnation as liberationist foundation for the new republic that was expected to emerge after the war, assimilationism gained in significance at one of the defining moments of the French twentieth century. Assimilationism applied to gender, nationality and ethnicity, elements that reinforced and conditioned each other in a complex web. It was a major element in France's approach to its population, positioning individuals in racialized and gendered categories that were then mobilized to impose limitations on them. In their idealized condition, assimilationist desires are for equality, not restriction. Being limited by its own essential categorizations, however, assimilationism contains implicit and often explicit grounds for inclusion or rejection. The assimilationist discourses and practices at liberation that I have explored explain the continuities not just between the government of Vichy and the republics that preceded and followed it, but between Vichy and its opponents. In this sense, I have expanded on Gérard Noiriel's work which examined the republican roots of Vichy's ethnic policies, but which paid little attention to resisters and took no account of gender.[1] Yet public and private resister expression, such as the clandestine press and women's diaries, showed the deep roots and varieties of thinking around gender and Jewishness, and the extent to which these issues were correlated. When links are made with demographers' writings on similar topics, we can establish a complicated, contradictory, but nonetheless coherent picture of how assimilationist thought in France operated vertically through socio-economic strata, and horizontally across political boundaries.

It was to restore an acute sense of lost certainty of what being French meant that the 'assimilatory project' became so fundamental at liberation. If the notion of a unitary and uncontested national identity is absurd for any modern nation, it had become impossible in France during the years of the occupation. There were so many competing, and yet insistent – at times murderously so – definitions of national identity, and the country was so carved into pieces that it was extremely unclear to anyone what 'being French' really meant. Nonetheless, a profound desire to define Frenchness was dear to nearly all political sectors. Vichy's National Revolution aimed to restore what it regarded as the lost values of its version of Frenchness. This included the wholesale rejection of some groups of people for whom 'being French' was held to be impossible. Parts of the resistance engaged in a counter-project that imposed an alternative set of values but which was no less categorical when it came to inclusion and exclusion. While resister categories were inclined to be based on political rather than ethnic or national factors, the tendency to slip into an essentialized taxonomy of ethnicity, nationality or sexuality was shared by the resistance and Vichy.

One of the major projects at liberation was the restoration of a national sense of unity. As the symbolic resurrection of the republic involved the physical creation of a new statue of Marianne, the female incarnation of the republic whose bust adorned public buildings, so she was contrasted to a new feminine figure who came to symbolize the suffering of France under the Nazis. There is no doubt that the inhabitants of France had suffered during the Nazi occupation, which began with the deaths of 112,000 soldiers in the six weeks of fighting in 1940, a rate higher even than that at Verdun in 1916.[2] About 1.5 million people, mostly men, had been taken to Germany and the economy had been ransacked. Tens of thousands of people had been executed, or perished in the killing centres and concentration camps. The number of individuals connected to those 'absent', often women, ran into millions. In many districts, hunger had been chronic, though elsewhere food was abundant. In this respect, there is little to be gained if France is compared to other occupied countries which experienced Nazi power and brutality to a greater extent; people in occupied France had scant idea of what was going on in the other zones, let alone in other countries. For all the profiteering that occurred in parts of the French economy, for many people, the experience of occupation was dreadful. But the image mobilized at liberation to remind them of this misery and to draw them together once again – a mother mourning the loss of her son – was not neutral, and nor should we expect it to have been. This representation of grieving maternity can be read either as one of the many individual mothers who *had* lost their sons, or as France itself. The image also reminded people of the nation's losses in 1918. At liberation, mothers were obviously not the only people to be bereaved, nor were young men the only ones to have died. The occlusion of other potential mourners becomes comprehensible if we take into account the period's insistent familialism and its bid to restore the heterosexual family as the nation's core unit. But was this image simply one of familialism?

Liberation and the restoration of the republic were full of contradictions. Vichy's anti-republican objectives had entailed its reinstatement of the link between church and state, and the promotion of Catholicism. It might be thought that, even if there were considerable overlaps in the populationist aims of Vichy and its successor republic, we might detect more rhetorical distance between the two in terms of their fundamental convictions regarding religion than was the case. In fact, liberation involved not only the historical recuperation of previous non-republican eras of French history that helped to hide Vichy, but the elevation of imagery that equated France with Mary mourning her dead son Jesus, one of Christianity's originating narratives. Just as support was almost universal for the ceremonial nationalization of the family that was Mothers' Day – support which certainly extended to the militantly secular and anti-Vichy French Communist Party – so the image of France as a Christian family bereaved in the loss of its sons was accorded widespread exposure. These inflections came at the moment that the secular republic superseded Catholic Vichy. The image, often deployed on Mothers' Day, suggested that women could fulfil national duties of mourning, and also maintain France's connection to the church. Gendered assimilatory discourses made the nation men's primary allegiance; in contrast, they provided women with not one but multiple allegiances, most obviously to the home. At liberation, these discourses opened the way for women to act as proxy for a nation still yearning for its links to the sacred. Reference to this Christianized mater dolorosa could, moreover, only consolidate the need for 'outsiders'. Whether these outsiders were constituted in terms of ethnicity, nationality, religion or gender non-conformity, they were then impelled to maintain the acts of dissimulation and hiding that they, or at least the survivors, had refined during the Vichy years.

As a *symbolic* entity, then, the new gendered republic in mourning was not much more welcoming as far as women were concerned than

Vichy. Let us not overstate the case here. The new government did put real legislative distance between Vichy and itself. After liberation, for example, the issue of women's equality started to come to the fore. Women could now vote, and steps were taken to ensure that they earned equal wages to men, though it would be many years before the wage gap began to close in any significant measure.[3] But it is much harder to distinguish the two regimes when it comes to the rhetoric, and indeed the practicalities, of the family. Home-based and reproductive, with Christian overtones, women's functions appeared to be restricted at liberation in ways that Vichy and its adherents would certainly have recognized.

This mobilization of a repository of Catholic images to understand the nation in mourning, and by extension the family, women and France as a symbolic whole, had implications for non-Christians. Before considering this symbolic France in more detail, it is worth referring briefly to some of the historiographic discussions that have emerged since the late 1990s, on the issue of non-Christians during this period. These reflect in particular on the historical significance of Jews and Vichy antisemitism.[4] Interest in Jews at liberation was confined neither to issues surrounding their deportation, which came to an end in August 1944, nor their return to France after May 1945. While the latter assumed great importance for the 2,190 individuals concerned, those close to them and the remaining Jewish inhabitants of France, it was rather insignificant for the nation as a whole. Western European fascination with Jews throughout the modern period – whether nominally 'pro-' or 'anti-Jewish' – represents worries that extend far beyond the numerically relatively insignificant Jewish population of a particular country. Analysis of this fascination can reveal ambivalences that lie at the heart of a culture and which are not necessarily about Jews as concrete individual subjects at all. At liberation, as before, immigrant assimilability or unassimilability was framed in terms derived in large measure from the language and beliefs used to describe Jews, whether or not their referents were in fact Jewish. Jewishness and its supposed attributes were elements woven in to the very fabric of Frenchness. We should take note, therefore, when some historiography from the turn of the twenty-first century argues that historians' focus on Jews has become excessive. These same historians have also suggested that, since very few people apart from those directly implicated showed much interest in the deportations, it is anachronistic for historians to concentrate on the subject.[5] This is seriously to misunderstand the cultural significance of 'the Jew' in modern western European thought, politics and society. More specifically, when Vichy's own anxiety about the Jew was so violent that they legislated for Jews' exclusion from the economy and then society as a whole, something rather serious was occurring that surely warrants historians' continued attention. Suggestions that historiography about Vichy antisemitism has come to dominate investigations into the period do not stand up to scrutiny.

Hostility to Jews did not end at liberation. While France saw nothing like the equivalent of the murderous pogroms that took place in Poland when the tiny number of Jewish survivors attempted to go home, former members of collaborationist organizations like the Parti Populaire Français did mobilize aggressive, and sometimes violent, demonstrations when Jews returned to Paris to reclaim their former homes.[6] These took place within what was occasionally a more generalized mood of antipathy. Madame Hanna, for instance, recounted how her mother faced the resentment of neighbours who, having taken advantage of their absence and with the probable connivance of the concierge, had entered their sealed apartment some time after July 1942 and removed their furniture. The mother's protestations over its rightful ownership did not result in the restitution of her property, even though she took her complaints to the police.[7] More seriously, a number of protests against the return of Jews were organized in Paris. Hundreds of demonstrators were reported to have gathered at various locations when Jews returned at the end of the war, and the following year, often with what was seen as the complicity of the police.[8] Demonstrators found encouragement in the poorly drafted legislation on the return of accommodation to former residents. This stipulated that it could only be retrieved on condition, first, that it had not been taken over by new tenants in 'good faith' and, second, that the original inhabitants had been forcibly removed. Exceptions to the obligation to return property were numerous. No claims could be made if the new tenants had previously become homeless through bombing, were evacuees, or 'refugees', that is, people who had moved within France, or were these people's spouses, parents, or children. Nor could those with a dependent who was a prisoner of war, political deportee, forced labourer or in the armed forces be asked to move.[9] So extensive were the exceptions to the rule of reclamation that lawyers handling the claims of Jews to their former housing regarded the situation as paralysed.[10] Antisemites took advantage of the fact that many Jews had fled 'of their own accord', and organized themselves into bands of 'tenants of good faith' to resist the return of accommodation to Jewish survivors.[11] While it is important not to exaggerate the number or frequency of these protests, it would also be a mistake not to recognize their political and cultural significance. Such an error would be comparable to the long-term occlusion from historical investigation of the women shaved at liberation. For all that Jacqueline Mesnil-Amar described herself as a tourist, many of the homecomings for absent Jews were far from the easy recuperation that the term 'tourism' suggests.

An additional factor complicated this. Who belonged to the nation and who did not continued to exercise government minds after liberation. It might be imagined that one could add the rider 'even if this no longer resulted in deportation for those who were deemed not to belong'. This, however, would be historically untrue. Precisely because of the rules about assimilation in the context of the Cold War, foreigners who 'got muddled up in politics,' as Madame Paulette put it, were subject to expulsion or internal exile, even if their numbers were far smaller than during the occupation, and the results nowhere near as devastating.[12]

Whether Jews at liberation regarded themselves as tourists, survivors or simply as French, there was no inevitability that France would seek to represent the period of occupation as one of suffering. Immigrant Jewish resisters – who by any standards had suffered abominably – represented themselves instead via images of strength and agency. Jewishness, they insisted, could not be encompassed in victimhood. Parallel stories of the fate of Jewish children during the occupation, discussed in the second chapter, reveal the dislocation between Jewish resister representations of survival against non-Jewish ones of Jewish powerlessness and mortality. It is in the context of Jewish agency that the implications for women of these stories of home and children can be understood. Where Jacqueline Mesnil-Amar stressed the number of Jewish children who had been murdered, *Droit et liberté* invoked tales of their capacity not only to survive, but to decide and act on their own survival tactics.[13] In terms of femininity, neither of these texts is unambiguous, but needs to be set within the wider picture of gender politics. At liberation, a relatively large number of women were newly elected to local or national political posts, in contrast to the pre-war era, when none had been elected and very few appointed to political office. For the vast majority of women in France, though, there was little room to concentrate on more public issues, and children represented both their traditional domain and one that would ensure the nation's future after a damaging war. In claiming children and the home as their terrain, though, *Droit et liberté* and Mesnil-Amar were doing more than underscoring the re-establishment of the home as a feminine ideal. They also countered Vichy's discursive constructions of the Jewish woman as not properly feminine. For Vichy's assertions that women's place was the home, and the educational efforts and propaganda that it developed to uphold this idea, were made only with respect to those it defined as French women. The Jewish home was transformed from a place of safety to one of fear, arrest and flight, as the minuscule number of Jews who survived in France and were able to remain in their homes during the occupation attests. Mesnil-Amar and *Droit et liberté*'s reconciliation with France at liberation involved a reassertion of their feminized humanity, a move that simultaneously broadened and closed down their, and other women's, fields of vision. Welcomed back into the realm of those who belonged, they were immediately confined to those patterns of belonging deemed appropriate to women.

These patterns were defined by maternalism, where still more contradictions emerge. The home was classified as women's ideal place, and the family as the supreme mechanism of assimilation, for here, stability and rootedness were held to reside. But the child's ability to assimilate was dependent on the prior assimilation of the mother. Anxiety about the ability of immigrant mothers to fulfil the assimilatory task allotted to them coalesced with general disquiet about immigration and the birth-rate. It was difficult for immigrant women with children to escape from the discursive paradox into which they were boxed. Encouraged by pro-natalist discourses to reproduce, they then found that their parenting skills were regarded with suspicion, and that their contribution to the French birth-rate derided as hiding the deficiency of 'French' births.[14] As far as Georges Mauco was concerned, while it was also the responsibility of mothers to Gallicize their offspring, their own lack of assimilatory potential as foreigners and as women would militate against their children's better assimilating interests. As we saw in chapter five, motherhood itself was regarded as both essential and as a condition that enforced restrictions on the child. At the same time, the family was idealized as the bedrock on which the nation would be reconstructed. The mother, romanticized and yet distrusted, was rarely able to escape the confines of her contradictory position. Moreover, in a situation that persists despite numerous legislative modifications, the immigrant status of the children of immigrants, even if they were entitled to French nationality, remained immanent.

This problem of the mother's influence on the child's access to language had wider social implications. Alfred Sauvy and Georges Mauco both reiterated that immigration was an invasion that was 'surely but silently' taking over France. It was, in fact, immigrants' incessant and incomprehensible chatter that they seemed to fear more than their quiescence. In 1945, an article never previously included in nationality legislation was introduced into the new Code de la Nationalité: applicants for naturalization would have to be able to speak French. Eighteen months after its introduction, ministers realized that, far from encouraging the population increase they so desired, the law was slowing down naturalizations, and therefore militating against assimilation. The tensions between the twin desires for assimilation and for a successful economy were becoming acute. The minister of population circulated officials in the field with a set of instructions to clarify the intentions of the law. It reminded them that, in light of national interests to increase both the number of children and the number of workers, the law's language requirements should not be applied too strictly. Priority cases in particular – miners, war and resistance veterans, industrial and agricultural workers, the small number of high-flying technologists, scientists, writers or artists, and fathers of three or more children – should still be naturalized and encouraged to change their foreign surnames despite any linguistic weaknesses they might exhibit.[15] But this compromise would inevitably lead to a downgrading of the unified nation represented in the ability of all its inhabitants to share what demographers and ministers believed to be the superior French language. No longer could the maxim 'if speaking signifies thinking in general, speaking French signifies thinking clearly' be seriously defended.[16] The problem was that many populationists continued to invoke an apparently immutable distinction between what they held to be the supremacy of rational Cartesian expression over foreign babble.

The one set of foreigners that the minister singled out as undesirable were those engaged in commerce. Is Mauco's hand visible here? His hatred of shopkeepers, based on his analysis of their trade as Jewish, was pronounced. Inasmuch as it was his proposals that were discussed and agreed by the Haut Comité Consultatif de la Population et de la Famille, and which went forward to become the foundations of the 1945 law (which was not discussed in parliament), his personal influence on the legislation was marked. The ministerial circular argued that in recent years, 'many hundreds of thousands' of foreign intermediaries and shopkeepers had taken up residence in France; from now on they were to be discouraged. It is quite feasible that shopkeepers themselves – who, along with farmers and middle-class employees, had joined collaborationist political organizations in higher proportions than other social groups – had agitated for this reminder.[17] But their interests cohered with more powerful ones represented in the new recourse to scientism and the structures established to sponsor it. It was scientific expertise, in psychology, econometrics and demography, as well as in industrial technology, that would triumph at liberation.

While this study has focused on a number of individuals, its overall aim has been to investigate the gendered and racialized structures of assimilationism. That said, the legislative framework of nationality and familialism constructed at liberation owed much to the expertise of a few strategic individuals whose interests keyed with the 'need' for immigrants and children. This need was most clearly expressed by Gaullists and, in this respect as in many others, they succeeded in putting their stamp authoritatively on post-war France. In the context of the gendering of assimilation, however, their success would have been less certain had it not corresponded so closely with the populationism supported elsewhere on the political spectrum. The HCCPF may have become a less significant body after de Gaulle's departure from government, but by that time, the main family and nationality legislation was already in place.

Liberation marked a crucial moment in the state's willingness to invest in science and technocracy as a new force for the future. Disasters of old, it was contended, could be planned out of existence, and potential hazards might be predicted and averted by a combination of social and natural sciences. The prevalence of planning in the realm of population was also related to both Vichy and Nazi Germany. France's victory over Nazi Germany in 1944–45 owed little to French scientific and technological advances. France's defeat in 1940 had been another matter. If anything had proved the necessity for France to develop along scientific lines, and that science extend beyond the traditional or natural sciences, it was believed to be the defeat. At the end of the war, everything would be subject to quantification, rational analysis and prediction. With a number of scientists installed as government advisers, the dynamic relation between the planners and the executive was established.[18]

Alfred Sauvy was one of the most important of these new advisers in the area of populationism. But his findings were based on dubious data. The arguments for population development that he developed with Robert Debré suggested that 'blood' was equivalent to 'nationality' and that permanent, recognizable characteristics accrued from it.[19] Likewise, despite the contradictions in Georges Mauco's propositions whereby Jews and other ethnic groups, or *ethnies*, were held to have permanent attributes and yet exist within an evolutionary system that could alter these characteristics, for him, the dangers of these *ethnies* were inherent. Herein lies a major problem of assimilationism. Its very articulation brings difference into being and its very project – to mould the characteristics of the non-French into those appropriate for France – becomes unviable if these characteristics are seen as bound to an immutable biology. Any assumed distinction between the biological and the cultural elements of racism in France becomes more blurred than is often thought.

The establishment and structure of the HCCPF and, concomitantly, of populationist legislation as a whole, was part of the move towards *planisme*. Regarded by communists (including the first minister of population, François Billoux) as anti-democratic, the Ministry of Population succeeded in drawing into its remit many areas of responsibility.[20] No longer was social security a matter for the Ministry of Labour, for example, or naturalization considered the responsibility of the Ministry of the Interior. The state, already more present under Vichy than its own rhetoric implied, broadened its scope at liberation. Sometimes this involved bringing private industry and banking under state authority, but it was also especially marked in the area of populationism. The scientific expertise collected within the membership of the HCCPF was hidebound by its interpretation of populationist needs in the most drastically restricted terms. Suspicion of the foreign, and fear of the feminine were convictions to which members gave full rein in the new Cold War demonization of the Soviet Union and parallel rehabilitation of Nazi Germany. All these elements informed their and other demographers' historicization of Vichy that permitted its implicit recuperation via its occlusion from demographic memory.

For all the government's apparent certainty about national identity at liberation, it remains unclear what being French really meant. So multifarious were France's inhabitants during the occupation (as they are today), that only the vaguest of gestures can be made towards a definition of national identity. In contrast, we can be rather more specific about how national identity was supposed to be formed, of what it consisted, and what elements were held to threaten it. Given the fear of the Jew and the feminine, examining these factors provides clues to assess and problematize national identity more clearly. Moreover, exploring Jewish women's lives during the occupation and discourses around Jewish femininity disrupts any universalizing tendencies to draw conclusions about women as a whole. The very condition of the modern Jew, defined by a refusal or inability of commitment to a singular identity, upsets the assimilationist project. Within this project, women were likewise regarded as incapable of alliance to a singular identity. The constructions of the foreignness of women, and the femininity of the foreign Jew cohered so as to undermine the assimilatory project at its inception. Who belonged to the category of the 'real French' was an issue that exercised many republican and anti-republican commentators at liberation. For all that the concept was illusory, this authenticity was explicitly expressed – most famously in de Gaulle's speech at the liberation of Paris on 25 August 1944 – and held to reside in a unique allegiance to the state. It was therefore incompatible with both Jewishness and femininity. This realization lay behind much twentieth-century antisemitism. Mauco's agony that Jews would not be properly French or historians' incredulity that they might not be properly Jewish, which were discussed in chapter two, both result from their differentiated failure to recognize the implicit meaning of this modern construction of Jewishness.

Individuals' ambivalence and lack of total identification with a nation are not very good rulers when it comes to measuring their commitment to improving conditions for themselves, others or their surroundings. On the contrary, it is those who confess to the deepest convictions about a nation and who seek its defence in the imposition of eternal divisions between one set of people and another who most endanger it. This is not a plea for tolerance, which is always dependent on its obverse, intolerance, nor is it one for enrichment. A state is not a fruit salad, and immigrants don't simply add flavour and variety, as some immigrant organizations purported at liberation.[21] In 1947, the Minister of Population noted that, when gauging the degree of an immigrant's assimilation, it was important for officials 'to investigate all the elements that permit one's appreciation of assimilation, most notably the applicant's behaviour during the occupation, which will reveal whether he has acquired the manners of thinking and reacting of the French population.'[22] It is unlikely that the minister intended any irony when he glossed over the sometimes ignoble 'manners' of parts of the French population with respect to the occupiers, and ignored that relatively large proportion of foreigners – anti-Nazi to the bone – who had been ardent resisters. This book has been about the impossibility of knowing precisely what 'behaving like a French person' meant. It suggests that, if the example of the 1940s has any pertinence, the attempt to impose ever more stringent definitions of national identity cannot be resolved. Reminding ourselves of these difficulties, and of the potential that fluid and multifarious identities might confer, have implications for our view of the past. In the context of mounting European disquiet about the 'foreign', they may also give us pause for thought in the future.

Notes

Chapter 1   Introduction: the long liberation

Place of publication is Paris unless otherwise stated.
1. AI, Madame Madeleine.
2. Julian Jackson, *France: The Dark Years 1940–1944* (Oxford: Oxford University Press, 2001), 132.
3. Louis-Ferdinand Céline, *L'Ecole des cadavres* (Denoël, 1938); Jean Giraudoux, *Pleins pouvoirs* (Gallimard, 1939); Pierre Drieu la Rochelle, *Gilles* (Gallimard, 1939).
4. AI, Madame Jeanne, on UFJ meeting *c*.1935, Belleville.
5. Philippe Burrin, *Living with Defeat: France under the German Occupation, 1940–1944* (1995; reprint, London: Arnold, 1996).
6. This ignores the *relève* scheme whereby some PoWs were exchanged for labourers in 1943, and the Jews shipped to occupied Poland, most of whom would not be returning.
7. Frédérique Boucher, 'Abriter vaille que vaille, se loger coûte que coûte', *Cahiers de l'IHTP* 5, 1989.
8. Kate Glazier, 'Liberation in Alsace – a Gendered Product', University of Sussex, 13–15 April 1994.
9. The emblematic case is described in Sarah Farmer, *Oradour. Arrêt sur mémoire* (Calmann-Lévy, 1994); see also Tzvetan Todorov, *Une Tragédie française: été 1944, scènes de guerre civile* (Seuil, 1994).
10. See Bonnie G. Smith, *The Gender of History: Men, Women, and Historical Practice* (1998; reprint, Cambridge, MA: Harvard University Press, 2000), 130–3, on the gendered historicization of big political events.
11. Miranda Pollard, *Reign of Virtue: Mobilizing Gender in Vichy France* (Chicago: University of Chicago Press, 1998).

Chapter 2   Narrating liberation

1. Renée Poznanski, *Etre Juif en France pendant la seconde guerre mondiale* (Hachette, 1994), 426.
2. AI, Madame Sarah recounts life in one of these orphanages.
3. Denis Peschanski, *Vichy 1940–1944: contrôle et exclusion* (Brussels: Complexe, 1997).

4. Bernard Laguerre, 'Les Dénaturalisés de Vichy 1940–1944', *Vingtième siècle*, no. 20 (October–December 1988).

5. Michael R. Marrus and Robert O. Paxton, *Vichy France and the Jews* (New York: Basic Books, 1981). On women in public office, see Linda L. Clark, *The Rise of Professional Women in France: Gender and Public Administration since 1830* (Cambridge: Cambridge University Press, 2000), chapter 8.

6. Mass killing was not on Vichy's agenda, but Vichy's actions helped the Nazis.

7. Denis Peschanski, Marie-Christine Hubert and Emmanuel Philippon, *Les Tsiganes en France 1939–1946* (CNRS, 1994), 147, 171.

8. Annette Wieviorka, *Déportation et génocide: entre la mémoire et l'oubli* (Plon, 1992); Serge Klarsfeld, *Vichy-Auschwitz: le rôle de Vichy dans la solution finale de la question juive en France*, 2 vols. (Fayard, 1985).

9. Miranda Pollard, *Reign of Virtue: Mobilizing Gender in Vichy France* (Chicago: University of Chicago Press, 1998).

10. W. D. Halls, *The Youth of Vichy France* (Oxford: Oxford University Press, 1981).

11. Gérard Noiriel, *Les Origines républicaines de Vichy* (Hachette, 1999).

12. Joshua Cole, *The Power of Large Numbers: Population, Politics, and Gender in Nineteenth-Century France* (Ithaca: Cornell University Press, 2000).

13. Vicki Caron, *Uneasy Asylum: France and the Jewish Refugee Crisis, 1933–1942* (Stanford: Stanford University Press, 1999).

14. Max Silverman, *Deconstructing the Nation: Immigration, Racism and Citizenship in Modern France* (London: Routledge, 1992), 19, 33.

15. *Ibid.*, 32.

16. Sharif Gemie, 'Docility, Zeal and Rebellion: Culture and Sub-Cultures in French Women's Teacher Training Colleges, *c.*1860–*c.*1910', *European History Quarterly* 24, no. 2 (April 1994); Jo Burr Margadant, *Madame le Professeur: Women Educators in the Third Republic* (Princeton: Princeton University Press, 1990).

17. Patrick Weil, *Qu'est-ce qu'un Français? Histoire de la nationalité française depuis la Révolution* (Bernard Grasset, 2002); Richard H. Weisberg, *Vichy Law and the Holocaust in France* (Amsterdam: Harwood Academic, 1996); Vincent Viet, *La France immigrée: construction d'une politique 1914–1997* (Fayard, 1998).

18. Jean Giraudoux, *Pleins pouvoirs* (Gallimard, 1939); Ralph Schor, *L'Opinion française et les étrangers en France 1919–1939* (La Sorbonne, 1985); Pierre-Jean Deschodt and François Huguenin, *La République xénophobe* (J.-C. Lattès, 2001).

19. Paul Smith, *Feminism and the Third Republic: Women's Political and Civil Rights in France, 1918–1945* (Oxford: Clarendon Press, 1996).

20. Maxime Blocq-Mascart, *Les Cahiers. Etudes pour une révolution française* (Organisation Civile et Militaire, June–September 1942).

21. Michael R. Marrus, *The Politics of Assimilation: A Study of the French Jewish Community at the Time of the Dreyfus Affair* (Oxford: Clarendon Press, 1971); Hannah Arendt, 'From the Dreyfus Affair to France Today', *Jewish Social Studies* 4, no. 3 (July 1942). Alternative interpretations are in Phyllis Albert Cohen, 'Israelite and Jew: How Did Nineteenth-Century French

Jews Understand Assimilation?', in *Assimilation and Community: The Jews in Nineteenth-Century Europe*, eds. Jonathan Frankel and Steven J. Zipperstein (Cambridge: Cambridge University Press, 1992); Phyllis Albert Cohen, 'L'Intégration et la persistance de l'ethnicité chez les Juifs dans la France moderne', in *Histoire politique des Juifs de France: entre universalisme et particularisme*, ed. Pierre Birnbaum (FNSP, 1990); Paula E. Hyman, *Gender and Assimilation: The Roles and Representation of Women* (Seattle: University of Washington Press, 1995); Marion A. Kaplan, *The Making of the Jewish Middle Class. Women, Family, and Identity in Imperial Germany* (New York: Oxford University Press, 1991); Robert S. Wistrich, 'Zionism and its Jewish "Assimilationist" Critics (1897–1948)', *Jewish Social Studies* 4, no. 2 (1998).

22. *Archives israélites*, vol. 1, 1840, 530. In Dominique Schnapper, *Juifs et Israélites* (Gallimard, 1980), 96.

23. Simon P. Sibelman, '*Le Renouvellement Juif*: French Jewry on the Eve of the Centenary of the Affaire Dreyfus', *French Cultural Studies* 3, no. 9 (October 1992), 264. Christine Piette, *Les Juifs de Paris (1808–1840): la marche vers l'assimilation* (Quebec: Presses de l'Université Laval, 1983), 173–4. Compare Marrus, *The Politics of Assimilation*; David H. Weinberg, *Les Juifs à Paris de 1933 à 1939* (Calmann-Lévy, 1974).

24. Pierre Birnbaum, *Un Mythe politique: 'la république juive'* (Fayard, 1988), chapter 2, 'Israélite, Juif ou Sioniste?'.

25. Adam Sutcliffe, *Judaism and Enlightenment* (Cambridge: Cambridge University Press, 2003).

26. Cohen, 'Israelite and Jew'. Alain Finkielkraut, *The Imaginary Jew* (1980; reprint, Lincoln: University of Nebraska Press, 1994), 66, suggests 'Juif' was abandoned *c*.1840.

27. Hyman, *Gender and Assimilation*.

28. Saul Friedländer, *Nazi Germany and the Jews*, vol. 1, *The Years of Persecution 1933–1939* (London: HarperCollins, 1997).

29. Norman Kleeblatt (ed.), *The Dreyfus Affair: Art, Truth, Justice* (Berkeley: University of California Press, 1987), 271, cited in Hyman, *Gender and Assimilation*, 23–4.

30. This list is not exhaustive, but all examples come from the author's interviews.

31. Sibelman, '*Le Renouvellement Juif*', 265.

32. Annette Wieviorka, *Ils étaient juifs, résistants, communistes* (Denoël, 1986), 329, attributes this to an instrumentalization by the PCF of Jewish resistance.

33. Some of the dozens of Jewish journals published after liberation are listed here. Dates refer to first issue: *Activité des organisations juives en France sous l'occupation*, 1947; *Actualités juives*, 1949; *Alyah. La montée vers la Palestine*, Marseilles, 1945; *Amandier fleuri. Cahiers de pensée et de vie juives*, Société de Publications Israélites Religieuses, 1949; *Ami*, OSE, 1949; *Ancien combattant juif*, Fédération des Associations d'Anciens Combattants et Volontaires Juifs, 1939; *Appel. Bulletin d'information de l'aide aux Israélites, victimes de la guerre*, 1947; *Arbeyter Vort*, Poale Tsion, 1950; *Arche de Noë*, Aumônerie de Jeunesse Juive, 1946; *Association Consistoriale Israélite de Paris*. 1945; *Au devant de la vie. Bulletin mensuel d'information des 'Jeunes de la LICA'*, 1945; *Bachaar*, Agudath

Israel; *Bleu et blanc. Cahiers mensuels du Mouvement de Jeunesse Sioniste à Nice*, Nice, 1945; *Bulletin de l'Union Séfaradite de France*, 1950; *Bulletin de nos communautés. Organe du judaïsme d'Alsace et de Lorraine*, Strasbourg, 1945; *Bulletin d'informations de l'union mondiale OSE*, 1957; *Bulletin du CDJC*, 1945; *Bulletin du Centre Israélite d'Information*, 1946; *Bulletin du Service Central des Déportés Israélites*, 1944; *Bulletin intérieur d'information du CRIF*, 1947; *Bulletin quotidien d'informations de l'Agence Télégraphique Juive*, 1945; *Cahiers sefardis*, Neuilly-sur-Seine, 1947; *Défense de l'homme*, 1949; *Défense*, 1948; *Droit de vivre*, LICA, 1930; *Droit et liberté*, UJRE, Paris/Marseilles, 1945; *Emouna-thenon. Bulletin de l'Union de la Jeunesse Juive Traditionaliste de France/Suisse*, 1948; *Folksgezunt*, OSE, 1950; *Gazette d'Israel*, Tunis, 1945; *Groupement des Artistes Juifs en France*, 1944; *Hamachkif-Observateur*, Parti Révisionniste, 1949; *Hillel*, Union Mondiale des Etudiants Juifs, 1946; *Images de la vie: l'actualité juive dans le monde*, 1950; *Information juive*, Comité Juif Algérien d'Etudes Sociales, Algiers, 1948; *Informations juives*, 1944; *Jeune combat*, Rassemble-ment de la Jeunesse Juive, 1944; *Kadimah*, Union Mondiale des Etudiants Juifs, 1947; *Lumières*, Eclaireurs Israélites de France, 1944; *Monde juif*, CDJC, 1946; *Mouvement National contre le Racisme. Bulletin d'information*, 1944; *Naïe presse*, UJRE, 1944; *Noar*, Association de la Jeunesse Juive, Casablanca, 1945; *Notre foi*, Agudath Israel; *Notre mouvement*; *notre parole*, 1945; *Notre voix*, 1944; *Nouvelle renaissance*, Union de la Résistance Juive, Toulouse, 1945; *Nou-velles*; *Nouvelles juives mondiales*, 1950; *OPEJ*, Œuvre de Protection des En-fants Juifs, 1946; *Parole. Hebdomadaire de l'actualité juive*, 1950; *Quand même*, Fédération des Sociétés Juives de France, 1944; *Quinzaine*, Centre Israélite d'Information/AIU, 1947; *Réforme*, 1945; *Renaissance*, Union de la Résistance Juive, Toulouse, 1944; *Réveil des jeunes*, Jeunesse Socialiste Juive 'Bund', 1944; *Revue d'histoire de la médecine hébraïque*, 1948; *Revue de la pensée juive*, 1949; *Riposte*, Mouvement Hébreu de Libération Nationale, 1947; *Samedi soir*, 1945; *Siona*, Mouvement des Jeunesses Sionistes, Grenoble, 1944; *Terre retrouvée*, Keren Kayemeth, 1944; *Unité*, Lyons, 1944; *Univers. Revue d'information et d'action pour l'union fraternelle entre tous les hommes*, Lille, 1946; *Unzer Shtimme*, Yidishn Sotsialistishn Medem Farband, 1935; *Unzer Veg*, 1945; *Vie juive*, Sec-tion Française du Congrès Juif Mondial, 1946; *Voix des camps*, Confédération Générale des Anciens Internés, des Déportés, des Prisonniers, des Victimes de l'Oppression et du Racisme, 1944; *Voix juive*, Tunis, 1944; *Yechouroun*, Mouvement Jeunesse Juive Traditionaliste, Lyons/Strasbourg, 1946; *Yedioth*, Bureau Européen de l'Agence Juive et de l'Organisation Sioniste Mondiale, 1945; *Yid un di velt*, 1959.

34. Zosa Szajkowski, *Jewish Education in France, 1789–1939*, Jewish Social Stud-ies Monograph Series, vol. 2, ed. Tobey B. Gitelle (New York: Columbia University Press, 1980); Lucien Lazare, *Rescue as Resistance: How Jewish Organizations Fought the Holocaust in France* (New York: Columbia University Press, 1996), 311.

35. On Jeunes Bâtisseurs de Belleville, see CDJC: DCXXIX-11-5; AI, Madame Sarah.

36. AI, Madame Rachel, Madame Hanna.

37. Lucien Lazare, *La Résistance juive: un combat pour la survie*, New edn (1987; reprint, Nadir, 2001), 236–8.

38. Consistoire Israélite de Paris, *La Communauté de Paris après la libération. Tableau d'ensemble* (1946), 60; AI, Madame Tony, Madame Rachele; Sylvie Lalario, 'Retours en France et réadaptations à la société française des femmes juives déportées' (Unpublished maîtrise, University of Paris VII, 1993).

39. Jacqueline Mesnil-Amar, *Ceux qui ne dormaient pas 1944–1946 (fragments de journal)* (Editions de Minuit, 1957).

40. *Ibid.*, 9.

41. Fabrice Virgili, *La France 'virile': des femmes tondues à la libération* (Payot, 2000).

42. On hiding as active, see Mark Roseman, *The Past in Hiding* (Harmondsworth: Allen Lane, 2000).

43. Mesnil-Amar, *Ceux qui ne dormaient pas*, 104.

44. *Ibid.*, 106.

45. Michel Bloit, *Moi, Maurice, bottier de Belleville* (L'Harmattan, 1993), 150–1.

46. Cf. AI, Madame Jeanne, chapter six below.

47. Jacqueline Mesnil-Amar, 'Ceux dont on ne parle pas', *Bulletin du Service Central des Déportés Israélites*, no. 4 (15 February 1945).

48. Mesnil-Amar, *Ceux qui ne dormaient pas*, 60–1.

49. *Combat* (19 March 1944).

50. Henri Frenay, *Bilan d'un effort* (Ministère des Prisonniers, Déportés et Réfugiés, 1945). AN: F[9] 3137.

51. Mesnil-Amar, *Ceux qui ne dormaient pas*, 60–1.

52. *Ibid.*, 119. Original emphasis.

53. *Ibid.*, 104.

54. David Knout, *Contribution à l'histoire de la résistance juive en France, 1940–1944* (Editions du Centre, 1947), 137, calls these '"Aryan" sounding' pseudonyms.

55. *Jeune combat* no. 22 (July 1944); *Notre voix* (September 1942).

56. Robert Gildea, *Marianne in Chains: In Search of the German Occupation 1940–45* (Basingstoke, Macmillan 2002), pp. 7–8.

57. Posters for the meeting: AN: 72AJ 1722 signed S. Commarmond; 72AJ 1721, 25 June 1945. See also Michael Kelly, 'Death at the Liberation: The Cultural Articulation of Death and Suffering in France 1944–47', *French Cultural Studies* 5, part 3, no. 15 (October 1994).

58. Jeanne Pakin, 'Les Enfants de nos déportés', *Droit et liberté*, 24 March 1945.

59. *Droit et liberté*, 27 April 1945. I am indebted to Sharon Muller and Judith Cohen of the United States Holocaust Memorial Museum for help in understanding the provenance of this photograph, and to NW Staatsarchiv Detmold: D 21 A, Zugang 95/88, no. 13.

60. E.g., *Point de vue*, 27 April 1945.

61. Kaunitz, in the Ruhrgebiet, was probably a stopping-off place for women concentration camp inmates being marched westwards by the SS. The photograph's original caption refers to a sub-camp liberated by the US 9th Army in April 1945 whose slave labourers manufactured munitions.

62. Radio speech, 8 May 1945 in Charles de Gaulle, *Discours et messages 1940–1946* (Berger-Levrault, 1946), 591.

63. *Bulletin du Service Central des Déportés Israélites*, no. 7 (15 May 1945). Original emphases.

64. Henry Rousso, 'The Historian, a Site of Memory', in *France at War: Vichy and the Historians*, ed. Sarah Fishman *et al.* (Oxford: Berg, 2000), 295; Henry Rousso, *La Hantise du passé: entretien avec Philippe Petit* (Textuel, 1998).

Chapter 3   Anticipating liberation: the gendered nation in print

1. Claude Bellanger, *Presse clandestine 1940–1944* (Armand Colin, 1961), 209. See National Union of Journalists, 'Hommage à la presse clandestine', 22–24 April 1943, in Françoise Bruneau, *Essai d'historique du mouvement né autour du journal clandestin 'Résistance'* (SEDES, 1951), 211. A Commission de la Presse and a Commission de l'Information et de la Propagande (based in Algiers) were established the same year. All three planned a post-liberation press based on resistance experience.
2. On compromises made by official publications, see Robert Pickering, 'The Implications of Legalised Publication', in *Collaboration in France: Politics and Culture During the Nazi Occupation, 1940–1944*, eds. Gerhard Hirschfeld and Patrick Marsh (Oxford: Berg, 1989). On the Propaganda Abteilung's inability to control publishing totally, see Rita Thalman, *La Mise au pas: idéologie et stratégie sécuritaire dans la France occupée* (Fayard, 1991), 179.
3. Pierre-André Taguieff, Grégoire Kauffmann and Michaël Lenoire (eds.), *L'Antisémitisme de plume 1940–1944: études et documents* (Berg International, 1999).
4. Joan Tumblety, 'Revenge of the Fascist Knights: Masculine Identities in *Je suis partout*, 1940–1944', *Modern and Contemporary France* 7, no. 1 (1999).
5. Pascal Fouché, *L'Edition française sous l'occupation 1940–1944* (Bibliothèque de Littérature française contemporaine, 1987), vol. 1, 266.
6. Claude Bellanger *et al.*, *Histoire générale de la presse française*, vol. 4, *De 1940 à 1958* (PUF, 1975).
7. E.g., Marie Granet, *Ceux de la résistance (1940–1944)* (Editions de Minuit, 1964).
8. At the Bibliothèque Nationale de France.
9. For an analysis based on economics and ownership, see J. W. Freiberg, *The French Press: Class, State, and Ideology* (New York: Praeger, 1981).
10. 'Entwicklung der Auflage der Pariser Tageszeitungen', in Gérard Walter, *La Vie à Paris sous l'occupation 1940–1944* (Armand Colin, 1960), 75; Eva Berg Gravensten, *La Quatrième Arme: la presse française sous l'occupation* (Den Franske Presse under den Anden Verdenskrig) (Lausanne: Esprit Ouvert, 2001).
11. Compare Reinhard Freiburg, 'Die Presse der Französischen Resistance. Technik und Positionen einer Untergrundpresse 1940–1944' (Ph.D. Dissertation, Freie Universität, 1962), 138 that *Combat* and *Défense de la France* were privately funded. See Laurent Douzou, *La Désobéissance: histoire d'un mouvement et d'un journal clandestins: Libération-sud (1940–1944)* (Odile Jacob, 1995), 70ff. on the bluff involved to launch the journal *Libération* when everything, including personnel, was in short supply.
12. Georges Piquet, *Presse clandestine: la vie secrète de la résistance*, Collection Révélations (Nathan, 1945); Marie Granet, *Défense de la France. Histoire d'un mouvement de résistance (1940–1944)* (PUF, 1960).

13. Jeanne List-Pakin, 'De certains aspects de la résistance', *Le Monde juif* 50, no. 152 (September–December 1994), 174; Paula Schwartz, 'La Repression des femmes communistes (1940–1944)', *Cahiers de l'IHTP*, 31, 27.

14. AI, Madame Fanny.

15. Bellanger *et al.*, *Histoire générale de la presse*, 4, 144ff.

16. David Diamant, *250 Combattants de la résistance témoignent: témoignages recueillis de septembre 1944 à décembre 1989* (L'Harmattan, 1991), 34.

17. Robert Salmon's 'insistence' on the 'necessity' of large-scale production of *Défense de la France* could only be made in the context of confidence, despite the dangers, of financing and directing such a large operation and having the requisite contacts within their social milieu. Granet, *Défense de la France*, 15ff.

18. Renée Rousseau, *Les Femmes rouges: chronique des années Vermeersch* (Albin Michel, 1983), 21.

19. Sarah Fishman, *We Will Wait: Wives of French Prisoners of War, 1940–1945* (New Haven: Yale University Press, 1991); Sarah Fishman and Geneviève Dermenjian, 'La Guerre des captives et les associations de femmes de prisonniers en France (1941–1945)', *Vingtième siècle*, no. 49 (January–March 1996).

20. Lucien Lazare, *Rescue as Resistance: How Jewish Organizations Fought the Holocaust in France* (New York: Columbia University Press, 1996), 26.

21. Michel Roblin, *Les Juifs de Paris. Démographie – economie – culture* (A. et J. Picard, 1952), 178.

22. E.g., *Jeunes Filles de France*, 31, February 1939.

23. *Combat*, December 1944, in Freiberg, *The French Press*, 1.

24. Bellanger *et al.*, *Histoire générale de la presse*, 4, 194.

25. See suggestions of posters and handouts in *Propagande féminine*, 1941; Dominique Veillon, *Le Franc-Tireur: un journal clandestin, un mouvement de résistance 1940–1944* (Flammarion, 1977), 164.

26. Olivier Wieviorka, *Une certaine idée de la résistance: défense de la France 1940–1949* (Seuil, 1995), 106–18.

27. Madeleine Vincent, conversation with author, 29 March 2001.

28. AI, Madame Hanna.

29. *Mères de France*, August 1941.

30. In H. R. Kedward, *Resistance in Vichy France: A Study of Ideas and Motivation in the Southern Zone 1940–1942* (Oxford: Oxford University Press, 1978), 277–8.

31. Jacques Adler, *The Jews of Paris and the Final Solution: Communal Response and Internal Conflicts, 1940–44* (Oxford: Oxford University Press, 1989), 188, 196–7; Renée Poznanski, *Etre Juif en France pendant la seconde guerre mondiale* (Hachette, 1994), 383–4.

32. AI, Madame Denise.

33. Marie-France Brive, 'L'Image des femmes à la libération', in *La Libération dans le Midi de la France*, ed. Rolande Trempé (Toulouse: Eché Editeur/UTM, 1986); see also Isabelle Pillet, 'Images de la femme dans la presse régionale, 1945–1975', *Revue du Nord* 63, no. 250 (1981).

34. Adé, 'A propos du Congrès de l'Union des Femmes Françaises', *Pour la vie* 1, no. 2 (October–December 1945), 72.

35. The authorities viewed such information as seditious. Yvonne Bruhat, *Les Femmes et la Révolution française 1789–1939* (Comité Mondial des Femmes contre la Guerre et le Fascisme, 1939), was on the 'Liste Otto' of banned publications.

36. *Libération* began international reports in January 1942. Douzou, *La Désobéissance*, 288.

37. Margaret L. Rossiter, 'Women in the French Underground Press', *Contemporary French Civilization* 4, no. 2 (1980); Joan Tumblety, 'Obedient Daughters of Marianne: Discourses of Patriotism and Maternity in the French Women's Resistance Press during the Second World War', *Women's History Notebooks* 4, no. 2 (summer 1997).

38. *L'Etincelle* (Parti Communiste de Boulogne-Billancourt), March 1942.

39. *L'Humanité de la femme*, December 1940; *Nous, les femmes*, no. 4, May 1941.

40. *Jeunes Filles de France*, no. spécial, March 1941.

41. Vichy France often presented itself as a tidy house. See the poster 'We must sweep out the Jews so that our house is clean', in Monique Lise Cohen and Valérie Ermosilla, *Les Juifs dans la résistance* (Toulouse: Bibliothèque Municipale, 1997), 20; and the contrasted crumbling and restored before and after Vichy houses in Miranda Pollard, *Reign of Virtue: Mobilizing Gender in Vichy France* (Chicago: University of Chicago Press, 1998), 3.

42. *Femmes de la Loire* (February–March 1944); *La Femme d'Eure et Loir* (25 August 1943); *La Femme comtoise*, no. 2 (1943).

43. Brive, 'L'Image des femmes', 397.

44. Dominique Veillon, 'The Resistance and Vichy', in *France at War: Vichy and the Historians*, ed. Sarah Fishman *et al.* (Oxford: Berg, 2000).

45. Nancy Miller, 'Changing the Subject: Authorship, Writing and the Reader', in *What Is an Author?*, eds. Maurice Biriotti and Nicola Miller (Manchester: Manchester University Press, 1993).

46. Tania Modleski, *Loving with a Vengeance: Mass-Produced Fantasies for Women* (London: Routledge, 1988); Jean Radford (ed.), *The Progress of Romance: The Politics of Popular Fiction* (London: Routledge and Kegan Paul, 1986). See also Margaret Homans, *Bearing the Word: Language and Female Experience in Nineteenth-Century Women's Writing* (Chicago: University of Chicago Press, 1986); Kate Flint, *The Woman Reader 1837–1914* (Oxford: Clarendon Press, 1993).

47. Jane Jenson, 'The Liberation and New Rights for French Women', in *Behind the Lines: Gender and the Two World Wars*, ed. Margaret Randolph Higonnet *et al.* (New Haven: Yale University Press, 1987); Jane Jenson, 'Représentations des rapports sociaux de sexe dans trois domaines politiques en France', in *Le Sexe des politiques sociales*, eds. Arlette Gautier and Jacqueline Heinen (Côté-femmes, 1993); Karen Offen, 'Body Politics: Women, Work and the Politics of Motherhood in France, 1920–1950', in *Maternity and Gender Policies: Women and the Rise of the European Welfare States, 1880s–1950s*, eds. Gisela Bock and Pat Thane (London: Routledge, 1991); Yvonne Knibiehler and Catherine Fouquet, *Histoire des mères du moyen-âge à nos jours* (Montalba, 1980); Hanna Diamond, 'Women's Experience during and after World War Two in the Toulouse Area 1939–1948.

Choices and Constraints' (unpublished D.Phil. thesis, University of Sussex, 1992).

48. *La Femme comtoise*, no. 2, 1943.

49. *Union des Femmes Françaises: bulletin d'information des comités*, no. 1 (1944).

50. Hilary Footitt, 'The First Women Députés: "Les 33 Glorieuses"?', in *The Liberation of France: Image and Event*, eds. H. R. Kedward and Nancy Wood (Oxford: Berg, 1995).

51. *Femmes à l'action* (Hyères). Sylvie Chaperon, *Les Années Beauvoir 1945–1970* (Fayard, 2000), 115ff, attributes the disappearance of women from politics to the cold war, and not to the gender politics already present in resister literature.

52. *Front national* (19 June 1945).

53. *Jeunes Filles de France*, no. spécial (March 1941); *La Voix des femmes du 18ème* (May 1943).

54. *Femmes françaises*, no. 1 (January 1944).

55. *Espérance* (Journal du Comité des Femmes de France de l'Allier) (March 1944).

56. *Jeunes Filles de France*, no. spécial (March 1941); *La Voix des femmes du 18ème* (May 1943).

57. C.f. Carolyn J. Dean, *The Self and its Pleasures: Bataille, Lacan, and the History of the Decentered Subject* (Ithaca: Cornell University Press, 1992), 71, on prostitution during the First World War; Luc Capdevila, *Les Bretons au lendemain de l'occupation: imaginaires et comportements d'une sortie de guerre (1944/1945)* (Presses Universitaires de Rennes, 1999), 409 on the uncertainty of national identity at liberation.

58. Alain Corbin, *Women for Hire: Prostitution and Sexuality in France after 1860* (Cambridge, MA: Harvard University Press, 1990).

59. Raymonde Machard, *Les Françaises. Ce qu'elles valent . . . Ce qu'elles veulent* (Flammarion, 1945), 83.

60. 'Mesures de barrage contre la prostitution' (26 June 1944). AN: F^{60} 895.

61. In Kedward, *Resistance in Vichy France*.

62. *La Lutte de classes*, no. 9 (February 1943).

63. *Femmes patriotes*, no. 1 (February 1944).

64. *Ibid*.

65. *Femmes françaises*, no. 1 (January 1944).

66. *L'Aurore* (December 1943).

67. Fabrice Virgili, *La France 'virile': des femmes tondues à la libération* (Payot, 2000).

68. *J'accuse*, no. 15 (15 June 1943).

69. Virgili, *France 'virile'*, 322–3.

70. *La Franc-Comtoise*, no. 1 (7 August 1942).

71. 'Français, femmes et mères françaises', in Gérard Silvain, *La Question juive en Europe 1933–1945* (J.-C. Lattès, 1985), 220.

72. *La Franc-Comtoise*, no. 1 (7 August 1942). Edition de Belfort et du Territoire. *Jeune combat*, no. 2 (5 July 1943) (Union de la Jeunesse Juive), also protested against the deportation of women and children.

73. *L'Humanité*, Edition spéciale féminine, no. 2 (2 October 1942).

74. *La Lutte de classes*, no. 9 (5 February 1943).

75. *La Voix des Dauphinoises* (July 1944).

76. Etienne Dejonghe, 'Les Départements du Nord et du Pas-de-Calais', in *De la défaite à Vichy*, vol. 2, *La France des années noires*, eds. Jean-Pierre Azéma and François Bédarida (Seuil, 1993), 503.

77. *La Voix de la femme juive* (15 August 1943).

78. *Appel des femmes* (Toulouse); *Espérance* (Allier); *Femmes à l'action* (Hyères, Var), all Zone sud.

79. *Notre voix* (15 March 1943).

80. *Notre voix* (15 February 1943).

81. Cf. the First World War figure of Joan of Arc, who symbolized women's connection to war, but was not used to prove their military equality to men. Margaret H. Darrow, *French Women and the First World War: War Stories of the Home Front* (Oxford: Berg, 2000), 58.

82. *L'Humanité de la femme*, December 1940; see Stéphane Courtois, *Le PCF dans la guerre: de Gaulle, la résistance, Staline ...* (Ramsay, 1980).

83. *Jeunes Filles de France*, no. 1 (October 1940).

84. *Jeunes Filles de France*, no. 12 (January 1942).

85. See also *La Clamartoise* (n.d.); *Femmes françaises*, no. 1 (January 1944); *Femmes patriotes*, no. 1 (February 1944); *L'Humanité*, Edition spéciale féminine, (March 1943); *Jeanne la Lorraine*, no. 3 (January 1944); *Cri des femmes* (1943); *Madelon du franc-tireur*, 1944; *La Voix des femmes de la Côte-d'Or* (January 1942).

86. *Action féminine: sud-ouest* (9 September 1944).

87. Abbé Robert Talmy, *Histoire du mouvement familial en France (1896–1939)* (UNCAF, 1962), vol. 1, 218–20.

88. Françoise Thébaud, *Quand nos grand-mères donnaient la vie: la maternité en France dans l'entre-deux-guerres* (Presses Universitaires de Lyon, 1986), 21.

89. Rousseau, *Les Femmes rouges*, 233n1; she also suggests that the PCF regarded Mothers' Day with contempt until the mid-1950s; Ania Francos, *Il était des femmes dans la résistance* (Stock, 1978), 122; Knibiehler and Fouquet, *Histoire des mères*, 319 ignores Vichy and suggests that the Fête des Mères only assumed importance after 1950. See Pollard, *Reign of Virtue*, 45–56; Francine Muel-Dreyfus, *Vichy et l'éternel féminin* (Seuil, 1996), 135–50.

90. Medals were available in bronze (five children), silver (eight) or gold (ten or more).

91. Karin Hausen, 'Mother's Day in the Weimar Republic', in *When Biology Became Destiny: Women in Weimar and Nazi Germany*, eds. Renate Bridenthal, Atina Grossmann and Marion Kaplan (New York: Monthly Review Press, 1984), 133–5; Pollard, *Reign of Virtue*, 48.

92. *Lutter et vaincre*, no. 2 (May 1941); *Jeunes Filles de France*, no. 6 (May 1941); *Femmes françaises* (May 1944).

93. *La Voix des femmes du XVIIIème* (May 1943). See also *Femmes de Provence* (May 1942).

94. The new certificate showed a man and a woman beneath a tree, children gambolling in the shade, mother sitting next to a cradle and father solicitous by her side, doves of peace fluttering in the branches. In Jacques Dupâquier, *Histoire de la population française*, vol. 4, *De 1914 à nos jours* (PUF, 1988), facing page 316.

95. *France-soir* (2 June 1945).

96. *Parisien libéré* (2 June 1945).

97. *La Croix* (5 June 1945).
98. Four of the women's medals were awarded posthumously.
99. *Population* 1, no. 1 (January–March 1946), 178; *Parisien libéré* (3 June 1945). See also 5 June 1945.
100. *Parisien libéré* (3 June 1945).
101. *La Croix* (4 June 1945).
102. *Front national* (7 June 1945).
103. *Maman*, no. 1 (3 June 1945).
104. *Ibid*. Original emphasis.
105. *Ibid*.
106. *Ibid*.
107. *L'Humanité* (5 June 1945). It had a 326,000 print run. Jean Mottin, *Histoire politique de la presse 1944–1949* (Bilans Hebdomadaires, 1949), 33.
108. *L'Humanité* (5 June 1945).
109. Nancy Scheper-Hughes, 'Maternal Thinking and the Politics of War', in *The Women and War Reader*, eds. Lois Ann Lorentzen and Jennifer Turpin (New York: New York University Press, 1998), 229.
110. Sara Ruddick, '"Woman of Peace". A Feminist Construction', in *The Women and War Reader*, 216, suggests that the mater dolorosa was a real person.
111. *Femmes françaises*, no. 2 (1 August 1945).
112. AN: F^9 3169.
113. Cécile Cerf in *Droit et liberté*, 15 June 1945.
114. *Ibid*.
115. *Témoignage chrétien* (1 June 1945) castigated members of the Catholic youth organization, JOC, for their violence. See also AN: F^9 3283; Jean-Pierre Vittori, *Eux, les S.T.O.* (Messidor, 1982).
116. Cf. Juliette Alex, *Trois compliments pour les tout petits à l'occasion de la Fête des Mères* (Macon: Robert Martin, 1945); Antoine Rigaud, *Deux poèmes pour la Fête des Mères* (Macon: Robert Martin, 1945); *La Journée des mères à la campagne* (Abbeville: Foyer Rural, 1946).
117. *Front national* (7 June 1945).
118. See emergency debate on suspected sabotage of paper supplies by former collaborators. JO (9 March 1945). Though note that much of this protest was initiated by Jacques Debû-Bridel, 'who doesn't know how to shut up': Lucie Aubrac, *La Résistance (naissance et organisation)* (Robert Lang, 1945), 111.
119. Pierre Gérard, 'La Presse à la libération dans la région de Toulouse', in *La Libération dans le Midi*, 344.
120. *Femmes françaises* (23 November 1944).
121. *Lucie Aubrac* (France: Claude Berri, 1998); Lucie Aubrac, *Ils partiront dans l'ivresse: Lyon, mai 43. Londres, février 44* (1984; reprint, Seuil, 1986).
122. Andrée Maire, Lucie Aubrac and Claire Vervin, *French Women Today* (New York: French Press and Information Service, 1944), 13.
123. Déclaration de Mme Lucie Aubrac (n.d.: 1944). AN: F^{22} 2052.
124. See also UFF, 'Les Femmes dans la résistance', in *Colloque tenu à l'initiative de l'Union des Femmes Françaises* (Editions du Rocher, 1977).
125. E.g. Elsa Triolet, *Les Amants d'Avignon* (Editions de Minuit, 1943).

126. A. Scheiber, *Un Fléau social. Le problème médico-policier de la prostitution* (Librairie de Médicis, 1946), 178.

127. *Front national* (25 July 1945); *Action féminine sud-ouest* (28 December 1944).

128. *Privilèges des femmes*, no. 3 (8 November 1945) and no. 7 (6 December 1945).

129. *Privilèges des femmes*, no. 3 (8 November 1945).

130. *Femmes françaises* (15 November 1945).

131. Lelong, one of the most important Paris couturiers, and Worth maintained their Paris houses throughout the occupation (unlike Schiaparelli and others). They were never purged. Dominique Veillon, *La Mode sous l'occupation. Débrouillardise et coquetterie dans la France en guerre (1939–1945)* (Payot, 1990), passim.

132. *Femmes françaises*, no. 6 (15 November 1945).

133. *Privilèges des femmes*, no. 1 (25 October 1945).

134. On the new turban fashion, see *Front national* (21 February 1945).

135. AI, Lucie Aubrac.

136. *Action* (13 July 1945); see also Lucie Aubrac, 'Témoignage: Le vote des femmes', *Matériaux pour l'histoire de notre temps*, no. 39–40 (July–December 1995), 64.

137. After the trial of Lyons Gestapo chief Klaus Barbie in 1987, doubt was cast on Lucie Aubrac's and her husband Raymond's activities as leaders of Libération-sud, especially by Gérard Chauvy, *Aubrac, Lyon 1943* (Albin Michel, 1997) and Barbie's lawyer, Jacques Vergès. See Jean-Marie Guillon, 'L'Affaire Aubrac, ou la dérive d'une certaine façon de faire l'histoire', *Modern and Contemporary France* 7, no. 1 (1999).

138. Aubrac, *Ils partiront dans l'ivresse*; Claire Gorrara, 'Reviewing Gender and the Resistance: The Case of Lucie Aubrac', in *The Liberation of France: Image and Event*, eds. H. R. Kedward and Nancy Wood (Oxford: Berg, 1995), 151.

139. Muel-Dreyfus, *Vichy et l'éternel féminin*, 75–6.

140. AN: F^9 3283.

141. Weill to Coigny, 16 November 1944. AN: F^9 3283.

142. Alexis Danan, *Maternité* (Albin Michel, 1936). Danan became editor of *Les Cahiers d'enfance* in 1953.

143. *Libération* (30 December 1944).

144. *Droit et liberté* (November 1944). The tale ends with Micou being given a scooter which she names 'Libération' and decorates with a tricolour ribbon.

145. AI, Madame Sara.

146. JO (30 July 1945), 1670.

147. Proposition de Résolution no. 327, JO (30 July 1945), 1669.

148. Commission consultative pour l'étude des questions familiales et de la protection des enfants de prisonniers, déportés et réfugiés, 25 October 1944. AN F^9 3184.

149. *Bulletin du Service Central des Déportés Israélites*, no. 7 (15 May 1945).

150. *Libération* (30 December 1944).

151. *Bulletin du Service Central des Déportés Israélites*, no. 3 (15 January 1945).

152. *La Terre retrouvée* (1 February 1945).

153. *L'Effort de l'immigration dans da reconstruction française* (CADI, 1946), 15.

154. *Unis* (24 March 1945).

155. *Unis* (2 June 1946).
156. *Droit et liberté* (7 February 1945).
157. See also Parti Socialiste SFIO, *Projet d'un statut des étrangers en France* (Fédération des Socialistes Etrangers de France, July 1945); Louis Petit, *Le Problème des immigrés dans la france libérée* (CADI, *c*.1945).
158. *Droit et liberté* (10 and 27 April 1945). *Jeune combat* (10 December 1944); Eric Schieber, *Un An de reconstruction juive en France* (ORT, 1946), 6; the Bundist Yidisher arbeter- en folks-froy-organisatsye (Organization of Jewish Working Women and Women of the People) in *Unzer Shtimme* (1 and 30 May 1945).
159. FDIF, *Femmes du monde entier. 5e anniversaire* (FDIF, 1950), 5.
160. *Jeunes Filles de France*, no. 1 (October 1940).
161. *MLN: bulletin intérieur du Mouvement de Libération Nationale*, no. 37 (January–February 1947).
162. Cf. 'Faire la guerre – abattre le fascisme: appel aux Françaises' (n.d., 1945) signed by numerous wives of ministers, women *députés*, women in the Comité Parisien de la Libération, CGT, Ceux de la Résistance, FLN, MRP, UFF and others. AN: F^1 3241.
163. Correspondence February–May 1947. CAC: 860269 1.
164. UFF, 'Deux ans d'activité au service de la famille française du premier Congrès national juin 1945 aux Journées Nationales de l'Union des Femmes Françaises', in *2e Congrès national* (UFF, 1947), 30–2. See paper sellers in the UFF film, *Union des femmes françaises*, France, 1947.
165. Perhaps by unilateral inclusion of all resisters. Denise Karnaouch-Poindron, 'L'UJFF et L'UFF: Réflexions sur leur histoire', *Pénélope*, no. 11 (Autumn 1984), 108.
166. *Femmes françaises* (June 1949). The UFF film emphasized that *Femmes françaises* was the magazine 'which struggles for the happy family'.
167. Raymond Aubrac funded *Privilèges*. AI, Lucie Aubrac.
168. See reports on care staff in deportee and PoW reception centres suspected of sexual relations with clients. AN: F^9 3247.

Chapter 4   Limiting liberation: 'the French for France'

1. Sauvy's assertions are difficult to verify since his war-time papers remain unavailable to researchers.
2. Bernard Mélamède, 'Comité intercommissarial pour la préservation et le développement de la population', 21 December 1943. CAC: 860269 1.
3. Parti Socialiste SFIO, *Projet d'un statut des étrangers en France* (Fédération des Socialistes Etrangers de France, July 1945), 12 and passim; André Graetz, 'Manque d'hommes', *Esprit* (December 1944); Jacquier-Bruère, *Refaire la France: l'effort d'une génération* (Plon, 1945), 8ff.
4. See, for example, the many publications of the ANCD; Joshua Cole, *The Power of Large Numbers: Population, Politics, and Gender in Nineteenth-Century France* (Ithaca: Cornell University Press, 2000).
5. Alain Girard and Jean Stoetzel, *Français et immigrés. L'attitude française. L'adaptation des Italiens et des Polonais*, Travaux et Documents, no. 19 (INED, 1953), 22.

6. Barbara Vormeier, 'La République française et les réfugiés et immigrés d'Europe Centrale: accueil, séjour, droit d'asile (1919–1939)', in *De l'éxil à la résistance: réfugiés et immigrés d'Europe centrale en France 1933–45*, eds. Karl Bartosek, René Gallissot and Denis Peschanski (Arcantère, 1989); Vincent Viet, *La France immigrée: construction d'une politique 1914–1997* (Fayard, 1998), 36.

7. Vicki Caron, *Uneasy Asylum: France and the Jewish Refugee Crisis, 1933–1942* (Stanford: Stanford University Press, 1999); Geneviève Dreyfus-Armand, *L'Exil des républicains espagnols en France: de la guerre civile à la mort de Franco* (Albin Michel, 1999); Pierre Milza and Denis Peschanski (eds.), *Exils et migration: Italiens et Espagnols en France, 1938–1946* (Harmattan, 1994).

8. Gisela Bock and Pat Thane (eds.), *Maternity and Gender Policies: Women and the Rise of European Welfare States 1880s–1950s* (London: Routledge, 1991); *French Historical Studies*, vol. 19, no. 3 (Spring 1996); Michael S. Teitelbaum and Jay Winter, *The Fear of Population Decline* (Orlando: Academic Press, 1985); Hervé le Bras, *Marianne et les lapins: l'obsession démographique* (O. Orban, 1991).

9. E.g. Alfred Sauvy, *Richesse et population: peuplement optimum, eugénisme et sélection, bien-être et répartition*, 2nd edn (1943; reprint, Payot, 1944), 229; Jean-François Gravier, *Paris et le désert français. Décentralisation équipement population* (Le Portulan, 1947), 83. Robert Debré, 'Rapport sur la création et l'organisation d'un Ministère de la population'. CAC: 860269 8; Graetz, 'Manque', 67; INED, 'Rapport au gouvernement: l'effet des mesures de politique démographique sur l'évolution de la fécondité', in *Natalité et Politique Démographique*, Travaux et Documents, no. 76 (PUF, 1976), 6.

10. Gravier, *Paris et le désert français*, 93–4.

11. Charles de Gaulle, 'Vers le renouveau national' (2 March 1945); 'Le lendemain de la victoire' (24 May 1945), in Charles de Gaulle, *Discours de guerre*, vol. 3, *Mai 1944–Septembre 1945* (Egloff, 1945), 169–86, 223–30.

12. Charles de Gaulle, *Mémoires de guerre*, vol. 3, *Le Salut* (1959; reprint, Geneva: Famot, 1981), 456.

13. *Libération* (25 May 1945).

14. Parti Socialiste, *Projet d'un statut*, 5.

15. *Population* 1, no. 1 (January–March 1946), 171, suggested just this, before explaining that before the Second World War, foreign workers were not allowed to work in areas such as medicine, the law, teaching, journalism, and could not change their occupation without authorization.

16. Alfred Sauvy, 'Besoins et possibilités de l'immigration française', *Population* 5, no. 2 (April–June 1950), 210; Alfred Sauvy, 'Evaluation des besoins de l'immigration française', *Population* 1, no. 1 (January–March 1946).

17. Georges Mauco, 'Le Code de la Famille', undated typescript. MP: 6.

18. François Billoux, *Quand nous étions ministres* (Editions Sociales, 1972), 127.

19. François Billoux, *La Renaissance française et la santé publique. Discours prononcé à l'Assemblée Consultative Provisoire* (PCF, 12 March 1945) (no pagination); Robert Prigent, 'L'Organisation du Ministère de la Santé Publique et de la Population', *Pour la vie*, no. 8 (February 1947), 48.

20. Andrès Horacio Reggiani, 'Alexis Carrel, the Unknown: Eugenics and Population Research under Vichy', *French Historical Studies* 25, no. 2 (2002); On other research organizations, see Jackie Clarke, 'Imagined Productive

Communities: Industrial Rationalisation and Cultural Crisis in 1930s France', *Modern and Contemporary France* 8, no. 3 (2000).

21. April 1945, in FFEPH, *Bulletin intérieur*, no. 2, 13. In Jacques Dupâquier, *Histoire de la population française*, vol. 4, *De 1914 à nos jours* (PUF, 1988), 23. Compare Robert Debré and Alfred Sauvy, *Des Français pour la France (le problème de la population)* (Gallimard, 1946), 237.

22. Decree of 19 January 1946.

23. The HCCPF was set up by *décret*, 4 March 1945, the Secrétariat by *ordonnance*, 4 April 1945, the Comité Interministériel by *décret*, 12 April 1945; *Espoir*, no. 21 (December 1977); Robert Debré, *L'honneur de vivre: témoignage* (Hermann & Stock, 1974), 399.

24. De Gaulle, *Le Salut*, 457.

25. See Paul-André Rosental, *L'Intelligence demographique: sciences et politiques des populations en France (1930–1960)* (Odile Jacob, 2003), a work published too recently to have been considered here.

26. Daladier to Comité Exécutif, Parti Radical, 4 June 1939 in Abbé Robert Talmy, *Histoire du mouvement familial en France (1896–1939)*, vol. 2 (UNCAF, 1962), 234; *Le Code de la Famille*, 2 December 1944. In BN.

27. Jacques Doublet, 'Le Code de la Famille: le Haut Comité de la Population et le décret-loi du 29 juillet relatif à la famille et à la natalité françaises', *Revue politique et parlementaire* (10 November 1939), 211.

28. Preamble to constitution of 27 October 1946 in Jacques Doublet, 'La Première Législation de la IVe République et la législation démographique', *Population* 6, no. 3 (July–September 1951), 398.

29. Robert Prigent, 'De la LOC Zone Occupée au Commissariat Général à la Famille en 1945', in *L'Action familiale ouvrière et la politique de Vichy*, ed. Groupement pour la Recherche sur les Mouvements Familiaux, Cahiers du GRMF (Forêt-sur-Marque: GRMF, 1985), 3, 86.

30. Louise Chevalley to Ministre de la Population, 21 September 1946. CAC: 860269 2.

31. Gravier, *Paris et le désert français*, 81.

32. Jean-François Gravier, *Etat, peuple, nation* (Vichy: Secrétariat Général à l'Information et à la Propagande, 1942).

33. Maxime Blocq, *Illusions capitalistes* (Les Œuvres Françaises, 1936).

34. Maxime Blocq-Mascart, *Les Cahiers. Etudes pour une révolution française* (Organisation Civile et Militaire, June–September 1942). See also Germaine Willard and Roger Bourderon, *Histoire de la France contemporaine, 1940–1947*, vol. 6 (Editions Sociales, 1980), 186; Gérard Silvain, *La Question juive en Europe 1933–1945* (J.-C. Lattès, 1985), 210–11; David Knout, *Contribution à l'histoire de la résistance juive en France, 1940–1944* (Editions du Centre, 1947), 194; Arthur Calmette, *L'O.C.M. Organisation civile et militaire: histoire d'un mouvement de résistance de 1940 à 1946* (PUF, 1961), 54n2; *Nouveau dictionnaire national des contemporains* (1964), 100.

35. Cf. Bureau Central de Renseignements et d'Action in London. Report, 28 January 1943 in Renée Poznanski, 'Reflections on Jewish Resistance and Jewish Resistants in France', *Jewish Social Studies* 2, no. 1 (1995), 138.

36. Blocq-Mascart, *Les Cahiers*, 125–87.

37. Fernand Boverat, *Patriotisme et paternité* (Bernard Grasset, 1913), 13–14.

38. Fernand Boverat, *Comment nous vaincrons la dénatalité?* (ANCD, 1938); Fernand Boverat, *Le Massacre des innocents* (ANCD, 1939); Fernand Boverat, *La Crise des naissances* (ANCD, 1932), and many others.

39. Fernand Boverat, *Une Doctrine de natalité* (FFEPH, 1943).

40. Fernand Boverat, *Niveau d'existence et charges de famille* (FFEPH, 1944); Fernand Boverat, *Le Premier Devoir: faire vivre la France. Enseignement nataliste et familial dans les Chantiers de la Jeunesse* (Lyons: ANCD, 1943); Fernand Boverat, *Le Routier et le problème de la natalité. Etude sociale de Fernand Boverat suivie d'une série de sujets proposés aux clans de routiers pour leurs cercles d'études et enquêtes* (Vichy: Eclaireurs de France, 1943).

41. Boverat to Mauco, 24 March 1945. CAC: 860269 2.

42. *Revue de l'Alliance Nationale contre la Dépopulation*, no. 368 (June–December 1944), 38.

43. The archives show how he bombarded the HCCPF secretary at every conceivable opportunity.

44. Son Michel became adviser and later prime minister to de Gaulle; grandson Jean-Louis was minister of the interior in the 1990s.

45. Debré, *L'Honneur de vivre*, 21–8.

46. *Ibid.*, 25; Robert Debré, *Ce que je crois* (Bernard Grasset, 1976), 22; Mauco to Joxe, 26 June 1945. CAC: 860269 8.

47. Renée Poznanski, *Les Juifs en France pendant la seconde guerre mondiale* (1994; reprint, Hachette, 1997), 372; Robert Debré, 'La Résistance médicale', in *La résistance intellectuelle*, ed. Jacques Debû-Bridel (Julliard, 1970), 191; Bruno Halioua, *Blouses blanches, étoiles jaunes. L'exclusion des médecins juifs en France sous l'occupation* (Liana Levi, 2000), 198ff.

48. Debré, *L'Honneur de vivre*, 221ff; Jacques Debû-Bridel (ed.), *La Résistance intellectuelle* (Julliard, 1970), 186–201.

49. Debré and Sauvy, *Des Français pour la France*; *Population* 1, no. 1 (January–March 1946).

50. Auguste Isaac, *La Plus Grande Famille, Association de Pères et Mères de Famille de Cinq Enfants au Moins: discours au déjeuner mensuel de l'Union du Commerce et de l'Industrie pour la Défense sociale* (La Plus Grande Famille, 1917).

51. *Pages sociales*, no. 17 (April–May 1946), 15; S. Collet, 'L'Action sociale des associations familiales: l'aide familiale de "La Plus Grande Famille" ', *Pour la vie* 1, no. 2 (October–December 1945). CAC: 860269 1. S. Collet, 'Associations féminines et associations familiales', *Pour la vie*, no. 13 (July–August 1947); Mme Collet, 'La Prolétarisation des classes moyennes en France', in *Niveau de vie des familles: congrès mondial de la famille et de la population*, 48–51, Problèmes familiaux dans le monde (UNAF, 1948).

52. Charles Flory, 'Le Second "Pour la vie" ', *Pour la vie*, no. 1 (July 1945).

53. Mme Olry Collet, 'Note sur l'immigration', May 1945. CAC: 860269 1.

54. Collet to Mauco, 10 September 1946. CAC: 860269 2. The delegation consisted of Prigent, Sauvy, Mauco, Boverat, Monsaingeon, Debré, Landry and Doublet. Jeanne Delabit, Simone Collet and Maxime Blocq-Mascart were excluded.

55. Michel Dreyfus, *Histoire de la CGT* (Brussels: Editions Complexe, 1995), 239–40. At the 1936 meeting which elected her to the position of *assesseur*,

only forty-two delegates among the 15,000 present representing 3,500 organizations were women. Delabit defended the rights of women workers in particular. See *Echo des Tabacs* (July–August 1937).

56. FDIF, 'Compte Rendu des travaux du Congrès', in *Congrès International des Femmes* (FDIF, 1946), xxi.

57. *Etudes syndicales* (FNSP, 1965), vol. 3, *La CGT-FO*, by Gérard Adam, 58–61. Four other members achieved similar longevity. Despite this unusually public and lengthy career, it is still very difficult to find much information about Jeanne Delabit.

58. Miranda Pollard, *Reign of Virtue: Mobilizing Gender in Vichy France* (Chicago: Chicago University Press, 1998), 113–4.

59. Jacques Doublet, 'Le Front du travail allemand' (Doctoral thesis, Faculté de Droit, Paris, 1937).

60. Alain Drouard, *Une Inconnue des sciences sociales: la Fondation Alexis Carrel 1941–1945* (La Maison des Sciences de l'Homme, 1992), 432.

61. Undated note. CAC: 860269 8.

62. CAC: 860269 8.

63. Adolphe Landry *et al.*, *Traité de démographie* (Payot, 1945); Adolphe Landry, *La Démographie française* (PUF, 1941); Adolphe Landry, *La Révolution démographique* (Bordeaux, 1934); Adolphe Landry, *La Démographie de l'ancien Paris. Extrait du Journal de la Société de Statistique de Paris, février 1935* (Editions Berger-Levrault, 1935).

64. Minutes, HCCPF, 18 May 1945. CAC: 860269 1; Loi no. 46-1835, JO 23 August 1946, 7,350

65. Jules Jeanneney, *Journal politique, septembre 1939–juillet 1942*, ed. Jean-Noël Jeanneney (Armand Colin, 1972), 427n171. The Comité National was formed of a number of Jewish organizations with some prominent non-Jewish support. See Bernard Schönberg, 'L'Aide aux réfugiés allemands', *Revue juive de Genève* 2, no. 5 (February 1934).

66. Alfred Sauvy, 'Adolphe Landry', *Population* 11, no. 4 (October–December 1956).

67. Michel Louis Lévy, *Alfred Sauvy: compagnon du siècle* (La Manufacture, 1990), 54. This work avoids the issue of whether Sauvy collaborated or not.

68. Alfred Sauvy, *Richesse et population* (Payot, 1943).

69. INED, *Les Travaux du Haut Comité Consultatif de la Population et de la Famille*, Travaux et Documents no. 1 (PUF, 1946), 11.

70. 'Allocution', in *Remise solennelle du Grand Prix de l'Académie des Sciences Morales et Politiques à M. Alfred Sauvy* (Palais de l'Institut, 1984); Alfred Sauvy, *La Vie en plus: souvenirs* (Calmann-Lévy, 1981).

71. Drouard, *La Fondation Alexis Carrel*, 177; Alain Drouard, 'Les Trois Ages de la Fondation Française pour l'Etude des Problèmes Humains', *Population* 38, no. 6 (November–December 1983); Laurent Thévenot, 'La Politique des statistiques: les origines sociales des enquêtes de mobilité sociale', *Annales: economies sociétés civilisations* 45, no. 6 (November–December 1990).

72. Among many examples of this, see the large IQ study started in 1943, quoted in Jean Sutter, *L'Eugénique. Problèmes – méthodes – résultats*, Travaux et Documents, no. 11 (INED, 1950), 171. See also *Population* 1, no. 4 (October–December 1946), 762–3.

73. Dupâquier, *Histoire de la population française*, 4, 24.
74. Alfred Sauvy, 'Introduction', *Population* 1, no. 1 (January–March 1946); Andrès Horacio Reggiani, 'Procreating France: The Politics of Demography, 1919–1945', *French Historical Studies* 19, no. 3 (spring 1996).
75. *Pages sociales*, 17 (April–May 1946).
76. Preface to Talmy, *Histoire du mouvement familial en France*, vol. 1, 5.
77. Maurice Monsaingeon, 'La Famille, être complet', *Pour la vie*, no. 1 (July 1945); Maurice Monsaingeon, 'Vie familiale, sécurité et responsabilité: la sécurité et la responsabilité dans la vie familiale', in *Economie, psychologie dans la vie familiale: journées familiales internationales*, 11–18, Problèmes familiaux dans le monde (Union Internationale des Organismes Familiaux, 1950).
78. Maurice Monsaingeon, *La Vraie Conception de la famille: sa place dans la société*, Collection Science et Charité, no. IX (Secrétariat Catholique des C Euvres Charitables et Sociales d'Hygiène et de Santé, May 1944), 23; Michèle Bordeaux, *La Victoire de la famille dans la France défaite: Vichy 1940–1944* (Flammarion, 2002), 281.
79. Maurice Monsaingeon, *Immigration et peuplement* (Centre National de Coordination des Activités Familiales, 1945), 2.
80. *Témoignage chrétien* (9 February 1945).
81. For arguments in favour of the family vote, see Debré and Sauvy, *Des Français pour la France*, 254; Sauvy, *Richesse et population*, 300; Pierre July, Olivier de Sesmaisons and Hélène de Suzannet, *Comment le Parti Républicain de la Liberté défend la famille* (PRL, 1946); André Toulemon, *Dialogue sur le suffrage familial. Suffrage universel intégral. Principes et objections* (ANCD, 1945). For counterviews, see M. Alvergnat, *Organisations familiales dans le monde: congrès mondial de la famille et de la population*, vol. 2, 85, Problèmes familiaux dans le monde (UNAF, 1947); Louise Weiss in *Aurore*, 26 (December 1944).
82. Article 21, Projet de Constitution, 30 January 1944 would allow two votes to fathers of more than three children.
83. Georges Mauco, *Les Etrangers en France: leur rôle dans l'activité économique* (Armand Colin, 1932).
84. Minutes, HCCPF, 30 April 1945. CAC: 860269 1.
85. Robert Debré, 'Rapport sur la création et l'organisation d'un Ministère de la population', 1945. CAC: 860269 8.
86. Bernard Mélamède, 'Note sommaire sur la situation démographique en France', 21 December 1943. AN: F^{60} 895.
87. See also Debré and Sauvy, *Des Français pour la France* analysed more fully below. Compare the stateless *peregrini sine civitate* of Roman Law. Marc Vichniac, *Le Statut international des apatrides* (Recueil Sirey, 1934), 7–8.
88. Patrick Weil, *Qu'est-ce qu'un Français? Histoire de la nationalité française depuis la Révolution* (Bernard Grasset, 2002).
89. INED, *Travaux du Haut Comité*, 46, 21.
90. *Population* 1, no. 1 (January–March 1946), 177–8.
91. Décret-loi 46-1835, 22 August 1946.
92. *Bulletin du Centre Israélite d'Information*, no. 3 (May 1946).
93. 'Circulaire du 23 avril 1947 relative à l'instruction des demandes de naturalisation', in *Population* 2, no. 3 (April–June 1947), 462.

94. J.-L. Mottier and Maurice Caillez, *Guide pratique des étrangers en France* (Librairie du Journal des Notaires et des Avocats, 1948), 42.

95. JO (3 November 1945), 7,194; JO (5 November 1945), 7,297.

96. CAC: 860269 8.

97. Debré and Sauvy, *Des Français pour la France*, 112.

98. *Ibid.*, 124.

99. *Ibid.*, 126.

100. *Ibid.*, 90.

101. *Ibid.*, 230. Cited in Patrick Weil, 'Racisme et discrimination dans la politique française de l'immigration 1938–1945/1954–1995', *Vingtième siècle*, no. 47 (July–September 1995), 88. See also Hervé Le Bras, *Le Sol et le sang* (La Tour d'Aigues: Editions de l'Aube, 1994).

102. Debré and Sauvy, *Des Français pour la France*, 230.

103. *Ibid.*, 231. Cf. similar late-nineteenth-century fears: Chambre des Députés, 16 March 1889, 595a, in Rogers Brubaker, *Citizenship and Nationhood in France and Germany* (Cambridge, MA: Harvard University Press, 1992), 105.

104. Debré and Sauvy, *Des Français pour la France*, 228.

105. Some members of the HCCPF believed that Germans were less 'desirable Nordics', though they still maintained that there were recognisable Nordic qualities. Minutes, 4 July 1945. CAC: 860269 1.

106. Georges Mauco, 'Projet pour un plan de l'immigration étrangère', April 1945. CAC: 860269 1.

107. 'Projet d'instructions définissant les grandes lignes de la politique d'immigration', July 1945. AN: F^1A 3345.

108. Louis Chevalier, 'Principaux aspects du problème de l'immigration', in *Documents sur l'immigration*, ed. Louis Chevalier *et al.*, Travaux et Documents, no. 2 (INED, 1947), 13–14.

109. Mauco, 'Projet pour un plan'. CAC: 860269 1.

110. Debré and Sauvy, *Des Français pour la France*, 230.

111. *Le Monde* (17 October 1945).

112. *Action* (2 November 1945).

113. Philippe Pétain, *Discours aux Français: 17 juin 1940–20 août 1944*, ed. Jean-Claude Barbas (Albin Michel, 1989), 60.

114. Compare the post-war development of the nuclear programme as nationalist enterprise. Gabrielle Hecht, *The Radiance of France: Nuclear Power and National Identity after World War II* (Cambridge, MA: MIT Press, 1998).

115. Boverat, *Patriotisme et paternité*.

116. Boverat, *Massacre des innocents*, 17.

117. *Ibid.*, 11.

118. Alfred Sauvy, 'La Prévision économique et l'organisation du travail', *Bulletin du Comité National de l'Organisation Française* 13, no. 2 (November 1938), 55–6.

119. Debré, *L'Honneur de vivre*, 398.

120. Adolphe Landry, *La Démographie française*, 2nd edn (1941; reprint, ANCD, 1942), 72.

121. Sauvy, *Richesse et population*, 314, 299 and passim.

122. *Ibid.*, 298.

123. The second edition was published in 1944.

124. J. E. Roy, *L'Avortement, fléau national. Causes – conséquences – remèdes* (1943; reprint, Jouve, 1944); Simone de Beauvoir, *Le Deuxième Sexe* (1949; reprint, Gallimard, 1979), 137.

125. *L'Avortement et les moyens anticonceptionnels*, La Famille d'aujourd'hui. Sa formation. Son développement, no. 4 (UNCAF, 1947), 37.

126. Paul Vincent, 'Statistique internationale du mouvement des naissances', *Population* 1, no. 2 (April–May 1946), 346–8; Adolphe Landry, 'La Politique sociale et démographique', *Petit congrès, Parti Républicain radical et radical-socialiste* (December 1944), 16.

127. Sauvy, *Richesse et population*, 297.

128. Debré and Sauvy, *Des Français pour la France*, 182–3.

129. Pollard, *Reign of Virtue*, 174–94. Francine Muel-Dreyfus, *Vichy et l'éternel féminin* (Seuil, 1996), 326, mistakenly attributes Vichy with prosecuting only one man for abortion.

130. Statistics for 1939–45 are not available.

131. Statistics of births, deaths and marriages; mid-year population estimates; and deaths of infants under one year old in B. R. Mitchell, *International Historical Statistics: Europe 1750–1988* (New York: Stockton Press, 1992), 100, 83–4, 119.

132. Doublet, 'Code de la Famille', 222.

133. Jacques Doublet, 'Politique démographique en Autriche', *Population* 2, no. 2 (April–June 1947), 298–9.

134. *Ibid.*, 301.

135. *Ibid.*, 298. See Charles A. Gulick, *Austria from Habsburg to Hitler*, vol. 2, *Fascism's Subversion of Democracy* (1948; reprint, Berkeley: California University Press, 1980), 1,403ff.

136. *Wien im Aufbau: Wohlfahrtswesen*, 9–10, in *ibid.*, 1,546. See also Doris Byer, 'Sexualität, Macht, Wohlfahrt: Zeitgemässe Erinnerungen an das "Rote Wien"', *Zeitgeschichte* 14, no. 11–12 (1987); Helmut Gruber, 'Sexuality in "Red Vienna": Socialist Party Concepts and Programs of Working-Class Life', *International Labor and Working-Class History* 31 (1987).

137. Ministère de la Justice to Président du Conseil, 12 June 1952, 3 October 1952. CAC: 860269 1.

138. E.g. Hervé Le Bras, *Les Trois France* (Odile Jacob, 1986), 45.

139. Alfred Sauvy and Sully Ledermann, 'La Guerre biologique, 1933–1945: population de l'Allemagne et des pays voisins', *Population* 1, no. 3 (July–September 1946).

140. Debré and Sauvy, *Des Français pour la France*, 124.

141. Friedrich Burgdörfer, 'Die neue deutsche Bevölkerungsentwicklung im gesamteuropäischen Rahmen mit besonderer Berücksichtigung der zahlenmäßig erfaßbaren Auswirkungen bevölkerungspolitischer Maßnahmen', in *Facteurs et conséquences de l'évolution démographique*, Congrès International de la Population (Hermann, 1938), vol. 7; see Glass to Mauco, 3 November 1948 (CAC: 860269 9), for a rare objection to Nazi race theorists rejoining the UIESP after the war.

142. Sauvy and Ledermann, 'La guerre biologique', 477.

143. As suggested in Lévy, *Alfred Sauvy*, 105.

144. Alfred Sauvy, Introduction to *Population* 1, no. 1 (January–March 1946).

145. Michel Chauvière, 'L'Expert et les propagandistes: Alfred Sauvy et le Code de la Famille de 1939', *Population* 47, no. 6 (November–December 1992), 1,449.

146. Alfred Sauvy, 'La Prévision économique', 56.

147. Ordonnance 45-2720, 2 November 1945.

148. William H. Schneider, *Quality and Quantity: The Quest for Biological Regeneration in Twentieth-Century France* (Cambridge: Cambridge University Press, 1990), chapter 6.

149. JO, 6 February 1946, 1,052.

150. Article 6. It was further updated in September 1946, when the medical exam had to include blood tests and x-rays. *Population* 1, no. 4 (October–December 1946), 770.

151. Judith Surkis, 'Secularization and Sexuality in Third Republic France, 1870–1920' (unpublished Ph.D. dissertation, Cornell University, 2001).

152. For medical reactions, see Anne Carol, *Histoire de l'eugénisme en France: les médecins et la procréation XIXe–XXe siècle* (Seuil, 1995), 339ff.

153. See e.g. Jean Audit and Marie Tisserand-Perrier, *L'Eugénique et l'euthénique (problèmes scientifiques et politiques)* (J.-B. Baillière et Fils, 1952), front cover. A 'tree of eugenics' is fed by roots labelled with diverse disciplines and factors (archaeology, genealogy, geology, anatomy, law, statistics, etc.).

154. Louis Chevalier, *Démographie générale* (Dalloz, 1951), 151–5; Alfred Sauvy, Preface to Sutter, *Eugénique*, 10.

155. On the Ecole des Parents, see Georges Mauco, 'Consultations psycho-pédagogiques', *Psyché* 2, no. 3 (1 January 1947).

156. Maxime Blocq-Mascart, *Chroniques de la résistance: suivies d'études pour une nouvelle révolution française par les groupes de l'OCM* (Corrêa, 1945), 506–7.

157. Sutter, *Eugénique*.

158. *Ibid*, 226.

159. *Ibid.*, 59.

160. Sauvy, *Richesse et population*, 79ff.

161. Alfred Sauvy, Preface to Sutter, *Eugénique*, 10.

162. Alfred Sauvy, 'Note sur le rythme necéssaire des naturalisations', 2 May 1945. CAC: 860269 1; Debré and Sauvy, *Des Français pour la France*, 232; 'Circulaire relative à l'instruction des demandes de naturalisation', 23 April 1947, *Population* 2, no. 2 (April–June 1947), 462–4.

163. Doublet, 'Politique démographique en Autriche', 301.

164. Hubert Thomas-Chevallier, *Le Racisme français* (Nancy: Imprimerie Georges Thomas, 1943), 118 offered a racist version of the pre-marital certificate.

165. INED, *Economie et population: les doctrines françaises avant 1800. Bibliographie générale commentée*, Travaux et Documents, no. 28 (PUF, 1956), xvi.

166. Anita Fage, 'Economie et population: les doctrines françaises avant 1800', *Population* 9, no. 1 (January–March 1954); Anita Fage, 'La Révolution française et la population', *Population* 8, no. 2 (April–June 1953); Anita Fage, 'Les Doctrines de population des encyclopédistes', *Population* 6, no. 4 (October–December 1951); Richard Cantillon, *Essai sur la nature du*

commerce en général. Texte de l'édition originale de 1755, avec des études et commentaires par Alfred Sauvy, Amintore Fanfani, Joseph J. Spengler, Louis Salleron (INED, 1952); see also André Toulemon, *Histoire des doctrines de la population* (Berger-Levrault, 1956).

167. Jean-Baptiste Say in Fage, 'La Révolution française', 336.
168. Sutter, *Eugénique*, 79.
169. Pierre-André Taguieff, Grégoire Kauffmann and Michaël Lenoire (eds.), *L'Antisémitisme de plume 1940–1944: études et documents* (Berg International, 1999), 29 refers to the 'integrity of the body'.
170. *L'Avortement et les moyens anticonceptionnels*, 37; Vincent, 'Statistique', 346–8; Sauvy, *Richesse et population*, 297; Debré and Sauvy, *Des Français pour la France*, 182–3; Landry, *Démographie française*, 72; Doublet, 'Politique démographique en Autriche', 301.
171. Max Lafont, *L'Extermination douce* (Latresne: Le Bord de l'eau, 2000).
172. Gérard Noiriel, *Les Origines républicaines de Vichy* (Hachette, 1999), 278.
173. See 'Enquête sur l'immigration étrangère dans les départements de l'est', December 1946–January 1947, on the 'complete failure' of Irish immigration. CAC: 860269 9.
174. Weil, 'Racisme', 78.
175. Mottier, *Guide pratique des étrangers*.
176. Georges Mauco, 'Le Problème de l'assimilation des étrangers en France: la population étrangère en France'. MP: 1.
177. Henri Mayeux and Jean H. Krailsheimer, *Guide pratique de la naturalisation française* (Centre d'Orientation Sociale des Etrangers, 1946), 18. All these matters were investigated in the FFEPH/INED study on assimilation. CAC: 760136.
178. Mauco, 'Le Problème de l'assimilation' examined immigrant health.
179. Raymond Sarraute, *Etude sur la situation des immigrés en France. De la libération à la repression* (Comité Français pour la Défense des Immigrés, 1953), 3.
180. See Sureté Nationale investigations on immigrant organizations' political allegiances. AN: F^{1}A 3345.
181. AI, Madame Paulette.
182. Sarraute, *La Situation des immigrés en France*, 19.
183. Ordonnance 45-2441, 19 October 1945, corrected 3 November and 3 December 1945, and 7 March 1946.
184. CAC: 760136; Girard and Stoetzel, *Français et immigrés*.
185. Robert Gessain and Madeleine Doré, 'Facteurs comparés d'assimilation chez des Russes et des Arméniens', *Population* 1, no. 1 (January–March 1946), 99. While at the FFEPH, Doré's co-author had hailed the 'scientific value' of George Montandon's work. Claude Singer, *L'Université libérée, l'université épurée (1943–1947)* (Les Belles Lettres, 1997), 307.
186. Alain Girard, *L'Institut National d'Etudes Démographiques: histoire et développement* (INED, 1986), 80.
187. Gessain and Doré, 'Facteurs comparés', 102, 108.
188. Madeleine Doré, 'Enquête sur la criminalité étrangère', June 1947. MP: 12.
189. Georges Mauco, 'Congrès mondial de la population et de la famille', *Psyché* 2, no. 9–10 (July–August 1947).

190. Debré and Sauvy, *Des Français pour la France*, 128. This echoes Sauvy, *Richesse et population*, 300.
191. Debré and Sauvy, *Des Français pour la France*, 183.
192. *Ibid.*, 188.
193. 'Elenco delle provvidenze adottate per l'incremento demografico dal regime sino al 31.12.1939-XVIII', 12 April 1940. AN: F[60] 498.
194. *Congrès mondial de la famille et de la population, Paris, 22–29 juin 1947* (UNAF, 1947); 'Sociology of Marriage and Family Behaviour 1945–56', *Current Sociology* 7, no. 1 (1958), 3, notes that after the United States, more literature on the family was published in France than anywhere else in the decade after the war.
195. Mauco, 'Congrès mondial'; Georges Mauco, 'Report on Relations between Parents and Children', in *World Congress for Family and Population: Congrès mondial de la famille et de la population* (UNAF, 1947).
196. Vote, 16 June 1945. CAC: 860269 8. Blocq-Mascart, Delabit and Prigent voted against. Familialism covered a broad political spectrum. See publications by the workerist Mouvement Populaire des Familles, and extreme right Union Républicaine des Familles Françaises, *Compte rendu de la grande réunion d'information organisée par l'URFF, à la salle Wagram, le mercredi 3 octobre 1945* (1945); Report, Renseignements Généraux on Union Républicaine des Familles, 11 October 1946. F[1]A 3355.
197. Girard and Stoetzel, *Français et immigrés*, 109.
198. 'Exil et travail social: les origines du SSAE', in *Accueillir*, ed. Jacqueline Costa-Lascoux (SSAE, October 1994), 198; Girard and Stoetzel, *Français et immigrés*, 24.
199. Armelle Mabon-Fall, *Les Assistantes sociales au temps de Vichy: du silence à l'oubli* (L'Harmattan, 1995).
200. Kevin Passmore, '"Planting the Tricolour in the Citadels of Communism": Women's Social Action in the Croix de Feu and Parti Social Français', *Journal of Modern History* 71, no. 4 (1999).
201. Kennedy to Owen, 10 August 1948. JDC: 328; Chevalley to Ministre de la Population, 23 September 1946. CAC: 860269 2.
202. Bernard Raffalli and Jacqueline Sauvageot, *Une Vigne sur la mer: deux siècles en Corse* (Bernard Grasset, 1980), 12; SSAE, *Rapport sur l'activité du SSAE en 1950* (SSAE, 1951).
203. Agenda, Conseil National des Femmes Françaises, 16 January 1946. CAC: 860269 2.
204. Chevalley to Mauco, n.d. CAC: 860269 7.
205. Mme L. Chevalley, 'Le Rôle du service social dans une politique générale d'immigration', *Cahiers du Musée Social*, no. 2–3 (1947), 68.
206. Lucie Chevalley, undated note on Statut des Etrangers (1945). CAC: 860269 7.
207. Chevalley, 'Rôle du service social', 68.
208. *Ibid.*, 69.
209. Mme L. Chevalley, 'Le Rôle des organismes sociaux d'assistance dans une politique générale d'immigration', *Bulletin d'information de l'Office Central des Œuvres de Bienfaisance*, no. 3 (March 1946), 77.
210. *Ibid.*, 78.

211. Cf. Laura Lee Downs, 'Les Marraines élues de la paix sociale? Les surintendantes d'usine et la rationalisation au travail en France 1917–1935', *Mouvement social*, no. 164 (July–September 1993).
212. AI, Madame Rivka.
213. Girard and Stoetzel, *Français et immigrés*, 71.
214. Mme Olry Collet, 'Note sur l'immigration', May 1945. CAC: 860269 1.
215. Georges Mauco, 'L'Aide à la famille', 1945. CAC: 860269 9.
216. Gérard Noiriel, *Le Creuset français. Histoire de l'immigration XIX–XXe siècles* (Seuil, 1988); Noiriel, *Origines républicaines*.
217. Abdelmalek Sayad, 'Qu'est-ce qu'un immigré', *Peuples-Méditerranée*, 1979, in Noiriel, *Creuset français*, 137–8.
218. Ministère du Travail et de la Sécurité Sociale, 4 June 1945. CAC: 860269 1.

Chapter 5   Controlling liberation: Georges Mauco and a population fit for France

1. Hervé Le Bras, *Les Trois France* (Odile Jacob, 1986), 208. Albert Demangeon, review of *Les Etrangers en France*, by Georges Mauco, in *Annales de géographie* 41, no. 232 (15 July 1932), prophesied that it 'will be the best source of documentation on these questions for a long time'.
2. Georges Mauco, *Les Etrangers en France: leur rôle dans l'activité économique* (Armand Colin, 1932); Pierre-André Taguieff, *La Force du préjugé: essai sur le racisme et ses doubles* (La Découverte, 1988); Gérard Noiriel, *Le Creuset français. Histoire de l'immigration XIX–XXe siècles* (Seuil, 1988).
3. Vicki Caron, *Uneasy Asylum: France and the Jewish Refugee Crisis, 1933–1942* (Stanford: Stanford University Press, 1999); Patrick Weil, 'Racisme et discrimination dans la politique française de l'immigration 1938–1945/1954–1995', *Vingtième siècle*, no. 47 (July–September 1995); Patrick Weil, 'Georges Mauco: un itinéraire camouflé,' in *L'Antisémitisme de plume 1940–1944: études et documents*, eds. Pierre-André Taguieff, Grégoire Kauffmann and Michaël Lenoire (Berg International, 1999).
4. CAC: 860269 1.
5. Noiriel, *Le Creuset français*; Max Silverman, *Deconstructing the Nation: Immigration, Racism and Citizenship in Modern France* (London: Routledge, 1992); Patrick Weil, *La France et ses étrangers: l'aventure d'une politique de l'immigration 1938–1991* (Calmann-Lévy, 1991); Ralph Schor, *L'Opinion française et les étrangers en France 1919–1939* (La Sorbonne, 1985); Vincent Viet, *La France immigrée: construction d'une politique 1914–1997* (Fayard, 1998).
6. Sigmund Freud, 'Family Romances' (Der Familienroman der Neurotiker – 1909), in *On Sexuality: Three Essays on the Theory of Sexuality and Other Works*, ed. Angela Richards, Penguin Freud Library (London: Penguin, 1991), 7, 222–3; personal details come from Georges Mauco, *Vécu 1899–1982* (Emile Paul, 1982).
7. As it was put by a third-year student in their paper *Entre nous*. MP: Box 1. When research was carried out, Mauco's personal papers were uncatalogued and kept in twelve boxes in private store at the Archives Nationales.

8. On the school's policy, see E. Devinat, *Livre de lecture et de morale: morale – leçons de choses – récitation* (Larousse, 1921), 4.

9. Mauco, *Vécu*, 64.

10. *Ibid.*, 63. The SPP's other founders were Marie Bonaparte, Edouard Pichon, Adrien Borel, Angelo Hesnard, Raymond de Saussure, Charles Odier, René Allendy, Georges Parcheminey, Rudolph Loewenstein, Eugénie Sokolnicka and Henri Codet.

11. René Martial, 'Conférence-programme pour les élèves des écoles normales d'instituteurs', *Société française de prophylaxie* 24, no. 4–5 (June–July 1924).

12. Georges Mauco, 'Les Etrangers en France. Etude géographique sur leur rôle dans l'activité économique' (Doctorat ès Lettres, University of Paris, A. Colin, 1932).

13. See also Edmond de Salses, *Livre d'or des valeurs humaines*, 2nd edn. (Editions du Mémorial, n.d.), 719.

14. JO, Lois et décrets, 1938, 5,492; Fatou to Mauco, 9 June 1938. MP: 6 congratulated Mauco's reinforcement of anti-foreigner laws. See also stringent suggestions for immigrants that foreshadow the occupation in Raymond Fatou, 'Note sur le patronage des étrangers à Marseille. Les apatrides. Nécessité d'une identification systématique des étrangers', in *Congrès international du patronage des libérés et des enfants traduits en justice* (Cahors: 1937).

15. On Grunebaum-Ballin and the Popular Front, see Pascal Ory, *La Belle Illusion: culture et politique sous le signe du Front Populaire, 1935–1938* (Plon, 1994), 151–4 and passim.

16. Mauco turned down the directorship, but remained on the executive committee. Minutes, 18 March 1946. MP: 2. The centre was in the sixteenth *arrondissement* of Paris.

17. P. Waelbroeck, International Labour Office, Geneva, to Mauco, 7 February 1936. MP: 6, on Mauco's submission of same article twice. Georges Mauco, *De l'inconscient à l'âme enfantine: la psychologie de l'enfant dans ses rapports avec la psychologie de l'inconscient* (Editions Psyché, 1948) was an unattributed edition of a book published ten years earlier, with an additional final paragraph on the Centre Psycho-Pédagogique: Georges Mauco, *La Psychologie de l'enfant dans ses rapports avec la psychologie de l'inconscient*, Bibliothèque Psychanalytique (Denoël, 1938). This was a reworking of Georges Mauco, 'La Psychologie de l'enfant dans ses rapports avec la psychologie de l'inconscient (d'après les travaux de Freud et de Piaget) 1 and 2', *Revue française de psychanalyse* 9, nos. 3 and 4 (1936). Familiar material was contained in new works on child psychology and sexuality between the 1950s and 1970s, as well as his reconsiderations of immigration.

18. Paul Vidal de la Blache and Lucien Gallois, *France économique et humaine*, Géographie Universelle, no. 6, ed. Albert Demangeon (Armand Colin, 1946–48).

19. Louis Chevalier, 'L'Ecole géographique française et la démographie', *Population* 2, no. 1 (January–March 1947).

20. Centre d'Orientation Sociale des Etrangers, 'Projet tendant à l'organisation de centres de propagation de culture française parmi les étrangers candidats à la naturalisation', August 1946. CAC: 860269 2.

21. Minutes, HCCPF, 30 April 1945. CAC: 860269 1.

22. Untitled typescript headed in Mauco's hand, 'G. Mauco 1939–40', in a file, 'Projet article "Révolution 1940"'. MP: 12.
23. *Ibid.*
24. Pierre Birnbaum, *Un Mythe politique: 'la république juive'* (Fayard, 1988), 196ff.
25. 'Révolution 1940'.
26. These were indebted to earlier psychiatric explorations. Henry Meige, *Le Juif errant à la Salpêtrière, étude sur certains névropathes voyageurs* (L. Bataille et Co, 1893), 76 saw Jews as 'asocial pariahs of pathological instability, incapable of putting down roots'.
27. Elisabeth Roudinesco, *La Bataille de cent ans: histoire de la psychanalyse en France*, vol. 1 (Ramsay, 1982), 398; Michel de Certeau, 'Psychoanalysis and its History', in Michel de Certeau, *Heterologies: Discourses on the Other* (Manchester: Manchester University Press, 1986), 12–13.
28. Gustave Le Bon, *Les Lois psychologiques de l'évolution des peuples* (Félix Alcan, 1894), 6.
29. The classic work on this is Eugen Weber, *Peasants into Frenchmen: The Modernization of Rural France 1870–1914* (Stanford: Stanford University Press, 1976).
30. Maurice Barrès, *Scènes et doctrines du nationalisme* (Plon, 1930), 10.
31. Jean-Marc Bernardini, *Le Darwinisme social en France (1859–1918): fascination et rejet d'une idéologie* (CNRS, 1997), esp. ch. 3.
32. Juliet Mitchell and Jacqueline Rose (eds.), *Feminine Sexuality: Jacques Lacan and the Ecole Freudienne*, trans. Jacqueline Rose (London: Macmillan, 1982), 14.
33. Sigmund Freud, 'Moses and Monotheism', (Der Mann Moses und die monotheistische Religion: drei Abhandlungen), in *The Origins of Religion*, ed. Albert Dickson, Penguin Freud Library (London: Penguin, 1990), 13, 339ff.
34. Freud to Ferenczi, 30 March 1922. In Peter Gay, *Freud: A Life for Our Time* (London: Macmillan, 1988), 601.
35. Freud to Zweig, 8 May 1932. In Sigmund Freud, *Briefe 1873–1939*, 3rd edn, ed. Ernst and Lucie Freud (1960; reprint, Frankfurt: S. Fischer Verlag, 1980), 426–7.
36. Sander L. Gilman, *Freud, Race, and Gender* (Princeton: Princeton University Press, 1993), 24–9.
37. Georges Mauco, 'L'Assimilation des étrangers en France', in *Le Règlement pacifique des problèmes internationaux* (Institut International de Coopération Intellectuelle/Société des Nations, 28 June–3 July 1937). Compare Debré and Sauvy's suspicion of immigrant clusters discussed in the last chapter. Robert Debré and Alfred Sauvy, *Des Français pour la France (le problème de la population)* (Gallimard, 1946), 231.
38. Georges Mauco, 'Le Problème de l'assimilation des étrangers en France: la population étrangère en France' (*c.*1948), 9–10. MP: 1.
39. Mauco, 'L'Assimilation des étrangers'.
40. The spelling of different nationalities emphasizes their Slavic nature – 'Yougo-Slaves', 'Tchéquo-Slovaques'. *Ibid.*, 22.
41. *Ibid.*, 22, 23, 37.
42. *Ibid.*, 62.

43. Mauco, 'Problème de l'assimilation', 78.
44. Mauco, 'L'Assimilation des étrangers', 81–2.
45. Article 11, Décret-loi, 2 May 1938. JO, Lois et décrets, 1938, 4,986.
46. Mauco, 'Note sur le projet de statut des étrangers', May 1945. CAC: 860269 1.
47. For views expressed in conservative, but pro-refugee, journals, see Georges Mauco, 'Le Mouvement de la population en Europe', *L'Europe nouvelle* (18 March 1939); Georges Mauco, 'Quelques conséquences du mouvement de la population en Europe', *L'Europe nouvelle* (8 April 1939).
48. Georges Mauco, *Rapport sur l'état sanitaire de la population étrangère en France* (n.d. (1947)), 17.
49. Cf. Adolphe Landry, *La Démographie française*, 2nd edn (1941; reprint, ANCD, 1942), 68.
50. Georges Mauco, 'Une Enquête en cours sur l'immigration agricole en France', in *Démographie statistique*, Congrès International de la Population (Hermann, 1938), 4, 4; Albert Demangeon and Georges Mauco, *Documents pour servir à l'étude des étrangers dans l'agriculture française* (Hermann, 1939).
51. H. R. Kedward, 'Rural France and Resistance', in *France at War: Vichy and the Historians*, ed. Sarah Fishman *et al.* (Oxford: Berg, 2000).
52. Mauco, 'Problème de l'assimilation'.
53. See Jackie Clarke, 'Imagined Productive Communities: Industrial Rationalisation and Cultural Crisis in 1930s France', *Modern and Contemporary France* 8, no. 3 (2000); Shanny Peer, *France on Display: Peasants, Provincials, and Folklore in the 1937 Paris World's Fair* (Albany: SUNY Press, 1998), 100ff; Ory, *La Belle Illusion*. See correspondence concerning the establishment of 'Jewish agriculture in France'. AN: 72 AJ 596. The success of farming projects in Palestine forms a significant contrast.
54. Caron, *Uneasy Asylum*, 164–7.
55. Mauco, Report, April–May 1946. CAC: 860269 9.
56. Ministre des Armées to Ministre de l'Intérieur, 28 September 1946; Minutes, 16 February 1946. AN: F¹A 3255.
57. Cf. Edouard Drumont, *La France juive*, vol. 1 (1886; reprint, La Librairie Française, 1986), 9.
58. Mauco, Report, April–May 1946. CAC: 860269 9.
59. Alexandre Parodi to General Menard, 20 March 1940; Call-up notice, 2 April 1940. MP: 10.
60. Anne Grynberg, *Les Camps de la honte: les internés juifs des camps français 1939–1944* (1991; reprint, La Découverte, 1999), 12.
61. *Ibid.*, 76–7. See also Denis Peschanski, *La France des camps: l'internement 1938–1946* (Gallimard, 2002); 'Le Temps des "indésirables": sur quelques camps d'internement français', *Le Monde juif*, no. 153, January–April 1995; Jacques Grandjonc and Theresia Grundtner (eds.), *Zone d'ombres 1933–1944: exil et internement d'Allemands et d'Autrichiens dans le sud-est de la France* (Aix-en-Provence: Alinéa, 1990); André Fontaine, *Le Camp d'étrangers des Milles 1939–1943 (Aix-en-Provence)* (Aix-en-Provence: Edisud, 1989); Claude Laharie, *Le Camp de Gurs 1939–1945: un aspect méconnu de l'histoire du Béarn* (Biarritz: J & D Editions, 1985); Jean-Jacques Bernard, *Le Camp de la mort lente: Compiègne 1941–42* (Albin Michel, 1944); Eric Malo, 'Le Camp de Noë

(Haute-Garonne) de 1941 à 1944', *Annales de Midi*, 100, no. 183 (1988); Equipe de Recherche en Civilisation Allemande de l'Université de Provence (eds.), *Les Camps en Provence: exil, internement, déportation 1933–1944* (Aix-en-Provence: Alinéa, 1984); Hanna Schramm and Barbara Vormeier, *Vivre à Gurs: un camp de concentration français 1940–1941* (Maspéro, 1979); Paul Lévy, *Un Camp de concentration français: Poitiers 1939–1945* (Sedes, 1995); Monique Lise Cohen and Eric Malo (eds.), *Les Camps du sud-ouest de la France 1939–1944: exclusion, internement et déportation* (Toulouse: Privat, 1994); Pierre Portier, *Le Camp du Vernet-d'Ariège ou les racines du désespoir: la vie du camp de sa création en 1917 à sa disparition en 1947* (Saverdun, 1997); Jacques Sigot, *Un Camp pour les Tsiganes . . . et les autres: Montreuil-Bellay 1940–1945* (Bordeaux: Wallada, 1983).

62. Etat-Major de l'Armée, 'Etrangers internés: recensement professionnel', 15 November 1939. MP: 12.
63. David Vogel, *Et ils partirent pour la guerre* (Denoël, 1993), 82–3.
64. JO, Lois et decrets, 4 December 1938, 13,615.
65. Captain Bonnicel, 'Compte rendu d'une mission . . . aux dépôts de la Légion Etrangère en France', 23 January 1940. MP: 12.
66. In the summer of 1942 alone, 9,862 Jews were transferred from Non-Occupied Zone camps to camps in the north, awaiting deportation. Serge Klarsfeld, *Vichy-Auschwitz: le rôle de Vichy dans la solution finale de la question juive en France. 1942*, vol. 1 (Fayard, 1983), 158–9.
67. Mauco to Minister of Interior, 15 May 1940. MP: 12.
68. Primo Levi, *If This Is a Man* (London: Abacus, 1999); Anita Lasker-Wallfisch, *Inherit the Truth 1939–1945: The Documented Experiences of a Survivor of Auschwitz and Belsen* (London: Giles de la Mare, 1996).
69. See Jacob Katz, *Out of the Ghetto: The Social Background of Jewish Emancipation 1770–1870* (Cambridge, MA: Harvard University Press, 1973); Monika Richarz, *Der Eintritt der Juden in die Akademischen Berufe: Jüdische Studenten und Akademiker in Deutschland, 1678–1848* (Tübingen: J. C. B. Mohr, 1974).
70. Jean-François Gravier, *Paris et le désert français. Décentralisation équipement population* (Le Portulan, 1947), 13; Georges Mauco, 'Les Commerçants dans la population française', *Annales de géographie* 55, no. 297 (January–March 1946). See also marked proofs of this article (originally 'L'Evolution de la population active en France et le développement des commerçants et in-termédiaires'). MP: 6; 'Circulaire du 23 avril 1947 relative à l'instruction des demandes de naturalisation' in J.-L. Mottier and Maurice Caillez, *Guide pratique des étrangers en France* (Librairie du Journal des Notaires et des Avocats, 1948), 389.
71. Mauco, *Etrangers en France*, 467.
72. Mauco, 'Quelques conséquences du mouvement de la population', 380. *L'Europe nouvelle*'s turn to the right provoked Louise Weiss, its feminist editor and future clandestine journalist, to resign the day before the 6 February 1934 riots. Louise Weiss, *Mémoires d'une Européenne*, vol. 2, *1919–1934* (Payot, 1969), 330–5.
73. Mauco, 'L'Assimilation des étrangers', 1937; Note on establishment of Centre d'Etudes du Problème des Etrangers en France, 1935. MP: 6; Mauco,

Rapport sur l'état sanitaire, 8; Mauco, 'Problème de l'assimilation', 62; Georges Mauco, 'L'Assimilation des étrangers en France', in *L'Assimilation culturelle des immigrants: union internationale pour l'étude scientifique de la population: assemblée générale*, 21–32, Communications présentées sous les auspices et éditées avec le concours de l'UNESCO (INED, 1950), 29.

74. André Pairault, *L'Immigration organisée et l'emploi de la main-d'œuvre étrangère en France* (PUF, 1926), 186–9. Pairault joined Mauco at the Centre d'Etudes du Problème des Etrangers. MP: 6. Weil, *France et ses étrangers*, 360 reproduces the table though attributes it to Mauco.

75. For personal accounts of North African workers in the automobile industry, see Yamina Benguigui, *Mémoires d'immigrés: l'héritage maghrébin*, France, 1997.

76. Silverman, *Deconstructing the Nation*, 25–7; Jane Freedman, 'Women and Immigration: Nationality and Citizenship', in *Women, Immigration and Identities in France*, eds. Jane Freedman and Carrie Tarr (Oxford: Berg, 2000).

77. Mauco, 'L'Assimilation des Etrangers', 1937.

78. Mauco, 'Problème de l'assimilation', 62.

79. *Résultats statistiques du recensement général de la population effectué le 7 mars 1926*, vol. 3: Population présente: résultats par département. Paris: 1930, 1–5; *Dénombrement de la Population, 1946*, 1947.

80. Patrick Fridenson, *Histoire des usines Renault: 1. Naissance de la grande entreprise* (Seuil, 1972), 207.

81. Mauco, 'L'Assimilation des étrangers', 1949, 29.

82. *Ibid.*, 29.

83. *Ibid.*, 21.

84. On Montandon's career, see Joseph Billig, *Commissariat Général aux Questions Juives (1941–1944)*, vol. 1 (Editions du Centre, 1955), 138–41; Marc Knobel, 'George Montandon et l'ethno-racisme', in *L'Antisémitisme de plume*, ed. Pierre-André Taguieff *et al*.

85. George Montandon, *L'Ethnie française* (Payot, 1935), 139–44.

86. *Ibid.*, 26.

87. *Ibid.*, 34, 169.

88. *Ibid.*, 228.

89. Georges Vacher de Lapouge, *Les Sélections sociales* (A. Fontemoing, 1896), 8.

90. Ferdinand de Saussure, *Cours de linguistique générale* (Payot, 1916), 312.

91. René Martial, *La Race française: le sol. Les racines. La souche. La croissance et les greffons (Arabes. Normands. Italiens. Hollandais, etc.). La greffe inter-raciale: la trilogie, histoire. Psychologie. Biologie. Le nouveau rejet ou transfusion sanguine ethnique* (Mercure de France, 1934), 8–14. Somewhat provocatively – and erroneously – Herman Lebovics translates 'ethnie' as *Volk*. As I demonstrate, the term *ethnie* is uniquely French. Herman Lebovics, *True France: The Wars over Cultural Identity, 1900–1945* (Ithaca: Cornell University Press, 1992), 42. Martial continued to publish on inherent racial differences until well after the war: René Martial, *Les Races humaines* (Hachette, 1955).

92. George Montandon, 'Commentaires sur les théories raciales de Gobineau', *Revue contemporaine*, no. 11 (25 August–25 September 1917); Arthur de Gobineau, *Essai sur l'inégalité des races humaines* (Firmin-Didot, 1855).

93. Montandon, *L'Ethnie française*, 145.

94. Joseph Billig, *Commissariat Général aux Questions Juives (1941–1944)*, vol. 2 (Editions du Centre, 1957), 288–97. *Jeune combat*, 28 January 1945, derided Montandon's pseudo-science, citing a case in which he certified two brothers, one as Jewish, the other Aryan.

95. *Ethnie française*, no. 1 (March 1941), 23.

96. *L'Ethnie française* appeared in March, April, May–June, July, September 1941; March 1942; January, May, July 1943; April 1944. See no. 6, 1, for note on its financial problems.

97. Pierre Albert, Gilles Feyel and Jean-François Picard (eds.), *Documents pour l'histoire de la presse nationale aux XIXe et XXe siècles* (CNRS, 1977), 78. This work cannot be relied upon for accuracy.

98. *Ethnie française*, no. 1 (March 1941), 1.

99. Undated, signed typescript with annotations in Mauco's hand. MP: 6.

100. Compare British eugenicist Karl Pearson's idea of 'germ plasm', the innate genetic imprint of each individual, immune to envorinmental influence.

101. Gérard Mauger, 'A quelle race appartenez-vous?', *Ethnie française*, no. 4 (July 1941).

102. Montandon, *L'Ethnie française*, 212–25.

103. George Montandon, *La Race. Les races: mise au point d'ethnologie somatique* (Payot, 1933).

104. See also Montandon, Preface to Frank H. Hankins, *La Race dans la civilisation: une critique de la doctrine nordique*, trans. and preface by George Montandon (Payot, 1935), 7.

105. Georges Mauco, 'L'Emigration étrangère en France et le problème des réfugiés,' *Ethnie française*, no. 6 (March 1942); Georges Mauco, 'La Situation démographique de la France', *Ethnie française*, no. 7 (January 1943).

106. Mauco, *Ethnie française*, no. 6 (March 1942), 8.

107. *Ibid.*, 11–12.

108. *Ibid.*, 13.

109. *Ibid.*, 14.

110. 'L'inquiétude et l'inversion sexuelle, la destruction de nos traditions sont les thèmes favoris des écrivains juifs', part of the 'Le Juif et la France' exhibition at Palais Berlitz in 1941. Pascal Ory, *Les Collaborateurs 1940–1945* (1976; reprint, Seuil, 1980), 158n4.

111. Mauco, *Ethnie française*, no. 6 (March 1942), 8.

112. Georges Mauco, 'La Situation démographique de la France', *Annales de géographie* 47, no. 271 (15 January 1939); Mauco to director of *Action*, 26 November 1947. MP: 12.

113. 'Déclaration au sujet de l'article de G. Mauco dans la Revue "Ethnie française"'. AN: F^{17} 16847.

114. *Ethnie française*, no. 7, 15.

115. Georges Mauco, 'La Situation démographique de la France depuis 1938'. Typed ms. MP: 6. Mauco noted the problems to statistical analysis and comparison caused by occupation-time changes, such as the reduction in the number of departments and population movement out of the country (deportations encompassed in an ambiguous 'etc.').

116. Weil, 'Racisme et discrimination', 83.

117. Mauco, *Vécu*, 104, states that Mauco was too ill to attend the trial in person.

118. Mauco, 'Les Etrangers en France et les inconvénients d'une immigration inorganisée', 31 August 1941. MP: 12.
119. Compare Fernand Boverat, *Le Massacre des innocents* (ANCD, 1939), 11.
120. Mauco, *Ethnie française*, no. 6 (March 1942), 13–14.
121. *Action*, 26 November 1947; Joseph André Bass in *Droit et liberté*, 15 May 1948. See also Pierre Hervé, *La Libération trahie* (Bernard Grasset, 1945); *Réveil des jeunes*, 1 February 1946.
122. President, Conseil Supérieur d'Enquête du Ministère de l'Education Nationale to Mauco, 4 June 1947. MP: 12. Thorez to Ministre de l'Education Nationale, 13 December 1946. AN: F^{17} 16847. Elisabeth Roudinesco, 'Georges Mauco (1899–1988): un psychanalyste au service du Vichy: de l'antisémitisme à la psychopédagogie', *L'Infini*, no. 51 (Autumn 1995) mistakenly asserts that Mauco underwent no *épuration*. On the purge in general, see François Rouquet, *L'Epuration dans l'administration française* (CNRS, 1993).
123. Mauco to director, *Action*, 3 December 1947. MP: 12. René Laforgue, his former analyst, was not Jewish. He was a member of the International League against Antisemitism (LICA) executive committee.
124. George Montandon, *Comment reconnaître et expliquer le Juif suivi d'un portrait moral du Juif* (Nouvelles Editions Françaises, 1940).
125. Mauco, 'Renseignements fournis par Mr Mauco au sujet de l'article paru dans "l'Ethnie française"', MP: 12.
126. Mauco, *Vécu*, 115.
127. *Ibid.*, 106. There is no archival evidence of death threats.
128. Claude Singer, *L'Université libérée, l'université épurée (1943–1947)* (Les Belles Lettres, 1997), 312. Knobel, 'George Montandon', 293 hedges his bets regarding Montandon's death.
129. George Montandon, 'Una soluzione "biologica" della questione ebraica', *La Difesa della Razza* 1, no. 5 (5 October XVI [1938]), 9–10.
130. *Le Droit de vivre*, 4 February 1939, 29 April 1939, 17 and 24 June 1939; *La Lumière*, 12 and 26 April 1940, 3 May 1940; *Nouvel âge*, 19 April 1940.
131. Montandon to *La Lumière*, 26 April 1940. CDJC: XCV-114.
132. George Montandon, 'L'Ethnie juive et le type racial juif: causerie donnée le 26 avril 1939 au Cercle Ernest Jouin', *Revue internationale des sociétés secrètes: bulletin bi-mensuel de la Ligue Anti-Judéomaçonnique 'Le Franc-Catholique'*, 12 (15 June 1939); George Montandon, 'La Solution ethnico-raciale du problème juif', *Contre-révolution: revue internationale d'études sociales*, 5 (April 1939).
133. Petit to Montandon, 5 September 1938; Montandon to Petit, 18 September 1938. CDJC: XCV-27 and 28.
134. Correspondence between Montandon and Darquier de Pellepoix, November 1938 and January 1939; and Vallery-Radot, December 1938 and January 1939. CDJC: XCV-41, 52, 59, 60. Montandon thanked Darquier for his 'friendliness' in publishing a report of Montandon's talk at the Sorbonne in *La France enchaînée*, 27 November 1938. CDJC: XCV-40.

Ory, *Les Collaborateurs*, 155, mentions that in 1940, Montandon announced imminent publication of a work, never to appear, entitled *L'Ethnie juive ou ethnie putain*. In fact, this was Giorgio Montandon,

' "L'ethnie putaine": determinazione psicologica dell'etnia giudaica', *La Difesa della Razza* 3, no. 1 (5 November XVIII [1940]). In an appeal to Catholic Italian readers, Montandon claimed in this article to have been published in the Belgian *Nouvelle revue théologique* and Mgr André Bressolles (ed.), *Racisme et christianisme* (Flammarion, 1939). Neither publication bears his name; on the contrary, both offer ripostes to Nazi racism, admittedly rather lukewarm. See also Giorgio Montandon, 'Il passaporto ancestrale', *La Difesa della Razza* 5, no. 18 (20 July XX [1942]).

135. Hans F. K. Günther, *Rassenkunde des jüdischen Volkes* (Munich: Lehmann, 1930).

136. Montandon to Günther, 23 October 1938. CDJC: XCV-31.

137. Sander L. Gilman, *The Jew's Body* (New York: Routledge, 1991), 126; Sander L. Gilman, 'Chicken Soup, or the Penalties for Sounding Too Jewish', *Shofar* 9, 1990.

138. Otto Weininger, *Geschlecht und Charakter, eine prinzipielle Untersuchung* (Vienna: W. Baumüller, 1903). Twenty-eight editions appeared between publication and 1947, and the work was translated into eleven languages, including Yiddish, Japanese and French.

139. MP: 9; correspondence between Mauco and PPF, 25 and 27 November 1942. MP: 12.

140. No article by Mauco appeared in the PPF's *Cahiers de l'émancipation*.

141. Mauco, *Vécu*, 107.

142. 'Renseignements fournis par Mr Mauco au sujet de l'article paru dans "l'Ethnie française" '. MP: 12.

143. Mauco to A. de Mijolla, 14 May 1987. MP: 8.

144. Mauco, *Vécu*, 81; Marie Bonaparte, *Derrière les vitres closes: les souvenirs d'enfance*, vol. 1, *A la mémoire des disparus* (London: Imago, 1952), 192ff; Célia Bertin, *Marie Bonaparte* (Plon, 1982), 319–21. See Freud to Max Eitingon (6 June 1938) on his reception in Paris. Freud, *Briefe*, 461.

145. International Union for the Scientific Study of Population Problems, 'Report by the President, Monsieur Landry', 6 September 1947. CAC: 860269 9.

146. Mauco, 'Le Code de la Famille', undated typescript. MP: 6. A corrected version was no less vitriolic.

147. Audition de M. Mauco devant Conseil Supérieur d'Enquête du Ministère de l'Education Nationale, 10 June 1947. AN: F^{17} 16847.

148. Conseil Supérieur d'Enquête du Ministère de l'Education Nationale, 14 October 1947. AN: F^{17} 16847.

149. Inspecteur d'Académie de Paris to Mauco and the director of the Collège J. B. Say, 23 February 1948. MP: 12.

150. Maurice Grandazzi, 25 June 1947. AN: F^{17} 16847.

151. Maurice Grandazzi, 12 June 1947. MP: 12.

152. J. Brilhac to Mauco, 27 November 1946. CAC: 860269 2.

153. Cf. Judith K. Proud, 'Plus Ça Change . . . ? Propaganda Fiction for Children, 1940–1945', in *The Liberation of France: Image and Event*, eds. H. R. Kedward and Nancy Wood (Oxford: Berg, 1995), 71.

154. Alain Drouard, *Une Inconnue des sciences sociales: la fondation Alexis Carrel 1941–1945* (La Maison des Sciences de l'Homme, 1992), 443.

155. ANCD to Minister of Information, 13 December 1944. CAC: 860269 2.

156. *Revue de l'Alliance Nationale contre la Dépopulation*, no. 368, June–December 1944, 38.

157. Robert Prigent, written question no. 343, JO, 15 May 1945, 1,055. This echoed the ANCD's pre-war efforts to show their films in every barracks in the country. Fernand Boverat, *Comment nous vaincrons la dénatalité?* (ANCD, 1938), 45. For the results of such initiatives, see Ministères de l'Education Nationale et de la Population, *Six leçons d'enseignement démographique* (1946).

158. Ministère de la Défense Nationale, Circular no. 14, appendix 1, no. 122 DN/CAB 2, 19 December 1949.

159. AN: F^9 3127; MP: 7.

160. Brilhac to Mauco, 27 November 1946. CAC: 860269 2; Mauco to Ministre de l'Education Nationale, 12 February 1947. CAC: 860269 2; Paul Haury and René Lugand, *Histoire et géographie: classe de sixième*, Enseignement démographique et familial (ANCD, 1945), 25 and other books in the series. They located the fall of Athens in moral decadence, disorder and love of luxury, evidenced by women's emancipation movements, while ancient Rome seems to have been rather like Vichy France, encouraging large families, colonization and a *retour à la terre*.

161. Paul Haury and René Lugand. *Histoire et géographie: classe de cinquième*. Enseignement démographique et familial (ANCD, 1945), 44.

162. J. Delteil, president of the ANCD to R. Pochtier, 2 February 1949. CAC: 860269 2.

163. Georges Mauco and Maurice Grandazzi, *La Démographie à l'école. Manuel à l'usage des maîtres* (ANCD, 1948), no pagination. Original emphasis.

164. *Ibid.*, 27.

165. *Ibid.*, 25–6.

166. Cheryl A. Koos, 'Gender, Anti-Individualism, and Nationalism: The Alliance Nationale and the Pronatalist Backlash against the *Femme Moderne*, 1933–1940', *French Historical Studies* 19, no. 3 (Spring 1996); Andrès Horacio Reggiani, 'Procreating France: The Politics of Demography, 1919–1945', *French Historical Studies* 19, no. 3 (Spring 1996); Mary Louise Roberts, *Civilization without Sexes: Reconstructing Gender in Postwar France, 1917–1927* (Chicago: Chicago University Press, 1994).

167. Compare the Soviet worker to the poster by Thébault and Fontséré, *Retroussons nos manches. Ça ira encore mieux!*, 1945, in Stéphane Marchetti, *Affiches 1939–1945: images d'une certaine France* (Lausanne: Edita Lazarus, 1982).

168. Queuille to ANCD president, 3 January 1948. MP: 1; Vote, HCCPF, 23 February 1949. CAC: 860269 2. See complaint, Pochtier to director, ANCD, 29 January 1949. CAC: 860269 2.

169. Ministère des Armées to Mauco, 19 November 1946. CAC: 860269 2.

170. The other countries were Switzerland, Sweden, Britain, Norway and Belgium. Georges Mauco, 'Le Mouvement de la population en Europe'. CAC: 860269 9.

171. Georges Mauco, 'Les Conséquences du déclin démographique et la nécessité d'une politique de la population', lecture to Ecole Navale. CAC: 860269 9.

172. Undated note on membership of PPF, MP: 12.
173. CAC: 860269 1.
174. Minutes, extraordinary general meeting, 28 November 1941, Association des Centres de Réadaptation Sociale des Jeunes Chômeurs. MP: 10.
175. Conseil d'administration, 28 July 1942, Association des Centres de Réadaptation Sociale des Jeunes Chômeurs. MP: 10.
176. Assemblée Général, 23 October 1941, Association des Centres de Réadaptation Sociale des Jeunes Chômeurs, MP: 10. For other involvement with Vichy organisms at this time see correspondence regarding the Centre Scientifique de la Main-d'Œuvre. Secretary of State for Labour to Mauco, inviting him to a meeting of the administrative council 'of which you are a member', 26 July 1944. MP: 10; Conseil d'administration, 28 July 1942, Association des Centres de Réadaptation Sociale des Jeunes Chômeurs, MP: 10. See Guy de Beaumont, *Guide pratique de l'orientation professionnelle*, Etudes Corporatives (Dunod, 1938).
177. 'Formation des cadres', Association des Centres de Réadaptation Sociale des Jeunes Chômeurs, MP: 10.
178. 'Formation éducative'. MP: 10.
179. Minutes, Direction de l'Hygiène Scolaire et Universitaire du Ministère de l'Education Nationale, 18 March 1946. MP: 2.
180. Georges Mauco, 'Le Centre Psycho-Pédagogique de l'Académie de Paris au Lycée Claude-Bernard,' *Psyché* 2, no. 13–14 (November–December 1947), 1,387.
181. Elisabeth Roudinesco, *Histoire de la psychanalyse en France*, vol. 2, *1925–1985* (1986; reprint, Fayard, 1994), 274–5.
182. André Berge, 'Le Centre Psycho-Pédagogique du Lycée Claude Bernard pour l'enseignement secondaire,' *A Criança Portuguesa* (1950–51), 81; Georges Mauco, 'Le Centre Psycho-Pédagogique de l'Académie de Paris au Lycée Claude-Bernard', *Sauvegarde: revue des associations régionales pour la sauvegarde de l'enfance et de l'adolescence* 2, no. 15–16 (November–December 1947), 60; Georges Mauco, 'Consultations psycho-pédagogiques', *Psyché* 2, no. 3 (1 January 1947), 50.
183. Mauco, 'Le Centre Psycho-Pédagogique', 1,401.
184. On a similar service for traumatized Jewish children, and Robert Debré's advice, see JDC: 324, 1946.
185. Sigmund Freud, 'Totem and Taboo', in *The Origins of Religion*, eds. James Strachey and Albert Dickson, Penguin Freud Library (London: Penguin, 1990), 13.
186. Mauco, *Etrangers en France*, 269.
187. *Ibid.*, 517.
188. Mauco, 'Consultations psycho-pédagogiques', 49.
189. Maurice Monsaingeon, *La Vraie Conception de la famille: sa place dans la société*, Collection Science et Charité, no. IX (Secrétariat Catholique des Œuvres Charitables et Sociales d'Hygiène et de Santé, May 1944), 23.
190. Ecole des Parents. MP: 7.
191. Mauco, 'Consultations psycho-pédagogiques', 49.
192. Weil, 'Racisme et discrimination', 91.
193. Mauco, 'Problème de l'assimilation', 61–2.

194. Mauco, 'L'Assimilation des étrangers', 1937; Mauco, *Etrangers en France*, 518.
195. Georges Mauco, *Le Meurtre d'un enfant et l'angoisse du schizophrène et de l'homosexuel* (PUF, 1979), 26; Carolyn J. Dean, *The Self and its Pleasures: Bataille, Lacan, and the History of the Decentered Subject* (Ithaca: Cornell University Press, 1992), 89.
196. Georges Mauco, 'Congrès mondial de la population et de la famille,' *Psyché* 2, no. 9–10 (July–August 1947), 987.
197. Mauco, *Vécu*, 84, passim.
198. Mauco, *Le Meurtre d'un enfant*, 136; Mauco, *Vécu*, 169.
199. Paul Mufraggi, 'Mémoire de proposition pour la médaille de la résistance', 8 September 1944. MP: 12. See also undated statement in MP: 9.
200. Dean, *The Self and its Pleasures*, 68.
201. E.g., Cesare Lombroso, *L'Anthropologie criminelle et ses récents progrès*, 3rd edn (Félix Alcan, 1896).
202. Dean, *The Self and its Pleasures*, 68.
203. See 'Situations et mesures à étudier', 30 April 1945. CAC 860269 1; Mauco and Grandazzi, *Démographie à l'école*, 26; Mauco, 'Les Etrangers en France et les inconvénients d'une immigration inorganisée', 31 August 1941. MP: 12; 'Conséquences du déclin démographique', 1946. CAC 860269 9.
204. Georges Mauco, 'L'Evolution rélle [*sic*] de la population française depuis un siècle et le déclin démographique de l'Europe occidentale', *c*.1949. MP: 6.
205. Mauco, 'L'Assimilation des étrangers', 1937, 113.
206. Weil, *France et ses étrangers*, 35. See e.g., Georges Mauco, 'L'Immigration étrangère en France', *Res Publica*, no. 6 (January–March 1946).
207. Roudinesco, 'Georges Mauco'.
208. Reggiani, 'Procreating France', 752–3.
209. Mauco, *Vécu*, 92.
210. See Georges Mauco, *La Paternité: sa fonction éducative dans la famille et à l'école* (Editions Universitaires, 1971), 138–9: the entrance of women into teaching resulted in a deplorable devaluation of the image of the father and a 'counter-education' for the child.

Chapter 6   Liberation in place: Jewish women in the city

1. *Vingt ans d'évolution de Paris: données statistiques 1954–1975. Population, logement, ménages* (APUR, n.d.) in Jeanne Brody, *Rue des Rosiers: une manière d'être juif* (Autrement, 1995), 28; Sophie Herszkowicz, *Lettre ouverte au Maire de Paris à propos de la destruction de Belleville* (Encyclopédie des Nuisances, 1994).
2. Willy Ronis, *Belleville-Ménilmontant* (Arthaud, 1984).
3. Robert Bober, *En remontant la rue Vilin*, France, 1992.
4. Georges Perec, *W ou le souvenir d'enfance* (Denoël, 1975); Nicole Priollaud, Victor Zigelman and Laurent Goldberg (eds.), *Images de la mémoire juive: immigration et intégration en France depuis 1800* (Aubanas: Liana Levi, 1994). The former rue Vilin is now part of a park.

5. Doris Bensimon and Sergio della Pergola, *La Population juive de France: socio-démographie et identité* (Jerusalem: Institute of Contemporary Jewry, 1984), 60, 63; Sylvie Strudel, *Votes juifs: itinéraires migratoires, religieux et politiques* (FNSP, 1996), 43.

6. Patrick Simon, 'Les Quartiers d'immigration: "ports de première entrée" ou espaces de sédentarisation? L'exemple de Belleville', *Espace, Populations, Sociétés*, no. 2 (1993), 380.

7. Gérard Jacquemet, 'Déchristianisation, structures familiales et anti-cléricalisme: Belleville au XIXe siècle', *Archives de Sciences Sociales des Religions* 57, no. 1 (1984).

8. AI, Mme Fanny.

9. Michel Roblin, *Les Juifs de Paris. Démographie – économie – culture* (A. et J. Picard, 1952), 157; Annette Wieviorka, *Ils étaient juifs, résistants, communistes* (Denoël, 1986).

10. Joseph Millner, 'Les Juifs de Belleville', *Journal des Communautés* 9, no. 141 (14 March 1958); Consistoire Israélite de Paris, *La Communauté de Paris après la libération. Tableau d'ensemble* (1946), 8–9.

11. *Ibid.*, 156; David Diamant, *Par-delà les barbelés. Lettres et écrits des camps et des prisons de France. Lettres jetées des trains de déportation. Ecrits d'Auschwitz. Créations journalistiques, littéraires et artistiques* (Un comité de familles de fusillés et de rescapés des camps de concentration, 1986); Clément Lépidis, *Belleville au Cœur* (Vermet, 1980); Patrick Simon and Claude Tapia, *Le Belleville des Juifs tunisiens* (Autrement, 1998), 84–7.

12. Madame Paulette, Madame Perla and Madame Fanny lived there before the war. Madame Hanna operated there during the liberation. Two remained – Madame Jeanne and Madame Nechuma, and Madame Magda lived within walking distance.

13. AI, Madame Denise, Madame Hanna.

14. Nancy L. Green, *The Pletzl of Paris: Jewish Immigrant Workers in the Belle Epoque* (New York: Holmes and Meier, 1986), 69–72.

15. Louis Chevalier, *Les Parisiens* (Hachette, 1967), 163.

16. Brody, *Rue des Rosiers*, 29.

17. Edward Said, *Orientalism* (1978; reprint, Harmondsworth: Penguin, 1985).

18. Earl of Cromer, *Modern Egypt*, vol. 2 (London: Macmillan, 1908), 146.

19. Brody, *Rue des Rosiers*, 25, 33.

20. David H. Weinberg, *Les Juifs à Paris de 1933 à 1939* (Calmann-Lévy, 1974), 22, 24.

21. Mauco to editor, *Réalités*, 12 February 1946. CAC: 860269 9.

22. Sauval mss, f° 86ff, BN, Baluze 212. In Robert Anchel, 'The Early History of the Jewish Quarters in Paris', *Jewish Social Studies* 2 (1940), 54.

23. Green, *The Pletzl of Paris*, 71.

24. Charlotte Roland, *Du Ghetto à l'occident: deux générations yiddiches en France* (Editions de Minuit, 1962), 130.

25. Robert Anchel, *Les Juifs de France* (J. B. Jamin, 1946), 71.

26. Wieviorka, *Ils étaient juifs*; Françoise Morier (ed.), *Belleville, Belleville: visages d'une planète* (Créaphis, 1994).

27. Groupe Juif du Parti Communiste, 'Directives générales pour la préparation de l'insurrection nationale', 1945 (Unpublished typescript), 270.

28. Renée Poznanski, 'Reflections on Jewish Resistance and Jewish Resistants in France', *Jewish Social Studies* 2, no. 1 (1995) provides a useful summary of the debate. See also Adam Rayski, 'La MOI: spécificité de la résistance juive,' in *De l'exil à la résistance*, eds. Karl Bartosek, René Gallissot and Denis Peschanski (Arcantère, 1989); Adam Rayski, *Le Choix des Juifs sous Vichy: entre soumission et résistance* (La Découverte, 1992); Patrick Binisti, 'Identité juive et résistance. Deux notions distinctes,' *Le Monde juif*, no. 152 (September–December 1994); David Knout, *Contribution à l'histoire de la résistance juive en France, 1940–1944* (Editions du Centre, 1947); David Diamant, *La Résistance juive. Entre gloire et tragédie* (L'Harmattan, 1993); David Diamant, *Les Juifs dans la résistance française 1940–1944 (avec armes ou sans armes)* (Le Pavillon Roger Maria Editeur, 1971); Stéphane Courtois, 'Que savait la presse communiste clandestine?', in *Qui savait quoi? L'extermination des Juifs, 1941–1945*, eds. Stéphane Courtois and Adam Rayski (La Découverte, 1987); Jacques Adler, 'Les Juifs dans la résistance communiste,' *Le Monde juif* 50, no. 152 (1994); Mosco, *Les terroristes à la retraite*, France, 1985; Jacques Adler, *The Jews of Paris and the Final Solution: Communal Response and Internal Conflicts, 1940–44* (Oxford: Oxford University Press, 1989); Annie Kriegel, 'De la résistance juive', *Pardès*, no. 2 (1985); Annie Kriegel, *Réflexions sur les questions juives* (Hachette, 1984); Lucien Lazare, *Rescue As Resistance: How Jewish Organizations Fought the Holocaust in France* (New York: Columbia University Press, 1996); Jacques Ravine, *La Résistance organisée des Juifs en France 1940–1944* (Julliard, 1973); Adam Rayski, *Nos illusions perdues* (Balland, 1985); Stéphane Courtois, Denis Peschanski and Adam Rayski, *Le Sang de l'étranger. Les immigrés de la MOI dans la résistance* (Fayard, 1989).
29. E.g., Groupe Juif, 'Directives générales'.
30. Lazare, *Rescue*.
31. Simon Schwarzfuchs, *Aux prises avec Vichy: histoire politique des Juifs de France, 1940–1944* (Calmann-Lévy, 1998).
32. Jacques Adler, *Face à la persécution: les organisations juives à Paris de 1940 à 1944* (Calmann-Lévy, 1985); Asher Cohen, *Persécutions et sauvetages: Juifs et Français sous l'occupation et sous Vichy* (Du Cerf, 1993); Rayski, *Choix*.
33. Claude Collin, *Jeune combat: les jeunes Juifs dans la MOI dans la résistance* (Presses Universitaires de Grenoble, 1998), 117.
34. AI, Madame Hanna, Madame Frida. On communist failure to ally with Hashomer Hatzair, see Adler, *Face à la persécution*, 177.
35. Adler, *Jews of Paris*, 178.
36. Serge Klarsfeld, *Vichy-Auschwitz: le rôle de Vichy dans la solution finale de la question juive en France. 1942*, vol. 1 (Fayard, 1983), 121.
37. Hanna Diamond, *Women and the Second World War in France 1939–1948: Choices and Constraints* (Harlow: Longman, 1999).
38. Paula Schwartz, '*Partisanes* and Gender Politics in Vichy France', *French Historical Studies* 16, no. 1 (Spring 1989).
39. Rita Thalmann, 'Femmes juives dans la résistance et la libération du territoire', *Le Monde juif* 50, no. 152 (September–December 1994), 179.
40. H. R. Kedward, *In Search of the Maquis: Rural Resistance in Southern France, 1942–1944* (Oxford: Clarendon Press, 1993), 89.

41. AI, Madame Rachel.
42. Tzvetan Todorov and Annick Jacquet, *Guerre et paix sous l'occupation: témoignages recuillis au centre de la France* (Arléa, 1996), 144.
43. Fabrice Virgili, *La France 'virile': des femmes tondues à la libération* (Payot, 2000), 74; Susan Jeffords, *The Remasculinization of America: Gender and the Vietnam War* (Bloomington: University of Indiana Press, 1989); Atina Grossmann, 'A Question of Silence: The Rape of German Women by Occupation Soldiers', *October*, no. 72 (1995); Alain Brossat, *Les Tondues. Un carnaval moche* (Levallois-Perret: Manya, 1992); Corran Laurens, ' "La Femme au turban": les femmes tondues', in *The Liberation of France: Image and Event*, eds. H. R. Kedward and Nancy Wood (Oxford: Berg, 1995); Luc Capdevila, 'La "Collaboration sentimentale": antipatriotisme ou sexualité hors-normes?', *Cahiers de l'IHTP* 31 (October 1995).
44. Virgili, *France 'virile'*, 324.
45. AI, Madame Hanna.
46. See the FFEPH/INED survey of Polish and Italian immigrant labour: CAC: 760138 TR 1275–9.
47. Karen Adler, ' "Un Mythe Necéssaire et Sacré"? Responses to the 50th Anniversaries of Liberation', *Modern and Contemporary France* 3, no. 1 (1995); 'Images de la Libération' exhibition, Paris Hôtel de Ville, July–October 1994.
48. Cf. Claudine Vegh, *Je ne lui ai pas dit au revoir: des enfants de déportés parlent* (Gallimard, 1979).
49. AI, Madame Rachel.
50. Jean Baldensperger, *Les Journées du 19 au 28 août 1944*. France, 1944.
51. Joan Ringelheim, 'Genocide and Gender: A Split Memory', in *Gender and Catastrophe*, ed. Ronit Lentin (London: Zed Books, 1997), 20.
52. AI, Madame Rachel; Virgili, *France 'virile'*, 288–9.
53. Michel de Certeau, *Heterologies: Discourses on the Other* (Manchester: Manchester University Press, 1986), 197.
54. Elizabeth Wilson, 'The Invisible *Flâneur*', in *The Contradictions of Culture: Cities, Culture, Women* (London: Sage, 2001).
55. Fernand Boverat, *Comment nous vaincrons la dénatalité?* (ANCD, 1938), 10.
56. Simon Kitson, 'The Police in the Liberation of Paris', in *The Liberation of France: Image and Event*, eds. H. R. Kedward and Nancy Wood (Oxford: Berg, 1995).
57. Claude Lévy and Paul Tillard, *La Grande Rafle du Vél d'Hiv (16 juillet 1942)* (Robert Laffont, 1967); The *rafle* began at 4 a.m. on 16 July 1942, and finished at 5 p.m. the following day.
58. AI, Madame Hanna. On Vincennes see Jean Laloum, *Les Juifs dans la banlieue parisienne, des années 20 aux années 50* (CNRS, 1998).
59. AI, Madame Madeleine. Cf. Gérard Noiriel, *Les Origines républicaines de Vichy* (Hachette, 1999), 184.
60. The aunt had a baby and so was spared. Madeleine was of French nationality, her parents stateless.
61. AI, Madame Perla.
62. AI, Madame Rachel.
63. AI, Madame Esther.
64. AI, Madame Nechuma.

65. AI, Madame Paulette.
66. *Ibid.*
67. Raymond Sarraute, *Etude sur la situation des immigrés en France. De la libération à la repression* (Comité Français pour la Défense des Immigrés, 1953).
68. See chapters four and five.
69. Bruno Halioua, *Blouses blanches, étoiles jaunes. L'exclusion des médecins juifs en France sous l'occupation* (Liana Levi, 2000), 202.
70. Serge Klarsfeld, *Vichy-Auschwitz: le rôle de Vichy dans la solution finale de la question juive en France. 1943–1944*, vol. 2 (Fayard, 1985), 393. Of 75,721 deportees from France, 1,647 men and 913 women survived; more women than men (892 to 863) survived from deportations in 1943 and 1944.
71. In Lévy and Tillard, *Grande Rafle*, 96.
72. AI, Madame Esther.
73. AI, Madame Hanna.
74. On the political weakness of the Parti Communiste Internationaliste, see AN: F^7 15284.
75. AI, Madame Magda.
76. AI, Madame Sara.
77. AI, Madame Fanny.
78. *Ibid.*
79. B. Honig, 'Toward an Agonistic Feminism: Hannah Arendt and the Politics of Identity', in *Feminists Theorize the Political*, eds. Judith Butler and Joan W. Scott (New York: Routledge, 1992), 231.
80. AI, Madame Paulette.
81. The most obvious example of this at the time of the event was the French state's bar on 'ostentatious' religious clothing in schools, generally Muslim girls' veils or headscarves. Rachel Bloul, 'Veiled Objects of (Post-)Colonial Desire: Forbidden Women Disrupt the Republican Fraternal Sphere', *Australian Journal of Anthropology* 5, no. 1–2 (1994).
82. Roblin, *Juifs de Paris*, 161.
83. AI, Madame Madeleine, Madame Hanna, Madame Magda.
84. AI, Madame Hanna, Madame Madeleine.
85. Atina Grossmann, 'Trauma, Memory, and Motherhood: Germans and Jewish Displaced Persons in Post-Nazi Germany, 1945–1949', *Archiv für Sozialgeschichte*, no. 38 (1998), 228.
86. *Ibid.*, 229.
87. AI, Madame Jeanne.
88. AI, Madame Sara.
89. See chapter two. Jacqueline Mesnil-Amar, *Ceux qui ne dormaient pas 1944–1946 (fragments de journal)* (Editions de Minuit, 1957), 60–1; AI, Madame Jeanne.
90. Anna Seghers, *Transit Visa* (London: Eyre and Spottiswoode, 1945), 15.
91. AI, Madame Madeleine.
92. A useful overview of the historiography of oral history is in Robert Perks and Alistair Thomson (eds.), *The Oral History Reader* (London: Routledge, 1998).
93. Annette Wieviorka, *L'Ere du témoin* (Plon, 1998).
94. *Ibid.*, 173. My emphasis.

95. Luisa Passerini, 'Mythbiography in Oral History', in *The Myths We Live By*, ed. Raphael Samuel and Paul Thompson (London: Routledge, 1990), 60.

96. H. R. Kedward, 'Resiting French Resistance', *Transactions of the Royal Historical Society* 6, no. 9 (1999), 280; Bonnie G. Smith, *The Gender of History: Men, Women, and Historical Practice* (1998; reprint, Cambridge, MA: Harvard University Press, 2000).

97. Wieviorka, *Ere*, 179.

98. AI, Madame Magda.

99. Note, *c*.28 April 1945. AN: F^9 3244.

100. Note, head of medical services, 2 June 1945. AN: F^9 3244.

101. AI, Madame Sara.

102. AI, Madame Madeleine.

103. Alistair Thomson, 'Memory as a Battlefield: Personal and Political Investments in the National Military Past', *Oral History Review* 22, no. 2 (Winter 1995).

104. Mark Roseman, 'Recent Writing on the Holocaust', *Journal for Contemporary History* 36, no. 2 (2001), 369.

Chapter 7   Conclusion

1. Gérard Noiriel, *Les Origines républicaines de Vichy* (Paris: Hachette, 1999).

2. Martin Alexander, 'Some Thoughts on the Defeat of 1940', unpublished paper, Society for the Study of French History, University of Nottingham, April 2003.

3. Abigail Gregory and Ursula Tidd (eds.), *Women in Contemporary France* (Oxford: Berg, 2000), 6.

4. Julian Jackson, *France: The Dark Years 1940–1944* (Oxford: Oxford University Press, 2001), 618–9; Henry Rousso, *La Hantise du passé: entretien avec Philippe Petit* (Paris: Textuel, 1998).

5. Éric Conan and Henry Rousso, *Vichy, un passé qui ne passe pas* (Paris: Fayard, 1994); K. H. Adler, 'Vichy History: the Obsessive Turn?', University of Oxford, November 2002.

6. Marc Hillel, *Le Massacre des survivants en Pologne 1945–1947* (Plon, 1989).

7. AI, Madame Hanna.

8. *Aurore*, 31 May 1945; *La Terre retrouvée*, 20 June 1945; *Humanité*, 6 June 1945; *Droit et liberté*, 31 May 1945; Alliance antiraciste, *Congrès national 21–22 juin 1947* (Alliance Antiraciste, 1947).

9. Ordonnance, 14 November 1944.

10. Raymond Sarraute and Jacques Rabinovitch, *Examen succinct de la situation actuelle juridique des Juifs* (Centre de Documentation des Déportés et Spoliés Juifs, 1945), 17–18.

11. AN: 72 AJ 598.

12. AI, Madame Paulette.

13. *Bulletin du Service Central des Déportés Israélites*, no. 7, 15 May 1945; *Droit et liberté*, 24 March 1945.

14. Georges Mauco and Maurice Grandazzi, *La Démographie à l'école. Manuel à l'usage des maîtres* (ANCD, 1948).

15. Circulaire du 27 avril 1947 relative à l'instruction des demandes de naturalisation in J.-L. Mottier and Maurice Caillez, *Guide pratique des étrangers en France* (Librairie du Journal des Notaires et des Avocats, 1948), 389.
16. Centre d'Orientation Sociale des Etrangers, August 1946. CAC: 860269 2.
17. Philippe Burrin, *Living with Defeat: France under the German Occupation, 1940–1944* (1995; reprint, London: Arnold, 1996), 468–70.
18. Alfred Sauvy, *La Prévision économique* (Vendôme: PUF, 1943).
19. Robert Debré and Alfred Sauvy, *Des Français pour la France (le problème de la population)* (Gallimard, 1946), 228.
20. François Billoux, *Quand nous étions ministres* (Editions Sociales, 1972), 127.
21. *L'Effort de l'immigration dans la reconstruction française. Rapport général et les principales interventions: 2e congrès national des immigrés de France* (Centre d'Action et de Défense des Immigrés, 1946), 15.
22. Circulaire du 27 avril 1947.

Bibliography

Archival sources

1. American Jewish Joint Distribution Committee

310–1   France. General 1944–49
318–23   France. 1945–51
324   France. Medical and mental health 1946–62
328   France. Refugees 1945–62
329–30   France. Relief supplies 1945–53
371   France. UJRE

2. Archives Nationales

72 AJ: Deuxième Guerre Mondiale
596   Correspondence, Jewish organizations, conferences
598   Post-liberation antisemitism
612   Press cuttings
1892   Concentration camps
1942–4   Centre de Formation Internationale
Posters:
1664   Centre d'Action et de Défense des Immigrés
1677   'La 5e colonne est toujours debout'
1721   'Tous déportés, prisonniers, combattants … sont invités'
1722   'Pour la paix du monde'
1732   'Ne gaspillez pas le pain!'

AJ 43: Organisation Internationale pour Réfugiés
1028   Post-war refugees in France

F¹A: Ministère de l'Intérieur
3241   Union des Femmes Françaises
3252   Population, health, social security, refugees
3253   Repatriation of prisoners and deportees
3255   Prostitution
3345–6   Foreigners in France 1944–47
3355   Political parties, women's movements, family associations

F⁷: Police
15283–5   Surveillance of political parties

F⁹: Ministère des Prisonniers, Déportés et Réfugiés
3107   Refugees, resistance, expulsions
3117   Legislation for deportees
3127   Repatriation to France
3137   Repatriation: propaganda
3140   Repatriation: propaganda
3162–3   Repatriation: non-French nationals
3169   Repatriation: press
3184   Protection of deportees' children
3190   Assistance to the absent
3244   Health service
3247   Social service
3252   Foreign refugees
3271   Repatriation of Jews
3283   Young women deportees
3792   Repatriation of foreigners
3821   Foreign refugees
3823   Refugees: social action
3827   Foreign refugees
3837   Foreign refugee social services

F¹⁷: Instruction Publique
16847   Epuration

F²²: Travail et Sécurité Sociale
2024   Workers' movements, 1943
2050   CFLN (Algiers): Social problems in liberated France
2052   Jews, Aubrac, 1944

F⁴¹: Information
350   Jewish problem
353   Divorce, family, 1945–47
453   Congrès International des Femmes, 1945

F⁶⁰: Premier Ministre
246   Feminist groups
395   Refugees: national defence, 1939–47
438   Elections, 1944–47
476   Festivals and ceremonies, 1945
492   Control of foreigners, 1945–47
498   Haut Comité de la Population, 1939–40
499   Naturalizations
507   Public order
603   Prostitution
606   Measures in favour of natality

894 Prisoners, deportees, refugees
895 Comité Intercommissarial pour Préservation et Développement de la Population
1411 Protection of pregnancy

Mauco Papers
(stored at the time of consultation in twelve uncatalogued boxes organized as follows)

1 Correspondence; Ecole normale d'Instituteurs; press cuttings; HCCPF
2 HCCPF; correspondence; child psychology centres
3 Enquiries into readaptation; psychoanalytic training; Centre Claude Bernard
4 Teaching materials; psycho-educative training; HCCPF; Centre Claude Bernard
5 Centre Claude Bernard; HCCPF; Report on ageing
6 Foreign immigration; *Ethnie française*; Centre d'Etudes du Problème des Etrangers; articles; Jewish refugees; racism and anti-racism
7 Immigrants; racism; schools; housing; health; political role; countries of emigration; demography; recruitment; HCCPF; Royal Commission on Population; Action psychologique; Ecole des Parents
8 Centre Claude Bernard; correspondence; HCCPF; psychoanalytic organizations; souvenirs
9 Correspondence; client notes; resistance
10 Psychoanalytic consultations and conferences; police; mobilization; correspondence; *Bulletins d'information et de documentation*, Gouvernement provisoire
11 Psychoanalysis and psychology; Egypt; correspondence; Union Internationale pour l'Etude Scientifique de la Population; Centre Claude Bernard; international conference on child education
12 War; refugees; German nationals; immigration; Riom trial; *Ethnie française*; foreigners in France; Légion des Volontaires Antibolchévique; hospital conditions; assimilation; Révolution 1940

3. Bibliothèque de Documentation Internationale Contemporaine

Dossiers:
Communist women and war
Women, 1951, Paris
Elections
MLN
Jews 1940–44
Liberation of Paris
Prostitution

4. Centre de Documentation Juive Contemporaine

XXVIII   UGIF
XCV   Montandon

CCCLXXIII   Women internees, 1939–40
DCXXIX   List-Pakin
DCXXX   List-Pakin

5. Centre des Archives Contemporaines

760136:   INED/Fondation Française pour l'Etude des Problèmes Humains
TR 1277–8   Enquiry into Adaptation of Italians and Poles in France 1951

860296: Haut Comité Consultatif de la Population et de la Famille
1   Members; meetings
2   Relations with other organizations; ANCD; Royal Commission on Population; immigrants' organizations
3   Projects
7   Immigration; North Africa; Foreigners' Statute; immigration in Europe
8   General Secretary; interministerial meetings on immigration; assimilation; various commissions
9   World family congress, 1947; immigration studies; Union Internationale pour l'Etude Scientifique des Problèmes de la Population; articles, correspondence, by Georges Mauco

6. Fondation Nationale des Sciences Politiques

Press dossiers:
Family
Female workers
Memory

Clandestine periodicals

Dates indicated where known.
14 Juillet. Journal des marraines de la Compagnie des Francs-Tireurs et Partisans Français 'LES TROIS GLORIEUSES'. February 1944.
93. Organe des héritiers de la Révolution française. 1942.
Amies du front
Appel aux femmes catholiques! Pour l'union de toutes les femmes de cœur pour sauver la famille pour libérer la France. Union des Comités des Femmes de France
L'Appel des femmes. Organe du Comité Féminin de Toulouse. Toulouse: September 1943.
Assistance française. Aux emprisonés, internés et déportés civils. A leurs familles et aux familles de patriotes fusillés. February–July 1944.
Assistance française. Bulletin de la visiteuse. June 1944 and n.d.
L'Aube. Le journal des femmes de l'Ile de France. 1941.
L'Aurore. Organe du groupe 'Esprit et Courage'. 1943.
Aux armes citoyens
Bulletin intérieur. Fédération des Jeunesses Communistes de France. Zone sud, March 1944.
Bulletin pour l'organisation et l'activité des femmes communistes. July 1943.

Les Cahiers. Etudes pour une révolution française. OCM. June–September 1942.

Le Carnet de la ménagère. Edité par les 'UNION DES MENAGERES' Région Parisienne. February–March 1944.

Chantier de Gaël. Feuille revendicative des ouvriers et ouvrières du camp. August 1941.

Chateaubriant. Bulletin spécial de l'ASSISTANCE FRANÇAISE réservé aux comités de veuves de fusillés. August 1944.

La Cinématographie française. May 1944.

La Clamartoise. 1943?

Combat du Languedoc. Publié par les Mouvements de Résistance Unis. July 1943.

Combat médicale. Organe des médecins du Mouvement National contre le Racisme.

Combat. Supplément Lyonnais. Organe des Mouvements de Résistance Unis. April 1943: no. 6.

Commune de Paris. Journal des marraines de la Compagnie de Francs-Tireurs et Partisans 'Commune de Paris'. February 1944.

Le Coq enchaîné... est là pour libérer la France. 733e jour de la LUTTE du PEUPLE FRANÇAIS pour sa LIBERATION. Lyons: 26 June 1942.

Cri d'alarme. Edité par la Commission de l'Enfance de l'Union des Femmes Françaises 'Région Parisienne'. February–April 1944.

Le Cri des femmes. Organe des Comités de Défense de la Famille. Lyon: 1943.

L'Ecole libératrice. Organe du Syndicat National des Instituteurs (reconstitué clandestinement). February–September 1944.

En avant. Journal de combat de la jeunesse juive. February–May 1943.

Espérance. Journal du Comité des Femmes de l'Allier. March 1944.

L'Etincelle. Journal édité par le Parti Communiste de Boulogne-Billancourt. March 1942.

L'Etincelle. Organe des Comités de la 4ème Internationale. November 1939–September 1940.

L'Etoile des Savoies. Organe du Comité des Femmes de France – région des Savoies. March 1944.

L'Etoile féminine. Edité par l'Union des Femmes de Romainville pour la Défense de la Famille et la Libération de la France. February 1943.

La Femme Comtoise. Organe de 'l'Union des femmes pour la Défense de la Famille et la Libération de la Patrie'. August 1943.

La Femme d'Eure et Loir. Journal des Femmes patriotes d'Eure et Loir. 25 August 1943.

Femmes. Edité par les femmes communistes de Choisy. January 1941.

Femmes. Edité par les femmes communistes de Vitry. January–April 1941.

Les Femmes à l'action! Organe du Comité des Femmes de France régions Aude-Hérault. July 1944.

Femmes à l'action! Organe du Comité des Femmes Hyéroises. February 1944.

Femmes d'Auvergne

Femmes de Belleville

Femmes de la Loire. Organe des Comités des Femmes de France de la Loire. March 1944.

Femmes de Limousin. Le 14 juillet a été partout un magnifique élan de patriotisme. Limousin: Limoges Comité Féminin du Limousin FFI, 1944.

Femmes de prisonniers. Journal féminin du Mouvement National des Prisonniers de Guerre et de Déportés. May–June 1944.

Femmes de Provence. Organe régionale d'union et de défense des femmes des Bouches du Rhône. May 1942–July 1943.

Femmes d'Orly

Femmes du Limousin. Comité Féminin du Limousin.

Femmes du Lot. Cahors: UFF.

Femmes françaises. Edité par 'France d'abord'. January–July 1944.

Femmes patriotes. Organe des Comités Féminins de la Résistance (MUR). February 1944.

Femmes varoises

La Franc-Comtoise. Journal des Comités Féminins de Franche-Comté. August 1942.

Français juifs. October 1940.

La France combattante des Côtes-du-Nord. Organe du Front National de Lutte pour la Libération de la France. October 1943.

Fraternité. Organe du Mouvement National Contre le Racisme (Zone sud). 1942–1944.

L'Humanité de la femme. Numéro spécial de l'Humanité. December 1940–March 1941.

L'Humanité des Paysans. Edition de la Corrèze. February 1941.

L'Humanité. Edition spéciale féminine. September 1942–June 1944.

L'Humanité. Organe central du Parti Communiste. 29 August 1942.

Information sur les atrocités nazies. September 1942.

Les Informations sociales. Bulletin d'information à l'usage des militants syndicalistes et des futurs cadres sociaux de la France liberée. June 1943–January 1944.

J'accuse. Journal de lutte contre le racisme. April 1942.

J'accuse. Organe de liaison des forces françaises contre la barbarie raciste. (From February 1943:) *Organe du Mouvement National contre le Racisme*. October 1942.

Jeanne la Lorraine. Journal des marraines du Groupe de Francs-Tireurs et Partisans 'Alsace-Lorraine'. January 1944.

Jeune combat. Organe de rassemblement de la jeunesse juive en lutte contre l'Hitlérisme et pour la libération de la France. July 1943–August 1944.

La Jeune ouvrière. Organe des jeunes cyndicalistes [sic]. 1944.

Le Jeune patriote. Edité par le Comité de la Jeunesse du Front National pour l'Indépendance de la France. 1943–44.

Jeune révolution. Bulletin révolutionnaire de la jeunesse française. Lyons: July 1944.

Jeunes Filles de France. Edité par la Fédération des Jeunesses Communistes de France. October 1940–July 1944.

Juifs de Paris. Milices patriotiques juives de Paris. 29 August 1944.

Les Lettres françaises. 1942–44.

La Liaison. Journal des familles des prisonniers. August 1941.

Libération de Bagnolet. Organe du Mouvement de la Libération Nationale. 1944.

Le Lot résistant. Organe des Lotois résistants, en collaboration avec la Fédération socialiste et la Section départementale de 'Libérer et Fédérer'. Souillac: no. 1: October 1943; no. 5: April 1944.

Lumières. Organe de la Section des Intellectuels du Mouvement National contre le Racisme. 1944.

La Lutte des classes. Organe du Groupe Communiste (4e Internationale). October 1942–March 1946.

Lutter et vaincre. Organe régional du Parti Communiste Français (SFIC) région Paris sud. 1942.

Le Madelon du franc-tireur. Journal des marraines des Francs-Tireurs et partisans région Parisienne. 1944.

Marianne. Journal des marraines du groupe de Francs-Tireurs 'République'. January 1944.

La Marraine du réfractaire. Organe des femmes patriotes de l'est. January 1944.

La Ménagère. Journal des Comités Féminins du Nord et du Pas de Calais. November 1943–February 1944.

La Ménagère. Journal des Comités Populaires Féminins du Pas-de-Calais. August 1941.

Ménagère de Bordeaux

Ménagère de Gentilly

Ménagère de l'Aisne

La Ménagère de Paris. December 1941–February 1942.

Ménagère de Villejuif

La Ménagère parisienne. Edité par l'Union des Femmes Françaises pour la Défense de la Famille et la Libération de la France. October 1943.

Mères de France. August 1941.

Mouvement National contre le Racisme. Bulletin d'information. July 1944.

Notre lutte. Organe local du Parti Communiste Français – 14e arrdt. 1941.

Notre parole. 1941–43.

Notre propagande. Bulletin intérieur à l'usage des groupes. 1941–43.

Notre voix. Organe de rassemblement des Juifs contre le fascisme oppresseur. Zone non occupée: September 1942–April 1944.

Nous, les femmes. Journal des femmes communistes du Canton de Villejuif. April 1941.

Nous . . . les femmes. Edité par le Comité Populaire des Femmes du 17e arrdt. January 1941.

Patriote française.

La Patriote parisienne. Journal édité par l'Union des Femmes pour la Défense de la Famille et la Libération de la France. July–November 1943.

Le Progrès. Organe du canton d'Argenteuil du Parti Communiste Français (SFIC). September 1940–August 1941.

Propagande féminine. Contre la famine qui menace nos petits. Les Comités Populaires Féminins, January–February 1941.

La Provence libre. Organe varois du Front National pour la Libération de la France. April 1944.

Quatre-vingt Treize! Journal des marraines de la Compagnie des Francs-Tireurs-Partisans (FTPF) 'TRIBUNE du PEUPLE'. UFF de la région parisienne, July 1944.

Quatre-vingt-treize. Organe des marraines des Francs-Tireurs et Partisans – détachement Victor Hugo. October 1943–January 1944.

Rubrique féminine de Créteil-Bonneuil. Journal du Comité des Femmes de Créteil-Bonneuil. January 1943.

La Rubrique féminine de Saint Maur. Journal du Comité Féminin de Saint-Maur. January 1943.

Sauvetage de la famille française. Organe de combat des femmes françaises dans le Front National. March 1943.

Trait d'union des familles de prisonniers de guerre. 1941–44.

Le Travailleur sétois. Parti Communiste Français SFIC, January 1942.

Unzer Wort. September 1940–March 1941.

L'Union des femmes de l'est. Journal des patriotes françaises unies pour la libération de la France. January 1944.

Union des Femmes Françaises pour la Défense de la Famille et la Libération de la France. Bulletin d'information des comités. 1944.

Vivandière

La Voix de la femme juive. Organe du Mouvement National Juif de Lutte contre le Fascisme (section féminine). 15 August 1943.

La Voix des dauphinoises. July 1944.

La Voix des femmes d'Arcueil. Edité par des ménagères. December 1942.

La Voix des femmes de Bourgogne. September–December 1941.

La Voix des femmes de la Côte d'Or. January 1942.

La Voix des femmes de la Marne. August 1941.

La Voix des femmes de Normandie. Organe des comités féminins de résistance de Seine-Inférieure. September 1943.

La Voix des femmes de Saône et Loire. June 1941.

La Voix des femmes du 18ème. May 1943.

La Voix des femmes. Département de la Seine-et-Oise. February 1942.

La Voix des Femmes. Edité par l'Union des Femmes pour la Défense de la Famille et la Libération de la France Comité du 20me arrondissement. May 1943.

La Voix des femmes. Gard: 27 January 1942.

La Voix des femmes. Journal des femmes du XIIIe édité par le Comité Populaire Féminin du XIIe [sic]. February 1941.

La Voix des femmes. Organe des comités populaires féminins. Zone sud: November 1941–March 1944.

Voix des lilas

La Voix féminine. Mensuel clandestin édité par les comités féminins de l'Aube et de la Haute-Marne. August 1941.

La Voix féminine. Organe mensuel des comités féminins. March 1941.

La Voix humaine. Organe des instituteurs antiracistes. February 1943.

La Voix populaire. Edité par les communistes d'Epinay. May 1941.

Other periodicals

Action

Action féminine: sud-ouest

Activité des organisations juives en France sous l'occupation

Actualités juives

Alyah. La montée vers la Palestine

Amandier fleuri. Cahiers de pensée et de vie juives

Ami

Ancien combattant juif

Annales de géographie

Appel. Bulletin d'information de l'aide aux Israélites, Victimes de la guerre

Arbeyter Vort

Arche de Noë

Association Consistoriale Israélite de Paris
Au devant de la vie. Bulletin mensuel d'information des 'Jeunes de la LICA'
Aube
L'Aurore
Bachaar
Bleu et blanc. Cahiers mensuels du Mouvement de Jeunesse Sioniste à Nice
Bulletin d'informations de l'union mondiale OSE
Bulletin de l'Union Séfaradite de France
Bulletin de nos communautés. Organe du Judaïsme d'Alsace et de Lorraine
Bulletin du CDJC
Bulletin du Centre Israélite d'Information
Bulletin du Service Central des Déportés Israélites
Bulletin intérieur d'information du CRIF
Bulletin mensuel féminin
Bulletin quotidien d'informations de l'Agence Télégraphique Juive
Cahier jaune
Cahiers antiracistes
Cahiers de l'émancipation
Cahiers sefardis
Cité soir
Combat
La Croix
Défense
Défense de l'homme
Déporté du travail
Difesa della Razza
Documents et informations (FDIF)
Droit de vivre
Droit et liberté
Echo de la résistance
Echo des tabacs
Emounathenon. Bulletin de l'Union de la Jeunesse Juive Traditionaliste de France/
    Suisse
Epoque
Ethnie française
La Femme
Femmes françaises
Figaro
Folksgezunt
France libre
France-soir
Front national
Gazette d'Israël
Groupement des artistes juifs en France
Hamachkif-Observateur
Hillel
L'Humanité
Images de la vie: l'actualité juive dans le monde

Bibliography

Immigration
Information juive
Informations juives
Jeune combat
Jeunes Filles de France
Jeunesse à l'action
Journal des combattants
Journal des communautés
Kadimah
Libération
Libération soir
Lumières
Maman
MLN: bulletin intérieur du Mouvement de Libération Nationale
Le Monde
Monde juif
Mouvement National contre le Racisme. Bulletin d'Information
Naïe Presse
Noar
Notre foi
Notre mouvement
Notre parole
Notre voix
Nouvelle renaissance
Nouvelle revue théologique (Belgium)
Nouvelles
Nouvelles juives mondiales
OPEJ, Œuvre de Protection des Enfants Juifs
Pages sociales
Parisien libéré
Parole. Hebdomadaire de l'actualité Juive
Patriote résistant
Point de vue
Population
Pour la vie
Privilèges des femmes
Quand même
Quinzaine
Réforme
Regards
Renaissance
Renovation
Res Publica
Réveil des jeunes
Revue d'histoire de la médecine hébraïque
Revue de l'Alliance Nationale contre la Dépopulation
Revue de la pensée juive
Riposte

Samedi soir
Siona
Témoignage chrétien
Terre retrouvée
Unir
Unis
Unité
Univers. Revue d'information et d'action pour l'union fraternelle entre tous les hommes
Unzer Shtimme
Unzer Veg
Vie juive
Voix des camps
Voix juive
Volontés
Yechouroun
Yedioth
Yid un di velt

Books and articles

Place of publication is Paris, unless otherwise stated.

Adam, Gérard. *Etudes syndicales*. Vol. 3, *La CGT-FO*. FNSP, 1965.

Adé. 'A propos du Congrès de l'Union des Femmes Françaises'. *Pour la vie 1*, no. 2 (October–December 1945): 71–5.

Adler, Jacques. 'Les Juifs dans la résistance communiste'. *Le Monde juif 50*, no. 152 (1994): 104–11.

Adler, Jacques. *Face à la persécution: les organisations juives à Paris de 1940 à 1944*, trans. André Charpentier. Calmann-Lévy, 1985.

Adler, Jacques. *The Jews of Paris and the Final Solution: Communal Response and Internal Conflicts, 1940–44*. Oxford: Oxford University Press, 1989.

Adler, K. H. ' "Un Mythe Necéssaire et Sacré"? Responses to the 50th Anniversaries of Liberation'. *Modern and Contemporary France 3*, no. 1 (1995): 119–26.

Adler, K. H. 'Vichy History: the Obsessive Turn?'. Unpublished paper, University of Oxford, November 2002.

Albert, Pierre, Gilles Feyel and Jean-François Picard (eds.), *Documents pour l'histoire de la presse nationale aux XIXe et XXe siècles*. CNRS, 1977.

Alex, Juliette. *Trois compliments pour les tout petits à l'occasion de la Fête des Mères*. Mâcon: Robert Martin, 1945.

Alexander, Martin, 'Some Thoughts on the Defeat of 1940'. Unpublished paper, Society for the Study of French History, University of Nottingham, April 2003.

Alliance antiraciste. *Congrès national 21–22 juin 1947*. Alliance Antiraciste, 1947.

'Allocution'. In *Remise solennelle du Grand Prix de l'Académie des Sciences Morales et Politiques à M. Alfred Sauvy*, 7–9. Palais de l'Institut, 1984.

Alvergnat, M. *Organisations familiales dans le monde: congrès mondial de la famille et de la population*, vol. 2, 85, Problèmes familiaux dans le monde. UNAF, 1947.

Anchel, Robert. 'The Early History of the Jewish Quarters in Paris'. *Jewish Social Studies 2* (1940): 45–60.

Anchel, Robert. *Les Juifs de France*. J. B. Jamin, 1946.

Arendt, Hannah. 'From the Dreyfus Affair to France Today.' *Jewish Social Studies* 4, no. 3 (July 1942): 195–240.

Aubrac, Lucie. *Ils partiront dans l'ivresse: Lyon, mai 43. Londres, février 44*. 1984; reprint, Seuil, 1986.

Aubrac, Lucie. *La Résistance (naissance et organisation)*. Robert Lang, 1945.

Aubrac, Lucie. 'Témoignage: le vote des femmes'. *Matériaux pour l'histoire de notre temps*, no. 39–40 (July–December 1995): 62–4.

Audit, Jean and Marie Tisserand-Perrier. *L'Eugénique et l'euthénique (problèmes scientifiques et politiques)*. J.-B. Baillière et Fils, 1952.

Audit, Jean and Marie Tisserand-Perrier. *L'Avortement et les moyens anticonceptionnels*. La Famille d'aujourd'hui. Sa formation. Son développement, no. 4. UNCAF, 1947.

Barrès, Maurice. *Scènes et doctrines du nationalisme*. 1902; reprint, Plon, 1930.

Beaumont, Guy de. *Guide pratique de l'orientation professionnelle*. Etudes Corporatives. Dunod, 1938.

Beauvoir, Simone de. *Le Deuxième Sexe*. 1949; reprint, Gallimard, 1979.

Bellanger, Claude, Jacques Godechot, Pierre Guiral and Fernand Terrour. *Histoire générale de la presse française*. Vol. 4, *De 1940 à 1958*, PUF, 1975.

Bellanger, Claude. *Presse clandestine 1940–1944*. Armand Colin, 1961.

Bendjebbar, André. *Libérations rêvées, libérations vécues 1940–1945*. Hachette, 1994.

Bensimon, Doris and Sergio della Pergola. *La Population juive de France: sociodémographie et identité*. Jerusalem: Institute of Contemporary Jewry, 1984.

Berge, André. 'Le Centre Psycho-Pédagogique du Lycée Claude Bernard pour l'enseignement secondaire'. *A Criança Portuguesa* (1950–1951): 81–5.

Bernard, Jean-Jacques. *Le Camp de la mort lente: Compiègne 1941–42*. Albin Michel, 1944.

Bernardini, Jean-Marc. *Le Darwinisme social en France (1859–1918): fascination et rejet d'une idéologie*. CNRS, 1997.

Bertin, Célia. *Marie Bonaparte*. Plon, 1982.

Billig, Joseph. *Commissariat Général aux Questions Juives (1941–1944)*. 3 vols, Editions du Centre, 1955–57.

Billoux, François. *La Renaissance française et la santé publique. Discours prononcé à l'Assemblée Consultative Provisoire*. PCF, 12 March 1945.

Billoux, François. *Quand nous étions ministres*. Editions Sociales, 1972.

Binisti, Patrick. 'Identité juive et résistance. Deux notions distinctes'. *Le Monde juif*, no. 152 (September–December 1994): 218–28.

Birnbaum, Pierre. *Un Mythe politique: 'la république juive'*. Fayard, 1988.

Blocq, Maxime. *Illusions capitalistes*. Les Œuvres Françaises, 1936.

Blocq-Mascart, Maxime. *Chroniques de la résistance: suivies d'études pour une nouvelle révolution française par les groupes de l'OCM*. Corrêa, 1945.

Blocq-Mascart, Maxime. *Les Cahiers. Etudes pour une révolution française*. Organisation Civile et Militaire, June–September 1942.

Bloit, Michel. *Moi, Maurice, bottier de Belleville*. L'Harmattan, 1993.

Bloul, Rachel. 'Veiled Objects of (Post-)Colonial Desire: Forbidden Women Disrupt the Republican Fraternal Sphere'. *Australian Journal of Anthropology* 5, no. 1–2 (1994): 113–23.

Bock, Gisela and Pat Thane (eds.), *Maternity and Gender Policies: Women and the Rise of European Welfare States 1880s–1950s*. London: Routledge, 1991.

Bonaparte, Marie. *Derrière les vitres closes: les souvenirs d'enfance.* Vol. 1, *A la mémoire des disparus*, London: Imago, 1952.

Bordeaux, Michèle. *La Victoire de la famille dans la France défaite: Vichy 1940–1944.* Flammarion, 2002.

Boucher, Frédérique. 'Abriter vaille que vaille, se loger coûte que coûte'. *Cahiers de l'IHTP* 5 (1989): 119–41.

Boverat, Fernand. *Comment nous vaincrons la dénatalité?* ANCD, 1938.

Boverat, Fernand. *La Crise des naissances.* ANCD, 1932.

Boverat, Fernand. *Le Massacre des innocents.* ANCD, 1939.

Boverat, Fernand. *Le Premier Devoir: faire vivre la France. Enseignement nataliste et familial dans les Chantiers de la Jeunesse.* Lyons: ANCD, 1943.

Boverat, Fernand. *Le Routier et le problème de la natalité. Etude sociale de Fernand Boverat suivie d'une série de sujets proposés aux clans de routiers pour leurs cercles d'études et enquêtes.* Vichy: Eclaireurs de France, 1943.

Boverat, Fernand. *Niveau d'existence et charges de famille.* FFEPH, 1944.

Boverat, Fernand. *Patriotisme et paternité.* Bernard Grasset, 1913.

Boverat, Fernand. *Une Doctrine de natalité.* FFEPH, 1943.

Brive, Marie-France. 'L'Image des femmes à la libération.' In *La Libération dans le Midi de la France*, ed. Rolande Trempé, 389–402. Toulouse: Eché Editeur/UTM, 1986.

Brody, Jeanne. *Rue des Rosiers: une manière d'être juif*. Autrement, 1995.

Brossat, Alain. *Les Tondues. Un carnaval moche.* Levallois-Perret: Manya, 1992.

Brubaker, Rogers. *Citizenship and Nationhood in France and Germany.* Cambridge, MA: Harvard University Press, 1992.

Bruhat, Yvonne. *Les Femmes et la Révolution française 1789–1939.* Comité mondial des Femmes contre la Guerre et le Fascisme, 1939.

Bruneau, Françoise. *Essai d'historique du mouvement né autour du journal clandestin 'Résistance'.* SEDES, 1951.

Burgdörfer, Friedrich. 'Die neue deutsche Bevölkerungsentwicklung im gesamteuropäischen Rahmen mit besonderer Berücksichtigung der zahlenmäßig erfaßbaren Auswirkungen bevölkerungspolitischer Maßnahmen'. In *Facteurs et conséquences de l'évolution démographique*, 7: 165–95. Congrès International de la Population. Hermann, 1938.

Burrin, Philippe. *Living with Defeat: France under the German Occupation, 1940–1944* (La France à l'heure allemande 1940–1944), trans. Janet Lloyd. 1995; reprint, London: Arnold, 1996.

Byer, Doris. 'Sexualität, Macht, Wohlfahrt: Zeitgemässe Erinnerungen an das "Rote Wien"'. *Zeitgeschichte* 14, no. 11–12 (1987): 442–63.

Calmette, Arthur. *L'O.C.M. Organisation civile et militaire: histoire d'un mouvement de résistance de 1940 à 1946.* PUF, 1961.

Cantillon, Richard. *Essai sur la nature du commerce en général. Texte de l'édition originale de 1755, avec des études et commentaires par Alfred Sauvy, Amintore Fanfani, Joseph J. Spengler, Louis Salleron.* INED, 1952.

Capdevila, Luc. *Les Bretons au lendemain de l'occupation: imaginaires et comportements d'une sortie de guerre (1944/1945).* Presses Universitaires de Rennes, 1999.

Capdevila, Luc. 'La "Collaboration sentimentale": antipatriotisme ou sexualité hors-normes?'. *Cahiers de l'IHTP* 31 (October 1995): 67–82.

Carol, Anne. *Histoire de l'eugénisme en France: les médecins et la procréation XIXe–XXe siècle.* Seuil, 1995.

Caron, Vicki. *Uneasy Asylum: France and the Jewish Refugee Crisis, 1933–1942.* Stanford: Stanford University Press, 1999.

Carroll, David. *French Literary Fascism: Nationalism, Anti-Semitism, and the Ideology of Culture.* Princeton: Princeton University Press, 1995.

Céline, Louis-Ferdinand. *L'Ecole des cadavres.* Denoël, 1938.

Chaperon, Sylvie. *Les Années Beauvoir 1945–1970.* Fayard, 2000.

Chauvière, Michel. 'L'Expert et les propagandistes: Alfred Sauvy et le Code de la Famille de 1939'. *Population* 47, no. 6 (November–December 1992): 1441–52.

Chauvy, Gérard. *Aubrac, Lyon 1943.* Albin Michel, 1997.

Chevalier, Louis. 'L'Ecole géographique française et la démographie'. *Population* 2, no. 1 (January–March 1947): 149–53.

Chevalier, Louis. 'Principaux aspects du problème de l'immigration'. In *Documents sur l'immigration,* eds. Louis Chevalier, Robert Gessain, G. de Longevialle, Jean Sutter. Travaux et Documents, no. 2. INED, 1947, 11–23.

Chevalier, Louis. *Démographie générale.* Dalloz, 1951.

Chevalier, Louis. *Les Parisiens.* Hachette, 1967.

Chevalley, Mme L. 'Le Rôle des organismes sociaux d'assistance dans une politique générale d'immigration'. *Bulletin d'information de l'Office Central des Œuvres de Bienfaisance,* no. 3 (March 1946): 77–85.

Chevalley, Mme L. 'Le Rôle du service social dans une politique générale d'immigration'. *Cahiers du Musée Social,* no. 2–3 (1947): 68–71.

Clark, Linda L. *The Rise of Professional Women in France: Gender and Public Administration since 1830.* Cambridge: Cambridge University Press, 2000.

Clarke, Jackie. 'Imagined Productive Communities: Industrial Rationalisation and Cultural Crisis in 1930s France'. *Modern and Contemporary France* 8, no. 3 (2000): 345–57.

Cohen, Asher. *Persécutions et sauvetages: Juifs et Français sous l'occupation et sous Vichy.* Du Cerf, 1993.

Cohen, Monique Lise and Eric Malo (eds.), *Les Camps du sud-ouest de la France 1939–1944: exclusion, internement et déportation.* Toulouse: Privat, 1994.

Cohen, Monique Lise and Valérie Ermosilla. *Les Juifs dans la résistance.* Toulouse: Bibliothèque Municipale, 1997.

Cohen, Phyllis Albert. 'Israelite and Jew: How Did Nineteenth-Century French Jews Understand Assimilation?'. In *Assimilation and Community: The Jews in Nineteenth-Century Europe,* eds. Jonathan Frankel and Steven J. Zipperstein, 88–109. Cambridge: Cambridge University Press, 1992.

Cohen, Phyllis Albert. 'L'Intégration et la persistance de l'ethnicité chez les Juifs dans la France moderne'. In *Histoire politique des Juifs de France: entre universalisme et particularisme,* ed. Pierre Birnbaum, 221–43. FNSP, 1990.

Cole, Joshua. *The Power of Large Numbers: Population, Politics, and Gender in Nineteenth-Century France.* Ithaca: Cornell University Press, 2000.

Collet, Mme. 'La Prolétarisation des classes moyennes en France'. In *Niveau de vie des familles: congrès mondial de la famille et de la population, Paris 1947.* Problèmes familiaux dans le monde. UNAF, 1948, 48–51.

Collet, S. 'Associations féminines et associations familiales'. *Pour la vie*, no. 13 (July–August 1947): 39–42.

Collet, S. 'L'Action sociale des associations familiales: l'aide familiale de "La Plus Grande Famille" ' *Pour la vie* 1, no. 2 (October–December 1945): 41–50.

Collin, Claude. *Jeune combat: les jeunes Juifs de la MOI dans la résistance*. Presses Universitaires de Grenoble, 1998.

Conan, Éric and Henry Rousso. *Vichy, un passé qui ne passe pas*. Fayard, 1994.

Conan, Éric and Henry Rousso. *Congrès mondial de la famille et de la population, Paris, 22–29 juin 1947*. UNAF, 1947.

Consistoire Israélite de Paris. *La Communauté de Paris après la libération. Tableau d'ensemble*. Consistoire Israélite de Paris, 1946.

Corbin, Alain. *Women for Hire: Prostitution and Sexuality in France after 1860*. Cambridge, MA: Harvard University Press, 1990.

Courtois, Stéphane, Denis Peschanski and Adam Rayski. *Le Sang de l'étranger. Les immigrés de la MOI dans la résistance*. Fayard, 1989.

Courtois, Stéphane. 'Que savait la presse communiste clandestine?'. In *Qui savait quoi? L'extermination des Juifs, 1941–1945*, eds. Stéphane Courtois and Adam Rayski, 103–12. La Découverte, 1987.

Courtois, Stéphane. *Le PCF dans la guerre: de Gaulle, la résistance, Staline...* Ramsay, 1980.

Danan, Alexis. *Maternité*. Albin Michel, 1936.

Darrow, Margaret H. *French Women and the First World War: War Stories of the Home Front*. Oxford: Berg, 2000.

de Certeau, Michel. *Heterologies: Discourses on the Other*, trans. Brian Massumi. Manchester: Manchester University Press, 1986.

de Gaulle, Charles. *Discours de guerre*. Vol. 3, *Mai 1944–septembre 1945*, Egloff, 1945.

de Gaulle, Charles. *Discours et messages 1940–1946*. Berger-Levrault, 1946.

de Gaulle, Charles. *Mémoires de guerre*. Vol. 3, *Le Salut*. 1959; reprint, Geneva: Famot, 1981.

Dean, Carolyn J. *The Self and its Pleasures: Bataille, Lacan, and the History of the Decentered Subject*. Ithaca: Cornell University Press, 1992.

Debré, Robert. 'La Résistance médicale'. In *La Résistance intellectuelle*, ed. Jacques Debû-Bridel, 185–201. Julliard, 1970.

Debré, Robert. *Ce que je crois*. Bernard Grasset, 1976.

Debré, Robert. *L'honneur de vivre: témoignage*. Hermann & Stock, 1974.

Debré, Robert and Alfred Sauvy. *Des Français pour la France (le problème de la population)*. Gallimard, 1946.

Debû-Bridel, Jacques (ed.), *La Résistance intellectuelle*. Julliard, 1970.

Dejonghe, Etienne. 'Les Départements du Nord et du Pas-de-Calais'. In *De la défaite à Vichy*. Vol. 2, *La France des années noires*, eds. Jean-Pierre Azéma, François Bédarida, 489–514. Seuil, 1993.

Demangeon, Albert and Georges Mauco. *Documents pour servir à l'étude des étrangers dans l'agriculture française*. Hermann, 1939.

Deschodt, Pierre-Jean and François Huguenin. *La République xénophobe*. J.-C. Lattès, 2001.

Devinat, E. *Livre de lecture et de morale: Morale – leçons de choses – récitation*. Larousse, 1921.

Diamant, David. *250 Combattants de la résistance témoignent: témoignages recueillis de septembre 1944 à décembre 1989*. L'Harmattan, 1991.

Diamant, David. *La Résistance juive. Entre gloire et tragédie*. L'Harmattan, 1993.

Diamant, David. *Les Juifs dans la résistance française 1940–1944 (avec armes ou sans armes)*. Le Pavillon Roger Maria Editeur, 1971.

Diamant, David. *Par-delà les barbelés. Lettres et écrits des camps et des prisons de France. Lettres jetées des trains de déportation. Ecrits d'Auschwitz. Créations journalistiques, littéraires et artistiques*. Un Comité de familles de fusillés et de rescapés des camps de concentration, 1986.

Diamond, Hanna. 'Women's Experience during and after World War Two in the Toulouse Area 1939–1948. Choices and Constraints'. Unpublished D.Phil. thesis, University of Sussex, 1992.

Diamond, Hanna. *Women and the Second World War in France 1939–1948: Choices and Constraints*. Harlow: Longman, 1999.

Donzelot, Jacques. *La Police des familles*. Editions de Minuit, 1977.

Doublet, Jacques. 'La Première Législation de la IVe République et la législation démographique'. *Population* 6, no. 3 (July–September 1951): 397–410.

Doublet, Jacques. 'Le Code de la Famille: le Haut Comité de la Population et le décret-loi du 29 juillet relatif à la famille et à la natalité françaises'. *Revue politique et parlementaire* (10 November 1939): 211–26.

Doublet, Jacques. 'Le Front du travail allemand'. Doctoral thesis, Faculté de Droit, 1937.

Doublet, Jacques. 'Politique démographique en Autriche'. *Population* 2, no. 2 (April–June 1947): 293–301.

Douzou, Laurent. *La Désobéissance: histoire d'un mouvement et d'un journal clandestins: Libération-sud (1940–1944)*. Odile Jacob, 1995.

Downs, Laura Lee. 'Les Marraines élues de la paix sociale? Les surintendantes d'usine et la rationalisation au travail en France 1917–1935'. *Mouvement Social*, no. 164 (July–September 1993): 53–76.

Dreyfus, Michel. *Histoire de la CGT*. Brussels: Editions Complexe, 1995.

Dreyfus-Armand, Geneviève. *L'Exil des républicains espagnols en France: de la guerre civile à la mort de Franco*. Albin Michel, 1999.

Drieu la Rochelle, Pierre. *Gilles*. Gallimard, 1939.

Drouard, Alain. 'Les Trois Ages de la Fondation Française pour l'Etude des Problèmes Humains'. *Population* 38, no. 6 (November–December 1983), 1,017–47.

Drouard, Alain. *Une Inconnue des sciences sociales: la Fondation Alexis Carrel 1941–1945*. La Maison des Sciences de l'Homme, 1992.

Drumont, Edouard. *La France juive*. Vol. 1. C. Marpon and E. Flammarion, 1886; reprint, La Librairie Française, 1986.

Dupâquier, Jacques. *Histoire de la population française*. Vol. 4, *De 1914 à nos jours*. PUF, 1988.

Earl of Cromer. *Modern Egypt*. Vol. 2. London: Macmillan, 1908.

L'Effort de l'immigration dans la reconstruction française. Rapport général et les principales interventions: 2e congrès national des immigrés de France. Centre d'Action et de Défense des Immigrés, 1946.

Equipe de recherche en civilisation allemande de l'Université de Provence, (eds.), *Les Camps en Provence: exil, internement, déportation 1933–1944*. Aix-en-Provence: Alinéa, 1984.

Exil et travail social: les orgines du SSAE. Special issue of *Accueillir*, 198, ed. Jacqueline Costa-Lascoux. SSAE, October 1994.

Fage, Anita. 'Economie et population: les doctrines françaises avant 1800'. *Population* 9, no. 1 (January–March 1954): 104–10.

Fage, Anita. 'La Révolution française et la population'. *Population* 8, no. 2 (April–June 1953): 310–36.

Fage, Anita. 'Les Doctrines de population des encyclopédistes'. *Population* 6, no. 4 (October–December 1951): 609–24.

Farmer, Sarah. *Oradour. Arrêt sur mémoire*. Calmann-Lévy, 1994.

Fatou, Raymond. 'Note sur le patronage des étrangers à Marseille. Les apatrides. Nécessité d'une identification systématique des étrangers'. In *Congrès international du patronage des libérés et des enfants traduits en Justice*. Cahors: 1937.

Fédération Démocratique Internationale des Femmes. 'Compte rendu des travaux du congrès'. In *Congrès International des Femmes*. FDIF, 1946.

Fédération Démocratique Internationale des Femmes. *Femmes du monde entier. 5e anniversaire*. FDIF, 1950.

Finkielkraut, Alain. *The Imaginary Jew* (Le Juif imaginaire). 1980; reprint, Lincoln: Nebraska University Press, 1994.

Fishman, Sarah and Geneviève Dermenjian. 'La Guerre des captives et les associations de femmes de prisonniers en France (1941–1945)'. *Vingtième siècle*, no. 49 (January–March 1996): 98–109.

Fishman, Sarah, Laura Lee Downs, Ioannis Sinanoglou, Leonard V. Smith and Robert Zaretsky (eds.), *France at War: Vichy and the Historians*. Oxford: Berg, 2000.

Fishman, Sarah. *We Will Wait: Wives of French Prisoners of War, 1940–1945*. New Haven: Yale University Press, 1991.

Flint, Kate. *The Woman Reader 1837–1914*. Oxford: Clarendon Press, 1993.

Flory, Charles. 'Le Second "Pour la vie"' *Pour la vie*, no. 1 (July 1945): 1–4.

Fontaine, André. *Le Camp d'étrangers des Milles 1939–1943 (Aix-en-Provence)*. Aix-en-Provence: Edisud, 1989.

Footitt, Hilary. 'The First Women Députés: "Les 33 Glorieuses"?'. In *The Liberation of France: Image and Event*, eds. H. R. Kedward and Nancy Wood, 129–41. Oxford: Berg, 1995.

Fouché, Pascal. *L'Edition française sous l'occupation 1940–1944*, Bibliothèque de Littérature française contemporaine, 1987.

Francos, Ania. *Il était des femmes dans la résistance*. Stock, 1978.

Freedman, Jane. 'Women and Immigration: Nationality and Citizenship'. In *Women, Immigration and Identities in France*, eds. Jane Freedman and Carrie Tarr, 13–28. Oxford: Berg, 2000.

Freiberg, J. W. *The French Press: Class, State, and Ideology*. New York: Praeger, 1981.

Freiburg, Reinhard. 'Die Presse der französischen Resistance. Technik und Positionen einer Untergrundpresse 1940–1944'. Unpublished Ph.D. Dissertation, Freie Universität, 1962.

Frenay, Henri. *Bilan d'un effort*. Ministère des Prisonniers, Déportés et Réfugiés, 1945.

Freud, Sigmund. 'Family Romances'. (1909) In *On Sexuality: Three Essays on the Theory of Sexuality and Other Works*, 7: 217–25, ed. Angela Richards, trans. James Strachey, Penguin Freud Library. London: Penguin, 1991.

Freud, Sigmund. 'Moses and Monotheism'. In *The Origins of Religion*, 13: 237–386, eds. James Strachey and Albert Dickson, trans. James Strachey, Penguin Freud Library. London: Penguin, 1990.

Freud, Sigmund. 'Totem and Taboo'. In *The Origins of Religion*, 13: 53–224, eds. James Strachey, Albert Dickson, trans. James Strachey, Penguin Freud Library. London: Penguin, 1990.

Freud, Sigmund. *Briefe 1873–1939*. 3rd edn. Edited by Ernst and Lucie Freud. 1960; reprint, Frankfurt: S. Fischer Verlag, 1980.

Fridenson, Patrick. *Histoire des usines Renault: 1. Naissance de la grande entreprise*. Seuil, 1972.

Friedländer, Saul. *Nazi Germany and the Jews*. Vol. 1, *The Years of Persecution 1933–1939*, London: HarperCollins, 1997.

Gay, Peter. *Freud: A Life for Our Time*. London: Macmillan, 1988.

Gemie, Sharif. 'Docility, Zeal and Rebellion: Culture and Sub-Cultures in French Women's Teacher Training Colleges, *c*.1860– *c*.1910'. *European History Quarterly* 24, no. 2 (April 1994): 213–44.

Gérard, Pierre. 'La Presse à la libération dans la région de Toulouse'. In *La Libération dans le Midi de la France*, ed. Rolande Trempé, 331–45. Toulouse: Eché Editeur/UTM, 1986.

Gessain, Robert and Madeleine Doré. 'Facteurs comparés d'assimilation chez des Russes et des Arméniens'. *Population* 1, no. 1 (January–March 1946): 99–116.

Gilman, Sander L. 'Chicken Soup, or the Penalties for Sounding Too Jewish'. *Shofar*, no. 9 (1990): 55–69.

Gilman, Sander L. *Freud, Race, and Gender*. Princeton: Princeton University Press, 1993.

Gilman, Sander L. *The Jew's Body*. New York: Routledge, 1991.

Girard, Alain. *L'Institut National d'Etudes Démographiques: histoire et développement*. INED, 1986.

Girard, Alain and Jean Stoetzel. *Français et immigrés. L'attitude française. L'adaptation des Italiens et des Polonais*. Travaux et Documents, no. 19. INED, 1953.

Giraudoux, Jean. *Pleins pouvoirs*. Gallimard, 1939.

Glazier, Kate. 'Liberation in Alsace – A Gendered Product'. Unpublished paper, Liberation: Image and Event, University of Sussex, 13–15 April 1994.

Gobineau, Arthur de, *Essai sur l'inégalité des races humaines*. Firmin-Didot, 1855.

Gorrara, Claire. 'Reviewing Gender and the Resistance: The Case of Lucie Aubrac'. In *The Liberation of France: Image and Event*, eds. H. R. Kedward and Nancy Wood, 143–54. Oxford: Berg, 1995.

Graetz, André. 'Manque d'hommes'. *Esprit* (December 1944): 65–81.

Grandjonc, Jacques and Theresia Grundtner (eds.), *Zone d'ombres 1933–1944: exil et internement d'Allemands et d'Autrichiens dans le sud-est de la France*. Aix-en-Provence: Alinéa, 1990.

Granet, Marie. *Ceux de la résistance (1940–1944)*. Editions de Minuit, 1964.

Granet, Marie. *Défense de la France. Histoire d'un mouvement de résistance (1940–1944)*. PUF, 1960.

Gravensten, Eva Berg. *La Quatrième Arme: la presse française sous l'occupation* (Den Franske Presse under den Anden Verdenskrig). Lausanne: Esprit Ouvert, 2001.

Gravier, Jean-François. *Etat, peuple, nation*. Vichy: Secrétariat Général à l'Information et à la Propagande, 1942.

Gravier, Jean-François. *Paris et le désert français. Décentralisation équipement population*. Le Portulan, 1947.

Green, Nancy L. *The Pletzl of Paris: Jewish Immigrant Workers in the Belle Epoque*. New York: Holmes and Meier, 1986.

Gregory, Abigail and Ursula Tidd (eds.), *Women in Contemporary France*. Oxford: Berg, 2000.

Grossmann, Atina. 'A Question of Silence: The Rape of German Women by Occupation Soldiers'. *October*, no. 72 (1995): 43–63.

Grossmann, Atina. 'Trauma, Memory, and Motherhood: Germans and Jewish Displaced Persons in Post-Nazi Germany, 1945–1949'. *Archiv für Sozialgeschichte*, no. 38 (1998): 215–39.

Groupe Juif du Parti Communiste. 'Directives générales pour la préparation de l'insurrection nationale'. 1945 (Unpublished typescript).

Gruber, Helmut. 'Sexuality in "Red Vienna": Socialist Party Concepts and Programs of Working-Class Life'. *International Labor and Working-Class History* 31 (1987): 37–68.

Grynberg, Anne. *Les Camps de la honte: les internés juifs des camps français 1939–1944*. 1991; reprint, La Découverte, 1999.

Guillon, Jean-Marie. 'L'Affaire Aubrac, ou la dérive d'une certaine façon de faire l'histoire'. *Modern and Contemporary France* 7, no. 1 (1999): 89–92.

Gulick, Charles A. *Austria from Habsburg to Hitler*. Vol. 2, *Fascism's Subversion of Democracy*, 1948; reprint, Berkeley: California University Press, 1980.

Günther, Hans F. K. *Rassenkunde des jüdischen Volkes*. Munich: Lehmann, 1930.

Halioua, Bruno. *Blouses blanches, étoiles jaunes. L'exclusion des médecins juifs en France sous l'occupation*. Liana Levi, 2000.

Halls, W. D. *The Youth of Vichy France*. Oxford: Oxford University Press, 1981.

Hankins, Frank H. *La Race dans la civilisation: une critique de la doctrine nordique*. Trans. and Preface by George Montandon. Payot, 1935.

Haury, Paul. Preface to *L'Ecole et la famille*. Commissariat Général à la Famille, 1943.

Haury, Paul. Preface to *L'Instituteur et son rôle dans la restauration de la famille française*. Secrétariat d'Etat à la Famille et à la Santé, 1943.

Haury, Paul and René Lugand. *Enseignement démographique et familial. Géographie*. 2 vols. ANCD, 1944–46.

Haury, Paul and René Lugand. *Enseignement démographique et familial. Histoire*. 2 vols. ANCD, 1945–46.

Haury, Paul and René Lugand. *Enseignement démographique et familial. Histoire et géographie*. 3 vols. ANCD, 1945.

Haury, Paul. *Exposé simple et clair de la question d'orient (1770–1913)*. Vuibert, 1913.

Haury, Paul. *Justice pour la famille ou la France est perdue! La dépression française et l'axe Rome–Berlin*. ANCD, 1938.

Haury, Paul. *La Campagne contre l'immoralité publique et pour le relèvement de la natalité dans les églises protestantes. Rapports présentés au VIIe Congrès National de la Natalité, Clermont-Ferrand, septembre 1925*. Saumur: Secrétariat de la Commission Protestante, 1925.

Haury, Paul. Review of *Les Etrangers en France*, by Georges Mauco. In *Revue de l'Alliance Nationale pour l'Accroissement de la Population Française* 33, no. 240 (July 1932): 209–13.

Hausen, Karin. 'Mother's Day in the Weimar Republic'. In *When Biology Became Destiny: Women in Weimar and Nazi Germany*, eds. Renate Bridenthal, Atina Grossmann and Marion Kaplan, 131–52. New York: Monthly Review Press, 1984.

Hecht, Gabrielle. *The Radiance of France: Nuclear Power and National Identity after World War II*. Cambridge, MA: MIT Press, 1998.

Herszkowicz, Sophie. *Lettre ouverte au Maire de Paris à propos de la destruction de Belleville*. Encyclopédie des Nuisances, 1994.

Hervé, Pierre. *La Libération trahie*. Bernard Grasset, 1945.

Hillel, Marc. *Le Massacre des survivants en Pologne 1945–1947*. Plon, 1989.

Homans, Margaret. *Bearing the Word: Language and Female Experience in Nineteenth-Century Women's Writing*. Chicago: Chicago University Press, 1986.

Honig, B. 'Toward an Agonistic Feminism: Hannah Arendt and the Politics of Identity'. In *Feminists Theorize the Political*, eds. Judith Butler and Joan W. Scott, 215–35. New York: Routledge, 1992.

Hyman, Paula E. *Gender and Assimilation: The Roles and Representation of Women*. Seattle: University of Washington Press, 1995.

Institut National d'Etudes Démographiques. 'Rapport au gouvernement: l'effet des mesures de politique démographique sur l'évolution de la fécondité'. In *Natalité et politique démographique*. Travaux et Documents, no. 76. PUF, 1976, 1–54.

Institut National d'Etudes Démographiques. *Economie et population: les doctrines françaises avant 1800. Bibliographie générale commentée*. Travaux et Documents, no. 28. PUF, 1956.

Institut National d'Etudes Démographiques. *Les Travaux du Haut Comité Consultatif de la Population et de la famille*. Travaux et Documents, no. 1. PUF, 1946.

Isaac, Auguste. *La Plus Grande Famille, association de pères et mères de famille de cinq enfants au moins: discours au déjeuner mensuel de l'Union du Commerce et de l'Industrie pour la Défense Sociale*. La Plus Grande Famille, 1917.

Jackson, Julian. *France: The Dark Years 1940–1944*. Oxford: Oxford University Press, 2001.

Jacquemet, Gérard. 'Déchristianisation, structures familiales et anticléricalisme: Belleville au XIXe siècle'. *Archives de sciences sociales des religions* 57, no. 1 (1984): 69–82.

Jacquier-Bruère (Michel Debré and Emmanuel Monick). *Refaire la France: l'effort d'une génération*. Plon, 1945.

Jeanneney, Jules. *Journal politique, septembre 1939–juillet 1942*. Edited by Jean-Noël Jeanneney. Armand Colin, 1972.

Jeffords, Susan. *The Remasculinization of America: Gender and the Vietnam War*. Bloomington: Indiana University Press, 1989.

Jenson, Jane. 'Représentations des rapports sociaux de sexe dans trois domaines politiques en France'. In *Le Sexe des politiques sociales*, eds. Arlette Gautier and Jacqueline Heinen, 59–84. Côté-femmes, 1993.

Jenson, Jane. 'The Liberation and New Rights for French Women'. In *Behind the Lines: Gender and the Two World Wars*, eds. Margaret Randolph Higonnet, Jane Jenson, Sonya Michel and Margaret Collins Weitz, 272–84. New Haven: Yale University Press, 1987.

July, Pierre, Olivier de Sesmaisons and Hélène de Suzannet. *Comment le Parti Républicain de la Liberté défend la famille*. PRL, 1946.

July, Pierre, Olivier de Sesmaisons and Hélène de Suzannet. *La Journée des Mères à la campagne*. Abbeville: Foyer Rural, 1946.

Kaplan, Marion A. *The Making of the Jewish Middle Class. Women, Family, and Identity in Imperial Germany*. New York: Oxford University Press, 1991.

Karnaouch-Poindron, Denise. 'L'UJFF et l'UFF: réflexions sur leur histoire'. *Pénélope*, no. 11 (Autumn 1984), 105–12.

Katz, Jacob. *Out of the Ghetto: The Social Background of Jewish Emancipation 1770–1870*. Cambridge, MA: Harvard University Press, 1973.

Kedward, H. R. 'Rural France and Resistance'. In *France at War*, ed. Sarah Fishman *et al.*, 125–44.

Kedward, H. R. *Resistance in Vichy France: A Study of Ideas and Motivation in the Southern Zone 1940–1942*. Oxford: Oxford University Press, 1978.

Kedward, H. R. 'Resiting French Resistance'. *Transactions of the Royal Historical Society* 6, no. 9 (1999): 271–82.

Kedward, H. R. and Nancy Wood (eds.). *The Liberation of France: Image and Event*. Oxford: Berg, 1995.

Kedward, H. R. *In Search of the Maquis: Rural Resistance in Southern France, 1942–1944*. Oxford: Clarendon Press, 1993.

Kelly, Michael. 'Death at the Liberation: The Cultural Articulation of Death and Suffering in France 1944–47'. *French Cultural Studies* 5, part 3, no. 15 (October 1994): 227–40.

Kitson, Simon. 'The Police in the Liberation of Paris'. In *The Liberation of France: Image and Event*, eds. H. R. Kedward and Nancy Wood, 43–56. Oxford: Berg, 1995.

Klarsfeld, Serge. *Vichy-Auschwitz: le rôle de Vichy dans la solution finale de la question juive en France*. Vol. 1, *1942*. Fayard, 1983.

Klarsfeld, Serge. *Vichy-Auschwitz: le rôle de Vichy dans la solution finale de la question juive en France*. Vol. 2, *1943–1944*. Fayard, 1985.

Knibiehler, Yvonne and Catherine Fouquet. *Histoire des mères du moyen-âge à nos jours*. Montalba, 1980.

Knobel, Marc. 'George Montandon et l'ethno-racisme'. In *L'Antisémitisme de plume 1940–1944: études et documents*, eds. Pierre-André Taguieff, Grégoire Kauffmann and Michaël Lenoire, 277–93. Berg International, 1999.

Knout, David. *Contribution à l'histoire de la résistance juive en France, 1940–1944*. Editions du Centre, 1947.

Koos, Cheryl A. 'Gender, Anti-Individualism, and Nationalism: The Alliance Nationale and the Pronatalist Backlash Against the *Femme Moderne*, 1933–1940'. *French Historical Studies* 19, no. 3 (spring 1996): 699–724.

Kriegel, Annie. 'De la résistance juive'. *Pardès*, no. 2 (1985): 191–209.

Kriegel, Annie. *Réflexions sur les questions juives*. Hachette, 1984.

Laborie, Pierre. *L'Opinion française sous Vichy: les Français et la crise d'identité nationale 1936–1944*. 1990; reprint, Seuil, 2001.

Lafont, Max. *L'Extermination douce*. Latresne: Le Bord de l'eau, 2000.

Laguerre, Bernard. 'Les Dénaturalisés de Vichy 1940–1944'. *Vingtième siècle*, no. 20 (October–December 1988): 3–15.

Laharie, Claude. *Le Camp de Gurs 1939–1945: un aspect méconnu de l'histoire du Béarn*. Biarritz: J & D Editions, 1985.

Lalario, Sylvie. 'Retours en France et réadaptations à la société française des femmes juives déportées'. Unpublished maîtrise, University of Paris VII, 1993.

Laloum, Jean. *Les Juifs dans la banlieue parisienne, des années 20 aux années 50. Montreuil, Bagnolet et Vincennes à l'heure de la solution finale*. CNRS, 1998.

Landy, Adolphe. 'La Politique sociale et démographique'. In *Petit congrès, Parti Républicain radical et radical-socialiste*, 19–21 December 1944.

Landry, Adolphe. *La Démographie française*. 2nd edn, 1941; reprint, ANCD, 1942.

Landry, Adolphe. *La Démographie française*. PUF, 1941.

Landry, Adolphe. *La Révolution démographique*. Bordeaux: 1934.

Landry, Adolphe. *La Démographie de l'ancien Paris. Extrait du journal de la Société de Statistique de Paris, Février 1935*. Editions Berger-Levrault, 1935.

Landry, Adolphe, Henri Bunle, Alfred Sauvy, Pierre Depoid and Michel Huber. *Traité de démographie*. Payot, 1945.

Lasker-Wallfisch, Anita. *Inherit the Truth 1939–1945: The Documented Experiences of a Survivor of Auschwitz and Belsen*. London: Giles de la Mare, 1996.

Laurens, Corran. '"La Femme au Turban": Les Femmes Tondues'. In *The Liberation of France: Image and Event*, eds. H. R. Kedward and Nancy Wood, 155–79. Oxford: Berg, 1995.

Lazare, Lucien. *La Résistance juive: un combat pour la survie*. New edn. 1987; reprint, Nadir, 2001.

Lazare, Lucien. *Rescue as Resistance: How Jewish Organizations Fought the Holocaust in France*, trans. Jeffrey M. Green. New York: Columbia University Press, 1996.

Le Bon, Gustave. *Les Lois psychologiques de l'évolution des peuples*. Félix Alcan, 1894.

Le Bras, Hervé. *Le Sol et le sang*. La Tour d'Aigues: Editions de l'Aube, 1994.

Le Bras, Hervé. *Les Trois France*. Odile Jacob, 1986.

Le Bras, Hervé. *Marianne et les lapins: l'obsession démographique*. O. Orban, 1991.

Lebovics, Herman. *True France: The Wars over Cultural Identity, 1900–1945*. Ithaca: Cornell University Press, 1992.

Lépidis, Clément. *Belleville au cœur*. Vermet, 1980.

Levi, Primo. *If This Is a Man*. London: Abacus, 1999.

Lévy, Claude and Paul Tillard. *La Grande Rafle du Vél d'Hiv (16 juillet 1942)*. Robert Laffont, 1967.

Lévy, Michel Louis. *Alfred Sauvy: compagnon du siècle*. La Manufacture, 1990.

Lévy, Paul. *Un camp de concentration français: Poitiers 1939–1945*. Sedes, 1995.

List-Pakin, Jeanne. 'De certains aspects de la résistance'. *Le Monde juif* 50, no. 152 (September–December 1994): 172–6.

Lombroso, Cesare. *L'Anthropologie criminelle et ses récents progrès*. 3rd edn. Félix Alcan, 1896.

Mabon-Fall, Armelle. *Les Assistantes sociales au temps de Vichy: du silence à l'oubli*. L'Harmattan, 1995.

Machard, Raymonde. *Les Françaises. Ce qu'elles valent... Ce qu'elles veulent*. Flammarion, 1945.

Maire, Andrée, Lucie Aubrac and Claire Vervin. *French Women Today*. New York: French Press and Information Service, 1944.

Malo, Eric. 'Le Camp de Noë (Haute-Garonne) de 1941 à 1944'. *Annales de Midi* 100, no. 183 (1988): 337–52.

Marchetti. *Affiches 1939–1945: images d'une certaine France*. Lausanne: Edita Lazarus, 1982.

Margadant, Jo Burr. *Madame le Professeur: Women Educators in the Third Republic*. Princeton: Princeton University Press, 1990.

Marrus, Michael R. and Robert O. Paxton. *Vichy France and the Jews*. New York: Basic Books, 1981.

Marrus, Michael R. *The Politics of Assimilation: A Study of the French Jewish Community at the Time of the Dreyfus Affair*. Oxford: Clarendon Press, 1971.

Martial, René. 'Conférence-programme pour les élèves des écoles normales d'instituteurs'. *Société française de prophylaxie* 24, no. 4–5 (June–July 1924): 67–8.

Martial, René. *La Race française: le sol. Les racines. La souche. La croissance et les greffons (Arabes. Normands. Italiens. Hollandais, etc.). La greffe inter-raciale: la trilogie, histoire. Psychologie. Biologie. Le nouveau rejet ou transfusion sanguine ethnique*. Mercure de France, 1934.

Martial, René. *Les Races humaines*. Hachette, 1955.

Mauco, Georges and Maurice Grandazzi. *La Démographie à l'école. Manuel à l'usage des maîtres*. ANCD, 1948.

Mauco, Georges. 'Congrès mondial de la population et de la famille'. *Psyché* 2, no. 9–10 (July–August 1947): 986–9.

Mauco, Georges. 'Consultations psycho-pédagogiques'. *Psyché* 2, no. 3 (1 January 1947): 47–52.

Mauco, Georges. 'L'Assimilation des étrangers en France.' In *L'Assimilation culturelle des immigrants: Union Internationale pour l'Etude Scientifique de la Population: Assemblée Générale*, 21–32. INED, 1950.

Mauco, Georges. 'L'Assimilation des étrangers en France.' In *Le Règlement pacifique des problèmes internationaux*. Institut International de Coopération Intellectuelle/Société des Nations, 28 June–3 July 1937.

Mauco, Georges. 'L'Emigration étrangère en France et le problème des réfugiés'. *Ethnie française*, no. 6 (March 1942): 6–15.

Mauco, Georges. 'L'Immigration étrangère en France'. *Res Publica*, no. 6 (January–March 1946): 28–40.

Mauco, Georges. 'La Psychologie de l'enfant dans ses rapports avec la psychologie de l'inconscient (d'après les travaux de Freud et de Piaget) 1 and 2'. *Revue française de psychanalyse* 9, nos. 3 and 4 (1936): 430–517, 658–710.

Mauco, Georges. 'La Situation démographique de la France'. *Annales de géographie* 47, no. 271 (15 January 1939): 85–90.

Mauco, Georges. 'La Situation démographique de la France'. *Ethnie française*, no. 7 (January 1942): 15–19.

Mauco, Georges. 'Le Centre Psycho-Pédagogique de l'Académie de Paris au Lycée Claude-Bernard'. *Psyché* 2, no. 13–14 (November–December 1947): 1387–401.

Mauco, Georges. 'Le Centre Psycho-Pédagogique de l'Académie de Paris au Lycée Claude-Bernard'. *Sauvegarde: revue des associations régionales pour la sauvegarde de l'enfance et de l'adolescence* 2, no. 15–16 (November–December 1947): 56–65.

Mauco, Georges. 'Le Mouvement de la population en Europe'. *L'Europe nouvelle* (18 March 1939): 295–6.

Mauco, Georges. 'Les Commerçants dans la population française'. *Annales de géographie* 55, no. 297 (January–March 1946): 54–7.

Mauco, Georges. 'Les Etrangers en France. Etude géographique sur leur rôle dans l'activité économique'. Doctorat ès Lettres, University of Paris, A. Colin, 1932.

Mauco, Georges. 'Quelques conséquences du mouvement de la population en Europe'. *L'Europe nouvelle* (8 April 1939): 379–81.

Mauco, Georges. 'Report on Relations between Parents and Children'. In *World Congress for Family and Population: congrès mondial de la famille et de la population*. UNAF, 1947.

Mauco, Georges. 'Une enquête en cours sur l'immigration agricole en France'. In *Démographie statistique*, 4: 83–5, Congrès International de la Population. Hermann, 1938.

Mauco, Georges. *De l'inconscient à l'âme enfantine: la psychologie de l'enfant dans ses rapports avec la psychologie de l'inconscient*. Editions Psyché, 1948.

Mauco, Georges. *La Paternité: sa fonction éducative dans la famille et à l'école*. Editions Universitaires, 1971.

Mauco, Georges. *La Psychologie de l'enfant dans ses rapports avec la psychologie de l'inconscient*. Bibliothèque Psychanalytique. Denoël, 1938.

Mauco, Georges. *Le Meurtre d'un enfant et l'angoisse du schizophrène et de l'homosexuel*. PUF, 1979.

Mauco, Georges. *Les Etrangers en France: leur rôle dans l'activité économique*. Armand Colin, 1932.

Mauco, Georges. *Rapport sur l'état sanitaire de la population étrangère en France*. N.d. (1947).

Mauco, Georges. *Vécu 1899–1982*. Emile Paul, 1982.

Mayeux, Henri and Jean H. Krailsheimer. *Guide pratique de la naturalisation française*. Centre d'Orientation Sociale des Etrangers, 1946.

Meige, Henry. *Le Juif errant à la Salpétrière, étude sur certains névropathes voyageurs*. L. Battaille et Co, 1893.

Mesnil-Amar, Jacqueline. *Ceux qui ne dormaient pas 1944–1946 (fragments de journal)*. Editions de Minuit, 1957.

Miller, Nancy. 'Changing the Subject: Authorship, Writing and the Reader'. In *What Is an Author?*, eds. Maurice Biriotti and Nicola Miller, 19–41. Manchester: Manchester University Press, 1993.

Millner, Joseph. 'Les Juifs de Belleville'. *Journal des communautés* 9, no. 141 (14 March 1958): 7.

Milza, Pierre and Denis Peschanski (eds.). *Exils et migration: Italiens et Espagnols en France, 1938–1946*. Harmattan, 1994.

Ministères de l'Education Nationale et de la Population. *Six leçons d'enseignement démographique*. 1946.

Mitchell, B. R. *International Historical Statistics: Europe 1750–1988*. New York: Stockton Press, 1992.

Mitchell, Juliet and Jacqueline Rose (eds.). *Feminine Sexuality: Jacques Lacan and the Ecole Freudienne*, trans. Jacqueline Rose. London: Macmillan, 1982.

Modleski, Tania. *Loving with a Vengeance: Mass-Produced Fantasies for Women*. London: Routledge, 1988.

Monsaingeon, Maurice. 'La Famille, être complet'. *Pour la vie*, no. 1 (July 1945): 5–19.

Monsaingeon, Maurice. 'Vie familiale, sécurité et responsabilité: la sécurité et la responsabilité dans la vie familiale'. In *Economie, psychologie dans la vie familiale: journées familiales internationales*, 11–18, Problèmes familiaux dans le monde. Union Internationale des Organismes Familiaux, 1950.

Monsaingeon, Maurice. *Immigration et peuplement*. Centre National de Coordination des Activités Familiales, 1945.

Monsaingeon, Maurice. *La Vraie Conception de la famille: sa place dans la société*. Collection Science et Charité, no. IX. Secrétariat Catholique des Œuvres Charitables et Sociales d'Hygiène et de Santé, May 1944.

Montandon, George. 'Commentaires sur les théories raciales de Gobineau'. *Revue contemporaine*, no. 11 (25 August–25 September 1917): 589–93.

Montandon, George. *Comment reconnaître et expliquer le Juif suivi d'un portrait moral du Juif*. Nouvelles Editions Françaises, 1940.

Montandon, George. *L'Ethnie française*. Payot, 1935.

Montandon, George. *La Race. Les races: mise au point d'ethnologie somatique*. Payot, 1933.

Montandon, George. 'L'Ethnie juive et le type racial juif: causerie donnée le 26 Avril 1939 au Cercle Ernest Jouin.' *Revue internationale des sociétés secrètes: bulletin bi-mensuel de la Ligue Anti-Judéomaçonnique 'Le Franc-Catholique'*, no. 12 (15 June 1939): 375–84.

Montandon, George. 'La Solution ethnico-raciale du problème juif'. *Contre-révolution: revue internationale d'études sociales*, no. 5 (April 1939): 19–34.

Morier, Françoise (ed.). *Belleville, Belleville: visages d'une planète*. Créaphis, 1994.

Mottier, J.-L. and Maurice Caillez. *Guide pratique des étrangers en France*. Librairie du Journal des Notaires et des Avocats, 1948.

Mottin, Jean. *Histoire politique de la presse 1944–1949*. Bilans Hebdomadaires, 1949.

Mouvement Populaire des Familles, Ouvrière Catholique Féminine and Jeunesse Ouvrière Catholique. *La Pensée ouvrière sur le problème de la formation de la jeunesse ouvrière*. MPF, 1945.

Mouvement Populaire des Familles. *La Mère de famille du milieu populaire face aux difficultés actuelles*. Editions Ouvrières, 1946.

Mouvement Populaire des Familles. *Travaux 45*. CCP-MPF, 1945.

Muel-Dreyfus, Francine. *Vichy et l'éternel féminin*. Seuil, 1996.

Noiriel, Gérard. *Le Creuset français. Histoire de l'immigration XIX–XXe siècles.* Seuil, 1988.

Noiriel, Gérard. *Les Origines républicaines de Vichy.* Hachette, 1999.

Nouveau dictionnaire national des contemporains. Loos-lez-Lille, 1964.

Offen, Karen. 'Body Politics: Women, Work and the Politics of Motherhood in France, 1920–1950'. In *Maternity and Gender Policies: Women and the Rise of the European Welfare States, 1880s–1950s*, eds. Gisela Bock and Pat Thane, 138–59. London: Routledge, 1991.

Ory, Pascal. *La Belle Illusion: culture et politique sous le signe du Front Populaire, 1935–1938.* Plon, 1994.

Ory, Pascal. *Les Collaborateurs 1940–1945.* 1976; reprint, Seuil, 1980.

Pairault, André. *L'Immigration organisée et l'emploi de la main-d'œuvre étrangère en France.* PUF, 1926.

Parti Socialiste SFIO. *Projet d'un statut des étrangers en France.* Fédération des Socialistes Etrangers de France, July 1945.

Passerini, Luisa. 'Mythbiography in Oral History'. In *The Myths We Live By*, eds. Raphael Samuel and Paul Thompson, 49–60. London: Routledge, 1990.

Passmore, Kevin. ' "Planting the Tricolour in the Citadels of Communism": Women's Social Action in the Croix de Feu and Parti Social Français'. *Journal of Modern History* 71, no. 4 (1999): 814–51.

Peer, Shanny. *France on Display: Peasants, Provincials, and Folklore in the 1937 Paris World's Fair.* Albany: SUNY Press, 1998.

Perec, Georges. *W ou le souvenir d'enfance.* Denoël, 1975.

Perks, Robert and Alistair Thomson (eds.). *The Oral History Reader.* London: Routledge, 1998.

Peschanski, Denis, Marie-Christine Hubert and Emmanuel Philippon. *Les Tsiganes en France 1939–1946.* CNRS, 1994.

Peschanski, Denis. *La France des camps: l'internement 1938–1946.* Gallimard, 2002.

Peschanski, Denis. *Vichy 1940–1944: contrôle et exclusion.* Brussels: Complexe, 1997.

Pétain, Philippe. *Discours aux Français: 17 juin 1940–20 août 1944.* Edited by Jean-Claude Barbas. Albin Michel, 1989.

Petit, Louis. *Le Problème des immigrés dans la France libérée.* CADI, c.1945.

Pickering, Robert. 'The Implications of Legalised Publication'. In *Collaboration in France: Politics and Culture During the Nazi Occupation, 1940–1944*, eds. Gerhard Hirschfeld and Patrick Marsh, 162–89. Oxford: Berg, 1989.

Piette, Christine. *Les Juifs de Paris (1808–1840): la marche vers l'assimilation.* Quebec: Presses de l'Université Laval, 1983.

Pillet, Isabelle. 'Images de la femme dans la presse régionale, 1945–1975'. *Revue du Nord* 63, no. 250 (1981): 737–73.

Piquet, Georges. *Presse clandestine: la vie secrète de la résistance.* Collection Révélations. Nathan, 1945.

Pollard, Miranda. *Reign of Virtue: Mobilizing Gender in Vichy France.* Chicago: Chicago University Press, 1998.

Portier, Pierre. *Le Camp du Vernet-d'Ariège ou les racines du désespoir: la vie du camp de sa création en 1917 à sa disparition en 1947.* Saverdun, 1997.

Poznanski, Renée. 'Reflections on Jewish Resistance and Jewish Resistants in France'. *Jewish Social Studies* 2, no. 1 (1995): 124–58.

Poznanski, Renée. *Etre Juif en France pendant la seconde guerre mondiale*. Hachette, 1994.

Poznanski, Renée. *Les Juifs en France pendant la seconde guerre mondiale*. 1994; reprint, Hachette, 1997.

Prigent, Robert. 'L'Organisation du Ministère de la Santé Publique et de la Population'. *Pour la vie*, no. 8 (February 1947): 48–52.

Prigent, Robert. 'De la LOC Zone Occupée au Commissariat Général à la Famille en 1945'. In *L'Action familiale ouvrière et la politique de Vichy*, 3: 79–87, ed. Groupement pour la Recherche sur les Mouvements Familiaux, Cahiers du GRMF. Forêt-sur-Marque: GRMF, 1985.

Priollaud, Nicole, Victor Zigelman and Laurent Goldberg (eds.). *Images de la mémoire juive: immigration et intégration en France depuis 1800*. Aubanas: Liana Levi, 1994.

Proud, Judith K. 'Plus Ça Change...? Propaganda Fiction for Children, 1940–1945'. In *The Liberation of France: Image and Event*, eds. H. R. Kedward and Nancy Wood, 57–74. Oxford: Berg, 1995.

Radford, Jean (ed.). *The Progress of Romance: The Politics of Popular Fiction*. London: Routledge and Kegan Paul, 1986.

Raffalli, Bernard and Jacqueline Sauvageot. *Une vigne sur la mer: deux siècles en Corse*. Bernard Grasset, 1980.

Ravine, Jacques. *La Résistance organisée des Juifs en France 1940–1944*. Julliard, 1973.

Rayski, Adam. 'La MOI: spécificité de la résistance juive'. In *De l'exil à la Résistance: réfugiés et immigrés d'Europe centrale en France 1933–45*, eds. Karl Bartosek, René Gallissot and Denis Peschanski, 245–53. Arcantère, 1989.

Rayski, Adam. *Le Choix des Juifs sous Vichy: entre soumission et résistance*. La Découverte, 1992.

Rayski, Adam. *Nos illusions perdues*. Balland, 1985.

Reggiani, Andrès Horacio. 'Alexis Carrel, the Unknown: Eugenics and Population Research under Vichy'. *French Historical Studies* 25, no. 2 (2002): 331–56.

Reggiani, Andrès Horacio. 'Procreating France: The Politics of Demography, 1919–1945'. *French Historical Studies* 19, no. 3 (spring 1996): 725–54.

Richarz, Monika. *Der Eintritt der Juden in die akademischen Berufe: Jüdische Studenten und Akademiker in Deutschland, 1678–1848*. Tübingen: J. C. B. Mohr, 1974.

Rigaud, Antoine. *Deux poèmes pour la Fête des Mères*. Mâcon: Robert Martin, 1945.

Ringelheim, Joan. 'Genocide and Gender: A Split Memory'. In *Gender and Catastrophe*, ed. Ronit Lentin, 18–33. London: Zed Books, 1997.

Roberts, Mary Louise. *Civilization without Sexes: Reconstructing Gender in Postwar France, 1917–1927*. Chicago: Chicago University Press, 1994.

Roblin, Michel. *Les Juifs de Paris. Démographie – économie – culture*. A. et J. Picard, 1952.

Roland, Charlotte. *Du ghetto à l'occident: deux générations yiddiches en France*. Editions de Minuit, 1962.

Ronis, Willy. *Belleville-Ménilmontant*. Arthaud, 1984.

Roseman, Mark. 'Recent Writing on the Holocaust'. *Journal for Contemporary History* 36, no. 2 (2001): 361–72.

Roseman, Mark. *The Past in Hiding*. Harmondsworth: Allen Lane, 2000.

Rosental, Paul-André. *L'Intelligence démographique: sciences et politiques des populations en France (1930–1960)*. Odile Jacob, 2003.

Rossiter, Margaret L. 'Women in the French Underground Press'. *Contemporary French Civilization* 4, no. 2 (1980): 179–91.

Roudinesco, Elisabeth. 'Georges Mauco (1899–1988): un psychanalyste au service du Vichy: de l'antisémitisme à la psychopédagogie'. *L'Infini*, no. 51 (autumn 1995): 69–84.

Roudinesco, Elisabeth. *Histoire de la psychanalyse en France*. Vol. 2, *1925–1985*. 1986; reprint, Fayard, 1994.

Roudinesco, Elisabeth. *La Bataille de cent ans: histoire de la psychanalyse en France*. Vol. 1. Ramsay, 1982.

Rouquet, François. *L'Epuration dans l'administration française*. CNRS, 1993.

Rousseau, Renée. *Les Femmes rouges: chronique des années Vermeersch*. Albin Michel, 1983.

Rousso, Henry. 'The Historian, a Site of Memory'. In *France at War*, ed. Sarah Fishman *et al.*, 285–302.

Rousso, Henry. *La Hantise du passé: entretien avec Philippe Petit*. Textuel, 1998.

Roy, J. E. *L'Avortement, fléau national. Causes – conséquences – remèdes*. 1943; reprint, Jouve, 1944.

Ruddick, Sara. ' "Woman of Peace". A Feminist Construction'. In *The Women and War Reader*, eds. Lois Ann Lorentzen and Jennifer Turpin, 213–26. New York: New York University Press, 1998.

Said, Edward. *Orientalism*. 1978; reprint, Harmondsworth: Penguin, 1985.

Salses, Edmond de. *Livre d'or des valeurs humaines*. 2nd edn. Editions du Mémorial, n.d.

Sarraute, Raymond. *Etude sur la situation des immigrés en France. De la libération à la repression*. Comité Français pour la Défense des Immigrés, 1953.

Sarraute, Raymond and Jacques Rabinovitch. *Examen succinct de la situation actuelle juridique des Juifs*. Centre de Documentation des Déportés et Spoliés Juifs, 1945.

Saussure, Ferdinand de. *Cours de linguistique générale*. Payot, 1916.

Sauvy, Alfred. 'La Prévision économique et l'organisation du travail'. *Bulletin du Comité National de l'Organisation Française* 13, no. 2 (November 1938): 45–56.

Sauvy, Alfred. 'Besoins et possibilités de l'immigration française'. *Population* 5, no. 2 (April–June 1950): 209–28.

Sauvy, Alfred. *La Prévision économique*. Vendôme: PUF, 1943.

Sauvy, Alfred. 'Evaluation des besoins de l'immigration française'. *Population* 1, no. 1 (January–March 1946): 91–8.

Sauvy, Alfred. *La Vie en plus: souvenirs*. Calmann-Lévy, 1981.

Sauvy, Alfred. *Richesse et population: peuplement optimum, eugénisme et sélection, bien-être et répartition*. 2nd edn. 1943; reprint, Payot, 1944.

Sauvy, Alfred. 'Adolphe Landry'. *Population* 11, no. 4 (October–December 1956): 609–20.

Sauvy, Alfred and Sully Ledermann. 'La Guerre biologique, 1933–1945: population de l'Allemagne et des pays voisins'. *Population* 1, no. 3 (July–September 1946): 471–88.

Scheper-Hughes, Nancy. 'Maternal Thinking and the Politics of War'. In *The Women and War Reader*, eds. Lois Ann Lorentzen and Jennifer Turpin, 227–33. New York: New York University Press, 1998.

Scheiber, A. *Un Fléau social. Le problème médico-policier de la prostitution*. Librairie de Médicis, 1946.

Schieber, Eric. *Un an de reconstruction juive en France*. ORT, 1946.

Schnapper, Dominique. *Juifs et Israélites*. Gallimard, 1980.

Schneider, William H. *Quality and Quantity: The Quest for Biological Regeneration in Twentieth-Century France*. Cambridge: Cambridge University Press, 1990.

Schönberg, Bernard. 'L'Aide aux réfugiés allemands'. *Revue juive de Genève* 2, no. 5 (February 1934): 181–5.

Schor, Ralph. *L'Opinion française et les étrangers en France 1919–1939*. La Sorbonne, 1985.

Schramm, Hanna and Barbara Vormeier. *Vivre à Gurs: un camp de concentration français 1940–1941*, trans. Irène Petit. Maspéro, 1979.

Schwartz, Paula. '*Partisanes* and Gender Politics in Vichy France'. *French Historical Studies* 16, no. 1 (Spring 1989): 126–51.

Schwarzfuchs, Simon. *Aux prises avec Vichy: histoire politique des Juifs de France, 1940–1944*. Calmann-Lévy, 1998.

Seghers, Anna. *Transit Visa* (Transit), trans. James A. Galston. 1944; reprint, London: Eyre and Spottiswoode, 1945.

Service Social d'Aide aux Emigrants. *Rapport sur l'activité du SSAE en 1950*. SSAE, 1951.

Sibelman, Simon P. '*Le Renouvellement Juif*: French Jewry on the Eve of the Centenary of the Affaire Dreyfus'. *French Cultural Studies* 3, no. 9 (October 1992): 263–76.

Sigot, Jacques. *Un camp pour les Tsiganes . . . et les autres: Montreuil-Bellay 1940–1945*. Bordeaux: Wallada, 1983.

Silvain, Gérard. *La Question juive en Europe 1933–1945*. J.-C. Lattès, 1985.

Silverman, Max. *Deconstructing the Nation: Immigration, Racism and Citizenship in Modern France*. London: Routledge, 1992.

Simon, Patrick and Claude Tapia. *Le Belleville des Juifs tunisiens*. Editions Autrement, 1998.

Simon, Patrick. 'Les Quartiers d'immigration: "ports de première entrée" ou espaces de sédentarisation? L'Exemple de Belleville.' *Espace, populations, sociétés*, no. 2 (1993): 379–88.

Singer, Claude. *L'Université libérée, l'université épurée (1943–1947)*. Les Belles Lettres, 1997.

Smith, Bonnie G. *The Gender of History: Men, Women, and Historical Practice*. 1998; reprint, Cambridge, MA: Harvard University Press, 2000.

Smith, Paul. *Feminism and the Third Republic: Women's Political and Civil Rights in France, 1918–1945*. Oxford: Clarendon Press, 1996.

Sociology of Marriage and Family Behaviour 1945–56. Special issue of *Current Sociology* 7, no. 1 (1958).

Strudel, Sylvie. *Votes juifs: itinéraires migratoires, religieux et politiques*. FNSP, 1996.

Surkis, Judith. 'Secularization and Sexuality in Third Republic France, 1870–1920'. Unpublished Ph.D. dissertation, Cornell University, 2001.

Sutcliffe, Adam. *Judaism and Enlightenment*. Cambridge: Cambridge University Press, 2003.

Sutter, Jean. *L'Eugénique. Problèmes – méthodes – résultats*. Travaux et Documents, no. 11. INED, 1950.

Szajkowski, Zosa. *Jewish Education in France, 1789–1939*. Jewish Social Studies Monograph Series, vol. 2, ed. Tobey B. Gitelle. New York: Columbia University Press, 1980.

Taguieff, Pierre-André. *La Force du préjugé: essai sur le racisme et ses doubles*. La Découverte, 1988.

Taguieff, Pierre-André, Grégoire Kauffmann and Michaël Lenoire (eds.). *L'Antisémitisme de plume 1940–1944: études et documents*. Berg International, 1999.

Talmy, Robert. *Histoire du mouvement familial en France (1896–1939)*. 2 vols. UNCAF, 1962.

Teitelbaum, Michael S. and Jay Winter. *The Fear of Population Decline*. Orlando: Academic Press, 1985.

Le Temps des 'indésirables': sur quelques camps d'internement français. Special issue of *Le Monde juif*, 50, no. 153 (January–April 1995).

Thalman, Rita. *La Mise au pas: idéologie et stratégie sécuritaire dans la France occupée*. Fayard, 1991.

Thalmann, Rita. 'Femmes juives dans la résistance et la libération du territoire'. *Le Monde juif* 50, no. 152 (September–December 1994): 177–82.

Thébaud, Françoise. *Quand nos grand-mères donnaient la vie: la maternité en France dans l'entre-deux-guerres*. Presses Universitaires de Lyon, 1986.

Thévenot, Laurent. 'La Politique des statistiques: les origines sociales des enquêtes de mobilité sociale'. *Annales: economies sociétés civilisations* 45, no. 6 (November–December 1990): 1,275–300.

Thomas-Chevallier, Hubert. *Le Racisme français*. Nancy: Imprimerie Georges Thomas, 1943.

Thomson, Alistair. 'Memory as a Battlefield: Personal and Political Investments in the National Military Past'. *Oral History Review* 22, no. 2 (winter 1995): 55–73.

Todorov, Tzvetan. *Une tragédie française: été 1944, scènes de guerre civile*. Seuil, 1994.

Todorov, Tzvetan and Annick Jacquet. *Guerre et paix sous l'occupation: témoignages recueillis au centre de la France*. Arléa, 1996.

Toulemon, André. *Dialogue sur le suffrage familial. Suffrage universel intégral. Principes et objections*. ANCD, 1945.

Toulemon, André. *Histoire des doctrines de la population*. Berger-Levrault, 1956.

Triolet, Elsa. *Les Amants d'Avignon*. Editions de Minuit, 1943.

Tumblety, Joan. 'Obedient Daughters of Marianne: Discourses of Patriotism and Maternity in the French Women's Resistance Press during the Second World War'. *Women's History Notebooks* 4, no. 2 (summer 1997): 1–6.

Tumblety, Joan. 'Revenge of the Fascist Knights: Masculine Identities in *Je suis partout*, 1940–1944'. *Modern and Contemporary France* 7, no. 1 (1999): 11–20.

Union des Femmes Françaises. 'Deux ans d'activité au service de la famille française du premier congrès national juin 1945 aux Journées Nationales de l'Union des Femmes Françaises'. In *2e Congrès national*. UFF, 1947.

Union des Femmes Françaises. 'Les Femmes dans la Résistance'. In *Colloque tenu à l'initiative de l'Union des Femmes Françaises 22–23 novembre 1975*. Editions du Rocher, 1977.

Union Républicaine des Familles Françaises. *Compte rendu de la grande réunion d'information organisée par l'URFF, à la salle Wagram, le mercredi 3 octobre 1945*. URFF, 1945.

Vacher de Lapouge, Georges. *Les Sélections sociales*. A. Fontemoing, 1896.

Vegh, Claudine. *Je ne lui ai pas dit au revoir: des enfants de déportés parlent*. Gallimard, 1979.

Veillon, Dominique. 'The Resistance and Vichy'. In *France at War*, ed. Sarah Fishman *et al.*, 161–77.

Veillon, Dominique. *La Mode sous l'occupation. Débrouillardise et coquetterie dans la France en guerre (1939–1945)*. Payot, 1990.

Veillon, Dominique. *Le Franc-tireur: Un journal clandestin, un mouvement de résistance 1940–1944*. Flammarion, 1977.

Vichniac, Marc. *Le Statut international des apatrides*. Recueil Sirey, 1934.

Vidal de la Blache, Paul and Lucien Gallois. *France économique et humaine*. Géographie universelle, no. 6. Edited by Albert Demangeon. Armand Colin, 1946–48.

Viet, Vincent. *La France immigrée: construction d'une politique 1914–1997*. Fayard, 1998.

Vincent, Paul. 'Statistique internationale du mouvement des naissances'. *Population* 1, no. 2 (April–May 1946): 343–51.

Virgili, Fabrice. *La France 'virile': des femmes tondues à la libération*. Payot, 2000.

Virgili, Fabrice. 'Les Tontes de la libération en France', *Cahiers de l'IHTP*, 31, October 1995: 53–66.

Vittori, Jean-Pierre. *Eux, les S.T.O.* Messidor, 1982.

Vogel, David. *Et ils partirent pour la guerre*, trans. Rosie Pinhas-Delpuech. Denoël, 1993.

Vormeier, Barbara. 'La République française et les réfugiés et immigrés d'Europe centrale: accueil, séjour, droit d'asile (1919–1939)'. In *De l'éxil à la résistance: réfugiés et immigrés d'Europe centrale en France 1933–45*, eds. Karl Bartosek, René Gallissot and Denis Peschanski, 13–25. Arcantère, 1989.

Walter, Gérard. *La Vie à Paris sous l'occupation 1940–1944*. Armand Colin, 1960.

Weber, Eugen. *Peasants into Frenchmen: The Modernization of Rural France 1870–1914*. Stanford: Stanford University Press, 1976.

Weil, Patrick. 'Georges Mauco: un itinéraire camouflé'. In *L'Antisémitisme de plume 1940–1944: études et documents*, eds. Pierre-André Taguieff, Grégoire Kauffmann and Michaël Lenoire, 267–76. Berg International, 1999.

Weil, Patrick. 'Racisme et discrimination dans la politique française de l'immigration 1938–1945/1954–1995'. *Vingtième siècle*, no. 47 (July–September 1995): 77–102.

Weil, Patrick. *La France et ses étrangers: l'aventure d'une politique de l'immigration 1938–1991*. Calmann-Lévy, 1991.

Weil, Patrick. *Qu'est-ce qu'un Français? Histoire de la nationalité française depuis la Révolution*. Bernard Grasset, 2002.

Weinberg, David H. *Les Juifs à Paris de 1933 à 1939*. Calmann-Lévy, 1974.

Weininger, Otto. *Geschlecht und Charakter, eine principielle Untersuchung*. Vienna: W. Baumüller, 1903.

Weisberg, Richard H. *Vichy Law and the Holocaust in France*. Amsterdam: Harwood Academic, 1996.

Weiss, Louise. *Mémoires d'une Européenne*. Vol. 2, *1919–1934*. Payot, 1969.

Wieviorka, Annette. *Déportation et génocide: entre la mémoire et l'oubli*. Plon, 1992.

Wieviorka, Annette. *Ils étaient juifs, résistants, communistes*. Denoël, 1986.

Wieviorka, Annette. *L'Ere du témoin*. Plon, 1998.

Wieviorka, Olivier. *Une certaine idée de la résistance: défense de la France 1940–1949*. Seuil, 1995.

Willard, Germaine and Roger Bourderon. *Histoire de la France contemporaine, 1940–1947*. Vol. 6. Editions Sociales, 1980.

Wilson, Elizabeth. 'The Invisible *Flâneur*'. In *The Contradictions of Culture: Cities, Culture, Women*, 72–89. London: Sage, 2001.

Wistrich, Robert S. 'Zionism and its Jewish "Assimilationist" Critics (1897–1948)'. *Jewish Social Studies* 4, no. 2 (1998): 59–111.

Films

Baldensperger, Jean. *Les Journées du 19 au 28 août 1944*. France, 1944.

Benguigui, Yamina. *Mémoires d'immigrés: l'héritage maghrébin*. France, 1997.

Berri, Claude. *Lucie Aubrac*. France, 1998.

Bober, Robert. *En remontant la rue Vilin*. France, 1992.

Mosco. *Les Terroristes à la retraite*. France, 1985.

UFF. *Union des Femmes Françaises*, France, 1947.

Index

259

Studies in the Social and Cultural History of Modern Warfare

10 *The Spirit of 1914: Militarism, Myth and Mobilization in Germany*
Jeffrey Verhey
ISBN 0 521 77137 4

11 *German Anglophobia and the Great War, 1914–1918*
Matthew Stibbe
ISBN 0 521 78296 1

12 *The Survivors of the Holocaust in Occupied Germany: Life Between Memory and Hope*
Zeer W. Mankowitz
ISBN 0 521 81105 8

13 *Commemorating the Irish Civil War: History and Memory, 1923–2000*
Anne Dolan
ISBN 0 521 81904 0

14 *Jews and Gender in Liberation France*
K. H. Adler
ISBN 0 521 79048 4